ON BROADWAY
A Journey Uptown Over Time

United States Custom House in lower Manhattan, Loew's 175th Street Theater lobby, and the Broadway Theater marquee, 1979 and 1988.

ON BROADWAY
A Journey Uptown Over Time

TEXT AND PRINCIPAL PHOTOGRAPHY BY

DAVID W. DUNLAP

RIZZOLI
NEW YORK

To Mother, Brother, and Bear

ILLUSTRATION CREDITS

Unless otherwise credited, photographs are by the author.

DD	The author, in the case of multiple credits
GRAY	Christopher Gray
GSW	*The Greatest Street in the World*
MCNY	Courtesy of the Museum of the City of New York
MET	Courtesy of the Metropolitan Opera
NYHS	Courtesy of the New-York Historical Society
NYI	*New York and Its Institutions*
VM	*Valentine's Manual* for 1865

Jacket photographs:

Front, *view of Broadway takes in the Roosevelt Building (far left), the Jacob K. Javits Federal Building, the former New York Life Insurance Home Office (with clocktower), the Marine Midland Building, One Wall Street, a bishop's-crook lamppost, and the Woolworth Building, 1979*

Back (above), *lobby of the Woolworth Building on lower Broadway, 1988*

Back (below), *rotunda of the John Crosby Brown Memorial Tower at Union Theological Seminary on upper Broadway, 1988*

(All photographs by David W. Dunlap)

First published in the United States of America in 1990 by
RIZZOLI INTERNATIONAL PUBLICATIONS, INC.
300 Park Avenue South, New York, N.Y. 10010

Designed by Abigail Sturges
Set in type by David E. Seham Associates, Inc.,
Metuchen, New Jersey

Library of Congress Cataloging-in-Publication Data

Dunlap, David W.
  On Broadway : a journey uptown over time / text and principal photography by David W. Dunlap.
    p.   cm.
  ISBN 0-8478-1181-6
  1. Broadway (New York, N.Y.)—History.
2. Broadway (New York, N.Y.)—Pictorial works.
3. New York (N.Y.)—History.   4. New York (N.Y.)—Description—Views.   I. Title.
F128.67.B7D86   1990
974.7'1—dc20   89-43558
                                        CIP

LC 89-43558
ISBN 0-8478-1181-6

Printed and bound by Dai Nippon Printing Company, Tokyo

ACKNOWLEDGMENTS

On Broadway has indeed been a journey. No one knows better how long this journey took than Roy Finamore, who has made room in his life for this book since 1985. He has influenced it—and me—at every turn. I have relied heavily and gratefully on his unfailing wisdom, insight, encouragement, and patience.

Barney Karpfinger, my agent, has been involved with the book more than a decade. His enthusiasm helped keep the project alive through several discouraging periods.

Stephanie Salomon did much more than edit the book and Abigail Sturges did much more than design it—although those two tasks alone were challenging enough. In addition, they gave a tremendous amount of time, care, energy, and intelligence to shaping this complex work. I am most grateful to Gianfranco Monacelli and Solveig Williams of Rizzoli for welcoming the project with such interest. Beth Kugler, Heidi King, Nancy Novick, and Victoria Geibel were instrumental in seeing it to completion.

Special thanks are due to Christopher Gray of the Office for Metropolitan History and Michael R. Miller of the Theatre Historical Society, who shared their knowledge and resources freely, providing data on more than 120 buildings. Dale Neighbors, at the New-York Historical Society, helped uncover many striking photographic images, a number of which are being published here for the first time.

Also of great help in offering information or illustrations were Susan E. Alpert, Lillian Ayala, Phyllis Barr, Val Coleman, Tom Frusciano, Larry Josephs, Jonathan Kuhn, Nathaniel Lieberman, Elizabeth J. Loeb, Joan McGann, Margaret Moore, Marjorie Pearson, Martha Ritter, Thomas Rosenbaum, Steve Rosenthal, Robert E. Selsam, Sally Sherwood, Mark P. Shiff, Vahe Tiryakian, Robert Tuggle, and Peter H. Wollenberg.

On Broadway includes many interior views, as well as a number of panoramas taken from special vantages. The following institutions and individuals made these photographs possible, and I thank them all for their gracious assistance: Apple Bank for Savings (Anthony M. Ronda and Phil Decker), Artkraft Strauss Sign Corporation (Tama Starr), Beacon Theater (Andrew Feltz), Broadway Barber Shop (Kay Demetriou), Citibank (Tony Burzo and William C. McGuire), Columbia University (Fred Knubel, Judith Leynse, Monica Miya, and Joe Patterson), Criterion Center (Charles B. Moss Jr.), First Baptist Church (Rev. Richard Daniel Burke), Arthur Gelb, Geto & deMilly (Ethan Geto), Grace Church (David L. Pearce), Guild Enterprises (Peter H. Elson), Church of the Intercession (Rev. Canon Frederick B. Williams), Jewish Theological Seminary (Irma L. Rabbino), H.J. Kalikow & Company (Peter S. Kalikow), Edward I. Koch, Lincoln Center for the Performing Arts (Joe McKaughan, Mary Loiselle, and Susanne Stevens), R.H. Macy & Company (Tara S. Gilani), Metropolitan Historic Structures (George

Henke), Metropolitan Opera (David M. Reuben), Nederlander Organization (Peter Russell), New York City Art Commission (Patricia Harris), New York City Council (Peg Breen), New York City Mayor's Office (George Arzt, Peter A. Gilvarry, and Larry Simonberg), New York City Transit Authority (Peter Barrett, Bob Previdi, and Eugene Wenz), New York Marriott Marquis Hotel (Kate McGrath), New York Philharmonic (Francis Little and Marcia Young), One Times Square Plaza (Steven M. Israel), Patterson & McLaughlin (Martin McLaughlin and Nikki Henkin), Marvin Schneider, Melvin Simon & Associates (Barbara Willis), Strand Book Store (Fred Bass and Richard Devereaux), Teachers College (Roy Campbell), Trinity Church Cemetery (Al Spagnoli), Trinity Parish (Toni Graff, Peter Albertis, and Angelica Roman), Union Theological Seminary (Steph Slater), United Christian Evangelistic Association (Kenneth Kolman and Shannon Grady), United Church (Rev. Dr. James Wyns), U.S. General Services Administration (Warren E. Gardner and Tom Trott), U.S. Postal Service (Gerald McCall of the Bowling Green Station and Vito Fortuna), Woolworth Corporation (Joe Grabowski and William B. Thomson), and Zabar's (Joy Watman).

I would also like to thank the staff at Modernage Custom Photo Labs—especially Jorge Coste, Alan Goldberg, and Ken Troiano—which produced the prints used in this book.

The *New York Times* has given me so many opportunities to learn about New York that it would be impossible to quantify my indebtedness. I can say, however, that my two editors in recent years, John Darnton and Michael Sterne, have been most accommodating and supportive.

Finally, it is with particular gratitude that I record the friends and colleagues who have joined me on Broadway walks, or watched for items of interest, or simply cheered me on with their kind words. These include Susan Anderson, George Anton, Dorothea and John Peter Boorsch, Deirdre Carmody, Arthur Cohen, Barbara Cohen, Mary D'Amour and Jim Condon, Dan Denton, Dick Foote and his family, Carlos Goez, Paul Goldberger, Paul Gunther, Bill Hamilton, Charlie Kaiser, John Kane and Hunter O'Hanian, Gretchen Leefmans and Al Siegal, Eden Lipson, Carole Lowenstein, Rich Meislin, Sally and Scotty Reston, Sam Roberts, Curt Sanburn, Marsha Shapiro, Dick Shepard, Marvin Siegel, David Steiert, Alfred Sturtevant, Sally Urang, Joe Vecchione, and Larry Yermack.

In a research work of this magnitude, omissions and errors are virtually inescapable. I apologize for any I have made, particularly to those architects whose work has not been duly credited.

CONTENTS

INTRODUCTION   1
With an explanation of the inventory

FINANCIAL DISTRICT   11
Bowling Green to City Hall Park

CIVIC CENTER / TRIBECA   43
City Hall Park to Canal Street

SOHO   67
Canal Street to Houston Street

NOHO / EAST VILLAGE   89
Houston Street to Fourteenth Street

UNION SQUARE / LADIES' MILE   111
Fourteenth Street to Twenty-second Street

MADISON SQUARE / THE TENDERLOIN   129
Twenty-second Street to Thirty-second Street

HERALD SQUARE / THE RIALTO / GARMENT CENTER   145
Thirty-second Street to Forty-first Street

TIMES SQUARE / THEATER DISTRICT / AUTOMOBILE ROW   163
Forty-first Street to Fifty-eighth Street

COLUMBUS CIRCLE / LINCOLN SQUARE   203
Fifty-eighth Street to Seventy-first Street

UPPER WEST SIDE   231
Seventy-first Street to Ninety-seventh Street

STRYKER'S BAY / MORNINGSIDE HEIGHTS   259
Ninety-seventh Street to Lasalle Street

HARLEM / MANHATTANVILLE / HAMILTON HEIGHTS   279
Lasalle Street to 168th Street

WASHINGTON HEIGHTS / INWOOD / MARBLE HILL   299
168th Street to 230th Street

NOTES   316
INDEX   324

Hudſons · River

BROADWAY IN 1988 *Frontispiece*
*At the foot of Broadway are the Washington Building,
Standard Oil Building, Two Broadway, and the
Custom House.*

BROADWAY IN 1661 *Left*
*The Heere Straat, as Broadway was called by the Dutch,
began outside the Fort (at the tip of the island) and ended
at the wall where Wall Street now runs. NYHS.*

I f New York City has a Main Street—one single thoroughfare that reflects its history and foretells its future, that embodies its power and poverty, that has been shaped by its overwhelming commercial and cultural ambitions—that street is Broadway. It is easily the longest street in Manhattan, running from the bottom of the island to the top. It is also one of the oldest streets. More remarkable, however, is its vitality. Broadway has always been at the heart of civic affairs and remains so today. The path of almost everyone who lives in or visits New York must cross it at some point. Here one can fight City Hall or get healed at an enormous medical center, attend the opera or the philharmonic orchestra, go to class at an Ivy League college or train for the rabbinate, shop at the world's largest department store and its best-known gourmet delicatessen, or plunge into that tarnished but electrifying entertainment precinct known as Broadway.

In diversity lies Broadway's greatest consistency. It has always worn a bewildering number of faces, trying to be almost everything to almost everyone. Witness this description, which sounds contemporary, although it was written three years after the Civil War:

Broadway is New York intensified,—the reflex of the Republic,—hustling, feverish, crowded, ever changing. Broadway is hardly surpassed by any street in the

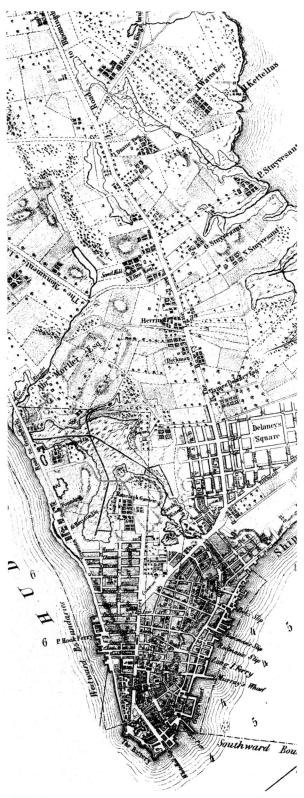

BROADWAY IN 1766-67

Before the Revolution, Broadway had reached Thomas Street. The Bloomingdale Road—to which Broadway would be joined—was a country highway. NYHS.

World. It is cosmoramic and cosmopolitan. In its vast throng, individuality is lost, and the race only is remembered.[1]

The first to walk upon Broadway were members of the Weckquaesgeek chieftaincy, an aggressive people who gathered along the Hudson River, largely between Dobbs Ferry and Tarrytown, New York. Their trail led to the southern tip of Manhattan Island, outlining Broadway's future course between Battery Place and Park Row. Perhaps the oldest surviving European reference to it comes from 1642, in the journal of the settler David Pietersen de Vries, who spoke of the "road over which the Indians from Wickquasgeck passed daily."[2]

This road recommended itself for further development, as it ran along a straight, high ridge of land.[3] It was incorporated into the plan of Nieuw Amsterdam and known variously as the Great Common Road, Great Highway or Public Highway, Public Wagon Road or Broad Wagon Way, Heere Straat or Heere Wegh. The last two names might have signified an upper-class area; indeed, the Dutch has been translated variously as Lord's Way or Gentlemen's Street.[4] What also set the Heere Straat apart was its uncommon breadth. In contrast to other streets, it was quite appreciably a broad way. After Nieuw Amsterdam was surrendered to the English in 1664, the Heere Straat took a new name that reflected this distinction. As early as 1665, the description "standing in the Broadway" was used to locate a house that was serving as a barracks.[5]

Well into the eighteenth century, the heart of New York was south of Wall Street, where the Dutch had built a protective palisade. Broadway did not go much beyond the tip of the Common (now City Hall Park), until 1760, when it was extended to Thomas Street. In 1793, a decade before the cornerstone was laid for the present City Hall, the Common was still considered the "upper end of Broad-way."[6]

What dictated Broadway's ultimate route was something happening far out of town: the creation of the Bloomingdale Road, beginning in 1703. This meandering country highway was linked to and consumed by Broadway in the nineteenth century, its course preserved almost exactly for three and a half miles, from Union Square to Eighty-seventh Street, in defiance of the street grid that was later imposed on Manhattan.[7] The old road began at Sixteenth Street and led to the countryside of Bloemendael, the "Vale of Flowers," as the Upper West Side was first called. It went through the hamlets of Harsenville (the Sixties and Seventies), Manhattanville (the 120s and 130s), and Carmansville (the 140s), then joined the road to the King's Bridge at the northern tip of the island.

In 1795, the Common Council ordered that Broadway be regulated as far as the Arch Bridge over the canal that is now Canal Street and, six years later, resolved to "continue Broadway until it meets the Bowery lane," at what is now Union Square.[8] This represented the union of the "two finest avenues in the city," in the words of John Lambert, an English visitor, in 1807. He also noted that although Broadway was more than two miles long, the pavement does not extend above a mile and a quarter: the remainder of the road consists of straggling houses. . . . In the vicinity of the Battery, and for some distance up the Broadway, they are nearly all private houses, and occupied by the principal merchants and gentry of New York; after which the Broadway is lined with . . . large commodious shops of every description . . . book stores, print-shops, music shops, jewellers, and silversmiths; hatters, linen-drapers, milliners, pastry-cooks, coach-makers, hotels, and coffee-houses. . . . The genteel lounge is in the Broadway, from eleven to three o'clock, during which time it is as much crowded as the Bond-street of London: and the carriages, though not so numerous, are driven to and fro with as much velocity.[9]

In 1811 the Commissioners of Streets and Roads presented the plan for Manhattan's gridiron layout. Their goal was to make it easier to buy, sell, and improve real estate, by establishing streets of "beautiful uniformity."[10] With their distaste for oddly shaped blocks, the commissioners viewed Broadway and the Bloomingdale Road as anathema. There was not much they could do about the portions that were already built up, but they proposed to keep Broadway on a straight line above Fourteenth Street, separate from the Bloomingdale Road, and to truncate both thoroughfares at Twenty-third Street.[11] Nothing came of this scheme.

Broadway kept moving uptown, although its reputation suffered in the 1830s and 1840s. Philip Hone, a civic leader and diarist, despaired of a city infested by gangs, "even in Broadway, where drunken frolics are succeeded by brawls . . . knives are brought out, dreadful wounds inflicted, and sometimes horrid murder committed."[12] George Templeton Strong, another prominent observer, commented: "It's a pity we've no street but Broadway that's fit to walk in of an evening. The street is always crowded, and whores and blackguards make up about two-thirds of the throng."[13]

"Broadway has ceased to be Broadway," declared the *New York Mirror* in 1836. Instead, the newspaper said,

it is nearly as much of a mere crowded thoroughfare as Fleet-street, London. . . . In one year, there will be scarcely a private residence or a boarding-house below Wall-street. The rise in rents and the price of bread, there, have already driven many up town. . . . A great portion of the retail business, drygood stores, etc., will soon reach as far as Prince-street. Ladies will, hereafter, scarcely extend their promenades farther down than the [City Hall] Park.[14]

Actually, Broadway was growing closer to its essential character: a bustling street of stores, theaters, and hotels. In 1842, Charles Dickens set out from the Carlton House, at Leonard Street, "situated in the best part of this main artery," and exclaimed:

Was there ever such a sunny street as this Broadway! The pavement stones are polished with the tread of feet until they shine. . . . No stint of omnibuses here! Half-a-dozen have gone by within as many minutes. Plenty of hackney cabs and coaches too; gigs, phaetons, large-wheeled tilburies, and private carriages. . . . Heaven save the ladies, how they dress! We have seen more colours in these ten minutes, than we should have seen elsewhere, in as many days.[15]

In outfitting these women, no merchant could approach A.T. Stewart,

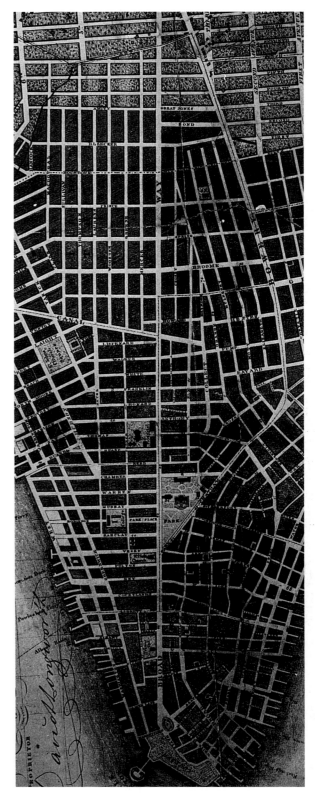

BROADWAY IN 1825
Amity Street (West Third Street) marked the upper reach of development. City Hall can be seen clearly in its park. Northwest of it is the New York Hospital. NYHS.

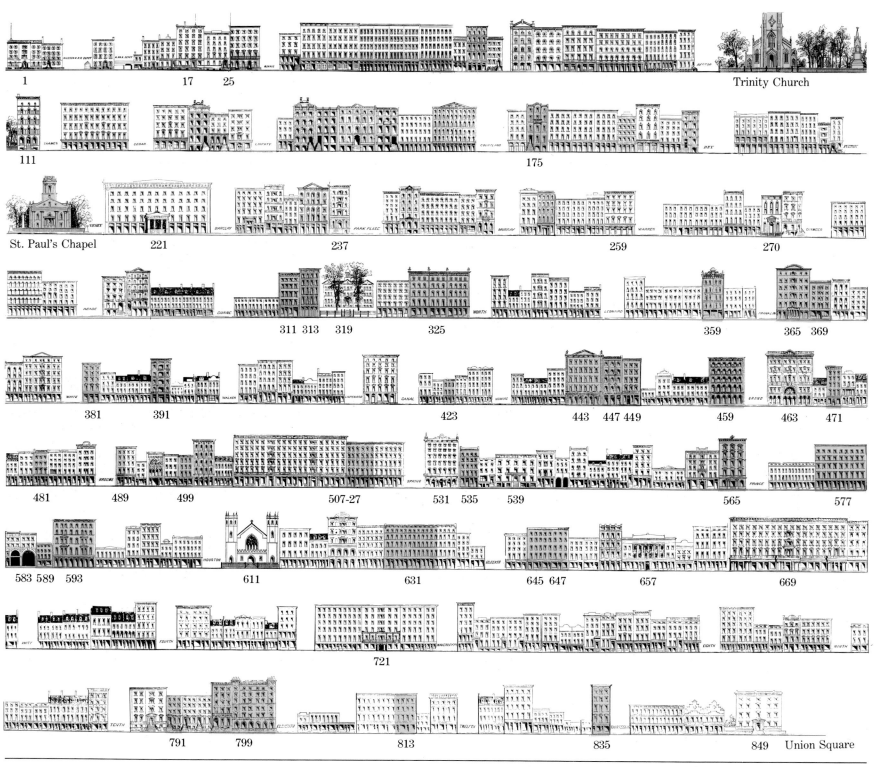

1   17   25   Trinity Church

111   175

St. Paul's Chapel   221   237   259   270

311 313   319   325   359   365 369

381   391   423   443   447 449   459   463   471

481   489   499   507-27   531 535   539   565   577

583 589   593   611   631   645 647   657   669

721

791   799   813   835   849   Union Square

BROADWAY IN 1865

WEST SIDE

Shaded buildings still exist; some quite altered.

1 Washington Hotel	
17 British Consulate	
25 Stevens House Hotel	463 Lord & Taylor
111 Trinity Building	471 Lake & McCreery
175 Germania Building	507-27 St. Nicholas Hotel
221 Astor House Hotel	531 Prescott House Hotel
237 Broadway Bank	539 Barnum's New Museum
259 D. Devlin & Company	565 Ball, Black & Company
270 Chemical Bank	583 San Francisco Minstrel Hall
319 New York Hospital	611 St. Thomas Church
359 Thompson's Saloon	647 Pfaff's Saloon
365 International Hotel	657 Stuyvesant Institute
423 Benjamin Lord House	669 La Farge House Hotel
443 D. Appleton & Company	721 New York Hotel
449 F. Booss & Brother	799 St. Denis Hotel
459 D. Devlin & Company	849 C.V.S. Roosevelt House

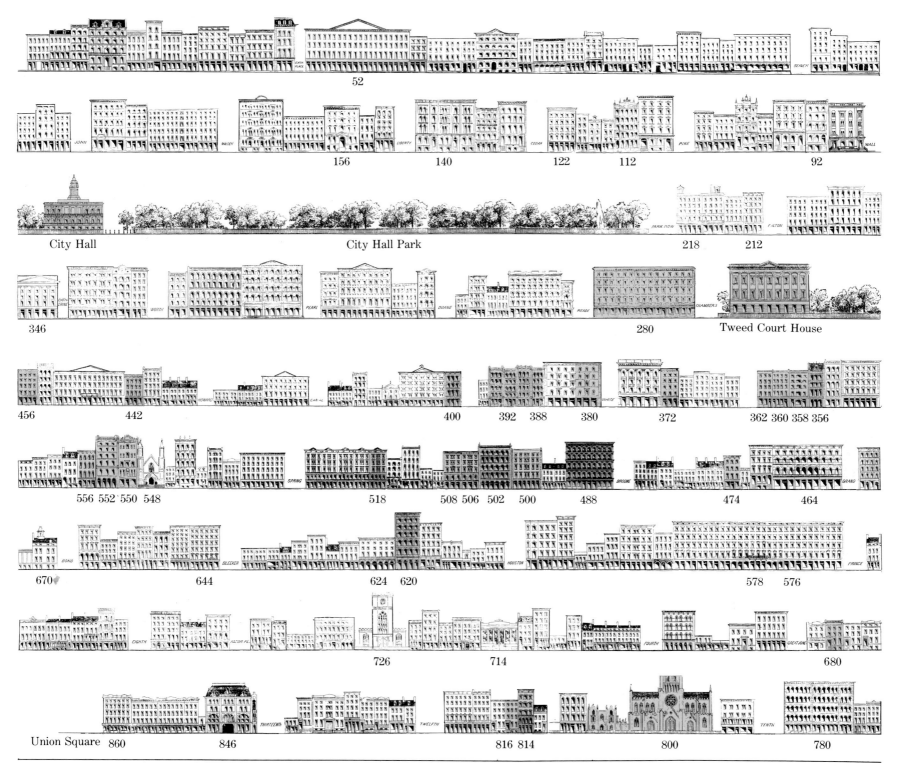

City Hall   City Hall Park   218   212

346   280   Tweed Court House

456   442   400   392 388   380   372   362 360 358 356

556 552 550 548   518   508 506 502 500   488   474   464

670   644   624 620   578 576

726   714   680

Union Square   860   846   816 814   800   780

BROADWAY IN 1865

EAST SIDE

*Shaded buildings still exist;
some quite altered.*

52 Exchange Court	112 New York Life	346 N.-Y. Society Library	556 Crouch & Fitzgerald	680 East River Savings Bank
92 Equitable Life	122 American Express	400 Florence's Hotel	576 Niblo's Garden	714 Colonnade Houses
	140 Mutual Life	464 Brooks Brothers	578 Metropolitan Hotel	726 Unitarian Church
	156 Manhattan Life	488 E.V. Haughwout Store	620 "Little Cary" Building	780 A.T. Stewart Store
	212 Knox Hat Store	502 C.G. Gunther's Sons	624 Olympic Theater	800 Grace Church
	218 Barnum's Museum	548 Fourth Universalist Church	644 Manhattan Savings Bank	846 Wallack's Theater
	280 Stewart's "Marble Palace"	550 Tiffany & Company	670 Samuel Ward House	860 Union Place Hotel

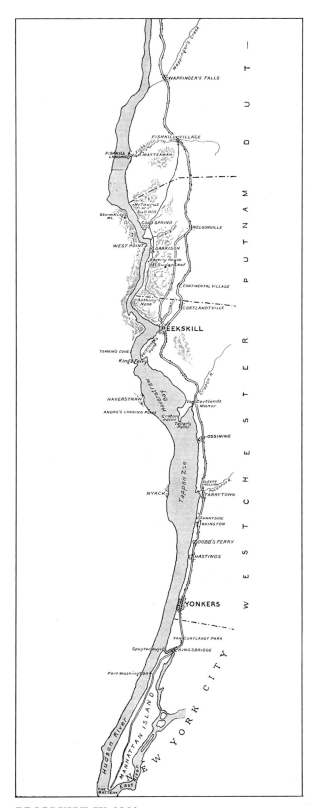

BROADWAY IN 1911

To bolster his assertion that Broadway was the longest modern street in the world, the historian Stephen Jenkins traced it to Albany, via the Albany Post Road. GSW.

who opened his "Marble Palace" department store at Broadway and Chambers Street in 1846, the year in which Grace Church, at Tenth Street, was consecrated. At the time, Union Square was the northern end of Broadway, practically speaking, and the street was gaining a sense of solidity. "Buildings now stand in Broadway that may go down to another century, for they are on a level with the wants and tastes of a capital," wrote James Fenimore Cooper in 1850.[16]

"The mania for converting Broadway into a street of shops is greater than ever," Hone marveled, as the 1850s began. "There is scarcely a block in the whole extent of this fine street of which some part is not in a state of transmutation."[17] In his book *What I Saw in New-York*, Joel H. Ross captured this chaotic feeling:

Broadway is like a boy who grows so fast that he can't stop to tie up his shoes. Every thing in the streets and on the walks is untied, unpacked, unrolled, unboxed. Doors, windows, walls, roofs, brick, stone, mortar, dust and splinters daily come tumbling down to make way for banks, stores, halls, hotels, shops, offices, &c., &c. . . . The clattering of legions of iron-bound hoofs, as though rushing to battle . . . the gong-like, tornado-like, oceanic, unceasing roar and tumult of this bustling street, make it less inviting than it otherwise would be to promenaders.[18]

Broadway could be most uninviting, indeed. In wintertime, Strong wrote, the street became a "long canal of mud syrup, all the sidewalks greasy with an abominable compound like melted black butter."[19] The ugliness and noise were by-products of a rapidly advancing city. In the 1850s, hotels, theaters, and stores moved to the areas north and south of Houston Street. David T. Valentine, whose manuals documented city life, expressed his belief in 1856 that "those who remember our great city artery twenty years since must, on reflection, often feel surprised, if not delighted, at the many splendid edifices which have been erected."[20] *Harper's Magazine* took a different view: "Twenty years ago it was a street of three-story red brick houses. Now it is a highway of stone, and iron, and marble buildings. . . . And yet, among all the costly and colossal buildings that have of late been erected how few show any real taste or grace."[21]

A new form for Broadway—spacious and verdant—was charted in 1868 from Fifty-ninth to 155th Street, as work began on the Boulevard, also known as the Grand Boulevard, a "great public drive, broad and long, where hundreds of fleet horses could be exercised in a single hour."[22] This was created by widening the bed of the Bloomingdale Road into two broad lanes, divided by small parks that were precursors of the malls that line upper Broadway today. Despite its different names, the Broadway-Bloomingdale-Boulevard-Kingsbridge Road amalgam was perceived as one road and described in 1868 as New York's longest street, running fifteen miles to Spuyten Duyvil Creek.[23] [The current figure for the Manhattan portion, according to Richard F. Shepard, a modern Broadway historian, is closer to seventeen miles.[24]]

The built-up portion of Broadway grew beyond Madison Square in the 1860s and the street became increasingly fragmented, with each neighborhood taking on a distinct quality. Financial houses stayed at the southern tip of Manhattan and the wholesale district remained in the blocks north of City Hall. At the same time, hotels, restaurants, theaters, gambling houses, and brothels reached as far north as Thirtieth Street, forming the Tenderloin district. Stores, which had once been inseparable from hotels and theaters, migrated to an area south of the Tenderloin. There, carriage-trade retailers formed perhaps the most elegant specialty district on Broadway, one that was known—after its patrons—as the Ladies' Mile.

In the late 1860s, Broadway grew more and more cosmopolitan. "To denizens of New York, society is usually known under the generic divisions of Broadway and Bowery," visitors were told, "the former being regarded as patrician, and the latter as plebeian."[25] Broadway was simply the "most wonderful street in the world," Edward Winslow Martin proclaimed unblushingly in his 1868 book, *The Secrets of the Great City*. He went on to say that

America, Europe, Asia, Africa, and even Oceanica, has each its representatives here. High and low, rich and poor, pass along these side-walks, at a speed peculiar to New York, and positively bewildering to a stranger. . . . Fine gentlemen in broadcloth, ladies in silks and jewels, and beggars in squalidness and rags, are mingled here in true Republican confusion. The bustle and uproar are very great, generally making it impossible to converse in an ordinary tone. . . . The street is full of all kinds of people, all of whom seem to be in high spirits, for Broadway is a sure cure for the 'blues.'[26]

"Whatever is purchasable can be had in Broadway," Junius Henri Browne remarked in a contemporary volume, *The Great Metropolis*, written at a time when the "last refinements of voluptuousness" could be found between Canal and Twenty-sixth streets.

Vice wears a fair mask at every corner, and Art smiles in a thousand bewitching forms. Hotels, and playhouses, and bazaars, and music-halls, and bagnios, and gambling hells are radiantly mingled together; and any of them will give you what you seek, and more sometimes. . . . Anything rare, or ripe, or dangerous, or dainty,—each and all are within your reach, if you can pay the price morally and materially.[27]

It was understood that in a state of upheaval and even chaos, Broadway had found a true identity. Here is a description from 1873:

The entire disregard of unity, the competition in costly and massive buildings, the diversity of material, as well as adornment, combine to make it as a highway of commerce, the paragon of the world, and in every pillar, façade and cornice proclaim it the special result of the energy and enterprise of a free, thriving people.[28]

That enterprise was soon to manifest itself in extraordinary physical development. The technological and aesthetic foundations for the skyscraping office tower were being laid at this time. Utilitarian commercial buildings gave way to expressions of corporate ego. Life insurance companies had "undertaken to excel all others in architectural enterprises" and, by the early 1870s, occupied "imposing business temples" on Broadway.[29] The passenger

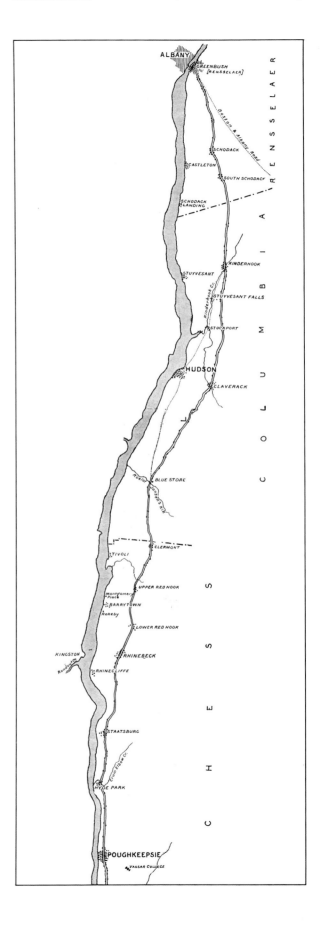

ABOUT THE INVENTORY

Accompanying each chapter is a compilation of structures—existing and demolished—that have aesthetic, architectural, cultural, historic, nostalgic, or social interest. It is meant to be informative and entertaining, but it is not exhaustive. Many buildings, generally the most nondescript, are not listed. The buildings shown in boldface were standing or underway in the spring of 1990.

With some exceptions, only those buildings with frontages on Broadway appear on the list. Buildings separated from Broadway only by a lawn or plaza are generally included (City Hall, the Metropolitan Opera House). For campuses such as Columbia University or Audubon Terrace, only buildings actually on Broadway are listed. Two major theaters that previously had entrances on Broadway, the Lunt-Fontanne and Mark Hellinger, are included.

Broadway is technically not mapped between 14th and 17th streets. Greeley Square and Times Square have blocks that appear geographically to be part of Sixth or Seventh avenues, but if they carry Broadway street numbers, they are included.

Because uptown chapters cover much territory in relatively few pages, a choice had to be made between many entries and no descriptions, or some descriptions at the expense of whole entries. The former was chosen, to keep the inventory complete. Sources used for the inventory can be found in the Notes.

elevator was introduced along Broadway in the late 1850s (although there are differing claims as to which building this distinction belongs). In 1888, New York's first true skyscraper, supported by a steel skeleton, was constructed on Broadway.

The 1880s were the beginning of a golden age for Broadway, which then boasted New York's best stores, on Ladies' Mile; its most fabled hotels and notorious nightspots, in the Tenderloin; and its finest theaters, on the Rialto, north of Thirty-fourth Street. Walt Whitman portrayed Broadway in 1888:

Thou portal—thou arena—thou of the myriad long-drawn lines and groups!
(Could but thy flagstones, curbs, façades, tell their inimitable tales;
Thy windows rich, and huge hotels—thy side-walks wide;)
Thou of the endless sliding, mincing, shuffling feet!
Thou, like the parti-colored world itself—like infinite, teeming, mocking life!
Thou visor'd, vast, unspeakable show and lesson![30]

Through the 1880s and early 1890s, the far reaches of Broadway—that is, almost anything north of Forty-second Street—were relatively undeveloped. Lacking rapid transit, the Grand Boulevard had not come close to living up to its name. Twenty years after being laid out, this unpaved thoroughfare was lined by a few churches, an armory, shanties, tenements, and yards filled with horses, cows, chickens, and goats. To the north, the Kingsbridge route was nothing more than an "ideal winding country road."[31]

The rural isolation of upper Manhattan ended at the turn of the century, when Columbia College moved to 116th Street, followed closely by Barnard College and Teachers College. Other vital institutions were also moving northward: the department stores to the Thirties, led by R.H. Macy & Company, and the theaters to the Forties, led by Oscar Hammerstein's Olympia. When the Olympia opened in 1895, the theater district stretched a mile and a half on Broadway, from Wallack's Thirteenth Street Theater to Hammerstein's at Forty-fourth Street.

Broadway, the Boulevard, and the Kingsbridge Road were consolidated under the name Broadway in 1899. It was not long before admirers were speaking of Broadway as the "Greatest Street in the World" and one of the longest—if one regarded it as a seamless part of the Albany Post Road.[32]

The last great uptown push came with the subway. Perhaps no other single project had so profound and almost instantaneous an impact on Broadway as the Interborough Rapid Transit railroad, which was built between 1900 and 1904. Downtown, powerful business interests saw to it that the subway did not run under Broadway properties (as had been envisioned by transit planners in 1895). Uptown, however, the railroad was free to proceed over and under Broadway, from Forty-second to 168th Street.[33] While the tracks were being laid, speculators readied themselves for an unprecedented wave of residential construction. Two weeks before the first train ran in October 1904, about 500 properties changed hands uptown, leading the *New York Times* to assert that "the 'subway boom,' for which the real estate market has been preparing for five years . . . has at last arrived."[34]

The people of the Weckquaesgeek chieftaincy found a good place at the tip of Manhattan Island to start their trail: a ridge of land so high that its steep contours can still be seen, in the way the small side streets slope downward from either side of Broadway. On this ridge, on this trail— so legend has it—the first Europeans to live on Manhattan spent the winter of 1613. They were sailors under the command of Captain Adriaen Block, forced ashore after their ship burned in the harbor. They occupied four huts at what is now 39 Broadway while building a new vessel, which they called *Restless*.[1]

Those who followed in the 1620s, to settle Nieuw Amsterdam for the West India Company, fashioned their largest thoroughfare from the Weckquaesgeek road. By the mid-1600s, it was known as the Heere Straat and was already home to some of the town's most prominent and notorious inhabitants. Their small, gable-roofed dwellings filled both sides of the street for several blocks. Among them were Pieter Laurenzen Cock, a Danish fur trader, whose tavern at One Broadway was reputedly where the first martini was mixed; Martin Cregier, one of the first burgomasters; Andries Hudde, the first surveyor-general of the province; Domine Johannes Megapolensis, the first Protestant missionary to the native Americans; Hendrick van Dyck, who provoked the last great attack by native dwellers on the settlers; and Augustine Herrman, a banker, lawyer, and dealer in slaves, furs, tobacco, wines, groceries, and dry goods.[2]

North of the settled area, around present-day Rector Street, the West India Company created a garden and orchard on the Heere Straat in the 1630s. Sometime before 1649, the first burying ground was established on the Heere Straat, straddling what today is Morris Street. A wall of wooden palisades was built in 1653, along the line of the present Wall Street, to guard against English attack. Where it crossed the Heere Straat was a portal called the Land Gate, through which cattle were driven to pasture in the common fields that are now City Hall Park.

Under the English, who took control of New York in 1664, the cemetery was moved north of the wall. From this period comes Broadway's oldest remaining object, the headstone of young Richard Churcher:[3]

HEAR . LYES . THE . BODY
OF . RICHARD . CHVRCH
ER . SON . OF . WILLIA
M . CHVRCHER . WHO .
DIED . THE . 5 OF . APRIL
1681 . OF . AGE 5 YEARS
AND . 5 . MONTHES

The boy's grave was not long to be on the outskirts of town. Members of the Church of England petitioned in 1696 for a "small piece of Land Lyeing without the North gate of the said Citty betwixt the King's Garden and the burying Place."[4] A charter was granted the next year to Trinity Parish, by the royal governor under King William III, with a quitrent of one pepper-

One Wall Street (left), Trinity Building and One Liberty Plaza (center), and Equitable Building (right), 1978.

George III statue and Bowling Green fence. NYHS, DD.

BOWLING GREEN

[0.51 acres] Within the park have been statues of *King George III*, by Joseph Wilton, which was destroyed, and *Abraham de Peyster*, by George Edwin Bissell, which was removed. Outside the park is the sculpture *Charging Bull*, by Arturo Di Modica. **Site of** the Parade; Broadway Shambles (also known as the Meat Market), 1684.

BOWLING GREEN FENCE
1771; damaged 1776. Landmark.

United States Custom House, 1988.

UNITED STATES CUSTOM HOUSE
1901-07, by Cass Gilbert. Landmark. [8 stories] The monumental allegorical statuary is integral to this massive Beaux-Arts composition. Daniel Chester French's statues of *Asia*, *America*, *Europe*, and *Africa* flank the entrance, high above which is a cartouche by Karl Bitter. Murals by Reginald Marsh are in the Rotunda. **Site of** Steamship Row, ca. 1815; Government House (also known as the Governor's Residence, Custom House), 1790-91, probably by James Robinson; Fort Amsterdam, 1626-35, by Crijn Fredericksz.

BATTERY PLACE

Washington Building in 1986 and ca. 1904. DD, NYHS.

w WASHINGTON BUILDING, No. 1

(Also known as the International Mercantile Marine Building, Field Building, United States Lines Building) 1882-84, by Edward Hale Kendall; rebuilt 1920-21, by Walter B. Chambers. [13 stories] Once red brick, with a four-story, copper mansard roof, it was reclad in limestone and streamlined. The mosaic coats of arms facing Broadway are those of Plymouth, London, Queenstown, Melbourne, New York, and Capetown. *Site of* Captain Archibald Kennedy mansion (also known as the Washington Hotel), 1760; John Watts house (also known as the Custom House); Martin Cregier house and tavern, 1656-59; Thomas Broen house (also known as the Pieter Laurenzen Cock house and tavern), 1644.

Captain Archibald Kennedy mansion. VM.

BOWLING GREEN OFFICES, No. 5-11

1895-98, by William James Audsley and George Ashdown Audsley, with Ludlow & Peabody. [23 stories] The base might be called Greco-Egyptian, with its battered pylons and lush anthemion vegetation. From it rises a boldly vertical white tower. *Site of* New York Central & Hudson River Railroad Depot, 1860; Atlantic Garden, 1852-55; Robert Livingston house; King's Arms Tavern (also

Tombstone of Abraham Williams in Trinity Church Yard, 1979.

Tombstone of Jemima Ross in Trinity Church Yard, 1979.

corn. Trinity Church was built and the first service held there in 1698. Five years later, Trinity was given the town cemetery as part of its churchyard, on the condition that it keep the fence in order and not charge more than three shillings for burials.[5]

By this time, the merchant Etienne De Lancey had built a stone mansion north of Trinity, at Cedar Street. It had a cupola on top, overlooking grounds that sloped down to the Hudson River. In 1733, the city's first official park was created when an open parcel at the foot of Broadway was "Inclosed to make A Bowling Green thereof with Walks therein, for the Beauty & Ornament of the Said Street as well as for the Recreation & delight of the Inhabitants of this City."[6] Overlooking the Bowling Green, Captain Archibald Kennedy of the Royal Navy built his gracious home at One Broadway in 1760. Its exterior was distinguished by Palladian features and its drawing room was perhaps the largest in the city.[7] The garden ran down to the Hudson, so that New York Bay and the New Jersey shore were in full view from its windows. Next door lived Kennedy's brother-in-law, John Watts, the last Royal Recorder in New York City, whose memorial statue is prominent in Trinity Church Yard.

No longer a rural retreat, De Lancey's mansion was converted in 1754

Tombstone of Richard Churcher in Trinity Church Yard—the oldest object on Broadway, 1988.

Tombstone in Trinity Church Yard, 1979.

Bowling Green Offices, 1986.

known as the Atlantic Garden, Atlantic Hotel, Burns's City Arms Tavern), 1730; Domine Johannes Megapolensis house, 1656.

CUNARD BUILDING, No. 25

1919-21, by Benjamin Wistar Morris, with Thomas Hastings. [23 stories] The central tower is flanked by projecting pavilions, on a strongly rusticated base with large arches. The statues of *Sea Horses and Riders* are by Rochette & Parzini and there are other nautical motifs throughout. Paintings and decorative work in the Great Hall and adjacent rooms are by Ezra Winter, John Gregory, Barry Faulkner, C. Paul Jennewein, and Samuel Yellin. *Site of* Consulate of Great Britain; Stevens House Hotel (also known as Delmonico's Hotel), 1846; Lucas Dircksen Inn, 1656; Burying Ground (also known as the Old Church Yard on the Heere Straat), 1640s, on either side of Morris Street.

STONE STREET

Produce Exchange. NYHS.

E **TWO BROADWAY**

1958-59, by Emery Roth & Sons. [32 stories] This behemoth has a grid of silvery windows and blue-gray spandrel panels. *Site of* New York Produce Exchange, 1882-84, by George B. Post; Albert Andriessen house, ca. 1645.

to the Province Arms Tavern, which became a hub of civic activity. It was where the governors and students of King's College (now Columbia University) celebrated laying the cornerstone for their new school in 1756 with a "very elegant Dinner."[8] At mid-century, residents were going as far north as Crown Street (now Liberty Street) to do their marketing. There, in the middle of Broadway, stood an eighty-four-foot-long shed known as the Oswego Market. In 1760, under the name of Great George Street, Broadway was extended as far as the "Ground of the Late Widdow Rutgers," or Thomas Street.[9]

Further evidence of New York's northward progress was the need felt by Trinity Parish in the early 1760s for a chapel of ease that would be more convenient for churchgoers in the outer reaches of the city. Trinity set aside a wheat field at the southeast corner of the Queen's Farm, which it had been given in 1705, and began building St. Paul's Chapel. Although it has long been believed that the architect was Thomas McBean, evidence came to light in the 1980s to suggest that St. Paul's may have been built by a Frenchman named Andrew Gautier. When the small country church was completed in 1766, it faced the Hudson, with an unobstructed view to the shore. (This explains its apparently backward orientation, with the tower and front porch

ST. PAUL'S CHAPEL

Views from 1979 to 1988 include the pulpit and organ case and a detail of the Broadway portico (lower right, facing page).

BEAVER STREET

Standard Oil Building in 1986 and ca. 1898. DD, NYHS.

E STANDARD OIL BUILDING, No. 26

(Also known as the Socony Mobil Building) 1884-86, by Ebenezer L. Roberts; expanded and enlarged 1896, by Francis Hatch Kimball; expanded and enlarged 1920-26, by Carrère & Hastings, with Shreve, Lamb & Blake. [27 stories] Its pyramidal peak, topped by a colossal oil lamp, crowns a complex mass that curves along Broadway, with a rusticated base. The original building was 10 stories, which is recalled by the presence of a tenth-floor cornice. The nineteenth-century structure is also distinguished from the 1920s enlargement by pilasters, instead of columns, atop the Broadway street wall. *Site of* Produce Exchange Bank, 1904-05, by Ernest Flagg; Welles Building (also known as the Seaboard National Bank), 1881, by Shaw & Anderson; Adelphi Hotel, 1827; John Jay house; Alexander Hamilton house; Play House (also known as the New Theater), 1735; Dirck Smit house, ca. 1659; Jacob Eldertsen house (also known as the Royal Oak Tavern), ca. 1657; Andries Hoppen house, ca. 1653; Abraham Pietersen tavern, ca. 1645.

HUDSON BUILDING, No. 32

(Also known as the Americus Building) 1896-98, by Clinton & Russell. [18 stories] This old-fashioned, buff-brick tower is squeezed among its neighbors. *Site of* David Provoost house, ca. 1650.

EMPIRE TRUST BUILDING, No. 42

1902-04, Henry Ives Cobb. [22 stories] The highly articulated façade has an unusual five-story ornament with curvilinear gables and large brackets. *Site of* Andries Hudde house, ca. 1640.

50 BROADWAY

1926-27, by H. Craig Severance. [35 stories] This is an almost planar, buff brick tower, with four-story pilasters. *Site of* Standard Arcade, 1914, by Severance & Van Alen; Tower Building, 1888-89, by

in the middle of the block, rather than on Broadway.) Built at a time of tumultuous relations between the colonies and the crown, St. Paul's was a loyalist bastion. It still has a gilded coronet and feathers atop the elevated pulpit, recalling the crest of the Prince of Wales. This may be the last symbol of British royalty in New York that has been undisturbed since the Revolution.[10]

While the chapel was under construction in 1765, 200 merchants gathered at the Province Arms Tavern to sign the Non-Importation Agreement, pledging to buy nothing from Great Britain while the Stamp Act was in force. After its repeal, grateful colonists ordered an equestrian statue of King George III in gilded lead, to be raised on the Bowling Green. To protect this centerpiece and prevent its setting from becoming a "Recepticle of all the filth & dirt of the Neighbourhood," the Common Council ordered an iron fence around the green in 1771.[11]

On the night of July 9, 1776, the Declaration of Independence was read at assemblies around the city. Afterward, a crowd descended on the Bowling Green and pulled down the King's statue to make musket balls, "so that his troops will probably have melted majesty fired at them." From the fence posts, the mob tore off ornaments, either crowns or balls, which were to be fired against the *Asia*, an enemy man-of-war.[12] The fence still stands, but the tops of the posts are broken and jagged—a mute, graphic, and poignant testament to New Yorkers' passion on the eve of revolution. General George Washington's headquarters were briefly in the Kennedy house at One Broadway until the British entered the city in September 1776. That same month, a terrible blaze swept up Broadway, destroying the Lutheran Church, south of Trinity, then Trinity itself, whose 140-foot steeple "resembled a vast pyramid of fire."[13]

After the Revolutionary War, Broadway played a role in the loose na-

St. Paul's Chapel, 1800; ruins of the first Trinity Church, after the great fire of 1776. VM.

tional government that existed under the Articles of Confederation, as New York was the capital. The Office of Congress was on Broadway and among the "Grand Departments of the United States," a directory listed "His Excellency John Jay, Esq. Secretary for foreign affairs, 8, Broadway."[14] When the new Federal Government came into existence in 1789 under the Constitution, New York remained the capital. When Washington was inaugurated as the President, he walked to St. Paul's for a thanksgiving service, accompanied by the Vice President, the Speaker of the House, and both houses of Congress. The chapel was used for this occasion because Trinity Church had not yet been rebuilt. There are only sketchy records of the service, so it must be left to imagine what prayers went up that afternoon, when the whole government was only hours old. For the next year and a half, Washington regularly attended St. Paul's, where he sat in a dignified, canopy-covered pew.[15] Today, a reconstructed version of the pew, on the north aisle, is marked by a painting of the United States seal.

Washington lived at 39 Broadway, which he leased from Alexander Macomb from February to August 1790, following France's chargé d'affaires as the tenant. Not quite an executive mansion, it was described simply as the "House, in the Broad Way, taken for the Residence of the President of the United States."[16] In his diary for February, Washington said that he "made a disposition of the rooms—fixed on some furniture of the Minister's (which was to be sold, and was well adapted to particular public rooms)—and directed additional stables to be built." Once settled, he wrote, "My office was in a front room below, where persons on business were at once admitted." When the capital moved to Philadelphia in 1790, Washington noted that his next residence "will not be so commodious as the house I left in New York."[17] Abigail Adams, the Vice President's wife, regretted that "when all is done it will not be Broadway."[18]

Tower Building (center). NYHS.

Bradford Lee Gilbert; Standard Oil Building; Hendrick Hendricksen house (also known as the English barracks), ca. 1655; Mathys Capito house, ca. 1650.

CHEMICAL BANK BUILDING, No. 52
(Also known as Exchange Court) 1896-98, by Clinton & Russell; completely rebuilt 1980-82, by Emery Roth & Sons. [21 stories] A modern box with silvery ribbons has been created from a 12-story masonry building whose façade boasted statues by John Massey Rhind. *Site of* Guaranty & Indemnity Building (also known as Exchange Court); Rutger Arentsen house, ca. 1640.

MORRIS STREET

W **29 BROADWAY**

1929-31, by Sloan & Robertson. [31 stories] This unusually narrow tower has alternating bands of white and dark gray bricks, and strong Art Deco motifs. *Site of* Columbia Building, 1890, by Youngs & Cable; Burying Ground, on either side of Morris Street.

HARRIMAN BUILDING, No. 39
(Also known as the Fred F. French Broadway Building) 1926-28, by Cross & Cross. [37 stories] A complex series of setbacks tops this golden-brick tower. *Site of* Second Presidential Mansion (also known as the Alexander Macomb mansion, Bunker's Mansion House hotel), 1786-87; Paulus Leendertsen van der Grift house, ca. 1649; Earliest European settlement on Manhattan, 1613, by Captain Adriaen Block and crew.

45 BROADWAY ATRIUM
1983, by Fox & Fowle. [32 stories] A six-story base with a deeply recessed entrance is topped by a saw-tooth tower of buff brick and clear glass ribbons. *Site of* Aldrich Court Building (also known as the Hamburg-American Building, United States Office Building), 1886, by Youngs & Cable.

Second Presidential Mansion, after becoming a hotel, 1830; second Trinity Church, 1791. VM.

47 BROADWAY

[5 stories] There is one bay, with large windows. *Site of* Hendrick van Dyck house and garden, ca. 1647.

ONE EXCHANGE PLAZA, No. 55

1982-84, by Fox & Fowle. [32 stories] This is an aesthetic mate for No. 45, with rounded corners, instead of jagged ones. *Site of* Wells, Fargo Building, 1902, by Benjamin W. Morris, Jr.; Goelet Building, 1880-81, by Babb, Cook & Willard and Architectural Iron Works; Ricketts's Amphitheater, 1795.

EXCHANGE ALLEY

w   ADAMS EXPRESS BUILDING, No. 61

(Also known as Chase National Bank headquarters) 1912-13, by Francis Hatch Kimball. [32 stories] Extraordinarily spare for its time, this white-brick tower has deeply punched windows and a great copper cornice. *Site of* Adams Express Building, 1865; Judson's Hotel.

American Express Building, 1988.

AMERICAN EXPRESS BUILDING, No. 65

(Also known as the American Bureau of Shipping Building) 1914-19, by Renwick, Aspinwall & Tucker. [22 stories] A two-story colonnade at the top crosses the deep light well over a dramatic coffered arch, with a huge eagle cartouche. *Site of* American Express Building; Wells, Fargo Building; John R. Livingston mansion (also known as the Branch of the Second Bank of the United States).

EMPIRE BUILDING, No. 71

(Also known as the Arcade Building) 1896-98, Francis Hatch Kimball. [23 stories] Its vast façade provides a surprisingly sympathetic backdrop for Trinity, with classically inspired arcades, colonnades, balconies, and decorative courses. *Site of* Empire Building; Grace Church, 1806-09; Union Trust Building; Hunter's Hotel; Lutheran Church, 1727-29,

The first Grace Church (left) and Trinity Church, 1828; City Hotel. VM.

The Broadway that she knew was still a street dominated by churches and mansions. The second Trinity Church was consecrated in 1790. St. Paul's had accepted the public monument to Major General Richard Montgomery in 1787 and built an elegant wooden steeple in 1794. Grace Church was begun at Rector Street in 1806. But among the two- and three-story houses, where members of prominent families like the Livingstons and Van Cortlandts lived, commercial buildings were rising by the century's end. In 1794, the City Hotel was begun on the site of the De Lancey mansion. This was the principal hotel in New York, "an immense building 5 stories in height," with seventy-eight rooms "fitted up and furnished in a tasteful, elegant, and convenient manner."[19]

A sign of Broadway's emerging mercantile vitality was this 1794 advertisement: "John Jacob Astor, No. 149 Broad-way, Corner of Crown-street, Gives Cash for all kinds of Furs."[20] Although real estate gave his dynastic family its economic backbone, Astor made his first fortune in the fur trade, while living in a small brick mansion at Broadway and Vesey Street. Philip Hone—Mayor, vestryman of Trinity, trustee of Columbia College, governor of the New York Hospital, patron of the arts, and diarist—moved to 235 Broadway in 1821, a block north of Astor's house.

By the early nineteenth century, the transformation of Broadway into a business thoroughfare was assured. The New York Chemical Manufacturing Company, founded in 1823 to make alum, borax, camphor, vitriol, and other substances, had also secured banking privileges for itself. A year after its founding, it opened its financial division—the Chemical Bank—in a three-story house at 216 Broadway.[21] Washington's home at 39 Broadway had become a hotel called Bunker's Mansion House, which was described in 1828 as having "much of the retirement and quiet of an elegant private residence."[22] In 1830, the Kennedy mansion at One Broadway was converted to the Washington Hotel.

Hone, meanwhile, was being driven to distraction by the growing commotion on Broadway. In 1834, Astor tore down the block between Vesey and

Barclay streets to build the Astor House hotel. "The dust and rubbish will be almost intolerable," Hone prophesied, "but the establishment will be a great public advantage, and the edifice an ornament to the city, and for centuries to come will serve, as it was probably intended, as a monument of its wealthy proprietor."[23] It did indeed assume the legendary proportions—although not the longevity that Hone predicted. Within a few years of its opening, it was described as being "among hotels, that which Niagara is among waterfalls."[24] Guests included Henry Clay, Charles Dickens, Nathaniel Hawthorne, Sam Houston, Washington Irving, Andrew Jackson, Abraham Lincoln, Jenny Lind, and Daniel Webster. At the heart of the building was a courtyard with a fountain, which eventually became a glass-domed restaurant and "any one who was anybody could be seen at the Astor Rotunda sooner or later."[25] Ten years after the Astor opened, Lorenzo and Joseph Delmonico opened a hotel at Broadway and Morris Street that became the Astor's chief competitor and helped establish the Delmonico name.

Broadway was also growing synonymous with entertainment, particularly after Phineas T. Barnum acquired the American Museum, at Ann Street, in 1841. His own hyperbole best described it: "STOREHOUSE OF EARTH'S NOVELTIES . . . A Million Curiosities . . . EIGHTH WONDER OF THE WORLD . . . MOVING WAX FIGURES . . . LIVING WHALES . . . MAMMOTH FAT WOMAN . . . Refined and pleasing entertainments."[26] Other attractions were the Wooly Horse, Ploughing Elephant, Fegee Mermaid and Charles S. Stratton, who was thirty-three inches tall and known as General Tom Thumb.

The second Trinity Church, which had proved to be structurally unsound, was pulled down in 1839. Two years later, work was begun on the third church, designed by Richard Upjohn. It was consecrated in 1846, when the "splendid vaultings of the solemn temple resounded with the

Empire Building, 1988.

by Chevalier; Lutheran Church, 1676; West India Company garden and orchard, 1630s, on either side of Rector Street.

EXCHANGE PLACE

Union Trust Building, 1897. NYHS.

E ONE WALL STREET, No. 80
(Also known as the Irving Trust Company headquarters) 1928-31, by Ralph Walker; expanded 1965, by Smith, Smith, Haines, Waehler & Lundberg. [50 stories] The original tower is a soaring, cloud-piercing limestone vision, combining Art Deco angularity with an almost Art Nouveau organic quality. The 36-story southern addition is sympathetic but not as subtle or complex. The mosaics in the main banking room are by Hildreth Meière. *Site of* Knickerbocker Trust Building (also known as the Irving Bank Columbia Trust Building), 1908, by McKim, Mead & White, incorporating part of the Consolidated Exchange; One Wall Street (also known as the Bandbox Building), 1906, by Barnett, Hayner & Barnett; Century Building (also known as the Arthur Building), 1901, by Bruce Price; Manhattan Life Insurance Building (also known as the Central Hanover Building), 1893-94, by Francis Hatch Kimball; Union Trust Building, 1889-90, by George B. Post; Consolidated Stock and Petroleum

Astor House, ca. 1895. NYHS.

TRINITY CHURCH

*Views from 1986 to 1988 include the Martyrs' Monument
(below right).*

Exchange, 1887-88, by E.D. Lindsey; American National Bank of New York; Public Petroleum Stock Exchange; Globe Hotel, 1846; Herman Le Roy house; Peter Schermerhorn house; Augustine Herrman house, 1656; Pieter Schaefbanck house, ca. 1650; Resolved Waldron house, ca. 1650; Petrus Stuyvesant orchard.

RECTOR STREET

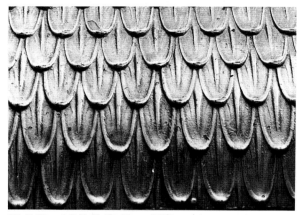

Wall Street I.R.T. Station, 1979.

w WALL STREET I.R.T. STATION
1904, by Heins & LaFarge. Interior Landmark. The stairways are covered by iron canopies with a lamb's-tongue pattern.

TRINITY CHURCH YARD
(Also known as the New Burial Place Without the Gate of the City) 1673. Landmark. Within the yard are the Martyrs' Monument (also known as the Soldiers' Monument), 1852-58; Firemen's Monument, 1865; Judge John Watts Monument, 1893, by George Bissell; and Trinity Church Yard Cross, 1914, by Thomas Nash. *Site of* Trinity Church, 1788-90, by James Robinson; Trinity Church, 1696-98; Lutheran Congregation House; Cornelis Jansen Pluvier house, ca. 1655; Jan Pietersen Verbrugge garden, ca. 1654; Land Gate of the Wall (also known as the City Gate), 1653.

TRINITY CHURCH
1841-1846, by Richard Upjohn. Landmark. Among its features are a tower clock, 1848, by James Rogers; front doors, 1891-96, by Richard Hunt, Karl Bitter, John Massey Rhind, and Charles Henry Niehaus; an altar and reredos, 1877, by Frederick Clark Withers; and a chancel window by Richard Upjohn and Abner Stephenson.
CHAPEL OF ALL SAINTS
1912-13, by Thomas Nash.
BISHOP WILLIAM T. MANNING MEMORIAL WING
1966, by Adams & Woodbridge.

notes of the grand organ and with the sounds of praise and adoration."[27] Its 284-foot Gothic spire was the tallest structure in New York for several decades and hundreds came to take in a panoramic view that was "unsurpassed on this continent."[28] The Martyrs' Monument, a sizable Gothic tower in its own right, was built in the north churchyard in 1858. Its nominal purpose was to honor soldiers and officers who died in British captivity, many of whom were buried nearby. Its secular purpose was to block attempts by the city to connect Albany and Pine streets through Trinity's property.[29]

Even at the time of its construction, Trinity Church reflected more of Broadway's past than its future. The real trendsetter was the Trinity Building, a speculative, multiple-tenant office building constructed in 1852 north of the churchyard, on the site of the Van Cortlandt mansion.[30] Among many occupants over the years were the Mutual Life Insurance Company, the Cunard Line, and Richard Upjohn, who designed it. On Cortlandt Street at this time, the ironmaker Daniel D. Badger gave New York its first major cast-iron business structure, the Gilsey Building, which set the architectural fashion for two decades.[31] An extraordinary survivor from this period of commercial development is the five-story Germania Building of 1865, which stands, upper stories intact, near Cortlandt Street. This was an office of the Germania Fire Insurance Company in the mid-1860s and the name is still visible on the façade.[32]

After the American Museum burned down in 1865—leaving a dead whale in the middle of Broadway, among other dreadful souvenirs—Barnum's site was taken by another flamboyant figure, James Gordon Bennett, for offices of the *New York Herald*. Depending on how one felt about the *Herald*, its costly marble palace by John Kellum could be seen as either the "most complete newspaper establishment in the world" or "proof of the profit that can be made . . . by unprincipled, demoralizing journalism."[33] The *Herald* was joined in 1874 by the *Evening Post*, which moved

New York Herald Building; Equitable Building of 1868–71. NYI.

to the corner of Fulton Street, one block south. Across Broadway in 1893 the *Mail and Express* completed an elaborately decorated, needle-like tower, designed by Carrère & Hastings.

More typical of Broadway than newspapers, however, were the financial institutions. An 1866 guide listed sixty-nine banks in New York; twenty-two of them had headquarters on Broadway.[34] One of the most important was the National Park Bank, next door to the Herald Building. Constructed in 1867 to designs by Griffith Thomas, the bank had a rotunda with ample room for its 125 employees—the largest number in any New York banking institution in the late nineteenth century—and a vault that was one of the strongest in the world.[35]

Even more impressive was the home office of the Equitable Life Assurance Society of the United States, at Cedar Street, which was begun in 1870 and later enlarged to cover the whole blockfront. Gargantuan in scale (each window opening was actually two stories high), it was the first office building in New York with elevators. Its rotunda had marble and onyx columns, a red granite entablature, and a stained-glass ceiling. Visitors came to Equitable to dine at the Café Savarin or meet at the Lawyers' Club or admire the view from the rooftop, where the Weather Bureau was located. Equitable exceeded the height of John Kellum's Mutual Life building, across Cedar Street, so Mutual added two extra floors. Not to be outdone, Equitable increased its building's height and exceeded Mutual again.[36]

By the very nature of their business, banks and insurance companies made Broadway the center of widespread economic networks, as did express companies, which transported bank notes, gold, and silver, and other valuables from city to city. They clustered on Express Row, a portion of Broadway north of Exchange Alley. There was the American Express Company, which moved to the row in 1875; Wells, Fargo & Company; and the Adams Express Company, whose headquarters were "fitted up in the best style of a banking-house" and whose stables were "as attractive as the queen's at Windsor Castle."[37]

Global networks in communication and industry were forming in the latter half of the nineteenth century and Broadway was at the heart of these as well. In 1875, the Western Union Telegraph Company—whose wires ran to every state and territory (except Arizona) and across the Atlantic Ocean—opened its tower-topped headquarters, designed by George B. Post, at Dey Street. Once a day, at noon, a ball was lowered on the tower, synchronized with the Naval Observatory in Washington. This time-keeping service was principally for ships' masters in the harbor, but on Broadway, "it was no unusual sight to see hundreds of faces turned anxiously upward about twelve o'clock."[38]

Another global network had its headquarters north of Bowling Green. In 1886, John D. Rockefeller and his associates moved the Standard Oil trust—the largest and richest manufacturing organization in the world—to 26 Broadway. From a modest, ten-story building there, 80 percent of the

Trinity Building, 1986 and 1988.

TRINITY BUILDING, No. 111

1904-07, by Francis Hatch Kimball; rooftop bridge added 1912; renovated 1988–1989, by Swanke Hayden Connell. Landmark. [21 stories] This Gothic slab is richly ornamented, marked by generous arched windows and gabled bays that echo but do not imitate Trinity Church. A copper-domed tower at top distinguishes this from the United States Realty Building next door. *Site of* Trinity Building, 1852, by Richard Upjohn; Van Cortlandt mansion.

WALL STREET

E ## TWO WALL STREET, No. 90

(Also known as the Banco Portugues do Atlantico, First National Bank of the City of New York) 1932-33, by Walker & Gillette. [22 stories] Oversized ornamentation, including gigantic granite brackets and five-pointed stars, dominates this tower. *Site of* United Bank Building (also known as the First National Bank), 1880, by Peabody & Stearns; Bank of the Republic; Equitable Life Building.

American Surety Building, 1979.

AMERICAN SURETY BUILDING, No. 100

(Also known as the Bank of Tokyo Building) 1894-96, by Bruce Price; expanded 1919-21, by Herman

Lee Meader; renovated 1975, by Kajima International. [22 stories] Eight allegorical figures by John Massey Rhind adorn the tremendous Ionic colonnade on the ground floor. Four more giant statues hover overhead. *Site of* Schermerhorn Building; Continental Insurance Company Home Office (also known as the Guardian Life Building), ca. 1860, by Griffith Thomas; Jacques Pryn house, ca. 1659.

PINE STREET

E   EQUITABLE BUILDING, No. 120

1912-15, by Ernest R. Graham; renovated 1983-90, by Ehrenkrantz, Eckstut & Whitelaw. [42 stories] Even now, this slab is astonishing for its sheer, daunting bulk. There is considerable refinement to the detailing, however. *Site of* Equitable Building, 1868-71, by Gillman & Kendall, enlarged 1886-88, by George B. Post; American Express Building; National Hotel, 1825; Athenaeum Reading Room, ca. 1824; John Trumbull house.

THAMES STREET

W   UNITED STATES REALTY BUILDING, No. 115

1906-07, by Francis Hatch Kimball; renovated 1988–90, by Swanke Hayden Connell. Landmark. [22 stories] Forms a pair with the Trinity Building. *Site of* Boreel Building, 1878-79, by Stephen Decatur Hatch; City Hotel, 1794-96; Etienne De Lancey mansion (also known as Burns's Tavern, City Tavern, Province Arms, Willett's), ca. 1700.

CEDAR STREET

W   LIBERTY PLAZA

[0.76 acres] *Site of* Liberty National Bank, 1902, by Cyrus L.W. Eidlitz; New York Title & Trust Building; Washington Life Insurance Building, 1897-98, by Cyrus L.W. Eidlitz; Western Union Building.

Marine Midland Building and Red Cube, *1978.*

E   MARINE MIDLAND BUILDING, No. 140

1967, by Skidmore, Owings & Merrill. [50 stories]

American Surety Building, 1979.

nation's refining capacity and 90 percent of its pipelines were controlled.[39] After the giant was broken up in 1909, the Standard Oil Company of New York remained at No. 26 and prospered.

Across from Standard, the old Washington Hotel at One Broadway was torn down in 1882 and replaced by the Washington Building, known for several years as the tallest office building in the world.[40] Its high copper roof and cupola, overlooking Battery Park, formed a landmark for travelers journeying through the harbor. (It is worth noting that despite all the tides of change that have washed over the tip of Manhattan Island, only three buildings have stood at One Broadway since the original land grant in 1643.) Also in 1882, construction began on the Produce Exchange, which was designed by George B. Post, using one of the earliest skeletal iron frameworks.[41] Wheat, corn, oats, rye, and barley were traded in a hall that was longer than an average city block, and the results were felt by farmers everywhere. Broadway also was home to the "Little Board," the Consolidated Stock and Petroleum Exchange, which came into existence in 1885. It competed for a time with the New York Stock Exchange, the "Big Board," but most of the Consolidated issues, as well as its brokers, were marginal.[42]

Broadway was not just a business street. Beginning in the 1880s, it was an architectural showcase as well. New York's first true skyscraper—a highrise with an iron frame—was the Tower Building, begun in 1888 at 50 Broadway, south of Exchange Place. Bradford Lee Gilbert, the architect, was asked by the owner of a twenty-one-foot lot to devise a plan that would yield a profitable building. "One day the idea came upon me like a flash that an iron bridge truss stood on end was the solution," Gilbert recalled.[43] The entire weight of this thirteen-story structure was carried by an interior skeleton, rather than by the exterior walls. The tower reached a height of 160 feet and showed that even the narrowest lots could be practicable building sites. The Corbin Building of 1889, for example, had a Broadway frontage of only twenty feet but was 135 feet high. Francis Hatch Kimball, the architect, turned the John Street façade into a richly embellished Romanesque fantasy in terra cotta. The apotheosis of skyscraping Romanesque was George B. Post's Union Trust Building of 1890. This rock-faced tower, south of Wall Street, was filled with soaring, monumental arches.

Beginning in the 1890s, bright, white towers started to replace smaller buildings of red brick and sandstone. The tallest building in the world was that of the Manhattan Life Insurance Company, completed in 1894, near Union Trust. It scraped the sky at 350 feet, the first building on Broadway to exceed the height of Trinity's steeple. The architect, Kimball, made an engineering breakthrough by sinking the foundations to bedrock with caissons, and was, with Gilbert and Post, one of the fathers of the skyscraper.[44]

The American Surety Building by Bruce Price, begun in 1894 at Pine Street, was one of the first to popularize the tripartite division of a façade into the elements of a Classical column: base, shaft, and capital.[45] The Bowling Green Offices, completed in 1898, north of Battery Place, presented a dazzling stylistic anomaly, with severely articulated upper stories and a florid Greco-Egyptian base. Its major historical association contrasts darkly with its aesthetic exuberance, for this was where families and friends of *Titanic* passengers gathered in April 1912 to get what news they could from the White Star Line.

At the foot of Broadway, the United States Custom House, designed by Cass Gilbert, symbolized the power of the Port of New York at a time when it accounted for much of the Federal Government's revenue. Seventy-five percent of America's worldwide commerce entered through New York, so it was fitting in 1907 that the city should get the "largest and most beautiful custom house in the world."[46] The enormous Rotunda was the heart of the

Bowling Green Offices, 1988.

Sleek and refined in manner, this black tower is enlivened by Isamu Noguchi's *Red Cube* sculpture. *Site of* Guaranty Trust Building (also known as the Morgan Guaranty Trust Building), 1911-13, by York & Sawyer; Mutual Life Insurance Company Home Office (also known as the First National Bank of New York), 1863-65, by John Kellum; Congress Hall Hotel, ca. 1830.

LIBERTY STREET

One Liberty Plaza, 1986.

W ONE LIBERTY PLAZA, No. 165

(Also known as Merrill Lynch headquarters, U.S. Steel Building) 1971, by Skidmore, Owings & Merrill. [54 stories] With some 2 million square feet, this dark, massive, and brutal building is one of the largest on Broadway. *Site of* Singer Building, 1897-99, by Ernest Flagg, enlarged 1906-08, by Flagg; City Investing Building (also known as the Benenson Building, Chemical Bank headquarters), 1906-08, by Francis Hatch Kimball; Gilsey Building (also known as the Benedict Brothers Building, Wessells Building), 1853-54, by J.W. Ritch and Daniel D. Badger; Rathbun's Hotel; John Jacob Astor fur business. *Near site of* Oswego Market (also known as the Broadway Market, Crown Market), 1738.

E WESTINGHOUSE BUILDING, No. 150

1923-24, Starrett & Van Vleck. [23 stories] This is a nondescript brown-brick box. *Site of* Williamsburgh City Fire Insurance Building, 1883, by F. C. Merry; Manhattan Life Insurance Building (also known as the Citizens' Insurance Building), ca. 1860, by John B. Snook.

LAWYERS' TITLE INSURANCE & TRUST BUILDING, No. 160

1907-08, by Clinton & Russell. [17 stories] A three-story colonnade above street level distinguishes this red-brick building. *Site of* Guernsey Building, 1881, by Richard Morris Hunt.

UNITED STATES CUSTOM HOUSE

Views from 1988 include the entrance hall (below),
ceiling of the Collector's Reception Room (below right),
and the Rotunda (left, facing page).

BROADWAY-MAIDEN LANE BUILDING, No. 170

(Also known as the Guardian Trust Building) 1901-02, Clinton & Russell. [18 stories] There is some spare ornamentation on this plain buff-brick tower.

CORTLANDT STREET

w 173 BROADWAY

[2 stories] A simple structure with a curved corner. *Site of* Waterman Building (also known as Pen Corner).

Germania Building, 1986.

GERMANIA BUILDING, No. 175

(Also known as the Century Twenty One Department Store) 1865. [5 stories] Despite alterations to the lower floors, the top of this cast-iron building is intact, with three-quarter-round Corinthian columns, plus a cornice with a hood mold.

177 BROADWAY

(Also known as the Century Twenty One Department Store, Crouch & Fitzgerald). [5 stories] Only the fenestration of this radically altered nineteenth-century building hints at its origin.

WALK-OVER BUILDING, No. 179

ca. 1907. [6 stories] A colossal central window bay, now painted over, is framed by a great segmental arch.

181 BROADWAY

[6 stories] This is a very simple brick and limestone grid.

183 BROADWAY

(Also known as J. Milhau's Son Dispensing Chemist). [5 stories] Like No. 177, this altered nineteenth-century building offers few clues as to its origin, except in the fenestration.

189-91 BROADWAY

[2 stories] *Site of* Mercantile National Bank, 1862.

operation—where millions of dollars were exchanged and dozens of foreign languages were spoken—but the Collector's Reception Room was no less grand, with walnut carvings and a gilded, coffered ceiling.[47]

In the new century, buildings along Broadway grew much taller and denser. They were unbound by stylistic convention—some were Gothic, some Classical, some Beaux-Arts. And they were unbound by zoning controls. In 1906, the roadbed of Thames Street was shifted to accommodate the United States Realty Building, enabling the developer to build over every square foot of ground. The Realty tower and its near twin, the Trinity Building, were designed by Francis Hatch Kimball and shaped like 300–foot-high slices of toast, turning Thames into a chilling, fathomless canyon. But the Trinity Building also overlooked Trinity Church from the north and that inspired a respectful, but not imitative, Gothic façade. (Kimball had designed the earlier Empire Building, at Rector Street, on the south side of the churchyard, and Montgomery Schuyler believed that the Empire and Trinity buildings together had the "effect of framing and protecting the relic."[48])

The "race of Titanic skyscrapers" surged ahead in 1906 with plans by the Singer Manufacturing Company for the world's tallest building, on the spot at Liberty Street where Astor once sold furs. The magnitude of the Singer project led the *Times* to declare that the "skyscraper is still *'ferae naturae.'* "[49] Ernest Flagg designed the red-and-green, mansard-topped tower, which bore a resemblance to his "Little" Singer Building in SoHo, with a large, glass-filled central bay under a broad arch. The shaft—added to an earlier, smaller building—rose 612 feet, more than twice the height of Trinity. Next door was the City Investing Building, another extravaganza by Kimball. It was the largest office building in the world, but, at thirty-four stories, it dwelled very much in Singer's shadow.[50]

Singer was eclipsed by the Metropolitan Life Tower at Madison Square, but in 1913 Broadway regained the distinction of having the tallest building on earth, with the dazzling Gothic spire that is today—as it was when built—headquarters for the F.W. Woolworth Company. The 792–foot Woolworth Building, between Barclay Street and Park Place, with its lacy white façade and its gleaming lobby of marbles and mosaics, was designed by Cass Gilbert for Frank W. Woolworth, who wanted a "building that would advertise the Woolworth five-and-ten-cent stores all over the world." When Gilbert asked him how tall this should be, Woolworth answered, "How high can you make it?"[51] The tower was nationally celebrated from the start. For its opening, President Woodrow Wilson pressed a button at the White House to set off 80,000 lights in the skyscraper. The Reverend Dr. S. Parkes Cadman called it the "Cathedral of Commerce" and said that the tower, "piercing space like a battlement of the paradise of God . . .inspires feelings too deep even for tears."[52] "What an 'uplift' there is in that sudden, rocketlike shooting of the white and channeled shaft," Montgomery Schuyler proclaimed. "How it cleaves the empyrean and makes the welkin ring."[53]

Not everyone was so enthusiastic about the unchecked race to the heavens. As early as 1898, after a heavy fire damaged the upper floors of the

Manhattan Life Insurance Building; Singer Building. NYHS, GRAY.

Postal Telegraph-Cable and Home Life buildings on Broadway, the question was raised of legally regulating tower heights.[54] The question came up again in 1908, when Equitable Life announced plans for a 909–foot skyscraper on the site of its headquarters, between Pine and Cedar streets. One critic said the building would create such great crowds that "people would have to walk in three layers, one above the other."[55] In 1912, after the old Equitable Building was destroyed by fire, new plans were announced: not for the world's tallest building, but for the world's biggest. Five months later, City Hall declared that the "time has come when an effort should be made to regulate the height, size, and arrangement of buildings," to preserve light and air, prevent congestion, and reduce fire hazards.[56]

Before this effort yielded its result—the 1916 Zoning Resolution—several more massive towers were built, including Equitable. "A City In Itself Housing 16,000 Souls," it had walls that rose forty-two stories straight up, without setbacks, and it cast a seven-acre shadow that reduced the value of surrounding properties.[57] With about 1.6 million square feet of floor space on a parcel of less than 50,000 square feet, the ratio of floor area to lot size was more than thirty-two to one. (Modern skyscrapers typically have floor-area ratios of about twenty to one, or less.)

Only slightly less dense were the Adams Express Building by Francis

MAIDEN LANE

E CUSHMAN BUILDING, No. 174

(Also known as the William Barthman Building) 1897-98, by C.P.H. Gilbert. [12 stories] A great, gabled copper roof with several overscaled dormers tops this chunky little tower. *Site of* Howard Hotel, 1839-40, by William Hurry. *Near site of* Oswego Market, 1772.

TITLE GUARANTEE & TRUST BUILDING, No. 176

1905-06, by Howells & Stokes; enlarged. [15 stories] Although the original façade of six-story-high Corinthian pilasters is intact, the building has been seriously compromised by a four-story addition.

180 BROADWAY

1901, by Clinton & Russell. [12 stories] This little tower has a deeply scored buff-brick façade.

182 BROADWAY

[2 stories] Under hideous modern signage lies a minor Art Deco gem with Bauhaus overtones. *Site of* Seventh National Bank (also known as the Chatham Bank).

DEY STREET

Telephone & Telegraph Building, 1988.

W TELEPHONE & TELEGRAPH BUILDING, No. 195

(Also known as the A. T. & T. Building) 1912-13 and 1916-17, by William Welles Bosworth; expanded 1921-23, by William Welles Bosworth; renovated 1983-85, by Eli Attia. [30 stories] Nine gleaming Greek colonnades, each colossal in itself, are wrapped around this dense office tower. *The Spirit of Communications* (also known as *Golden Boy*), a sculpture by Evelyn Beatrice Longman Batchelder, once adorned the building's pyramidal peak, but has been removed. The *Four Elements*, bas-relief panels by Paul Manship, remain. *Site of* Mail and Express Building, 1890-93, by Carrère & Hastings, with

WOOLWORTH BUILDING

Views from 1988 and 1989.

Western Union Building. NYHS.

sculpture by F. Martiny; Western Union Building, 1873-75, by George B. Post, enlarged, by Henry J. Hardenbergh; Franklin House hotel.

JOHN STREET

Corbin Building, 1989.

E   **CORBIN BUILDING, No. 192**
(Also known as the Chatham National Bank Building) 1888-89, by Francis Hatch Kimball. [9 stories] Magnificent arches, in a variety of sizes and treatments, add drama to this vast red-brick and terra-cotta façade.

CHILDS RESTAURANT, No. 194-96
1911, by J.C. Westervelt. [3 stories] Antefixes, dentiled cornices, and fretwork characterize this finely detailed façade.

GIRARD BUILDING, No. 198
1902, by Walter H. Wickes. [12 stories] This very narrow tower has a six-story copper bay at center, with oversize decoration throughout.

204-10 BROADWAY
[2 stories] Contemporary signage detracts from this streamlined building. *Site of* Evening Post Building, 1874, by C.F. Mengelson.

Hatch Kimball, at Exchange Alley, and the Telephone and Telegraph Building, at Dey Street, both begun in 1912. At the time, American Telephone and Telegraph held a 30 percent interest in Western Union, whose building had occupied the Dey Street site. They joined headquarters in the new, column-girdled tower—topped by an allegorical statue known as *Golden Boy*—which also took in the general offices of the New York Telephone and Western Electric companies. The architect, William Welles Bosworth, said he aimed for "simplicity and dignity combined with an impression of enduring strength."[58] He achieved his goal in the hypostyle hall that is the lobby, an ivory-colored forest of massively fluted columns.

The A.T.&T. lobby was not the last word in sumptuousness, however. That distinction belongs to the Cunard Building of 1921, at Morris Street, which still evokes the luxury of ocean travel, even in its modern incarnation as a post office. The ticket office was the "most imposing entrance hall ever created for the booking of trans-atlantic passengers and freight," with "mural decorative effects probably unsurpassed in the annals of commercial building construction."[59] It is 183 feet long, with a grand, octagonal rotunda whose dome is sixty-eight feet high (about six stories). The ceiling murals by Ezra Winter, devoted to explorers and mythical sea creatures, are painted in a luscious palette of magenta, raspberry, gold, and blue. Map murals nearby testify to the geopolitical past: French and British colonies and the old Chinese republic.

Two doors down from Cunard, the International Mercantile Marine Company remodeled the Washington Building in 1921 to serve as its headquarters. This gigantic shipping combine—including the White Star Line—was created by J.P. Morgan and controlled 120 vessels at the time it moved into One Broadway. There are still iron railings with anchor-like "I.M.M." ligatures, map murals, an inlaid compass on the floor, and entrances marked "FIRST CLASS" and "CABIN CLASS." Ringing the building are the mosaic arms of twenty principal ports of call. One Broadway was later headquarters for the United States Lines.

Across the street, the Standard Oil Building was expanded southward to Beaver Street in the 1920s and given a new tower, with a pyramidal peak modeled on the Mausoleum at Halicarnassos. The three-part structure (the original from 1886, a northern addition from 1896, and the new southern addition) got a uniform façade, whose deep rustication and monumental arches complemented the Cunard Building. Because of its association with Standard Oil, the address 26 Broadway was "incorporated into the language of America as having a sweeping significance."[60] Meanwhile, with the expansive regional Bell System, A.T.&T. was growing into a huge corporate entity—the biggest company on earth.[61] And just as No. 26 meant oil, No. 195 became synonymous with the telephone. It, too, had a Halicarnassos-style peak, topped with a winged allegorical figure known popularly as *Golden Boy*. The building was also expanded in the 1920s, to fill the whole blockfront, to Fulton Street.

A clean aesthetic break with these corporate monuments came in the late 1920s and early '30s, when a number of Art Deco or Modernist towers were

TELEPHONE & TELEGRAPH BUILDING
Views from 1979 to 1988.

CUNARD BUILDING

Views from 1988 include Ezra Winter's ceiling murals in the Great Hall.

FULTON STREET

w **FULTON STREET I.R.T. STATION**
1904, by Heins & LaFarge. Interior Landmark.

Loew Footbridge and St. Paul's Chapel, ca. 1867. NYHS.

ST. PAUL'S CHURCH YARD
Landmark. Within the yard are the George
Frederick Cooke Monument (also known as the
Actors Monument), 1821, by W. & J. Frazee;
Thomas Addis Emmet Monument, 1833; and William
James MacNeven Monument, ca. 1865. ***Near site of***
Loew Footbridge, 1866-67.

ST. PAUL'S CHAPEL OF TRINITY PARISH
1764-66, attributed to Thomas McBean, possibly by
Andrew Gautier; wood steeple added 1794, by James
Crommelin Lawrence. Landmark. Monument to
Major General Richard Montgomery, by J.J.
Caffieri. The altar and "Glory" carving are by Pierre
Charles L'Enfant.

*National Park Bank,
ca. 1910. NYHS.*

E **WESTERN ELECTRIC BUILDING, No. 222**
1959-61, by Shreve, Lamb & Harmon Associates. [31
stories] This blandly pink building is obtrusive in its
bulky massing. The lobby mural is by Buell Mullen.
Site of National Park Bank of New York, 1904, by
Donn Barber, with murals by Albert Herter; St.

built. There was 29 Broadway, at Morris Street, as effervescent as it was
narrow. There was the sober, almost brutal Two Wall Street, which was completed in 1933 for the First National Bank, an elite old institution which later
merged with the National City Bank, forerunner of Citibank. Far larger and
more refined was One Wall Street, whose central shaft was clad in an undulating curtain of limestone. The Irving Trust Company moved its headquarters
into this tower in 1931 with a dramatic, military-style operation in which $3
billion in gold, currency, and securities were transported from the bank's old
headquarters in the Woolworth Building.[62]

With the Depression, the Second World War, and the post-war emergence of mid-Manhattan as the prime office district, lower Broadway fell into
a twenty-five-year hiatus. Its reemergence, beginning in the late 1950s, came
at the expense of some of its finest landmarks. Even the Woolworth Building's Gothicism fell out of favor, although the company always kept the tower
exquisitely maintained while it was growing into a 7,000-store giant. The Produce Exchange was replaced by a glass-and-steel monster, Two Broadway, in
1959. Another graceless modern box, the Western Electric Building of 1961,
replaced the second National Park Bank, which had a grand vaulted interior,
and the St. Paul Building by George B. Post, which was once the third tallest
building in New York.[63] (The Chase Bank, which merged with the Park Bank
in 1929, still has a branch at that location.)

The Guaranty Trust Building of 1913, designated by the Municipal Art
Society as worthy of preservation, was replaced in 1967 by the Marine Midland Building. Faced with a trapezoidal site, between Cedar and Liberty
streets, the architects at Skidmore, Owings & Merrill chose to smooth over
the odd shape with a skin of mat-black aluminum and dark glass.[64] The result
is the epitome of cool 1960s International Style. Then, for a delightful aesthetic surprise, it was offset with a bright red, twenty-eight-foot rhombohe-
dron by Isamu Noguchi.

The Singer Company sold its tower in 1963 and moved out. The Municipal
Art Society identified the building as a landmark worth preserving and Nathan Silver praised its "spectacular lobby of colored marble, bronze, and
glass-saucer domes." But the once-proud tower earned the unhappy distinction in 1967 of being the tallest building ever demolished.[65] Even more unfor-
tunately, it was replaced by One Liberty Plaza. U.S. Steel, the co-developer,
requested a structure that would express the notion of steel and Skidmore,
Owings & Merrill replied with brutal, black, six-foot spandrel girders
throughout.[66]

One Liberty Plaza later became the headquarters of Merrill Lynch &
Company, the giant financial house, and the Bank of Tokyo Trust Company
rebuilt the American Surety Building, but the arrival of new corporate titans
was the exception. Standard Oil, which had evolved into Socony Mobil, left
in 1956 for East Forty-second Street. Cunard left in 1968 for Fifth Avenue.
The Customs Service left in 1971 for the World Trade Center. American Express left in 1975 for Water Street, although it kept a bureau at 65 Broadway.
A.T.&T. left in 1983 for Madison Avenue. And Irving Trust was taken over

ONE WALL STREET

Views from 1988 and 1989 include a detail of the façade.

Paul Building, 1895-99, by George B. Post, with statues by Karl Bitter; New York Herald Building, 1867, by John Kellum; National Park Bank, 1867-68, by Griffith Thomas; Knox's Great Hat and Cap Establishment, ca. 1850; Dr. Scudder's Museum (also known as Barnum's American Museum), 1830; Chemical Bank; Spring Garden House (also known as the John Elkin Public House, Hampden Hall).

VESEY STREET

w ASTOR BUILDING, No. 217

(Also known as the Franklin Society Building) 1915, by Charles A. Platt. [7 stories] Somewhat evocative of the old Astor House, this building has a severely plain, rusticated façade. *Site of* Astor House hotel (also known as the Park Hotel), 1834-36, by Isaiah Rogers; Walter Rutherfurd house; Aaron Burr house (also known as the Official Residence of the Vice President); John Jacob Astor house, 1792-95; King's Farm House (also known as the Drover's Inn).

TRANSPORTATION BUILDING, No. 225

1926-28, by York & Sawyer. [44 stories] This oddly proportioned buff-brick tower is topped by a copper hip roof.

BARCLAY STREET

Woolworth Building, 1978.

w WOOLWORTH BUILDING, No. 233

1911-13, by Cass Gilbert; renovated 1977-81, by the Ehrenkrantz Group. Exterior and Interior Landmark. [58 stories] This copper-crested, 792-foot Gothic stalagmite of granite, limestone, and terra cotta is brilliantly faceted. The exterior carvings are by Donnally & Ricci. The lobby mosaics are by Heinigke & Bowen, the lunettes by C. Paul Jennewein, and grotesques by Tom Johnson. *Site of* National Broadway Bank, rebuilt 1877, by David & John Jardine; American Hotel (also known as Cozzens Hotel), 1826-27; Philip Hone house.

Telephone & Telegraph Building, 1988.

by the Bank of New York in 1988, after which its name disappeared from One Wall Street.

Despite the corporate exodus, lower Broadway was—in some respects—looking like its old self as the 1980s ended. Minus *Golden Boy*, which A.T.&T. spirited uptown, the 195 Broadway building was restored by its new owner in the 1980s, as were a number of other towers, including the Trinity and United States Realty Buildings, Adams Express, and Equitable. Another enduring Broadway presence was the ticker-tape parade. Among the heroic and celebrated figures who had been honored through the years under a deluge of paper in the canyon of lower Broadway were Theodore Roosevelt (who may have been the first), a Prince of Wales, Charles Lindbergh, Douglas MacArthur, John Glenn, the first lunar astronauts, Pope John Paul II, Vietnam veterans, the American hostages from Iran, the 1984 Olympic team, and the New York Mets in 1969 and 1986.[67]

Two other ceremonial events on Broadway were particularly evocative of its history. In 1976, two hundred years to the day after her ancestor's statue was pulled down at the Bowling Green, Queen Elizabeth II called at Trinity Church. She was given 279 peppercorns from the Rector of Trinity, as "rent past due the Monarchy" since the Charter of 1697.[68] In 1989, at St. Paul's Chapel, the bicentenary of the Federal Government was celebrated. President George Bush sat where Washington had worshipped after the first inauguration and listened, as his predecessor had, to the singing of the *Te Deum*. A great national circle had been drawn, beginning and ending on Broadway.

Ticker-tape parade in 1986 for the New York Mets, looking south over City Hall Park. Neal Boenzi/The New York Times.

New York City Department of City Planning

CIVIC CENTER TRIBECA

CITY HALL PARK TO CANAL STREET

View south in 1988 includes the Federal Plaza (left), the Woolworth Building (center), and the World Trade Center.

Broadway clings to tradition in the blocks north and south of Chambers Street. What looks at first like a drab streetscape—office towers, lofts, and parking lots—turns out, on closer inspection, to have a fine nineteenth-century character. There is City Hall and its park, the Tweed Court House, A.T. Stewart's store, and more than twenty other structures that have stood since the mid-1800s. These buildings reflect Broadway's long-standing role as the seat of government and as a dry-goods center. In the 1970s and '80s, government kept growing, while the wholesale trade shrank. The borders of Chinatown expanded from the east and loft dwellers moved in from the north. The area was christened TriBeCa (the triangle below Canal Street), and its social fabric—part residential, part mercantile, part civic—became as heterogeneous as its architecture.

Bridewell, 1805. VM.

City Hall Park, 1986.

Post Office (left) and National Park Bank, 1890. NYHS.

In the eighteenth century, Chambers Street was the edge of town, where large or unwanted institutions were placed. Broadway virtually came to an end after its intersection with the High Road to Boston, the present-day Park Row. Within the large V formed by these two roads was the Common, which would become City Hall Park. The first Alms House was built on the Common in 1735 for "Needy Persons and Idle Wandring Vagabonds, Sturdy Beggars" and "unruly and ungovernable Servants and Slaves," so that "such Poor as are able to work, may not Eat the Bread of Sloth & Idleness, and be a Burthen to the Publick."[1] In 1775, a city prison called the Bridewell was begun next to the Alms House. This was branded a "school for guilt" because it placed the "aged and crafty felon in the same room, with the boy, who has committed some trifling depredations."[2] North of the Bridewell and Alms House was the graveyard for African-Americans, where most of the slaves who lived in lower New York were buried. "Not even a dedication of their burial-place was made by the church authorities," said an 1865 history. "The locality was unattractive and desolate."[3]

Such isolated tracts of land were ideal for large-scale construction. The Society of the Hospital in the City of New York in America received its charter in 1771, "having for its object the Relief of the indigent & diseased."[4] The society purchased five acres north of Duane Street and began building the New York Hospital. At the time, the city's first major waterworks were also under construction. As planned in 1774 by the engineer Christopher Colles, the heart of the system was a reservoir on Broadway, north of Franklin Street. Water was to run in pitch-pine pipes through every street and lane, where it could be drawn from perpendicular conduits at 100–yard intervals.[5]

Remote though it was, the area played a significant role in the events leading to the Revolution. In May 1766, to mark the repeal of the Stamp Act, the patriots' group known as the Sons of Liberty raised a mast near the Alms House. It carried a board with the word "Liberty" on it and was called the Liberty Pole. In August, the pole was cut down by the British soldiers. The Sons of Liberty erected a second, third, and fourth pole, which were brought down in turn. The fifth Liberty Pole was still standing on July 9, 1776. That evening, American troops formed a hollow square on the Common, with General Washington on horseback in the middle, and listened as the Declaration of Independence was read aloud. Washington later informed Congress that

E CITY HALL PARK

[8.8 acres] On Broadway is a statue of *Nathan Hale*, by Frederick MacMonnies (pedestal by Stanford White), a Liberty Pole from 1921, and the George Delacorte Fountain. *Site of* United States Post Office, 1875, by A.B. Mullett; Liberty Poles, 1766-76.

City Hall, 1979.

CITY HALL

1803-12, by John McComb Jr. and Joseph François Mangin; renovated 1859, by Leopold Eidlitz;

View north in 1979 includes Grace Church in the distance.

renovated 1902-15; completely rebuilt 1954-56, by
New York City Public Works Department and
Shreve, Lamb & Harmon Associates. Exterior and
Interior Landmark. [4 stories] There have been
several statues of *Justice* on the cupola, the earliest
by John Dixey. *Site of* the Bridewell, 1775-76, by
Theophilus Hardenbrook; Alms House, 1735-36;
Dugdale and Searle's Rope Walk, 1719; Wind Mill on
the Commons, 1663-64, rebuilt 1695.

CITY HALL I.R.T. STATION

1904, by Heins & LaFarge. Interior Landmark. The
unique character of this station comes from the
Guastavino vaults and sweeping green- and white-
tiled arches over its curved platform.

Tweed Court House, 1987.

TWEED COURT HOUSE

(Also known as the New York County Court
House). 1861-72, by Thomas Little and John Kellum;
enlarged 1877-81, by Leopold Eidlitz. Exterior and
Interior Landmark. [4 stories] There is sorrow and
romance to the ghostly gray decay of this Italianate
façade. *Site of* Alms House (also known as the New
City Hall, New York Institution), 1796-97.

PARK PLACE

w ### 250 BROADWAY

1961, by Emery Roth & Sons. [29 stories] A stack of
glass boxes. *Site of* Importers' and Traders'
National Bank, 1907-08, by Joseph H. Freedlander;
Varick Building, 1870, by R.G. Hatfield; Bixby's
Hotel, 1854; W. & J. Sloane's Carpet Wareroom;
Mechanics' Hall, 1802-03.

MURRAY STREET

w ### POSTAL TELEGRAPH-CABLE BUILDING, No. 251-55

(Also known as the Home Life Building). 1892-94,
by Harding & Gooch. Proposed landmark. [14

the "measure seemed to have their most hearty assent."[6] There was not much
time to celebrate, however. By mid-September, the British controlled New
York. They turned the Bridewell into a dungeon for 800 prisoners, who "died
like rotten sheep, with cold, hunger and dirt."[7] They also used the unfinished
hospital as a garrison.

It was not until well after the war's end—and a riot in 1788 to protest
the practice of grave-digging by medical students—that the New York Hospital finally opened, in 1791. The main building, known as the Central Hospital,
accommodated 200 patients and was surrounded by spacious grounds. It was
reached from Broadway along an allee lined with elm trees. "No spot on the
whole island could be better chosen on which to build a hospital," it was noted
in 1817. "The elevation of the building secures to the sick all the advantages
of a free circulation of air."[8] An insane asylum opened on the south grounds
in 1808, but was later moved far north on the island, to Bloomingdale.

The Common was still thought of as a fitting place for an Alms House in
1796, when the second one was begun. But at the beginning of the nineteenth
century, New York decided to build its new City Hall directly south of the
Alms House, thereby moving government and the courts "almost to the ex-
tremity of the city," as the *Daily Advertiser* said in 1802. That decision helped
raise property values and spurred Broadway's transformation into a well-to-
do avenue, as the newspaper predicted: "Gentlemen of the long robe, and
those whose duties are connected with public offices, will naturally fix their
residence in the vicinity."[9] The architects Joseph François Mangin and John
McComb Jr. were chosen in 1802. The cornerstone was laid in 1803. What
followed over the next decade was a civic undertaking of vast proportion,
consuming each year an amount equal to almost half the city's revenues.[10] Of
course, there were those who believed that "objects of far greater importance
demand the attention of the Corporation": paving, lighting, adequate fire pro-
tection, and street cleaning.[11] But the building project pressed ahead—with
economic concessions like the substitution of brownstone for marble in the
rear—and in 1811, the Common Council met there for the first time. Mayor

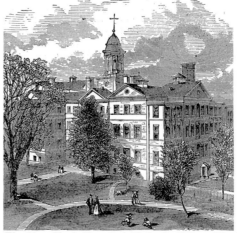
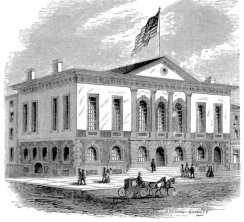

The New York Hospital Main Building; Washington Hall, 1828. NYI, VM.

View north in 1819 includes City Hall. MCNY.

De Witt Clinton moved in the next year. "The City Hall is the most prominent, and most important building in New-York," an 1817 guide book proclaimed. "It is the handsomest structure in the United States; perhaps of its size, in the world."[12]

Inside, the public chambers radiated from the top of a dramatic, double-sided, flying staircase in a central rotunda. At center was the room set aside for the Governor's use when he was in town. The Governor's Room was also a portrait gallery, filled with paintings by John Trumbull and John Wesley Jarvis, among others. In the southwest corner of the Hall was the Common Council Chamber, an elegant room with a circular array of columns and pilasters under a shallow dome. The Court of Sessions and the Court of Oyer and Terminer were conducted in the building's northwest corner. "These being courts of criminal jurisdiction," it was said, "they excite much interest and draw a large concourse of auditors. The largest room in the Hall is, therefore, appropriated to their use."[13] The room had a delicacy and dignity far surpassing the proceedings that occurred within.

After City Hall's cornerstone was laid, the stretch of Broadway along the Park and to the north became the seat of fashion, with assembly halls, cultural institutions, clubs, theaters, churches, stores, and hotels. The General Society of Mechanics and Tradesmen opened Mechanics' Hall, at Park Place, in 1803. John McComb Jr. designed Washington Hall, at Reade Street, which was completed in 1812. This assembly place and hotel was an important social and political center—"none hold a higher rank."[14] The second Alms House became the New York Institution in 1816, home to such organizations as the New-York Historical Society, the New-York Society Library, and the American Museum (forerunner of Barnum's). Masonic Hall, begun in 1826, north of Duane Street, had a ballroom ornamented by Gothic traceries and arches, with a dance floor suspended on elastic springs. Its granite façade and great oak door reminded viewers of "ancient abbeys, castles, and other edifices of the gothic ages."[15]

stories] Highly unusual recessed window frames run through this buff-brick tower, whose monumental entrance portico was ruined by modernization. *Site of* Peale's Museum and Gallery of the Fine Arts, 1825; Montagne's Tavern, ca. 1750.

HOME LIFE BUILDING, No. 256-57

1892-94, by Napoleon LeBrun & Son. Proposed landmark. [16 stories] Its steeply peaked copper roof slices the skyline and its ornately garlanded base has arched windows, oculi, pediments, and columns.

Beach Pneumatic Subway Terminal. NYI.

ROGERS, PEET BUILDING, No. 258-59

1899-1900, by John B. Snook; expanded ca. 1912. Proposed landmark. [8 stories] This façade has an articulated grid of wide bays with large, 4-over-4 windows. *Site of* D. Devlin & Company Store (also known as the Beach Pneumatic Subway Terminal), ca. 1850, by John B. Snook; Tiffany & Young Store.

WARREN STREET

W **CITY HALL BUILDING, No. 260-61**

1906, by James B. Baker. [12 stories] A white-brick box. *Site of* United States Life Insurance Building.

CORN EXCHANGE BANK BUILDING, No. 265-67

(Also known as the Civil Service Retired Employees Association World Headquarters). 1936, by Fellheimer & Wagner. [5 stories] Its simple modernist façade is overwhelmed by the signage.

ARTHUR LEVITT STATE OFFICE BUILDING, No. 270

1928-30, by E.H. Faile & Company. [28 stories] A spartan, white-brick tower. *Site of* Chemical National Bank, 1905-07, by Trowbridge & Livingston; National Shoe and Leather Bank, 1893, by Josiah Cleveland Cady; Remsen Building (also known as the New York Athenaeum, New-York Historical Society), ca. 1832.

CITY HALL

Views from 1979 to 1988 include the Rotunda (facing page).

CITY HALL

Views from 1988 show the original Common Council Chamber (left, facing page); the Governor's Room, with a portrait of Governor George Clinton by John Trumbull (right, facing page); and the Board of Estimate Chamber (below).

CHAMBERS STREET

Broadway Chambers, 1988.

w BROADWAY CHAMBERS, No. 273-77

1899-1900, by Cass Gilbert. Proposed landmark. [18 stories] Atop a red-brick façade is a monumentally embellished arcade of great depth, plasticity, and color. *Site of* Irving House Hotel, 1848.

279-83 BROADWAY

[3 stories] *Site of* first A.T. Stewart store.

287 BROADWAY

1871-72, by John B. Snook. Landmark. [6 stories] With leafy cresting atop its mansard roof, pediment-framed dormers, stout columns, and large arched windows, this is a cast-iron gem.

A.T. Stewart's "Marble Palace," 1987.

E A.T. STEWART'S "MARBLE PALACE," No. 280

(Also known as the Sun Building). 1845-46, by John B. Snook of Joseph Trench & Company; expanded 1850-51, by Trench & Snook; enlarged 1884, by Edward D. Harris. Landmark. [7 stories] The Renaissance Revival façade is full of subtle details, like the projecting and receding pavilions and the human-mask keystones. The *Sun* clock and thermometer were added after 1917. *Site of*

New York's first club on the London model—a gathering place for patrician citizens—was the Union Club, begun in 1837 at 343 Broadway, south of Leonard Street. Its elite members had the use of dining, reading, billiard, and card rooms.[16] Across Broadway, a massive, temple-fronted structure was begun in 1838 to house the venerable New-York Society Library. This was the city's "public library," offering books, periodicals, and newspapers in a "large and airy apartment" that was open fourteen hours a day.[17] At the Apollo Rooms, south of Canal Street, professional musicians met in 1842 to form a society for the "advancement of instrumental music."[18] Eight months later, in the same hall, this Philharmonic Society gave its first concert, including Beethoven's Fifth Symphony. In 1847, the Broadway Theater, which could seat 4,000 patrons, opened south of Worth Street. It won a reputation as "one of the best arranged places of amusement in New York."[19]

Outside the social whirl, but of major political importance, was the Broadway Tabernacle Congregational Church, which was founded in 1840 and became a cornerstone of Abolitionism. It occupied a site on Worth Street, directly north of where the slaves' burial ground had been, and its pastor was said to have influenced President Abraham Lincoln's opinion on emancipation.[20]

Nearby were several notable retailers. Charles Lewis Tiffany and John B. Young opened a store in 1837 at Warren Street that sold Japanese and Chinese goods, papier-mâché, terra cotta, umbrellas, walking sticks, fans, stationery, pottery, and bric-a-brac. Within eight years they boasted that their "establishment is the largest of its kind in the country, if not in the world, and has become one of the attractions of the city."[21]

The merchant prince of his day, Alexander Turney Stewart, took over a failing dry-goods store at 283 Broadway in 1823. By the 1840s, on the site of Washington Hall, he was building on an unprecedented scale. Stewart's "mar-

A.T. Stewart's "Marble Palace," also known as the Sun Building, 1987.

ble palace," designed by John B. Snook, was not just a storefront but, eventually, the entire blockfront between Chambers and Reade streets. Hone called it "spacious and magnificent beyond anything of the kind in the New World, or the Old either." "There are numerous superior shops in Broadway, but the most preeminently magnificent is 'Stewart's,'" a visitor, Lady Emmeline Wortley, declared in 1849.[22] The building's Italian Renaissance design reflected a new, more conspicuous, image on the part of the city's wealthy merchants and captured the imagination of the public.[23] Other Renaissance-style buildings of distinction, presumably inspired by Stewart's, included 311, 372, 380, and 383 Broadway.

Broadway in the 1850s had become "the 'Main Artery' of the Metropolis," and was completely thronged—"from the Chinaman with his long cue, and the Arab with his turban, to the Paris fop and the London cockney . . . and elegant women—matrons and their daughters—decorated like Birds of Paradise."[24] There were two favored spots for refreshment, both of which still stand. "Ladies, when on shopping excursion, very frequently betake themselves to Taylor's or Thompson's," it was noted in 1857.[25] Taylor's Saloon, in the International Hotel at Franklin Street, "carries off the palm from all the rest, by the splendour of its furniture and appointments, which seem rather suited to a fairy palace than a sublunary café and restaurant."[26] Thompson's was at 359 Broadway, a building that also housed Mathew Brady's daguerreotype gallery.

By 1860, when Brady left, TriBeCa's golden age had come to a close. The Union Club moved uptown in 1850. The Society Library quit its Broadway home in 1853. In 1854, the New York Institution burned down and Tiffany relocated. Masonic Hall was razed in 1856, and the Broadway Theater was torn down three years later.

"Great wholesale stores stand where the pretty shops stood," *Harper's*

Details of the Sun Building façade, including a corner clock, 1988 and 1979.

Washington Hall, 1809-12, by John McComb Jr.; Burial-Place for Negroes, Slave and Free.

READE STREET

w EAST RIVER SAVINGS INSTITUTION BUILDING, No. 291

(Also known as the National Council of the Y.M.C.A.). 1910-11, by Clinton & Russell. [19 stories] A yellow-brick tower rises from imposing, four-story pilasters. *Site of* Tradesmens National Bank, 1860.

BARCLAY BUILDING, No. 303

(Also known as the Ungar Building). 1902-05, by Stockton B. Colt. [18 stories] A simple but crisply detailed red-brick and limestone tower.

E CITY VEHICLE CONTROL CENTER, No. 300

Paved lot. *Site of* Dun & Bradstreet Building (also known as the R.G. Dun Building), 1898, by Harding & Gooch; Vincent Building. *Proposed site of* Foley Square Federal-Municipal Office Building.

DUANE STREET

w MUTUAL RESERVE FUND LIFE BUILDING, No. 305-09

(Also known as the Langdon Building). 1892-94, by William H. Hume. Proposed landmark. [14 stories] The vitality of this early granite tower comes through in its rock-faced base and clustered piers.

311 BROADWAY

1858. Proposed landmark. [5 stories] Expansive windows with exquisitely articulated architraves fill this Italianate stone façade.

313-15 BROADWAY

1861. Proposed landmark. [5 stories] Heavy brackets support cornices at every story, adding complexity and depth to this stone façade.

McDONALD'S, No. 317

1972. [1 story] *Site of* "Thomas Twin," 1869, by David & John Jardine and Daniel D. Badger; Ranelagh Pleasure Gardens, ca. 1750.

E JACOB K. JAVITS FEDERAL BUILDING, No. 306-34

(Also known as 26 Federal Plaza). 1963-69, by Kahn & Jacobs, Office of Alfred Easton Poor, Eggers & Higgins; enlarged 1975-77, by Kahn & Jacobs, Poor & Swanke, Eggers Partnership. [42 stories] A 2.7-million-square-foot metaphor for the huge and faceless bureaucracy within. *Site of* Citizens' Central National Bank, 1896, by John T. Williams; Central National Bank, ca. 1865; Tefft-Weller Building, ca.

1860, by Kellum & Son and Daniel D. Badger;
Broadway Theater, 1846-47; Gem Saloon; Masonic
Hall (also known as Gothic Hall), 1826-27, by Hugh
Reinagle.

THOMAS STREET

w **METROPOLITAN LIFE HOME OFFICE, No. 319**
(Also known as the "Thomas Twin"). 1869, by David
& John Jardine and Daniel D. Badger. Landmark. [5
stories] Nearly 70 rounded, oversized, deeply
recessed, and generously detailed windows
rhythmically punctuate this cast-iron façade. *Near
site of* the New York Hospital: Main Building -
Central Hospital, 1773-75, burned 1775, rebuilt 1775-
91; expanded 1803; Lunatic Asylum, 1806-08; North
Hospital, 1841; South Hospital, 1853.

319 Broadway; 325–31 Broadway, 1987.

325-31 BROADWAY
1863-64. Proposed landmark. [5 stories] These three
buildings share a common cornice and marble
façade, in which deep, segmental-arched pockets
contain each window. The ensemble has survived
remarkably well—even the roofline urns.

WORTH STREET

w **335-37 BROADWAY**
1924, by Jardine, Hill & Murdock. [13 stories] A
severe and restrained buff-brick building.

PARKING LOT, No. 343-47
Site of Langdon, Batcheller & Company; Jacob Le
Roy House (also known as the Union Club); Mount
Vernon Gardens Theater (also known as Ranelagh
Gardens, White Conduit House), 1767.

E **336-44 BROADWAY**
1930. [1 story] *Site of* James H. Dunham &
Company (also known as Carter; Kirtland &

380–82 Broadway; 390 and 388 Broadway, 1988.

Magazine said in 1862, "and if you go below Canal Street of an evening there
is something ghostly in the gloom of the closed warehouses."[27] Stewart moved
his retail operations to Tenth Street that year, but kept his wholesale business in the "marble palace," where it was in good company. Wholesalers had
begun moving to Broadway after the Great Fire of 1835 drove them from
Pearl Street. By the middle of the century, Broadway was filled with dealers
in cottons, dress goods, flannels, ginghams, laces, linens, satins, silks, vel-
vets, and woolens, as well as notions, ribbons, and trimmings. A distinctive
architecture developed at this time, using tall, thin columns that reminded
some viewers of sperm whale oil candles. "Sperm candle" buildings, such as
388, 392, and 394 Broadway, typically had two arcades of two stories each
and glass-filled façades—ideal for inspecting, modeling, and cutting fabric.

Hemmed in by businesses, the once-rural New York Hospital found itself
by the mid-1860s in a dense urban setting. Tremendous pressure was placed
on the governors to release the grounds for development. The city refused
to give aid, and private philanthropy evaporated. Meanwhile, more charity
patients than ever were being admitted. As a result, the debt reached
$100,000 by 1868, when the governors finally began leasing the grounds. The
hospital was entirely suspended in 1870. "It is saddening to see this time-
honored Institution . . . crowded into obscurity," an observer eulogized in
1872, "when the suffering population needs its accommodations more than

ever."[28] The hospital would not operate again for five years, when it reopened on Fifteenth Street.

Thomas Street was cut through the old hospital grounds along the path of the tree-lined allee. On either side of the new street, mirror-image buildings, with ironwork by Daniel D. Badger, went up in 1869. The one on the north, which still stands, became the Metropolitan Life Insurance Company Home Office in 1870.[29] Metropolitan was one of a number of insurance companies that moved into the blocks around City Hall. In 1868, New York Life began a lavish headquarters on the site of the Society Library. This design, by Griffith Thomas, was so much of a departure from the relative anonymity of most business buildings that one chronicler felt compelled to reassure readers that they "need not be alarmed at the report of the millions lavished by the managers of these [life insurance] companies on imposing business temples."[30] John B. Snook, architect of the "marble palace," designed an elaborate Italianate-Second Empire office building across the street, in 1871. Another highly ornamented cast-iron gem, the landmark James White Building, was constructed ten years later at Franklin Street. Its façade was filled with boughs, berries, leaves, and rosettes. In sober contrast was the Chemical National Bank, which had settled into an exceedingly modest building near Chambers Street in 1850 and became known as the "plainest and smallest of New York banks, with the most valuable stock."[31]

One of the clearest signs of change in this section of Broadway came in 1870 when, on the site where Tiffany opened, New York got its first underground railroad. The Beach Pneumatic Subway traveled one block under Broadway, from Warren to Murray Street. Its inventor, Alfred Ely Beach, dug his 312–foot tunnel in secret, fearing that the political boss, William M. Tweed, would exact a fortune to grant a franchise. Beach counted on the

New York Life Insurance Company Home Office of 1868–70. NYI.

Company), 1858; Broadway Tabernacle Congregational Church (also known as the Sixth Free Presbyterian Church), 1835-36.

CATHARINE LANE

E NEW YORK LIFE INSURANCE HOME OFFICE, No. 346

1894-98, by Stephen Decatur Hatch and McKim, Mead & White. Exterior and Interior Landmark. [13 stories] Stretching 400 feet from a clocktower pavilion ringed by huge eagles, this building forms a monumental wall. The tower clock is by the E. Howard Watch & Clock Company; a sculpture above it, by Philip Martiny, was removed. *Site of* New York Life Insurance Company Home Office, 1868-70, by Griffith Thomas, expanded 1879; New-York Society Library (also known as D. Appleton & Company Publishers), 1838-40, by Frederic Diaper.

LEONARD STREET

W AYER BUILDING, No. 349

1895, by Robert Maynicke. [9 stories] A spartan and narrow white brick building. *Near site of* Contoit's New-York Garden, 1805-10.

THOMPSON'S SALOON, No. 359

(Also known as the Mathew Brady studio). 1852. Proposed landmark. [5 stories] With four different kinds of window treatments, plus rosettes and other embellishments, this small façade has great variety.

James White Building; Broadway-Franklin Building, 1988.

JAMES WHITE BUILDING, No. 361-63

(Also known as Albert G. Hyde & Sons Textiles, Scientific American). 1881-82, by William Wheeler Smith. Landmark. [6 stories] There is a complex relation between this building's strong grid pattern, its rhythmic, free-standing columns and its delicate adornments, like branches and berries.

COLUMNS OF IRON AND STONE

Views from 1979 and 1988 show 380–82 Broadway (below), the Metropolitan Life Home Office at 319 Broadway (right), and 390, 392, and 394 Broadway (facing page).

E BROADWAY-LEONARD BUILDING, No. 350

1903-04, by Frederick C. Browne. [12 stories] A stark, buff-brick façade with deep, vertical windows. *Site of* Carlton House Hotel, 1837.

BROADWAY COURT, No. 356

Before 1865. [5 stories] Among flat arches and three-quarter-round columns are huge frames into which small modern windows have been squeezed.

358 BROADWAY

1857. [5 stories] Most of the old architectural fabric has been removed, leaving ground-floor pilasters and the segmental-arch window shapes.

360 BROADWAY

1860. [5 stories] Highly articulated architraves distinguish this building from its neighbors.

362 BROADWAY

Before 1865. [5 stories] The drip molding over its windows has deteriorated badly.

FRANKLIN STREET

International Hotel, and a façade detail, 1987 and 1988.

W INTERNATIONAL HOTEL, No. 365-67

(Also known as Taylor's Saloon, Ninth National Bank). 1853, by Thomas & Son and Daniel D. Badger. [6 stories] Much has been removed from this great antebellum survivor, but the ground-floor pilasters remain, as do arched windows, with arched side lights, on the second and sixth floors.

SOLOMON & HART UPHOLSTERY STORE, No. 369

ca. 1860, by F.A. Petersen. [5 stories] Three floors, with handsomely simple architraves, are intact.

373-75 BROADWAY

(Also known as the Mosler Safe Building). 1901, by Robert Maynicke. [6 stories] A deep cornice sits atop a simple but articulated façade.

momentum of public enthusiasm to sustain the railroad. He made the Warren Street waiting room an elegant salon, with a grand piano, fountain, paintings, frescoes, and goldfish tank. From there, one boarded a cylindrical car—with upholstered benches, built-in tables, and porthole-shaped windows—that was pushed through the nine-foot-wide tube by a column of air. The subway was a sensation, but Beach never got a franchise, thanks to Tweed, and finally gave up.[32] (When the first modern subway train ran in 1904, it left from an almost equally ornate station one block away, under City Hall.)

Boss Tweed had a project of his own, behind City Hall. Its enduring nickname, the Tweed Court House, immortalizes the politician and the ring that profited from its construction. The New York County Court House was begun in 1861 and was supposed to cost $250,000. The *New York Times* noted ten years later that the structure, not yet finished, had already drained nearly $6.5 million from the public treasury. For example, one day's cabinet work had cost $125,830.56. "Just imagine . . . the weary days and the sleepless nights, that it must have cost the 'Boss' to procure all these sums," a *Times* editorial sneered. "The Tweed monument and the new Court-house are . . . one and the same."[33]

Besides corruption, the Tweed Court House symbolized the way in which government offices were spreading along Broadway. The United States Post Office took over the south end of City Hall Park in 1875 for its "mammoth 'Bird Cage' in granite," whose uppermost peak was 160 feet high.[34] Stewart's store was converted to office use in 1884, and served as a municipal building through the early twentieth century.[35]

City Hall I.R.T. Station, 1988.

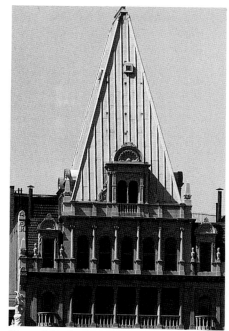

Home Life Building, 1988.

Government's chronic and insatiable need for more space nearly resulted in an unthinkable misadventure. In 1893, the demolition or removal of City Hall was all but a fait accompli. Mayor Thomas F. Gilroy sought to replace the hall, he said, because it was "utterly unsuited for office purposes for the departments of a great city."[36] Admittedly, it did not evoke the most uplifting images. "Here Tweed and his fellow-bandits despoiled the city," the *Times* said. "Here foul-mouthed, illiterate, be-diamonded Aldermen divided plunder wrested from the taxpayers . . . In this hall corruption held high carnival and spat upon the laws . . . In this hall corrupt Aldermen and officials of higher station laughingly discussed their indictments."[37] Fortunately for posterity, fonder sentimentalists prevailed and Gilroy was thwarted. After the consolidation of greater New York City in 1898, an enormous new Aldermanic Chamber (now the Council Chamber) was created in City Hall.[38] The Board of Estimate took over the old Common Council Chamber for committee meetings and, for its public hearings, convened in the former criminal courtroom.

Near City Hall in the 1890s, there was a wave of construction by the insurance industry. The Mutual Reserve Fund Life Association began its Romanesque headquarters at Duane Street in 1892. The Home Life Insurance Company scraped the sky with its copper-peaked tower between Murray and Warren streets, completed in 1894 and described at the time as the "severest kind of Italian Renaissance and plain and simple in its beauty."[39] (Home Life still had offices in the building ninety years later.) New York Life began a vast expansion of its home office in 1894, by Stephen Decatur Hatch and McKim, Mead & White, who replaced the original building with a dramatic clocktower pavilion surmounted by an eagle, atop a fifteen-foot globe, resting on the shoulders of four Atlases. The clock below had faces twelve feet in

WILLIAMS BUILDING, No. 377-79

1896, by John T. Williams. [11 stories] The buff-brick façade is a forceful grid of recessed two-window bays and delicate ornament.

E BROADWAY-FRANKLIN BUILDING, No. 366

(Also known as the Broadway Textile Building, Collect Pond House). 1907, by Frederick C. Browne. [12 stories] Rough-faced masonry, garlanded brackets with monumental female faces, marble columns, and huge, scrolled keystones provide this building with strong character. ***Near site of*** New York Water Works Reservoir (also known as the Colles Reservoir), 1774-75, by Christopher Colles.

368 BROADWAY

1880, by John B. Snook. [5 stories] A simple brick building with chamfered piers.

370 BROADWAY

1880, by David & John Jardine. [5 stories] Rosette panels and geometric leaf forms decorate this strong, red-brick façade.

372 BROADWAY

ca. 1865, by Samuel A. Warner. [5 stories] This handsome building—its windows framed differently at each floor—is in exceptional condition. The window hoods, brackets, keystones, architraves, and cornice are all intact.

MANDARIN PLAZA, No. 374

1989-90, by Daniel Pang & Associates. [25 stories] This flat, pink- and brown-brick slab is utterly out of context. ***Site of*** Sweetser, Pembrook & Company, 1860, radically altered; William B. Astor House (also known as the Union Club).

WHITE STREET

W 381 BROADWAY

1851, by John B. Snook. [5 stories] The outlines of its second-floor pediments are still visible.

383 BROADWAY

[5 stories] Once a twin of the ruined No. 381, this Italianate relic has deep window hoods on brackets and chunky, triangular pediments.

GROSVENOR BUILDINGS, No. 385-87

1875, by Charles Wright. [5 stories] Under a colossal common pediment, two buildings share an iron and glass façade, with flat arches and simple columns.

TWEED COURT HOUSE

*Views from 1988 show Room 201–02, a former courtroom
(below left and on facing page, a detail of the floor tiles),
and the Rotunda (below right and on facing page).*

NEW YORK LIFE BUILDING

Views from 1988 include Marvin Schneider, a volunteer,
tending the tower clock.

diameter and a bell that weighed 5,000 pounds. Aware of architecture's symbolic power, New York Life sought an image of prosperity, integrity, and permanence.[40]

Other towers nearby included one of Cass Gilbert's earliest major works, the Broadway Chambers, which pioneered the use of color to differentiate a skyscraper's base (granite), shaft (red brick), and capital (polychrome tile and copper).[41] A miscellaneous cast of companies filled the rest of the area. Next door to Home Life, and almost simultaneously, the Postal Telegraph-Cable Company—the "only successful rival which the Western Union has ever found"—completed its headquarters.[42] Stewart's store became the Sun Building in 1919 with the arrival of the "newspaperman's newspaper," as the *Sun* was known.[43] The credit-reporting firms of R.G. Dun, at 290 Broadway, and Bradstreet, at 279 Broadway, competed until 1933, when they merged as Dun & Bradstreet. The company that made Remington typewriters operated from 327 Broadway, near Worth Street, a building that still stands.[44]

New construction came to a virtual standstill in the twentieth century and the area's commercial appeal declined. Two decades after building a new headquarters at Chambers Street, Chemical Bank moved downtown in 1928 to be closer to Wall Street. That year, New York Life, having outgrown its headquarters, moved to Madison Square. But the civil servants and wholesalers remained. Perhaps the most dramatic change to the area before World War II came with the demolition in 1938 of the Post Office. Preservationists were delighted, as they had long lobbied against "this perversion of their beautiful park . . . the monstrous pile . . . unsighlty in the last degree."[45] Miraculously, the Post Office was not replaced by a larger building, but by parkland.

The *Sun* expired in 1950, leaving behind a four-faced clock over Chambers Street, bearing the motto, "The Sun—It Shines for All." The "marble palace" was almost immediately scheduled for demolition and was apparently doomed through the 1960s.[46] Today, it is a landmark and the clock is periodically revived through voluntary efforts. Agitation for removal of the Tweed Court House, because of its infamous associations, was quite intense at times and lasted until the 1970s. However, the building was designated a landmark in 1984, having emerged from Tweed's shadow to be recognized as an important monument, with a five-story rotunda and other features that constitute "one of New York's grandest and most important nineteenth-century interior spaces."[47]

City Hall, too, endured long enough to be venerated. But what has been transmitted to our time is, in certain respects, a replica. The façade—Corinthian capitals, medallions, oak-leaf-and-acorn swags, keystones, egg-and-dart and acanthus-leaf modillions—is not the product of antique craftsmanship but was made, in part, by machine, and is younger than the United Nations headquarters. Beginning in 1954, the top four inches of City Hall's crumbling marble exterior were stripped away with pneumatic drills and replaced by a limestone veneer. In all, 15,000 new stones were anchored to the old wall with bronze rods.[48] Inside, the original Mayor's Office, used by the chief executive

391 BROADWAY
Before 1865. [5 stories] Delicate fluted columns, ornamented spandrels, balustrades, and keystones fill this cast-iron façade.

393 BROADWAY
1867, by Nicholas Whyte. [5 stories] With flat arches and simple pilasters, this stands in sober contrast to No. 391.

395 BROADWAY
1899, by Robert Maynicke. [15 stories] The smooth surface of this building has been punched with deep windows. A band course is set into each story, with a vigorous arcade at the top.

E **380-82 BROADWAY**
Before 1865. [5 stories] Marble pavilions with quoined edges compose this marvelous Italianate façade, which was once part of a larger building. Window pediments and hoods are different on each floor. There is rich molding throughout and a Corinthian colonnade.

384-86 BROADWAY
1882, by Jarvis Morgan Slade. [6 stories] Embellished lintels, free-standing colonettes, and large windows form a grid in this red-brick façade.

388 BROADWAY
ca. 1860, by King & Kellum and Daniel D. Badger. [5 stories] The arches in this transparent façade spring from exceptionally tall and thin columns, which recall sperm whale oil candles.

390 BROADWAY
Before 1865. [5 stories] The façade of this old building is virtually a glass curtain wall.

392 BROADWAY
Before 1865. [5 stories] With "sperm-candle" columns, this building is similar to No. 388.

394 BROADWAY
Before 1865. [6 stories] A rusticated façade and mansard roof distinguish this building from its neighbors with "sperm-candle" columns.

396-98 BROADWAY
1898, by William H. Birkshire. [10 stories] A slender and severe buff-brick tower.

WALKER STREET

W **401-03 BROADWAY**
1929-30, by Jardine, Hill & Murdock. [26 stories] A copper hip roof and seven setbacks top this energetic, orange-brick Jazz Age tower. *Site of*

Citizens' National Bank, 1875, by David & John Jardine.

MANUFACTURERS TRUST BANK, No. 407

(Also known as the Manufacturers Hanover Trust). 1926, by A.F. Gilbert. [1 story] A single, large arch is framed by Ionic pilasters in this limestone façade. *Site of* Ninth National Bank (also known as the Columbia Bank), 1869-71, by Ebenezer L. Roberts.

E FLORENCE'S HOTEL, No. 400

Before 1865. [4 stories] In this hybrid structure, the Broadway façade has deep windows, flat arches, and three-quarter-round columns. On the Walker Street mid-block, the style drifts toward Italianate, with big window pediments.

CALHOUN ROBBINS FANCY GOODS STORE, No. 408-10

1866. [5 stories] There are a dozen two-story bays in this masonry building, framed by "sperm-candle" pilasters and topped by segmental and round arches.

412 BROADWAY

[5 stories] A rather delicate projecting bay, four stories tall, dominates the façade. *Site of* Apollo Rooms (also known as Euterpean Hall, Broadway Theater), 1836-37.

416 BROADWAY

1898, by Jordan & Giller. [9 stories] The façade has an almost membranous quality in the taut, thin skin created by its many windows. *Site of* New York & New Haven Railroad Depot, 1851.

LISPENARD STREET

W NATIONAL CITY BANK, No. 415

(Also known as Citibank). 1927, by Walker & Gillette. [3 stories] The power of this Art Moderne box, with a double-eagle relief over its entrance, is diluted by modern signage. *Site of* Brandreth House Hotel, ca. 1860, by Charles Mettam and Daniel D. Badger.

Grosvenor Buildings, 1987.

as late as Fiorello LaGuardia, was transformed into the Mayor's Reception Room, or Blue Room. (The Mayor now has a much smaller office in the northwest corner.)

By far the most overwhelming project in the Civic Center district during the last half of the twentieth century was the Jacob K. Javits Federal Building—the largest United States Government building outside the Washington area—which sits between Duane and Worth streets.[49] It holds more than eighty agencies and 8,100 employees.

Broadway became something of a residential street in the 1970s and '80s, as artists and other urban pioneers, driven out by high costs in SoHo, took over the old lofts in what came to be called TriBeCa. And Chinese businesses, many of them in the garment and fabric trade, began filling Broadway storefronts and loft buildings. In the vicinity of Canal Street, cast-iron or marble columns still framed windows filled with bolts of colorful cloth, as they had since the middle of the 1800s.

Meanwhile, the tiny jewel box of City Hall was nobly filling its role as the governmental seat—designed for a town of 100,000; serving a city of more than 7,000,000. And City Hall Park was playing an even more ancient role. It was still an open-air cradle of public protest, as it had been since pre-Revolutionary days. One might find the park ringed by taxi drivers or pushcart peddlers, objecting to municipal regulation. One might find protesters attacking the city's handling of the AIDS epidemic or homeless people camped under the trees in a tent city. By coming to this verdant triangle to express their rage, they all joined a great civic tradition and refreshed the ancient democratic drama. The protesters might not have had time to notice, but just outside the Mayor's windows in City Hall, there still stood a Liberty Pole.

Textile dealer, 1979.

TEXTILES

FABRICS INC

ESPANOL

New York City Department of City Planning

SOHO

CANAL STREET TO HOUSTON STREET

473–75 Broadway, 1979.

Broadway south of Houston Street is a youthful avenue in antique garb. There are a surprising number of antebellum vestiges in brownstone and marble, squeezed among gigantic grids formed by cast-iron façades and cliffside walls of masonry lofts. Some of the glamour of the nineteenth century is still evident: the Ball, Black & Company jewelry store, the E.V. Haughwout fancy-goods emporium, C.G. Gunther's Sons furriers, and D. Appleton booksellers. Yet, the sense of SoHo is that of a young neighborhood, both in development and population, waking up from a long existence as a manufacturing and wholesale quarter. Its acronymic name and artistic reputation date from the 1960s, when lofts were recycled as studios, galleries, and dwellings; when SoHo reclaimed its place—as TriBeCa would a decade later—in the city's social fabric.

Stone Bridge over the canal at Canal Street, 1800. VM.

SoHo began in rural isolation. As the nineteenth century opened, much of the area was the Nicholas Bayard farm. To get there from the city, which was not yet much more than the tip of Manhattan Island, one would have taken the Middle Road, as the suburban extension of Broadway was then called. That crossed a small canal, along the line of Canal Street, over an arched bridge that the British had probably built during their occupation.[1] Benjamin Lord's house, which still stands at 423 Broadway, looked out on this rural scene: a stone bridge with "long square timbers on either side . . . to prevent a fall into the sluggish stream—some fifteen feet below."[2] A roadside inn, known later as the Broadway House, greeted the visitor who made it as far north as Grand Street. In 1828, north of Prince Street, William Niblo opened a summer resort and amusement ground called Niblo's Garden. It was "handsomely lighted, and decorated with paintings, mirrors, &c. The walks are bordered with shrubbery and flowers in great variety. Fire works are occasionally exhibited; and in the Saloon [are] theatrical and musical entertainments."[3]

The neighborhood achieved considerable cachet in the 1840s, after John Jacob Astor, founder of the Astor dynasty and then the wealthiest man in the country, moved to 585 Broadway, between Prince and Houston streets. His brick dwelling was a fairly plain affair on the outside, but was "furnished in princely style" and "adorned by costly works of art"—in all, "one of the most pretentious New York homes."[4] At 482 Broadway, south of Broome Street, lived James Henry Roosevelt, whose legal career had been cut short when he was paralyzed in his 20s. He spent his life giving "quiet attention to the improvement of his fortune."[5] In addition to socially prominent residents, the neighborhood was graced by the First Unitarian Church, built in 1845 between Spring and Prince streets, whose interior was "finished in more complete gothic style" than perhaps any other building in New York.[6] In 1847, the Century Association, a group of "gentlemen engaged or interested in Letters or the Fine Arts," began meeting at 495 Broadway, north of Broome Street.[7]

View south in 1979 includes the Silk Exchange Building (left), Loubat Stores (center), and St. Nicholas Hotel (right).

SOHO-CAST IRON HISTORIC DISTRICT

This designation covers every building on the west side of Broadway, from Canal to Houston Street, and on the east side, from Howard to Houston Street.

CANAL STREET

W BENJAMIN LORD HOUSE, No. 423

1822-23. [3 stories] It is amazing that this small Federal house, with incised lintels, has survived. The shape of the original pitched roof can be seen on the south elevation. ***Near site of*** Stone Bridge (also known as the Arch Bridge), ca. 1776-83.

LE BOUTILLIER BROTHERS STORE, No. 425

1869, by Griffith Thomas. [5 stories] This small cast-iron building has a large broken pediment.

Le Boutillier Brothers Store and A.J. Dittenhoffer Warehouse, 1987.

A.J. DITTENHOFFER WAREHOUSE, No. 427-29

1870-71, by Thomas R. Jackson. [5 stories] A great pediment crowns this sculptural and splendidly detailed cast-iron composition of four powerful arcades with richly ornamented spandrels.

E OLTARSH BUILDING, No. 420-22

(Also known as the Pearl River Department Store). 1927, by R. Hall and D.M. Oltarsh. [3 stories] A plain brick box.

CANAL CINEMA

Rebuilt 1988 as a shopping mall.

424-26 BROADWAY

1885. [6 stories] There are flat arches and pilasters with foliate capitals on this façade.

428-32 BROADWAY

[6 stories] Stout, red-brick pilasters with florid capitals mark this vigorous Victorian design.

HOWARD STREET

W　FRANKLIN NATIONAL BANK, No. 433

(Also known as the European American Bank).
1967, by Eggers & Higgins; landscape by Zion &
Breen. [1 story] A mock-Colonial pavilion.

D. APPLETON & COMPANY BUILDING, No. 443

1860, by Griffith Thomas. [5 stories] Great richness
characterizes this façade: arched windows framed by
colonettes, window hoods on brackets, a balcony
with urns, and a monumental roofline pediment.

447 BROADWAY

1860. [5 stories] A lively composition marked by tall
pilasters and arched windows with large keystones.

F. BOOSS & BROTHER FURRIERS, No. 449

1855-56. [5 stories] Beautifully articulated
architraves and pediments adorn this small building.

GLOBE-WERNICKE BUILDING, No. 451-53

1869; rebuilt 1916. [5 stories] A bas-relief globe tops
this flat façade.

BELDING BROTHERS BUILDING, No. 455-57

1867-68. [5 stories] A rectilinear design of oversized
windows, with a rounded pediment.

D. DEVLIN & COMPANY STORE, No. 459-61

1860-61. [5 stories] Four rhythmic arcades,
springing from three-quarter-round columns, make
this an imposing presence on the corner.

E　MERCHANTS BANK BUILDING, No. 434-38

1895-96, by Ralph S. Townsend. [9 stories]
Monumental in its details, this white-brick building
has two arcades and a deep copper cornice. *Site of*
Howard House hotel, 1853.

440 BROADWAY

1938. [2 stories] This is a strongly horizontal, Art
Moderne composition.

CONTINENTAL HOTEL, No. 442

Before 1865. [4 stories] Almost all original
architectural fabric has been removed.

444 and 452 BROADWAY

1876-77, by August Schweitzer and Emile Gruwé. [5
stories] These twin buildings, separated by No. 446-
50, both have tracery arches over their large
windows. *Site of* Mitchell's Olympic Theater (also
known as the American Theater), 1837, rebuilt.

Niblo's Garden, 1828; Tattersall's Stables and Mitchell's Olympic Theater, 1840. VM.

Notwithstanding the presence of homes, churches, and clubs, however, Broadway's destiny was as a vibrant throughfare, rather than a refined enclave. The pattern was set by Niblo's Garden, which was gradually transformed from a summer resort into a phenomenally long-lived theatrical enterprise by that name. The Olympic Theater opened in 1837, between Howard and Grand streets, and became the most popular playhouse in New York, with productions always "calculated to excite mirth."[8] James Wallack took over the Lyceum Theater, near Broome Street, in 1852. It was the first of several Broadway houses run by his family, which was then at the pinnacle of New York theatrical circles. At least a half dozen minstrel halls were on Broadway at mid-century. The Chinese Hall, with curiosities like wax figures purporting to show how prisoners were tortured in China, came under P.T. Barnum's control in 1865, after he was burned out of his Ann Street museum.

Adjoining Niblo's Garden, the Metropolitan Hotel opened in 1852. It was a favorite of dry-goods buyers because it was so close to the wholesale district and it was briefly considered the "largest and most magnificent of the kind in the world."[9] But it was quickly eclipsed. "The entire length of Broadway seems to have been measured for a new suit of marble," *Gleason's Pictorial* exclaimed in 1852. "The far-famed Metropolitan Hotel with its multiplied splendors of furniture and luxurious elegances is to be outdone by still another Broadway hotel."[10] That was the St. Nicholas, at Spring Street. Its façade was a snowy white expanse, but all that remains of the "Hotel *par excellence*" are two door fronts at 521 and 523 Broadway, once part of its north wing. They scarcely capture the glory of this 600-room hostelry, where marble was under foot, frescoed ceilings were overhead, and 400 people could be seated in the dining room. Every guest room had hot and cold water, gas, and steam heat. The Bridal Chamber—a "fairy-like apartment"—had white satin walls and a white satin canopy over the bed, suspended from carved work in the ceiling, overlaid with gold, all of it illuminated by four crystal

Metropolitan Hotel. GSW.

chandeliers.[11] Both hotels were designed by John B. Snook, although Griffith Thomas may have had a hand in the St. Nicholas.

Among the hotels and theaters were the elegant stores. The Brooks Brothers—Daniel, Edward, Elisha, and John—moved to the corner of Grand Street in 1858, on the site of the Broadway House. "Our Custom Department claims particular attention," they boasted, "being a Circular Room lit from a dome 68 feet high, and finished in a superior style of art." Their most illustrious customer was President Abraham Lincoln. (For his second inauguration

St. Nicholas Hotel, ca. 1870. NYHS.

446-50 BROADWAY

1876-77, by John B. Snook. [5 stories] A common façade—large square windows and three-quarter-round columns—unites two buildings. *Site of* Broadway Circus (also known as Christy & Wood's Minstrel Hall, City Assembly Rooms, Fellow's Opera House, Tattersall's Stables), 1812-16, rebuilt ca. 1855, by A. Winnam.

456 BROADWAY

1854. [5 stories] Narrow, segmental arched windows punctuate this red-brick façade.

458 BROADWAY

1895-96, by Alfred Zucker. [9 stories] A fairly plain, small, yellow-brick tower.

GRAND STREET

w PARKING LOT, No. 461
Site of Lord & Taylor Store (also known as the Grand Building), 1859-60, by Griffith Thomas.

LAKE & McCREERY STORE, No. 471

(Also known as Ubsdell, Pierson & Lake). 1855, storefront by Daniel D. Badger. [5 stories] The cornice and cast-iron pilasters are mostly intact.

473-75 BROADWAY

1894-95, by Ralph S. Townsend. [9 stories] Fine, restrained detail abounds on this limestone façade.

477-79 BROADWAY

1869-70, by H.W. Smith & Sons. [5 stories] Expansive windows are framed by flat arches and three-quarter-round columns.

481 BROADWAY

1855-56. [4 stories] The façade has been stripped but the windows retain their segmental-arch shape.

483-85 BROADWAY

1869-70, by Robert Mook. [5 stories] Stout columns characterize this square and deep composition. *Site of* Wallack's Lyceum Theater (also known as the Broadway Theater, Brougham's Lyceum, New York Theater), 1850.

SILK EXCHANGE BUILDING, No. 487

(Also known as the French Telegraph & Cable Building). 1895-96, by John T. Williams. [12 stories] Bristling magnificently with ornament, this small tower also has an enormous copper cornice.

Mills & Gibb Building, 1986.

E MILLS & GIBB BUILDING, No. 462-68

1879-80, by John Correja. [6 stories] Free-standing columns and serrated lintels compose a cast-iron grid that is astonishingly modern in its simple power. *Site of* Brooks Brothers Store, 1857-58; Broadway House Hotel, 1815; Abraham Davis Tavern, ca. 1796.

472 BROADWAY

1934. [1 story] *Site of* Hall of the General Society of Mechanics and Tradesmen (also known as the Apprentices' Library, Bryant's Minstrel Hall, Christy's Minstrel Hall, Mechanics' Hall), 1847.

JANE McNEVIN HOUSE, No. 474

1863. [4 stories] This brick dwelling has segmental-arched window heads and an intact cornice.

476 BROADWAY

1902-03, by Robert Maynicke. [11 stories] Two gigantic Ionic columns frame the ground floor.

Roosevelt Building, 1986.

ROOSEVELT BUILDING, No. 478-82

1873-74, by Richard Morris Hunt. [5 stories] Broad expanses of glass, in very wide bays, framed by arches with delicate tracery. *Site of* James Henry Roosevelt house.

Belding Brothers Building and D. Devlin & Company Store, 1990.

they made a special overcoat, and Lincoln was wearing a Brooks Brothers suit on the night he went to Ford's Theater.)[12] Lord & Taylor opened across the street from Brooks in 1860, in a building by Griffith Thomas "whose extravagant ornamentation would be regarded as a fault by persons of more moderate taste than New Yorkers." During the Draft Riots of 1863, a massive civil insurrection, the store was defended with barricades of merchandise.[13] On the third corner of the Grand Street intersection was the uptown branch of D. Devlin & Company, clothiers and furnishers, which is still standing.

Under the trademark statue of *Atlas* bearing a large clock, Tiffany & Company welcomed customers to 550 Broadway, between Spring and Prince streets, with diamonds, pearls, silverware, watches, clocks, and other fancy

D. Appleton & Company Building, 1990.

goods—a "Bazaar of wealth and magnificence."[14] Tiffany was "only one of the fatted calves," it was noted in 1864, because "Ball and Black have gorged themselves as well upon the exorbitant demand for jewellry." Ball, Black & Company, already renowned for tending the "Diamond Palace of Broadway," at Murray Street, moved in 1861 to a handsome five-story Renaissance-style building, designed by John Kellum, at the corner of Prince Street.[15] (Four floors were later added, but the original marble façade is preserved.) Another particularly distinguished Italianate marble building, north of Howard Street, served as headquarters for the publishing house of D. Appleton & Company in the early 1860s. It was designed by Griffith Thomas and is still standing.

A few doors north of Tiffany's, Crouch & Fitzgerald offered trunks, va-

MERCHANTS' AND TRADERS' BANK, No. 486

1882-85, by Lamb & Rich. [6 stories] A dark and heavy façade with sweeping brick arches.

BROOME STREET

w 489 BROADWAY

1860. [5 stories] The cornice and richly detailed architraves add life to this façade.

491 BROADWAY

1896-97, by Buchman & Deisler. [12 stories] An abundance of subtle detailing enriches this tower.

491 Broadway, Butler Brothers Haughwout & Company Store, 1987.

BUTLER BROTHERS STORE, No. 495-97

(Also known as the Cossitt Building, New Era Building). 1892-93, by Alfred Zucker. [9 stories] A grand, bright-green, two-story mansard roof sits atop large arches and bas-relief spandrels. *Site of* Grover & Baker Sewing Machine Building, 1860, by George Johnson and Daniel D. Badger; Century Association; American Art Union.

499 BROADWAY

ca. 1865. [5 stories] This little building has nicely detailed window heads and a cornice.

PARKING LOT, No. 501

Site of W. & J. Sloane Store (also known as the Francis Bannerman Store and Military Museum), ca. 1855, by Thomas & Son and Daniel D. Badger.

LOUBAT STORES, No. 503-11

1878-79, by John B. Snook. [6 stories] Three buildings share an almost modern façade, with a rectilinear grid formed by simple columns.

DE FOREST BUILDING, No. 513-17

1884, by Lamb & Rich. [7 stories] This robust, red-brick Victorian gem has pediment-topped bays and deeply recessed windows, many flanked by free-standing columns. *Site of* St. Nicholas Hotel.

E. V. HAUGHWOUT STORE

Views from 1978 and 1988.

ST. NICHOLAS HOTEL, No. 521-23

1851-54, by John B. Snook or Griffith Thomas. [6 stories] Most of the hotel was replaced by new buildings to the north and south. This remnant, from the middle portion, has a large cornice with leafy scrollwork brackets.

525-27 BROADWAY

[9 stories] A simple, red-brick tower. *Site of* St. Nicholas Hotel.

E   E. V. HAUGHWOUT & COMPANY STORE, No. 488-92

(Also known as the Broadway Manufacturers Supply Corporation). 1856-57, by John P. Gaynor and Daniel D. Badger. Landmark. [5 stories] The power of its rhythmic symmetry, meshed with its extravagantly detailed arch orders, is compelling.

494 BROADWAY

1866. [4 stories] This building has segmental-arched windows and an intact cornice.

496 BROADWAY

1866. [5 stories] A restrained series of well-defined segmental arches marks this façade.

500 BROADWAY

1859. [5 stories] A handsome, antebellum, masonry composition with finely detailed architraves.

C. G. GUNTHER'S SONS STORE, No. 502-04

1860, by Kellum & Son and Daniel D. Badger. [5 stories] This exceptionally exuberant and vertical façade, which almost leaps upward, has two tremendous rows of "sperm-candle" columns.

506 BROADWAY

1854-56. [3 stories] There are fine antebellum details: shouldered architraves, a grand pediment, and round arched windows.

508 BROADWAY

1854. [5 stories] This is the twin of No. 506 and it is whole, complete to the roofline pediment.

510 BROADWAY

1878, by William Bloodgood. [5 stories] A cornice bursting with ornament sits above flat arches.

GILBERT MANUFACTURING BUILDING, No. 512-16

1881-82, by Lamb & Wheeler. [6 stories] Strongly vertical window bays run through this red-brick façade. *Site of* Hebrew Synagogue (also known as Harrigan & Hart's Theatre Comique, Thalia Theater, Wood's Minstrel Hall), rebuilt 1862.

Façade details at 550 and 552–54 Broadway, 1988.

lises, hat boxes, and carpet bags, soliciting the patronage of anyone spending the summer in the country or making the tour of Europe. At F. Booss & Brother, south of Grand Street, were furs in all forms—caps, capes, coats, stoles, gloves, mufflers, collars, and sleigh robes. The carpet dealers of W. & J. Sloane did business at 591 Broadway, near Houston Street, a building whose twin at No. 593 is well preserved.

Ubsdell, Pierson & Lake, north of Grand Street, boasted that no other house "presents as large, rich and well selected a variety of Silks in Robes, Pattern Dresses, Stripes, Plaids."[16] (This firm evolved into Lake & Mc-Creery, predecessor of James H. McCreery & Company, whose store still stands at Eleventh Street.) In 1868, the firm that eventually became Hackett, Carhart & Company, an important manufacturing clothier, was founded at the northeast corner of Canal Street.[17]

Given their close relation to the dry-goods trade, sewing-machine manufacturers were very much part of the scene. I. M. Singer & Company had a showroom on Grand Street, beginning in the 1850s. Singer was later to commission two of Broadway's architectural masterpieces but its mid-century home paled in contrast to the Grover & Baker sewing-machine showroom, north of Broome Street: one enormous Gothic arch, almost four stories high, filled with glass, traceries, and quatrefoils.

C.G. Gunther's Sons Store, 1988.

518 BROADWAY

1855. [5 stories] Akin to Nos. 506 and 508, this has a grand pediment and shouldered architraves.

BANK OF NAPLES BUILDING, No. 520-22

(Also known as the Savoy Trust Company). 1900-01, by Buchman & Fox. [11 stories] Balconies, pediments, medallion-like keystones, and a copper balustrade embellish this façade.

Bayard Building amd 530 Broadway, 1986.

BAYARD BUILDING, No. 524-28

1902-03, by Arthur H. Bowditch. [11 stories] While simple compared to its resplendent neighbors, this white-brick building has a highly articulated façade.

SPRING STREET

w **529 BROADWAY**

[2 stories] A black-and-aluminum Art Deco building. *Site of* Prescott House Hotel, 1852.

535 BROADWAY

1852. [5 stories] Almost bereft of any details.

537-41 BROADWAY

1868-69, by Charles Mettam. [5 stories] These two buildings share a façade that has intricate flat arches, three-quarter-round columns, and a cornice with pediments and urns. *Site of* Chinese Hall (also known as Barnum's New Museum, Buckley's Minstrel Hall), 1851.

543 BROADWAY

1902-03, by John W. Stevens. [10 stories] A broad, three-story arch marks this narrow marble tower.

545 BROADWAY

1885, by Samuel A. Warner. [6 stories] Slender colonettes run through this rectilinear façade.

547 BROADWAY

1888, by O.P. Hatfield. [6 stories] This red-brick building has an elegant semi-circular fire escape.

The Grover & Baker façade was the product of Daniel D. Badger's Architectural Iron Works, as were many other storefronts along Broadway. Coincident with the mercantile development of the 1850s and 1860s—and influencing it, as well—was the widespread use of cast iron. In her history of this building material, Margot Gayle enumerated its attractions: Because relatively few and slender columns were needed to support a façade, big windows were possible. Iron columns allowed for high ceilings and open floor areas. Façade pieces, cast in almost any delicate or intricate architectural style, could be assembled easily, quickly, and cheaply.[18]

If stores were measured by design alone, E.V. Haughwout & Company's cast-iron building, completed in 1857, would surely have been foremost. This rich evocation of Venetian architecture was Badger's finest moment. And its contents were equal to its exterior. Eder V. Haughwout supplied the White House with china during Lincoln's presidency. The Broadway store sparkled and gleamed with silver tea services, urns, kettles, casters, salvers, baskets, goblets, tureens, dishes, and pitchers; sharing space with glassware, bronzes, chandeliers, clocks, paintings, and statuary. Haughwout even carried its own champagne.[19]

Another glorious iron front by Badger, a few doors north, was the home of the renowned furrier C. G. Gunther's Sons, beginning in 1866. The Gunther

ROUSS BUILDING, No. 549-55

(Also known as the Blechman Building). 1889-90, by Alfred Zucker; enlarged 1900. [12 stories] The name of Charles Broadway Rouss spills across the rusticated façade. Above are four gable-topped bays.

"LITTLE" SINGER BUILDING, No. 561-63

(Also known as the Paul Building). 1902-04, by Ernest Flagg. [12 stories] A nine-story bay is recessed behind delicate balustrades and colonettes, framed at the top by a tracery arch. *Site of* Henry Wood's Marble Hall (also known as the Manufacturers' and Merchants' Bank), 1857; Church of St. George the Martyr, 1847.

BALL, BLACK & COMPANY JEWELERS, No. 565-67

(Also known as the Metropolitan Savings Bank). 1859-60, by John Kellum; enlarged. [9 stories] The lower five stories are marble—a powerful, handsome, Italianate work, whose windows have colossal pediments. The yellow-brick addition tried to be sympathetic.

E 530 BROADWAY

1897-98, by Brunner & Tryon. [11 stories] Abundant decoration has been confidently applied throughout, and there is a tremendous arcade and cornice. *Site of* Collamore House hotel, 1851.

532-34 BROADWAY

1896-97, by Ralph S. Townsend. [10 stories] This is virtually identical to No. 832-34, also by Townsend. On a complex façade, ornament has been lavished— swags, fretwork, and guilloche patterns.

536-38 BROADWAY

1901-02, by DeLemos & Cordes. [11 stories] Deep, six-story bays framed by four great lion heads.

540 Broadway, 1979.

540 BROADWAY

1867, by David & John Jardine. [5 stories] The façade has almost lace-like incised decoration.

A.J. Dittenhoffer Warehouse (top); Roosevelt Building, 1979.

store was built in the "sperm candle" style, with tall, narrow columns. More in the spirit of Haughwout, with deep and elaborate stone-like arches, was a warehouse at Howard Street that was begun in 1870 for the A. J. Dittenhoffer dry-goods concern.

The cast-iron Roosevelt Building of 1874 was a significant departure toward modernity and away from the use of iron to imitate stone. It was designed by Richard Morris Hunt and had a nearly transparent façade, filled with great expanses of glass. It occupies the site of James Henry Roosevelt's home and was built to provide income to his principal benefaction, the Roosevelt Hospital.[20]

Another remarkably modernistic design was the Mills & Gibb Building of 1880, at Grand Street, which dispensed with almost all large-scale orna-

A.J. Dittenhoffer Warehouse, 1979.

542-44 BROADWAY

1864. [5 stories] On the top floor are three draped female figures—caryatids manquées.

546-48 BROADWAY

1866 and 1874, by John Correja. [5 stories] A huge, flat façade of square, oversized windows. *Site of* Fourth Universalist Church (also known as the Unitarian Church of the Divine Unity), 1845.

TIFFANY & COMPANY STORE, No. 550

(Also known as the International Silver Company Building). 1854, by Robert G. Hatfield; refaced 1901. [5 stories] Tiffany's trademark *Atlas Clock*, by Henry Frederick Metzler, adorned this building until the late 1860s. The façade was later turned into a cast-iron and glass expanse.

552-54 BROADWAY

1855, by John B. Snook. [6 stories] Vibrant and rhythmic, this façade is common to two buildings. It is enlivened by segmental and round-arched windows with highly detailed architraves.

CROUCH & FITZGERALD STORE, No. 556

1855. [4 stories] With deep hood molds and a chunky cornice, the upper stories of this red-brick building have a robust antebellum charm.

560-66 BROADWAY

1883-84, by Thomas Stent. [6 stories] This forceful, polychrome building of brick and iron, with its deep, segmental-arched window bays, is vivid, sculptural, and colorful—yet it is also quite disciplined.

PRINCE STREET

w ROGERS, PEET STORE, No. 569-75

1881-82, by Thomas Stent. [6 stories] Every floor on the façade of this red-brick and masonry Victorian delight is different, with deep arches, tiny colonettes nestled in pockets, and pilasters placed throughout.

577-81 BROADWAY

1860, by Cornell Iron Works and Daniel D. Badger (storefronts). [5 stories] Projecting window hoods and deep, articulated architraves add drama to this marble façade, carried across three buildings.

ASTOR BUILDING, No. 583-87

1896-97, by Cleverdon & Putzel. [12 stories] This taut and complex façade has exceptionally deep windows and two major colonnades. *Site of* Buckley's Minstrel Hall (also known as the San Francisco Minstrel Hall, Tony Pastor's Theater), 1856; John Jacob Astor house.

mentation in favor of a compellingly simple grid. Mills & Gibb was the largest American importer of laces, embroideries, linens, hosiery, notions, and trimmings.[21] Its presence on Broadway, where Brooks Brothers had been, symbolized the shift to wholesaling after the Civil War, when many shops, hotels, and theaters moved to Union Square and beyond. The neighborhood lost little of its vitality but much of its stylishness, although there were some distinguished late arrivals. In 1882, the conservative old clothier Rogers, Peet moved its flagship store to a robust, red-brick, Victorian building, designed by Thomas Stent, at Prince Street. Catercorner was 560 Broadway, an exceptionally handsome red-brick and iron store built by William Astor in 1884 and also designed by Stent. Six years later, Charles Broadway Rouss opened his enormous wholesale dry-goods house, a hybrid of granite and iron, south

560-66 BROADWAY
Views from 1979 to 1988.

NINETEENTH-CENTURY STORES

View at left, from 1979, shows 491 Broadway and Butler Brothers Store (right); view below, from 1990, shows the Ball, Black & Company and Rogers, Peet stores.

TURN-OF-THE-CENTURY LOFTS

Views from 1979 and 1987 show the Merchants Bank Building (left, this page), blockfront from the Havemeyer to Manhattan Mercantile buildings (right, this page), Silk Exchange Building (top, facing page), and Havemeyer Building (bottom, facing page).

"LITTLE" SINGER BUILDING

Views from 1979 and 1987 include part of the Ball, Black
& Company Jewelers Building (facing page).

JUDAH HAMMON HOUSE, No. 589

1832-33. [4 stories] This is an ancient brick dwelling with a simple dentiled cornice.

W. & J. SLOANE STORE, No. 591

1859; rebuilt 1900. [6 stories] A grand-peaked gable dominates this façade. This once matched No. 593.

593 BROADWAY

1860. [5 stories] This exceptional marble façade has arched windows, fine architraves, quoins, and large arched pediments on brackets.

597 BROADWAY

1867, by John Kellum. [5 stories] Large windows under flat arches alternate with generous ornament.

AYER BUILDING, No. 601

1916-17, by J. Odell Whitenack. [12 stories] Notable for an eight-story wall sculpture by Forrest Myers.

E   HAVEMEYER BUILDING, No. 568-78

1896-97, by George B. Post. [12 stories] A series of mammoth buildings stretches 392 feet along Broadway. This façade has banded piers, florid spandrel panels, and heroic arches among tall Ionic columns. *Site of* Metropolitan Hotel, 1849-52 by John B. Snook; Niblo's Garden, 1843, rebuilt 1846-49 and 1872; Sans Souci Theater, 1828; Niblo's Garden, 1822; James Fenimore Cooper house.

580-90 BROADWAY

1897, by Buchman & Deisler. [12 stories] Three buildings share a façade—a six-story arcade with elaborate spandrels, giant brackets, Ionic columns, and pediment-framed windows.

LYONS BUILDING, No. 594-96

1897-98, by Buchman & Deisler. [12 stories] The splayed lintels have been turned into geometric abstractions. There are Ionic columns at top.

MANHATTAN MERCANTILE BUILDING, No. 598

1897-98, by Robert Maynicke. [12 stories] This narrow tower, with a single large bay, ends the mammoth row. *Site of* Washington Hall (also known as White's Opera House), 1850-51.

600-02 BROADWAY

1883-84, by Samuel A. Warner. [6 stories] In a starkly rectilinear cast-iron façade, free-standing columns frame very large windows. *Near site of* Revere House hotel.

of Prince Street. (Rouss had legally changed his middle name to Broadway, in honor of the thoroughfare. "People might smile at the adoption of so singular a cognomen," the *Times* said, "but they never failed to remember it."[22]) His architect, Alfred Zucker, also designed a store for the Butler Brothers, dealers in novelty goods and notions, on the site where the Century Association first met and Grover & Baker sold sewing machines.

It was clear by the 1880s that cast iron had seen its day. One guidebook said disparagingly that iron buildings "are very abundant in New York, and are one of its most distasteful features."[23] The loft building itself continued to serve well, however, as the district switched to manufacturing, wholesaling, and warehousing. The basic building type was expanded in the 1890s to a massive, twelve-story form, richly—sometimes riotously—ornamented at the top, with deep colonnades and heavy cornices. One of the largest loft structures was the Havemeyer Building, designed by George B. Post in 1895 to replace the Metropolitan Hotel.

Floating almost ethereally in the midst of the heavy masonry architecture of its day was the "Little" Singer Building at Prince Street, completed in 1904. The L-shaped tower may be thought of as an aesthetic heir to the Roosevelt Building, a glass wall topped by delicate arches. It was designed by Ernest Flagg and got its diminutive name when Flagg later created the world's tallest building for the sewing-machine company, at Broadway and Liberty Street.

Architecturally, SoHo virtually froze in the twentieth century. It also declined as an industrial quarter and had to survive a period in which age and dilapidation were regarded as fatal flaws, calling for wholesale demolition. Plans advanced for the Lower Manhattan Cross-Town Expressway, an elevated road along Broome Street that would have taken out the Haughwout Building, among many others. But something else happened at the same time. Lofts—large, light, and, several decades ago, inexpensive—were readapted by artists who found a last resort in SoHo.[24] What began as an underground movement gained implicit official endorsement and impetus with the scuttling of the expressway in 1969, the legalization of some loft dwellings in 1971, and the creation of the twenty-six-block SoHo Cast Iron Historic District in 1973.

Although SoHo was a vital artistic quarter, Broadway was at the cultural outskirts. It remained a hybrid Latin and Chinese bazaar, where cheap clothes were sold from boxes, bins, and racks on the sidewalks. Hand-lettered signs testified to sweatshops behind the elegant façades—"Se necesitan operarias con experiencia para la Singer." It was not until the late 1980s that Broadway developed its own art scene, drawing from western SoHo and the East Village. The New Museum of Contemporary Art moved in 1983 to the spot between Prince and Houston streets where John Jacob Astor had lived. So many art dealers were clustered in the vicinity, particularly at the Havemeyer and 560 Broadway buildings, that an observer of the art world could decree flatly in 1989: "If you do the rounds of the galleries, you must include Broadway."[25]

Blockfront north of Grand Street, 1986.

NOHO EAST VILLAGE

HOUSTON STREET TO FOURTEENTH STREET

Grace Church, with the Chrysler Building in the distance, 1979.

Broadway is distinctly striated north of Houston Street, with almost every era of its growth recorded by striking architectural souvenirs in a marvelously incongruous jumble. They attest to its days as the city's most fashionable neighborhood (Grace Church and the St. Denis Hotel), as a premier shopping district (the old McCreery and Wanamaker stores), as an industrial precinct (the Cable and Roosevelt buildings), as an eastern outpost of Greenwich Village (a half dozen New York University buildings and several apartment towers), and as a western outpost of the East Village (storefronts and street corners that still exude a kind of counter-cultural funk). In the 1980s, under the name of NoHo, the district was recreated again, as a thriving, youth-oriented shopping precinct and social scene, with the older layers preserved and even revitalized.

our large farms originally filled the area, those of Anthony L. Bleecker (around Bleecker Street), Elbert Herring, Hendrick Brevoort, and Robert Richard Randall. Had Randall's will of 1801 been followed, his estate would have become an "Asylum, or Marine Hospital, to be called 'Sailors' Snug Harbor' for the purpose of maintaining and supporting aged, decrepit and worn-out sailors."[1] Randall, a shipmaster and merchant, envisioned sailors farming the tract and living in the house that stood near what is now Broadway and Ninth Street. However, the will was challenged by relatives and by the time the last claim was settled, in 1830, the property was too valuable to be used as a sprawling retreat. The trustees purchased a site on Staten Island instead and the farm was divided into leaseholds that provided Snug Harbor with a generous income.

Another legacy of the farming period is the bend that Broadway makes at Tenth Street, the first jog in its uptown journey. A favorite New York legend has it that the street was deflected at the insistence of Hendrick Brevoort, who owned the land and cherished a particular tree that stood in the proposed path of Broadway. A prosaic and slightly more credible explanation is that the bend was engineered to align Broadway with the Bowery Road, making for a smoother and more direct junction with the angle of the Bloomingdale Road at Sixteenth Street.[2]

As the farming period ended, the first big attraction to draw outsiders to the area was a country resort called Vauxhall Gardens, which extended to the Bowery, south of Astor Place. It opened in the summer of 1805 and offered concerts, fireworks, an equestrian statue of Washington, and, in its verdant acreage, pleasantly pastoral relief from the city. "The walks are ornamented with Pillars, Arches, Pedestals, Figures, &c. the whole of which when illuminated, cannot fail to create pleasure," the proprietor boasted. Fruits, sweets, wines, and liquors were served. The orchestra played on an elevated bandstand in the midst of the trees, to "romantic effect."[3]

The newly created St. Thomas congregation was worshipping in a large room at Broadway and Broome Street in 1824, when the vestry decided to build at Houston Street, despite objections that this "very noisy" intersection would disturb services. St. Thomas Church was completed in 1826, one of the first works of Gothic Revival in New York. Despite its barn-like proportions, it was admired as a "sort of castle with its two towers and its stone walls . . . a small Westminster Abbey."[4] In a similar vein, the Unitarian Church of the Messiah, south of Astor Place, was begun in 1838. Elaborately painted, it was said to "represent very nearly the interior of Westminster Abbey."[5]

For a while in the 1830s and '40s, this was the "swell" part of town.[6] David Prall, founder of a far-flung drug company and "one of the fastest of the fast young men that New York could then boast," lived near Houston Street.[7] Samuel Ward, a powerful banker and old-school New Yorker, lived at Bond Street. Next to the house was Ward's painting gallery, the first private building constructed as an art gallery in America.[8] From the outside, it was a windowless marble box on Broadway, and it excited the curiosity of thousands of passers-by over the decades. Ward sold an adjacent parcel on Great

View south in 1988 includes the John Wanamaker Store (left), Sinclair Building (center), and Astor Place Plaza (right).

HOUSTON STREET

Cable Building, 1987.

W   CABLE BUILDING, No. 611-21

1892-93, by McKim, Mead & White. [9 stories] Three great arched courses wrap around this chamfer-cornered mass, which has a deep copper cornice. In the ironwork is a "BCT" ligature, for the Broadway Cable Traction Company. **Site of** St. Thomas Episcopal Church, 1824-26, by Joseph R. Brady, with the Rev. John McVickar, rebuilt after 1851, by Wills & Dudley.

ANGELIKA FILM CENTER

1989, by Igor Josza and Don Schimenti. [6 theaters with 1,146 seats]

623 BROADWAY

1881, by John B. Snook. [5 stories] A simple cast-iron grid of flat arches and three-quarter-round columns.

625 BROADWAY

1896, by David W. King. [12 stories] Three deep cornices and splayed lintels enrich a fairly restrained façade.

NOHO BUILDING, No. 627-29

1894, by Louis Korn. [10 stories] There are two prominent five-story bays, friezes, lion heads, and a large cornice.

631-35 BROADWAY

Before 1865. [5 stories] These three modest antebellum buildings, once part of a longer row, have finely detailed architraves, with segmental-arched window hoods.

E   "LITTLE CARY" BUILDING, No. 620

1858-59, by John B. Snook and Daniel D. Badger. [6 stories] The texture of stonework is splendidly evoked by this cast-iron façade, with its rusticated spandrels and piers, small Corinthian columns, entablatures, and arches. **Site of** David Prall house.

622-26 BROADWAY

1881, by Henry Fernbach. [6 stories] Three-quarter-round columns create the frame of this deep and rectilinear iron façade. *Site of* Laura Keene's Varieties (also known as the Olympic Theater), 1856, by John M. Trimble.

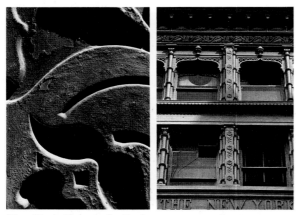

New York Mercantile Exchange, 1987 and 1979.

NEW YORK MERCANTILE EXCHANGE, No. 628-30

1882, by Herman J. Schwarzmann, with Buchman & Deisler. [6 stories] With colonettes in the form of bamboo, giant lilies in deep relief, roses strewn everywhere, and a leafy frieze, this cast-iron façade is lush and exotic.

632-34 BROADWAY

1899, by Robert Maynicke. [12 stories] Lion heads run along the cornice, above a façade with finely articulated architraves.

COE ESTATE BUILDING, No. 636-38

1896, by George B. Post. [12 stories] These seven-story-high, three-quarter-round, Roman-brick columns look as sturdy as tree trunks. Giant arches spring from their composite capitals.

EMPIRE STATE BUILDING, No. 640

1897, by DeLemos & Cordes. [9 stories] Two large, arched windows dominate the Broadway façade.

BLEECKER STREET

w **643 BROADWAY**

1878, by Stephen Decatur Hatch. [6 stories] This modest red-brick building has heavy hood molds with starkly geometric patterning.

645 BROADWAY

Before 1865. [6 stories] Segmental arched windows and a big, bracketed cornice mark this simple structure.

St. Thomas Church, 1823; Grace Church. VM, GSW.

Jones Street to former Mayor Philip Hone, who moved uptown in 1836. While building his new residence, Hone rented one of the Colonnade Houses, near Fourth Street, a marble pair with a common portico framed by huge granite columns. Impressed by the locale, Hone said the house was "delightfully situated."[9] A half mile uptown, in a large brick house overlooking Union Square, Cornelius Van Schaack Roosevelt spent a quarter of a century, beginning in the 1840s. One of his grandsons, President Theodore Roosevelt, remembered about the house that "we children much admired both the tessellated floor and the circular staircase" in the high front hall.[10]

Broadway lost a good deal of its residential flavor in the 1840s, the "noise and bustle of the great thoroughfare having driven [away] all the wealth and fashion."[11] Into the area came such institutions as the New-York Historical Society, which occupied the large Stuyvesant Institute building, between Bleecker and Third streets, from 1837 to 1841. It was succeeded there by the New York University Medical School, headed by Dr. Valentine Mott, which graduated its first class in 1842. At the Stuyvesant hall, the school had dissecting, chemistry, and lecture rooms, a library, and museum.[12] A few doors north, at 663 Broadway, the National Academy of Design opened its new galleries in 1850. It was said that its "collection of models from the Antique is the most complete in the country."[13]

There was no greater symbol of the neighborhood's advance than the construction, beginning in 1843, of Grace Church, one of the most important in the city, aesthetically and socially. Directly above the first bend in Broadway, the church is visible as far south as City Hall Park. Its architect, James Renwick Jr., knew how to handle so special a site, raising a delicate, white tower that seems to float over Broadway and has been known on a wintry sunset to look like "a pinnacle of alabaster, or a great crystal of rose quartz."[14] Like the contemporary Trinity Church, Grace is an artifice in that its Gothic elements are more decorative than structural. But it grew by accretion, as a

Gothic complex might: the Rectory was added in 1847, Grace Chantry in 1879, and Grace House in 1881.

Grace Church was a social as well as a religious entity. Pews rented for extravagant prices. "The word of God," Hone wrote, "will cost the quality who worship in this splendid temple about three dollars every Sunday. This may have a good effect; for . . . if they do not go regularly to church they will not get the worth of their money."[15] The most important person at Grace was the sexton, Isaac Hull Brown, who ruled society when society centered on Grace. "To be married or buried within its walls has been ever considered the height of felicity," it was said in 1869. "For many years, Brown has stood at the entrance to fashionable life."[16]

At mid-century, fashion meant Broadway. The New York Hotel, from Washington to Waverly Place, opened in 1847 as "one of the most ultra fashionable houses of the city, and the favorite resort of the Southerners."[17] In 1850, the Union Place Hotel was built at Fourteenth Street. Known later as the Morton House, it was favored by actors and journalists.[18] Preeminent among hotels was the St. Denis, at Eleventh Street, which was designed by Renwick and opened in 1853. Sarah Bernhardt, Colonel William "Buffalo Bill" Cody, and Presidents Abraham Lincoln and Ulysses S. Grant stayed there.

One of the Colonnade Houses in 1889, after the southern portion was demolished. NYHS.

PFAFF'S SALOON, No. 647
Before 1865. [6 stories] A companion to No. 645.

Façade of W. & J. Sloane Building after 1979 fire.

BLEECKER COURT, No. 649-59
(Also known as the W. & J. Sloane Carpet Warehouse). ca. 1867; rebuilt 1979-81, by Avinash K. Malhotra. [6 stories] Behind four nineteenth-century façades—all with three-quarter-round columns and pronounced cornices—is a completely new apartment building. No. 649-51 has a triangular pediment. No. 653 has a rounded pediment. No. 655 is a virtual twin of No. 653, but with balconies. No. 657-59 is taller and also has balconies. *Site of* Stuyvesant Institute (also known as the New York University Medical College, Lyceum of Natural History, New-York Historical Society, Young Men's Christian Association), 1837-40.

661 BROADWAY
1891, by Brunner & Tryon. [8 stories] This delightful orange-brick tower, an ornamented sliver of a building, has handsome iron bays and a pyramidal roof with a peaked dormer.

663-65 BROADWAY
1910, by Victor Hugo Koehler. [12 stories] The building's grid—strongly articulated, almost modern in its simplicity—is graced by elegant spandrels. *Site of* National Academy of Design, 1850; Marble Houses (also known as the Raleigh Hotel, Tremont House), ca. 1825.

NEW YORK UNIVERSITY: MERCER STREET RESIDENCE, No. 667-81
1981, by Benjamin Thompson Associates. [21 stories] A wide, tall, and expressionless brick façade rises over a tiny, marginal, sidewalk park. *Site of* Grand Central Hotel (also known as Broadway Central Hotel, University Hotel), 1870, by Henry Engelbert; La Farge House (also known as the Southern Hotel), 1854-56, by James Renwick Jr.; Tripler's Hall (also known as Burton's New Theater,

GRACE CHURCH

Views from 1979 and 1988 include the Huntington Close pulpit (left, facing page).

Laura Keene's Varieties, Metropolitan Hall, Winter Garden), 1850, by John M. Trimble, rebuilt.

E   MANHATTAN SAVINGS INSTITUTION, No. 644-46

1889-90, by Stephen Decatur Hatch. [9 stories] This turreted sentinel has tremendously complex arched window bays—much like those at Hatch's Roosevelt Building—in a vibrant façade of orange brick and sandstone.

648 BROADWAY

1891, by Cleverdon & Putzel; enlarged 1898, by Robert T. Lyons. [10 stories] This brick-edged iron building has a lacy fanlight and delicate leaded windows on the ground floor.

650 BROADWAY

[5 stories] The colonettes look almost as thin as pencil leads and they separate giant sash windows.

652 BROADWAY

1906, by Frederick C. Browne. [12 stories] This white-brick, ornamented sliver has a central bay with lovely wrought iron work.

654 BROADWAY

1882, by Jarvis Morgan Slade. [6 stories] There is one wide and exceptionally deep bay, framed by delicate, spindly colonettes.

BINGHAM BUILDING, No. 666

1903, by Rossiter & Wright. [12 stories] Very large arches in the base and an anthemion-topped entrance enliven this sober composition.

BOND STREET

Brooks Brothers Store, 1987.

E   BROOKS BROTHERS STORE, No. 670-74

1873-74, by George E. Harney. [5 stories] This robust, red-brick façade is full of incised decoration, like deep masonry archivolts with serrated edges;

St. Denis Hotel, ca. 1890. NYHS.

Alexander Graham Bell demonstrated the telephone at the hotel in 1877, arranging for the transmission from Brooklyn of the song "Hold the Fort" and the air "The Last Rose of Summer." The St. Denis, which is still standing, was known for the "absolute coziness of its public rooms, which, indeed, do not seem in the least like parts of a hotel, but rather like pleasant nooks in a refined home. . . . From their windows one can watch the vast and perpetual human tides flow up and down Broadway."[19]

Another major gathering place in the years before the Civil War was Charlie Pfaff's basement saloon, a few doors north of Bleecker Street, which was the headquarters of Bohemia. Its patrons included William Dean Howells, George Farrar Browne (known as Artemus Ward), and Ada Clare, the Queen of Bohemia. More than anyone else, however, Walt Whitman was identified closely with Pfaff's,

. . . where the drinkers and laughers meet to eat and drink and carouse,
While on the walk immediately overhead past the myriad feet of Broadway. . . .[20]

Adding considerably to this artistic melange were some of New York's most important theaters at mid-century. Tripler's Hall, one of the largest music halls in the world, was built in 1850 near Third Street.[21] It was rebuilt after a fire and then considerably remodeled in 1859, emerging as the Winter Garden. Edwin Booth was the lessee in 1865. He and John Wilkes Booth appeared together there in *Julius Caesar*, not long before the younger brother killed President Lincoln. Laura Keene, a famous English actress who had briefly managed Tripler's Hall, opened her Varieties theater, just above Houston Street, in 1856. Five years later, James Wallack opened a theater

St. Denis Hotel and James H. McCreery & Company Store, 1987.

at Thirteenth Street that was to become, for two decades, the "most famous amusement house in the United States." Indeed, it was asserted that even "London has no theatre that can equal Wallack's in comfort, size and beauty combined," except for the Drury Lane.[22] Even the Church of the Messiah was renovated as a playhouse in the 1860s. No theatrical enterprise took root there, however. It was under at least sixteen managements in as many years, and there were those who suspected that the place was jinxed by its religious origins.[23]

The theaters were accompanied by considerable commercial development. The big dry-goods house of Hearn Brothers (later James A. Hearn & Son) moved to 775 Broadway in 1856. Three years later, David Prall's home gave way to an extremely elaborate, iron-fronted building, by John B. Snook and Daniel D. Badger, that housed a chandelier maker and a velocipede dealer. John Daniell started a ribbon and silk business at Eighth Street in 1861 that was to grow into a ten-building complex.

Casting a shadow over every other enterprise was A.T. Stewart & Company, which arrived in 1862. As soon as it opened at Tenth Street, the area was transformed into the "ladies' shopping-ground," where "carriages are in possession of the roadway, and throngs of women in elegant costumes flock in and out of the shops."[24] Stewart's emporium, designed by John Kellum, may have been the largest cast-iron building ever constructed and was the largest store of its time. It was also the progenitor of the modern department store.[25] Many people called it the "marble palace," so well did the white cast iron work its deception. And it was no less imposing inside. In the great central rotunda, the "successive floors rise one above another like the tiers

each floor has a different window treatment. *Site of* Samuel Ward house and art gallery, ca. 1833.

676 BROADWAY

1873. [5 stories] A rich and exuberant composition, with roofline pediment, three-quarter-round columns (a different order at each floor), arched windows, and pronounced rustication.

678 Broadway, 1979.

678 BROADWAY

1874, by David & John Jardine. [5 stories] In this cast-iron façade, with incised and relief ornamentation, the window arches look like machine parts, reminiscent of hinges and piston rods.

EAST RIVER SAVINGS BANK, No. 680

Before 1865. [4 stories] This is a handsome and severe marble building, with a strong cornice.

682 BROADWAY

1902, by J.W. Stevens. [10 stories] This simple, refined marble tower has five-story pilasters. *Site of* Philip Hone house, 1837.

3rd STREET

w ### 250 MERCER STREET, No. 683-97

1978-79, by Henry George Greene. Most structures on this block were combined into a single apartment building, including all four facing Broadway:

BUTCHERS' AND DROVERS' BANK

1899, by W. Wheeler Smith. [13 stories] There are gargantuan triple keystones and splayed lintels on the façade of this red-brick tower.

687-91 BROADWAY

1884 and 1887, by J.A. Wood. [7 stories] These twin buildings with delicate, free-standing colonettes, are highly rectilinear. *Site of* the Union Club.

MERCHANTS' BUILDING

ca. 1905. [16 stories] Giant twelve-pane windows give this white-brick tower a powerful industrial appearance. There are also six-foot-high masonry owls on the fourth floor.

GREAT JONES STREET

E 684 BROADWAY

1904, by Frederick C. Browne. [12 stories] The features of this façade are masterfully exaggerated— scrolled brackets, lion-head cornice brackets, intricate six-story bays.

TOBÉ-COBURN SCHOOL, No. 686

[2 stories] A spare limestone box.

SILK BUILDING, No. 692-94

1909, by Clinton & Russell. [12 stories] This spartan white-brick tower has a narrow façade on Broadway but a tremendous 275-foot expanse on Fourth Street. *Site of* Female Normal and High School (the original Hunter College).

4th STREET

W HEBREW UNION COLLEGE-JEWISH INSTITUTE OF RELIGION: BROOKDALE CENTER, No. 705

1978-79, by Abramovitz, Harris & Kingsland. [5 stories] This brick box with dark, horizontal window strips is unexpressive and noncontextual.

NEW YORK UNIVERSITY: ANDRÉ & BELLA MEYER HALL OF PHYSICS, No. 707-13

1971, by Philip Johnson and Richard Foster, with Wank, Adams & Slavin. [12 stories] Varied colors of overly red stone, arranged randomly, work against the simple vertical composition.

Furniture Workers Building, 1978.

E FURNITURE WORKERS BUILDING, No. 700

1890, by George B. Post. [8 stories] Powerful and compelling, this orange-brick façade has an extraordinary four-story arcade that springs from a rusticated base with a sweeping entrance arch. Above a second arcade are terra-cotta masks with amusing expressions. *Site of* Vauxhall Gardens (also known as Sperry Gardens), 1805.

in an opera-house" and "one can witness as busy and interesting a scene as New York affords . . . from the poor woman whose scanty garb tells too plainly the story of her poverty, to the wife of the millionaire whose purchases amount to a small fortune."[26] Fifteen thousand customers would come on an average day in 1872 and sales totaled $60,000, one-quarter of that spent on silks. This was not necessarily New Yorkers' favorite place to shop, however, as James D. McCabe Jr. sniffed: "The salesmen have the reputation of being rude and often insolent."[27]

Along the aesthetic lines of Stewart's was the James H. McCreery & Company store, another spectacular cast-iron mercantile palace by Kellum, which opened in 1870. For twenty years, McCreery's shared its home on Eleventh Street with the Methodist Book Concern. Broadway was an ideal location for a major publisher and bookseller, and the Methodist house was in respectable company: Charles Scribner's Sons, G.P. Putnam's Sons, August Brentano, E.P. Dutton & Company, and Dodd, Mead & Company were all nearby.

McCreery's, which took over the cast-iron building entirely in 1890, was best known for its silk department and it was "preeminently the place at which ladies find materials for dresses, whether they desire simple house-gowns or full wedding trousseaux."[28] Other major retailers in the vicinity included W. & J. Sloane, which moved uptown in 1867. Its "Carpet Ware-house" was a handsome building at 649–55 Broadway, north of Bleecker Street. Brooks Brothers moved to the site of Samuel Ward's house in 1874, where their richly eclectic building still stands. The first floor had ready-made clothing, with custom and military goods on the second, and workrooms or storerooms above. The 1870s also saw the establishment of a new toy store in New York City, at 765 Broadway, by a thirty-four-year-old Baltimore merchant named Frederick August Otto Schwarz.[29]

It was a measure of the area's vitality that the carpet manufacturer Elias S. Higgins believed it was ready for the "most palatial hotel in America." His

"Little Cary" Building, 1988.

James H. McCreery & Company Store. NYI.

Grand Central Hotel (later Broadway Central) opened in 1870, opposite Bond Street. Designed by Henry Engelbert, this massive Second-Empire pile spread its marble wings 175 feet along Broadway and was not only the nation's largest hotel but "one of the most conspicuous objects on the street."[30] It could seat 600 diners and house 1,200 guests, who trod on seven acres of carpets, presumably made by Higgins. The hotel went from celebrated to legendary in 1872 when Edward S. Stokes killed James "Jubilee Jim" Fisk Jr., the notorious partner of Jay Gould, in a bitter struggle over the mistress they had shared. Four years later, the hotel gained another historical footnote as the host of the first meeting of the National League of Professional Base-Ball Clubs.[31]

Incongruously in the midst of this bustling neighborhood, Hunter College

A.T. Stewart Store. NYHS.

704-06 BROADWAY

1895, by DeLemos & Cordes. [10 stories] Generous in proportion, this white-brick tower with a wide central bay has two seventh-floor pediments on which nude figures, in stone, recline langorously.

708 BROADWAY

1896, by Cleverdon & Putzel. [10 stories] The top of this ornamented sliver has tiny arcades, miniature pediments, enormous medallions, and masks. *Site of* August Brentano bookseller.

710 BROADWAY

1894, by Cleverdon & Putzel. [10 stories] This is an exuberant, buff-colored, ornamented sliver, with exquisite decorative courses and four-story rounded buttresses.

712 BROADWAY

1891-93, by Alfred Zucker. [8 stories] There are delicate spandrels in this rectilinear façade.

714 BROADWAY

1896, by Buchman & Deisler. [11 stories] This ornamented sliver has a massively rusticated façade. *Site of* Colonnade Houses (also known as the Philip Hone house), 1833.

716 Broadway, 1988.

716 BROADWAY

1890, by Alfred Zucker. [6 stories] Two of the best gargoyles on Broadway are here. So, too, are rope-twist colonettes, leeringly demonic bracket masks, and foliate pilasters.

718-20 BROADWAY

1906, by Charles E. Birge. [11 stories] Contrasted to its neighbors, this is a fairly plain white-brick tower. *Site of* Hope Chapel Baptist Church (also known as Kelly & Leon's Theater), 1850, remodeled 1853.

EMPORIUMS

Views from 1979 show the James H. McCreery & Company Store (above), and Brooks Brothers Store.

Grand Central Hotel; Harrigan & Hart's New Theatre Comique. NYI, GSW.

was begun in 1870 under the name of the Female Normal and High School. The school, headed by Dr. Thomas Hunter, leased part of a business building at 694 Broadway. There was not nearly enough room, however, and it moved in 1874 to more hospitable surroundings on Lexington Avenue.[32] St. Thomas Church had already fled the area. In 1865, the rector complained: "We are now planted in the center of the worst neighborhood in this city, the most degraded and the most completely surrendered to the purpose of crime."[33] A year later, the congregation moved to Fifth Avenue.

Not even Grace Church was immune to wrenching social change. Virtually in its front yard, one of the city's largest bread lines formed in the late 1800s. Fleischmann's Vienna Model Bakery, next door, offered one-third of a loaf of bread to each of the 350 or so homeless men who gathered there every night. Its proprietor believed that a "man who begged for bread and would call for it at midnight was really worthy."[34]

In the latter half of the nineteenth century, the theater district drained away, by transformation or trauma. The Winter Garden burned in 1867. Laura Keene's second theater, later known as the Olympic, was razed in 1880. The Church of the Messiah, which had become Harrigan & Hart's New Theatre Comique, burned in 1884. (It was replaced by what may have been New York's first thematic, indoor shopping mall: Old London Street, an arcade of vaguely Elizabethan shopfronts, half-timbered and thatch-roofed. This was an "attempt to reproduce a fragment of ancient London, and to combine it with nineteenth-century retail shop-keeping."[35])

Two playhouses endured into the twentieth century. Wallack's Theater, later known as the Star, did not close until 1901. The Union Square Theater, built next door in 1871, saw George M. Cohan's stage debut in the 1890s and stayed open, as a cinema, until 1936.[36] It was still standing in 1990, as was the northeast wing of the Morton House.

722 BROADWAY

1895, by Francis A. Minuth. [9 stories] Four bearded, stone faces stare down from the seventh-floor cornice. Other bracket masks and a pretty copper dormer distinguish this ornamented sliver.

JOHN WANAMAKER WAREHOUSE AND GARAGE, No. 726-30

1916, by William Steele & Sons; enlarged. [10 stories] This industrial design, with its big, horizontal windows, is proof that old buildings can be just as heedless of context as recent ones. *Site of* Old London Street, 1887; Unitarian Church of the Messiah (also known as the Broadway Athenaeum, Globe Theater, Harrigan & Hart's New Theatre Comique, Lucy Rushton's), 1838-39, rebuilt 1864-65, rebuilt 1881, by Francis Hatch Kimball; Colonnade Hotel, 1830-33 (an entrance to La Grange Terrace on Lafayette Street).

TREFFURTH'S CAFE, No. 732

1885. [4 stories] The name of the restaurant endures in exuberant script on the façade.

734 BROADWAY

1872, by David & John Jardine. [5 stories] In this elaborate cast-iron façade, oversized windows under segmental arches are set between powerful three-quarter-round columns with Corinthian capitals.

736 BROADWAY

1897, by Louis Korn. [11 stories] There are giant leafy brackets on this ornamented sliver.

738 BROADWAY

1867. [5 stories] This is a classic old façade of flat arches and three-quarter-round columns.

ASTOR PLACE PLAZA, No. 740-44

1910-12, by Francis Hatch Kimball. [12 stories] The white-brick mass wraps confidently around the corner, with a rhythmic, vertical façade of seven-story bays.

WASHINGTON PLACE

w **NEW YORK COMMERCIAL BUILDINGS, No. 715-27**

(Also known as the Guggenheimer Building). 1894-96, by Robert Maynicke. [12 stories] Tied together by a tremendous copper cornice, this ensemble is powerful and massive. *Site of* New York Hotel, 1847.

NEW YORK UNIVERSITY, No. 715

There are three recessed window bays among six-story pilasters.

NEW YORK UNIVERSITY, No. 719

This portion has a large central bay in iron, with ornamented spandrels, framed by six-story pilasters.

NEW YORK UNIVERSITY: TISCH SCHOOL OF THE ARTS, No. 721

Before some unsympathetic alterations, this was the mirror image of No. 719.

NEW YORK UNIVERSITY, No. 727

Once the mirror image of No. 715, the ground floor has been altered, with more of the original façade retained than at No. 721.

WAVERLY PLACE

w HILARY GARDENS, No. 729

1972, by Joseph Feingold. [36 stories] Far too large for its setting, this orange-brick tower is made even more alien by being isolated in a plaza.

GEORGETOWN PLAZA, No. 743

1960, by Boak & Raad. [31 stories] This monumentally bland buff-brick tower, like its neighbor, is disproportionately huge and set off in a plaza. The yellow balconies look like an afterthought.

ASTOR PLACE

E ONE ASTOR PLACE, No. 746-50

(Also known as the Astor Place Building). 1881, by Starkweather & Gibbs. [7 stories] This chunky, robust, Victorian red-brick fantasy is a total delight. Countless fine embellishments, like keystone masks and foliated panels, give it sculptural depth.

SINCLAIR BUILDING, No. 752-54

1908, by William H. Gompert. [12 stories] Giant, geometric cornice brackets dominate this white-brick façade. *Site of* Sinclair House hotel.

8th STREET

w THE HAMILTON, No. 757

1950, by H.I. Feldman. [6 stories] This drab modern structure wraps around a large court. *Site of* F.A.O. Schwarz Toy Bazaar; American Hotel (also known as the John Daniell Sons & Sons Store).

E JOHN WANAMAKER STORE, No. 756-70

1904-10, by D.H. Burnham & Company; expanded 1926. [14 stories] Ranks of powerful, three-story arches march along the street and a distinct, inscribed grid runs through this massive white façade. It was once joined to the Stewart store, across Ninth Street, by the Bridge of Progress. The murals in the bank lobby are by Andrew B. Karoly. *Site of* New York Philharmonic Society, by Kellum & Son.

Astor Place Building, 1988.

Garment manufacturing spread uptown in the 1870s and '80s. A stalwart landmark of the old days, the Roosevelt house on Fourteenth Street, was torn down shortly after Cornelius died in 1871. The Domestic Sewing Machine Company had Griffith Thomas design a florid, domed headquarters on the spot, overlooking what was sometimes called "Sewing Machine Square."[37] After Brooks Brothers departed in 1884, its store was taken over by a large wholesale clothing manufacturer. Another factory was created from the beau-

Furniture Workers Building, 1988.

Cable Building, 1979.

tiful Astor Place Building that Orlando B. Potter had intended to be a combination store and hotel.[38]

Towering loft buildings rose throughout the area in the 1890s. Because new technology permitted construction of skyscrapers on house-sized lots, it was not uncommon to see ten-story buildings only twenty-five feet wide, looking like ornamented slivers, invested with whimsy, exuberance, and great decorative detail. More substantial works included 700 Broadway, at Fourth Street, which was designed by George B. Post in 1890. With its double course of powerfully articulated arches, this massively Romanesque building recalled Post's Produce Exchange on the Bowling Green. Its tenants included hatters, furriers, dressmakers, and suppliers of flowers, feathers, and notions. Another architectural gem was the Roosevelt Building of 1893, in what had been Cornelius Roosevelt's backyard, on Thirteenth Street. It was designed by Stephen Decatur Hatch and built by a partnership of Roosevelt's sons. The building was home to Hackett, Carhart clothiers and its rooftop was used in the 1890s as the first movie studio of the American Mutoscope & Biograph Company.[39] Hatch also designed an effusive, turreted tower in 1889 for the Manhattan Savings Institution, which had long been in the neighborhood.

A striking sign of change in the area was the coming in 1893 of the Cable Building, center and powerhouse of the Broadway cable-car system, to the spot where St. Thomas Church had stood. From colossal wheels and "hundreds of tons of ponderous machinery" in the building's basement, four cables emerged and ran under Broadway: two for regular service, two for emer-

9th STREET

W **RANDALL HOUSE, No. 771**
1958, by Boak & Raad. [14 stories] A dull wall of red brick. *Site of* James A. Hearn & Son Store; "Minto" Estate-Sailors' Snug Harbor (also known as the Robert Richard Randall house), ca. 1766.

E **STEWART HOUSE, No. 772-86**
1958, by Sylvan Bien. [21 stories] This is a thoughtlessly scaled and poorly arranged white brick mass. *Site of* A.T. Stewart Store (also known as the John Wanamaker Store), 1862, by John Kellum.

10th STREET

W **NEW YORK UNIVERSITY: BRITTANY RESIDENCE HALL, No. 787-89**
(Also known as the Brittany Hotel). 1928-29, by Farrar & Watmough; remodeled 1966. [16 stories] This plain red-brick tower has some surprises: 40-pane casement windows and neo-Gothic terra-cotta detailing.

791 BROADWAY
Before 1865. [4 stories] Badly damaged in a 1987 fire, it still has its dentiled cornice and some 2-over-2 windows.

ST. DENIS HOTEL, No. 797-99
1852-53, by James Renwick Jr.; rebuilt 1875 and 1917. [6 stories] Stripped of detail in 1917 (the section at No. 797 was radically altered), it retains a rusticated ground-floor façade on Eleventh Street. There is a rather grand staircase inside. The northern portion has been painted to show where decorative courses used to run.

E **GRACE CHURCH, No. 800**
1843-46, by James Renwick Jr. Landmark. Altar and reredos by James Renwick Jr., pulpit by William Welles Bosworth, chancel window by James Renwick Jr. and Clayton & Bell, and transept windows by Clayton & Bell.
HUNTINGTON CLOSE
1909-11. *Site of* Fleischmann's Vienna Model Bakery.
GRACE CHANTRY
1878-79, by Edward T. Potter. A small marble chapel that presents a five-sided apse to Broadway, with lancet windows. The Huntington Close pulpit of 1910 was designed by William W. Renwick and Jules Edouard Roiné, sculptor.
GRACE HOUSE - SEXTON'S OFFICE, No. 802
1880-81. A three-story tower is the focal point, with an octagonal peaked roof, quatrefoil courses, and lancet windows with flowing tracery. The garden was designed in 1881 by Vaux & Company.

BY STEPHEN DECATUR HATCH

Views from 1979 to 1988 show the Roosevelt Building (facing page) and Manhattan Savings Institution (this page).

GRACE CHURCH RECTORY, No. 804

1846-47, by James Renwick Jr. Landmark. Set back in the garden, it features a large central porch, with delicately detailed projecting bays.

THE RENWICK, No. 806-08

(Also known as the Domestic Publishing Building). 1888, by Renwick, Aspinwall & Russell. [6 stories] Though in brick, not marble, it complements Grace Church with many Gothic-inspired touches: lancet arches, cinquefoil arches, and molding.

810 BROADWAY

1907, by Rouse & Sloan. [8 stories] This white, ornamented sliver has a glass-filled central bay and is topped by a steep gable and finials.

812 BROADWAY

(Also known as the Gurbob Building). 1868. [5 stories] A broken pediment embellishes this façade of flat arches and three-quarter-round columns.

814 BROADWAY

(Also known as the Gurbob Building). Before 1865. [5 stories] Delightfully elaborate hood molds, a bracketed cornice, and a broken pediment.

816 BROADWAY

Before 1865. [5 stories] This building reveals its great age through half-story attic windows.

HEWLETT HOUSE, No. 818

1961, by A.H. Salkowitz. [13 stories] Its glazed white bricks and strip windows are inappropriate and wholly out of context.

11th STREET

w   JAMES H. McCREERY & COMPANY STORE, No. 801-807

(Also known as the Cast-Iron Building, Methodist Book Concern). 1868-70, by John Kellum; ironwork by J.B. & W.W. Cornell; rebuilt 1972-73, by Stephen B. Jacobs. [6 stories] Above a colossal ground-floor colonnade are rhythmic, grand, and seemingly endless arcades, springing from three-quarter-round columns. The original design has been compromised by a new penthouse.

KEEP MANUFACTURING COMPANY, No. 809-11

1887, by Joseph M. Dunn. [5 stories] A strong iron grid of segmental arched windows.

813 BROADWAY

Before 1865. [4 stories] A cornice and some 4-over-4 windows are all that remain of original detailing.

John Wanamaker Store, 1988.

gency backup. One pair ran to the Battery, the other to Fiftieth Street.[40] "The cable cars come down Broadway as the waters come down at Lodore," Stephen Crane wrote. "The cars, by force of column and numbers, almost dominate the great street, and the eye of even an old New Yorker is held by these long yellow monsters which prowl intently up and down, up and down, in a mystic search."[41]

Growth in industry meant a loss in social life, an infirmity on which the Broadway Central Hotel sought to capitalize in 1895. "At 6 o'clock the offices and great wholesale houses surrounding the hotel are closed," it promised, "and Central Broadway becomes as quiet as a village street."[42] Yet, there was abundant life in the daytime, thanks to John Wanamaker, who recreated Stewart's store in 1896 as the New York outpost of his Philadelphia-based empire. At the turn of the century, it could still be said, Eighth Street was "where Broadway emerges from its wholesale chrysalis and expands into a fashionable retail shopping district. The life of the street is cheerier for the change, which is quickly seen in the greater gayety and brighter color of the crowd. . . . Somehow even the cable cars do not seem so aggressive."[43]

Wanamaker's outgrew Stewart's cast-iron palace, but rather than move uptown, as most stores did, it expanded in place, beginning in 1904. Land was cheaper downtown and Wanamaker was convinced that wherever he operated, the crowds would come. The mammoth new John Wanamaker Store, between Eighth and Ninth streets, was joined to Stewart's by the double-deck Bridge of Progress. The centerpiece of the new building was the two-story "House Palatial," with twenty-two rooms, a hall, staircases, and a Summer Garden. Wanamaker's was the first department store to sell airplanes and the first to have a permanent department of Modernist furniture and decorative objects.[44] The store did not go out of business until 1954, and even then to general surprise. Writing its obituary, Meyer Berger said New Yorkers "had come to love the place, its soft-spoken salespeople, its suave—but not too suave—floorwalkers, its mellow indoor bells, the concerts in the great Wanamaker Auditorium, the air of quiet gentility that always lay, sort of reverent and hushed, over its well-stocked counters."[45]

Throughout the first half of the twentieth century, Broadway's essential profile, a street of wholesale textile dealers and garment makers, remained very much the same, although conditions were growing worse and worse. Things got so bad that the Fire Commissioner was moved to call it a "fourth-rate, shabby, deplorable neighborhood" in 1958, after a flash fire in a textile printing plant and underwear factory at 623 Broadway killed twenty-four people.[46]

The area was not completely desolate, however. In the 1950s, the East Village attracted new Bohemians. Although Broadway was on the margin, it did take on some of the intellectual and artistic qualities of that neighborhood. The New York University campus reached Broadway in 1965 when N.Y.U. bought the Brittany Hotel, at Tenth Street, for use as undergraduate quarters, and the colossal New York Commercial Buildings, from Washington to Waverly Place, which now house the Tisch School of the Arts, and other university operations. Nearby was the Strand Book Store, which moved from Fourth Avenue in the 1950s.

Residential development began on a large scale in 1958 with Stewart

Children's clothes for sale by a sidewalk vendor, 1979.

815 BROADWAY

1897. [2 stories] Tiny scale and delicate detail make this an unusual commercial front.

WELD BUILDING, No. 817-19

(Also known as the Anderson Building, Meyer-Jonasson Skyscraper, Sprague Building). 1895, by George B. Post. [14 stories] Its seven-story arcade has diamond-sharp piers of Roman brick, rotated 45 degrees, that resolve in arches high above the street.

12th STREET

w **821 BROADWAY**

1906, by S. Sass. [11 stories] This red-brick tower has a tall, turreted corner and strong arches.

825 BROADWAY

[8 stories] Oddly shaped, semi-circular balconies jut from this modern, red-brick façade.

827-31 BROADWAY

1866. [4 stories] These two buildings are linked by a common façade of flat arches, three-quarter-round columns, and quoins, topped by cornices with triangular pediments.

833 BROADWAY

1878, by Charles H. Nichols. [5 stories] Slender, free-standing colonettes and incised geometric designs enliven this façade.

835 BROADWAY

Before 1865. [5 stories] There is not much left of the original but a cornice with large brackets.

E **NATIONAL BUILDING, No. 828**

1902, by William H. Birkmire. [11 stories] This strongly geometric and articulated façade is organized in five-story bays.

830 BROADWAY

1896. [11 stories] There are deep windows and little blind arches in the façade of this thin, white tower.

832-34 BROADWAY

1896, by Ralph S. Townsend. [10 stories] This is virtually identical to No. 532-34, also by Townsend. On an already complex façade, ornament has been lavished—heavy swags, fretwork courses, and guilloche patterns in the pilasters.

836-38 BROADWAY

1876. [6 stories] This is a great remnant of the nineteenth century, quite intact in its crisp detailing, grandly proportioned windows, steep mansard roof, and dormers with pediments.

840 BROADWAY

1899, by Robert Maynicke. [12 stories] This handsome white tower, with elegantly detailed architraves, has a chamfered corner and a two-story arcade.

13th STREET

W   ROOSEVELT BUILDING, No. 839

1893, by Stephen Decatur Hatch. [9 stories] The complex and heavily ornamented façade is dominated by giant arched bays of tautly arranged windows, between three-story Roman-brick pilasters. The corner buttress is topped by a great copper knob.

Domestic Sewing Machine Building. NYHS.

UNION BUILDING, No. 849-53

1928-29, by Emery Roth. [23 stories] A stark buff-brick tower with a nervously articulated grid. *Site of* Domestic Sewing Machine Building, 1872, by Griffith Thomas; Cornelius Van Schaack Roosevelt house, ca. 1846.

E   ROGERS, PEET BUILDING, No. 842

(Also known as the Village Voice offices). 1902, by Clinton & Russell. [8 stories] The red-brick façade is divided into bays topped by large segmental arches. There are copper dormers on the mansard roof. *Site of* Wallack's Theater (also known as the Germania Theater, Star), 1860-61, by Thomas R. Jackson, remodeled 1883 and 1889.

VACANT LOT, No. 850-60

Site of Morton House Hotel (also known as the Hotel Churchill, Union Place Hotel).

UNION SQUARE THEATER and MORTON HOUSE

Nothing remains on Broadway of the hotel or theater. But the auditorium house exists on the 14th Street midblock, as does a wing of the hotel, with pediment-framed windows.

Georgetown Plaza (left) and Astor Place Building, 1987.

House, a huge apartment tower that replaced the Stewart store, which burned in 1956 as it was being prepared for demolition. In later years, other fire-damaged stores were salvaged for residential purposes. McCreery's, which had become a shoe and handbag factory, burned in 1971. Instead of being scrapped, it was renovated as an apartment house. The W. & J. Sloane building burned in 1979. Its façades were saved to form a nineteenth-century veneer for a modern apartment building. Nothing could save the Broadway Central Hotel, however. In its final years, it straddled two worlds. It housed the six-theater Mercer Arts Center but was also "one of the worst 'welfare hotels,' " a "cesspool of squalor and crime."[47] More than 300 people were living there in 1973 when the building collapsed, killing four.

Almost twenty years after the closing of Wanamaker's, Broadway got its "first major department store for the hip," as the *Village Voice* described the Unique Clothing Warehouse, south of Astor Place.[48] The *Voice* itself moved in 1980 to Thirteenth Street, where Rogers, Peet had once done business. Publishers settled again in the area in the 1970s and '80s, and bookstores like Shakespeare & Company and Untitled II opened. The Hebrew Union College-Jewish Institute of Religion, the Western Hemisphere's oldest and largest institution of Jewish higher education, moved to Fourth Street from West Sixty-eighth Street in 1979.[49]

This revitalization attracted wide notice. "Things are changing on Lower Broadway faster than anyone had probably ever thought possible," the *Times* said in 1984, adding, a year later, that "it has become the momentary locus of hip."[50] Even as the street came ostentatiously and noisily back to life, however, one old quality endured that had been appreciatively described in 1876: "In the midst of the bustle of this babel of business, the observer will be surprised to discover even one spot where peace and quiet and solemnity reign supreme, and his eye will sparkle with delight as he distinguishes through the trees the graceful contour of Grace Church."[51]

James H. McCreery & Company Store (left), 810 Broadway (center), and the Renwick (right), 1987.

UNION SQUARE LADIES' MILE

FOURTEENTH STREET TO TWENTY-SECOND STREET

George Washington *at Union Square, with the Empire State Building in the distance, 1987.*

Broadway is graced with remarkable architectural remnants north of Union Square. They testify to its residential period in the early nineteenth century (more than a dozen old houses still exist) and to its commercial phase in later years. Most important, they speak of the role that Broadway played, beginning in the late 1860s, as the heart of the fancy shopping district, where well-to-do women spent their days and a good deal of money besides. This was the Ladies' Mile, the realm of Arnold, Constable and Lord & Taylor and Gorham Silver and W. & J. Sloane. Its souvenirs are abundant, cohesive and, in many cases, still quite glorious. Seven decades of abandonment did not extinguish their allure. By the late 1980s, the newly designated Ladies' Mile Historic District and the newly rebuilt Union Square Park were regaining a fair measure of their gilded age vitality.

Buck's Horn Tavern. VM.

This designation covers every building on the west side of Broadway, from 17th to 24th Street, and on the east side, from 17th Street through 928-30 Broadway, north of 21st Street.

14th STREET

Abraham Lincoln in Union Square, 1986.

UNION SQUARE

[3.59 acres] Within the park are statues of *George Washington*, by Henry Kirke Brown, with J.Q.A. Ward (pedestal by Richard Upjohn); *Mohandas Gandhi*, by Kantilal B. Patel; *Marquis de Lafayette*, by Frédéric-Auguste Bartholdi; and *Abraham Lincoln*, by Henry Kirke Brown; the Independence Flagstaff (also known as the Charles Francis Murphy Memorial), 1926-30, by Anthony de Francisci (pedestal by Perry Coke Smith); the Union Square Drinking Fountain (also known as the James Fountain), 1881, by Karl Adolph Donndorf; and the Bandstand.

ntil the middle of the nineteenth century, the most eventful moment in the area's history had occurred in 1783, when George Washington entered New York City to reclaim it after seven years of British occupation. (His statue once stood at the southeast corner of Union Square Park, where he was received by the citizenry.[1]) Other than that excitement, this was a bucolic realm, dotted by country estates: Rose Hill, which belonged to the Stuyvesants and later to John Watts; Gramercy Seat, which belonged to James Duane; and Roxborough, which belonged to Cornelius Tiebout. The city was safely distant. In 1822, for example, the Bank of the Manhattan Company (predecessor of Chase Manhattan) opened temporary quarters near Eighteenth Street, while yellow fever ravaged New York.[2] The most prominent landmark was the Buck's Horn Tavern, a road house opposite the Abingdon Road to Chelsea, which ran along the line of Twenty-first Street.

In 1811, the Street Commissioners tried to smooth out the awkward junction of Broadway and the Bowery Road by designing "Union Place," a long and slender trapezium beginning at Tenth Street and narrowing to a point at Sixteenth Street. That concept was shrunk a few years later and, in 1832, the idea was discarded entirely because of its "shapeless and ill-looking form." With that, Union Square was created.[3]

As if ushering in the first major period of development, the fountains of Union Square "exhibited all the forms of aquatic magnificence" in 1842, when fresh water first arrived from the new Croton aqueduct system.[4] Within a decade, Union Square had become the "most fashionable portion of the city."[5] The merchant Henry Parish had a mansion and conservatory on one corner of Seventeenth Street. Robert Goelet had a large house opposite. His brother, Peter, lived at Broadway and Nineteenth Street, where his home attracted much attention. "Everybody that passes his courtyard stops to look through the iron railing at his superb peacocks, golden pheasants, silver pheasants, California quail, and so on."[6] The Goelets owned a significant amount of Manhattan, perhaps second only to the Astors in the impressiveness of their holdings, and they played a major role in developing Broadway.[7]

Along with the mansions were more modest row houses, several of which

17th STREET

From 17th to 18th Street, west side, 1986.

w   ROBERT GOELET HOUSE, No. 857
1847-48; rebuilt 1884, by Joseph M. Dunn. [4 stories]
Altered beyond recognition from the original, this

Arnold, Constable & Company Store (left) and the Gorham Silver Manufacturers Building (center).

building has a delicate commercial façade of cast-iron and glass.

NANCY S. EDWARDS HOUSE, No. 859

1841; remodeled 1869 and 1897. [3 stories] The upper story and bracketed cornice of this brick dwelling are intact.

MOSES L. JACKSON HOUSE, No. 861

1841-42; remodeled 1889. [4 stories] The upper two stories and bracketed cornice are intact.

JOHN FERRIS HOUSE, No. 863

(Also known as Huyler's Candy Store). 1841-42; remodeled 1885, by C.B.J. Snyder. [4 stories] Three upper stories of this old brick dwelling are pretty much intact, as is the cornice.

E.W. CLAWSON HOUSE, No. 865

1843; rebuilt 1869. [5 stories] This façade has round, segmental, and flat arches.

DITSON BUILDING, No. 867-71

(Also known as the Whiting Silver Manufacturing Company). 1882-83, by George W. Pope. [5 stories] This fairly simple and solid façade is enlivened by modest touches like gables and brick brackets.

E PARISH BUILDING, No. 860

(Also known as the Butler Building, Lienau Building, Thonet Brothers Depot, Andy Warhol's Factory). 1883-84, by Detlef Lienau; remodeled 1925, by F.H. Dewey & Company. [6 stories] The vigorous original building was considerably watered down to its current yellow-brick version. **Site of** Henry Parish house (also known as the Union League Club).

From 17th to 18th Street, east side, 1987.

ROW HOUSE, No. 862

1847-48; remodeled 1921, by John B. Snook & Sons. [4 stories] It is astonishing that these brick row houses have survived in any form. Old window

Jacob Cram House, 1988.

can still be found between Seventeenth and Eighteenth streets and between Twenty-first and Twenty-second streets. Although it is remarkable that any of them survived, perhaps the single most interesting house is 922 Broadway, the remnant of a row built in about 1854 for Jacob Cram. This was converted to a "large and pleasant hotel" called the Bancroft House, which was "furnished with accommodations that cannot fail of giving satisfaction to the most fastidious."[8]

Although the Fifth Avenue Hotel proved in 1860 that society would venture as far as Twenty-third Street, Broadway between Union and Madison squares did not pick up momentum until after the Civil War. Its first major commercial development—the Mortimer Building of 1862, an exquisite Italianate structure at Twenty-second Street that was designed by Griffith Thomas—was occupied for seven years by Bryant, Stratton & Packard's Business College, which taught bookkeeping, law, arithmetic, and penmanship.[9]

Arnold, Constable & Company Store, 1979.

heads remain at No. 862; delicate iron pilasters were added later.

ROW HOUSE, No. 864

1847-48. [4 stories] Mostly stripped of original architectural fabric, this building still has half-height attic windows.

ROW HOUSE, No. 866

1847-48. [4 stories] Of all the houses in the row, this one is in the best condition, with window heads intact on three stories and a simple dentiled cornice.

ROW HOUSE, No. 868

1847-48. [4 stories] Somewhat stripped of detail, this building has remnants of the old window heads.

H. BERGDORF TAILORING SHOP, No. 870

1847-48; rebuilt 1915, by Arthur Sutcliffe. [4 stories] The old brick façade is now broken by bands of horizontal windows.

HAWES BUILDING, No. 872

1847-48; rebuilt 1901, by Frederick Jacobson. [4 stories] Two wide bays with quoined surrounds and big scallop keystones create a striking and unusual façade. ***Site of*** Bank of the Manhattan Company branch.

18th STREET

Arnold, Constable & Company Store, 1987.

It took the dry-goods merchant Aaron Arnold, whose "marble palace" was at Canal and Mercer streets, to see that the city's retail center was going to keep moving uptown. Where a row of cheap little stores had stood, between Eighteenth and Nineteenth streets, Arnold and the merchant Edwin Hoyt began a remarkable dual development in 1868: two enormous marble buildings with a uniform Second Empire façade, designed by Griffith Thomas. The south building was owned by Hoyt, the north building by Arnold, who lived near Twenty-first Street.[10]

Arnold, Constable & Company, which opened its spacious Nineteenth Street store in 1869, was "one of the greatest . . . dry-goods establishments in the world."[11] It took care of wealthy customers—on which it had a near monopoly—"from cradleside to graveside," providing children's wear and mourning clothes and practically everything in between.[12] Silks, dress goods, and furnishings filled the first floor; furs and apparel, the second; with three top floors given to upholstery, carpets, and Oriental rugs. The Hoyt Building,

w HOYT BUILDING, No. 873-79

(Also known as Aitken, Son & Company, A.A. Vantine & Company). 1868, by Griffith Thomas; expanded 1888, by DeLemos & Cordes; expanded 1901, by Thomas H. Styles. [6 stories] Together with the Arnold, Constable store, the Hoyt Building forms a massive, looming ensemble. Its marble façade has 48 enormous arched windows—larger than double doorways—capped by keystones and separated by three-quarter-round columns.

ARNOLD, CONSTABLE & COMPANY STORE, No. 881-87

(Also known as the A.B.C. Carpet Store). 1868-69, by Griffith Thomas; expanded 1872 and 1876, by Thomas. [7 stories] This structure has everything the Hoyt Building has and more: a two-story mansard roof, dominated by an enormous center pavilion and topped by leafy cresting. The total length of this magnificent rooftop, along all façades, is about 540 feet.

E MacINTYRE BUILDING, No. 874

1890-92, by R.H. Robertson. [11 stories] A slender, pyramidally peaked tower that is an architectural beacon over Ladies' Mile. There is vigorous ornamentation throughout the façade and oversized arches on the ninth floor.

Hess Building, 1987.

HESS BUILDING, No. 876-78

1883-84, by Henry Fernbach. [6 stories] This robust, red-brick Victorian building has a forceful center bay and prominent mansard.

W. & J. Sloane Store, 1987.

W. & J. SLOANE STORE, No. 880-88

(Also known as the A.B.C. Carpet Store). 1881-82, by William Wheeler Smith; expanded 1898, by

Mortimer Building, 1987.

at Eighteenth Street, had two major tenants. Aitken, Son & Company dealt in ribbons, lace, and trimmings, and ranked with Arnold, Constable for quality.[13] A.A. Vantine & Company, an Oriental bazaar, scoured China, Egypt, India, Japan, Persia, and Turkey for ivory, jewelry, brass, teakwood, and porcelain; for fans, screens, carved furniture, perfumes, lamps, chinaware, umbrellas, and kimonos.[14]

Lord & Taylor quickly followed the rival Arnold, Constable to Ladies' Mile. Its new store, which opened in 1870, was so large that it straddled two properties: that of the Badeau family, on Twentieth Street, and the Goelets in mid-block. From a distinctive corner tower, Lord & Taylor's cast-iron façade stretched 100 feet along Broadway. Although "one of the most massive structures on the island," it was "so profusely and tastefully ornamented that one almost forgets that it is a place of business" and it was also admired as a work of iron that did not try to pretend to be stone, as "its wealth of filigree acknowledges with all honesty what it is made of."[15] Inside, Lord & Taylor's attractions included an elevator "as luxurious as the grand salon of the first class steamboats," a "stock of goods equal in costliness and superior in taste to anything that can be bought at Stewart's," and show windows that were "among the sights on Broadway."[16]

The dry-goods firm of J. & C. Johnston moved into the Mortimer Building in 1872. The store was known in its day for carrying the latest fashions from France, but its enduring significance was that—given the design of the Mortimer Building—it fronted both on Broadway and Fifth Avenue. "The encroachments of commerce on the heretofore restricted thoroughfare of Fifth-avenue has at last made a gigantic stride," the *Times* reported.[17] In four years' time, Arnold, Constable was also on Fifth Avenue, having stretched westward from Broadway, creating a remarkable 540-foot-long mansard roof in the process. The west façade was a near replica of the Broadway front, but in cast-iron.

LORD & TAYLOR STORE

Views from 1979.

Smith. [6 stories] Great expanses of glass provide a sense of lightness, while the complex brick and terra-cotta detailing, ornamented pilasters, and articulated cornices endow the façade with a feeling of considerable solidity.

19th STREET

w GORHAM SILVER MANUFACTURERS BUILDING, No. 889

1883-84, by Edward Hale Kendall. Landmark. [8 stories] A delicate, taut composition, this façade is etched by a fine-line grid of masonry courses and brick piers. Its roof is punctuated by dormers and gables.

EDWARD A. MORRISON & SON STORE, No. 893

1844; rebuilt 1873-74; refaced 1975. [3 stories] This has been reduced to a metal-screen façade.

LORD & TAYLOR STORE (Goelet portion), No. 897

(Also known as the Saint Laurie Building). 1869-70, by James H. Giles; rebuilt and reclad 1914, by John H. Duncan; renovated 1983, by Beyer Blinder Belle. [5 stories] On first glance, this relatively chaste limestone façade appears unrelated to No. 901. But its fenestration pattern matches the original Lord & Taylor building. This portion was remodeled with a gilded and green marble streetfront.

Lord & Taylor Store. NYI.

LORD & TAYLOR STORE (Badeau portion), No. 901

1869-70, by James H. Giles. Landmark. [5 stories] Like a cast-iron ghost, this dilapidated structure eerily dominates Ladies' Mile. Its mansard-roofed tower greets the intersection obliquely. Among free-standing colonettes are deeply recessed windows with shouldered arches.

W. & J. Sloane Store, 1986.

"Here you may see the gayest of the gay, their costly costumes with pride display." Such was the state of Broadway above Union Square in 1876, as one guide book told it.[18] But Ladies' Mile also began diversifying in the 1870s. Among the retail palaces was a modest business called the Bell Telephone Company of New York, at 923 Broadway, with 252 business subscribers, twenty-two residential customers, and long-distance lines up to thirty miles.[19] Park & Tilford, the world's largest retail grocery operation, had its general offices at 917 Broadway.[20] W. & J. Sloane, which stood "indisputably at the head of the carpet and rug industry of this country," moved to Nineteenth Street in 1882, where it served the Astors, Morgans, and Vanderbilts, and provided carpets for the coronation of Czar Nicholas II of Russia.[21] The Thonet Brothers' bentwood furniture store was housed in the Parish Building, which was completed in 1884 on the site of Henry Parish's mansion. Also that year, Brooks Brothers relocated to Twenty-second Street and David S. Hess, a well-known furniture dealer and decorator, moved in next to Sloane.[22]

The most dazzling spot on Ladies' Mile must have been the Gorham Sil-

Gorham Silver Manufacturers Building, 1987.

Lawrence A. Wien Center for Dance and Theater, 1987.

E LAWRENCE A. WIEN CENTER FOR DANCE AND THEATER, No. 890-92
1897-98 and 1898-99, by John B. Snook & Son. [8 stories] A gray brick box with a pronounced grid of large, two-window bays separated by pilasters. *Site of* Peter Goelet house.
LOEWS 19TH STREET EAST THEATER
1989-90, by Rubin Architects. [6 theaters with 1,806 seats]

GOELET BUILDING, No. 900
(Also known as the Shoninger Brothers Building). 1886-87, by McKim, Mead & White; enlarged 1905-06, by Maynicke & Franke. [10 stories] A structure of tremendous power, it rounds the corner with a great sweep of giant arches. Its windows are grouped in three-bay panels of patterned brickwork on a luscious, orange background.

20th STREET

Warren Building, 1986.

W WARREN BUILDING, No. 905-07
1890-91, by McKim, Mead & White. [8 stories] A riot of ornamentation—arches, swags, medallions, pediments, brackets, rosettes, and quoins—encrusts this small, Roman-brick, chamfer-cornered building.

ver Manufacturers Building, at Nineteenth Street, which opened in 1884. Among its "objects of art indisputably perfect" were amphoras, candelabra, goblets, loving cups, and punch bowls carved to show vine leaves, grapes, bacchanals, nymphs, and satyrs—"like a trip through fairyland, so gorgeous is the display."[23] With bachelor apartments upstairs, the Gorham was an unusually early mixed-use building. Like so much else in the neighborhood, it was developed by the Goelets.[24] (Amid all this building, Peter Goelet's mansion stood until 1897.)

In the early 1890s, Herman Bergdorf sold dresses and suits at 870 Broadway—before he went into partnership with Edwin Goodman. As late as 1899, it could still be said that Broadway "caters to only one class . . . the favored ones who spend money for pastime as much as for necessity, and Fashion's costumers might call it their living show place."[25]

Nonetheless, profound changes were already under way, with the rise of multiple-tenant, speculative office and loft buildings. The Goelets engaged McKim, Mead & White in 1886 to design the six-story Goelet Building, a boldly detailed and brightly colored mass that wraps around the corner of

GOELET BUILDING
Views from 1986 to 1988.

WILLIAM FAIRMAN HOUSE, No. 909

1843-44. [3 stories] The upper floor is intact on this old brick dwelling.

ALBERT HORN HOUSE, No. 911

ca. 1830. [3 stories] A companion to No. 909.

913 BROADWAY

1874; altered 1934. [2 stories] There is a large bay of three flat arches on the second floor.

THE BROADWAY BUILDING, No. 915-19

1925-26, by Joseph Martine. [20 stories] This massive, buff-brick building has a chamfered corner. It rises in setbacks, some of them crenellated, appearing as a fortress in the sky. *Site of* Park & Tilford Grocers, 1876, by David & John Jardine.

E   902-10 BROADWAY

1912-13, by Robert T. Lyons. [20 stories] At the base of an otherwise plain white-brick tower are two-story entrance arches in a vaguely Tudor Revival style. *Site of* Continental Hotel.

912-20 BROADWAY

1916-17, by Schwartz & Gross. [16 stories] The best part of this building is an extravagant entrance pediment with two putti.

21st STREET

W   BRADISH JOHNSON BUILDING, No. 921-25

1917-18, by Maynicke & Franke. [16 stories] This spare, yellow-brick tower has three-story pilasters at top and bottom. *Site of* Bell Telephone Company.

SARAH MILLS HOUSE, No. 927

1857-58. [5 stories] The dentiled archivolts in the upper three floors are quite distinctive.

SINGER COMPANY SHOW ROOMS, No. 929

ca. 1846. [3 stories] The third floor and the cornice of this altered brick dwelling are intact. This is tied to Nos. 931 and 933 as the Gordon Novelty Company.

SARAH DYCKMAN HOUSE, No. 931

ca. 1846. [3 stories] It still has its cornice, but has otherwise been much altered.

HARVARD CLUB, No. 933

(Also known as the Sarah Dyckman house). ca. 1846; remodeled. [3 stories] This has large window hoods and an intact cornice with the numbers "933." The storefront, added later, has a delicately detailed bay on the second floor.

Brooks Brothers Store, 1884. NYHS.

Twentieth Street. George Henry Warren, a prominent financial and civic leader, chose McKim, Mead & White in 1891 to design the Warren Building, catercorner from Goelet. This was a three-dimensional catalogue of ornament, with an eclectic tenancy to match: jewelers, cleaners and dyers, real-estate agents, carpeting concerns, and garment and millinery companies. The MacIntyre Building of 1892, by R.H. Robertson, created the skyline signature for Ladies' Mile: a gabled, pyramidal tower more than twelve stories high.

In 1887, the year that the Goelet Building was completed, the first Labor Day parade was staged in Union Square. The first socialist-sponsored May Day parade occurred three years later.[26] As the square became a focal point for unionists, socialists, and anarchists, the old stores slipped away to Fifth Avenue. Gorham left in 1901 (and later merged with the successors to Ball, Black & Company), Sloane in 1912, Vantine in 1913, Lord & Taylor in 1914 (for Thirty-eighth Street, where it still does business), and Arnold, Constable in 1915. Brooks Brothers also moved in 1915, to Madison Avenue and Forty-fourth Street, where it remains.

By the end of the 1930s, Union Square was the "center of America's radical movement."[27] The change from Ladies' Mile had been so rapid and complete that New York utterly forgot the old shopping district. Many buildings were kept as manufacturing lofts or warehouses or small offices, not exquisitely maintained—but not demolished, either. Perhaps the most unusual fate was that of Lord & Taylor. The Goelet family reclaimed its midblock portion and reclad it with limestone in 1914. Only the corner portion, which they did not own, retained its cast-iron façade.

WARREN BUILDING
View from 1987.

MacINTYRE BUILDING

Views from 1987.

Mortimer Building, 1986.

MORTIMER BUILDING, No. 935-39
(Also known as the Albert Building, J. & C. Johnston Store). 1861-62, by Griffith Thomas. [6 stories] One of the most refined buildings on Broadway, this Renaissance Revival gem is considerably sophisticated and subtly articulated. There are rounded and triangular window pediments and window hoods—different on each floor—above exquisitely detailed architraves.

E JACOB CRAM HOUSE, No. 922
(Also known as the Bancroft House hotel, Hotel Courte). ca. 1854. [5 stories] This red-brick house is an astonishing survivor of its time—its mansard roof is intact, with pediment-framed dormers and roof slates. It also has 2-over-2 windows and some pilasters from the old cast-iron storefront.

928-30 BROADWAY
1909-10, by William H. Birkmire. [12 stories] Delicate detailing enriches this fairly slender white-brick tower.

BROOKS BROTHERS STORE, No. 932-38
1883-84, by Charles C. Haight; rebuilt 1937, by Seelig & Finklestein; rebuilt 1986-87, by Architects Unlimited. [5 stories] This structural shell has had two entirely new façades since it was the Brooks Brothers flagship. The current round-edged, Postmodern incarnation has broad stucco bands alternating with strips of casement windows. *Site of* Abbey's Park Theater, 1873-74. *Near site of* Buck's Horn Tavern.

The area's slow, steady enervation after World War II reached a nadir in the 1970s, by which time much of Union Square Park had become the undisputed province of drug dealers. Many storefronts, including those of Lord & Taylor and Gorham, were given over to novelty jobbers. Yet Ladies' Mile was never entirely without signs of fashionable life, however incongruous. Andy Warhol moved his Factory into the old Parish Building in the early 1970s. Lofts elsewhere were put to use as photo studios or rehearsal spaces and the 890 Broadway building, on the corner where Goelet's peacocks once strutted, became a center of the dance and theater world, through a redevelopment by the choreographer Michael Bennett.[28]

The rebuilding of Union Square Park in the early 1980s dispersed the drug dealers and opened it again to strolling and sitting. It also opened the surrounding area to redevelopment by powerful real-estate concerns. At the same time, popular interest was awakening in the history of New York's retail institutions. That became a focus of books like *Manhattan Manners, End of the Road for Ladies' Mile?* and *Great Merchants of Early New York*, and a preservation movement grew even as development pressures did. In 1989, the Ladies' Mile Historic District was created by the Landmarks Preservation Commission, covering almost all of Broadway from Seventeenth to Twenty-fourth Street. By that time, market forces had already furnished some tantalizing echoes of the past. The Goelet portion of the Lord & Taylor store—renamed the Saint Laurie Building—was again in the business of making and selling fashionable apparel in an elegant setting. And the W. & J. Sloane and Arnold, Constable stores were home to the A.B.C. Carpet Company. "It's a perfect place to sell beautiful rugs," said the company president, Jerry Weinrib. "It worked 100 years ago and it's working today."[29]

Gordon Novelty Company, 1979.

Independence Flagstaff in 1979, before it was rehabilitated during the reconstruction of Union Square.

New York City Department of City Planning

MADISON SQUARE THE TENDERLOIN

TWENTY-SECOND STREET TO THIRTY-SECOND STREET

Broadway's history has been all but forgotten just north of Madison Square. Now a center for the toy industry and a thriving Korean business quarter, it is a far cry from the days in the nineteenth century when the area was so wicked it was called "Satan's Circus." What remains of the old Tenderloin district are a smattering of little buildings and two of New York's great old hostelries, the Gilsey House and Grand Hotel. The other hotels are gone, as are the theaters and most of the restaurants. There is nonetheless a palpable sense of the past, thanks to the thickly verdant expanse of Madison Square and thanks to the way the Flatiron Building looms over the district. It still looks as if its magnificent prow might cleave the rest of Broadway as it steams northward, exactly as it did when the once-naughty Tenderloin was transformed into a stolid business quarter.

Flatiron Building, 1986.

To the grounds of what would become Madison Square—at the Y-shaped intersection of the Bloomingdale and Eastern Post roads—the poorest of New York's poor were brought for burial in a potter's field during the last years of the eighteenth century. There were few neighbors to complain. Isaac Varian lived on the west side of the Bloomingdale Road. His homestead, supposedly built in part from a ship's cabin, stood just north of what would be Twenty-sixth Street.[1] Casper Samler had a farm of nearly forty-five acres across the road from Varian. Although his home was on the eastern edge of the farm, there was also a gambrel-roofed cottage near the road that was later known as the last farmhouse on lower Broadway.[2]

The only big development in the early nineteenth century was the United States Arsenal, which was built at the junction in 1807. It was later converted into the House of Refuge, the first institution in the nation to separate delinquent children from adult criminals, with the goal of reforming them.[3]

When the Street Commissioners looked at these environs in 1811, they saw a virtual *tabula rasa* and envisioned something mighty: the "Parade," a 239-acre field for military maneuvers, stretching from Twenty-third to Thirty-fourth Street, Third to Seventh Avenue. The Parade was by far the largest open space on their gridiron plan—Central Park still being decades away from conception—and it would have marked the terminus of Broadway and the Bloomingdale Road. But the plan was shrunk to ninety acres in 1814 and then abandoned. Madison Square was established in 1837. The Post Road, which would have bisected the park, was closed in 1839.

Nearby was Madison Cottage, a roadhouse where a number of stage lines started and numberless country excursions ended. "There was a special magnetism about the snug little barroom, always trim as a lady's boudoir,

Casper Samler farmhouse, 1869. NYHS.

Madison Square, 1979.

22nd STREET

Flatiron Building, 1988.

W FLATIRON BUILDING, No. 945-53
(Also known as the Fuller Building). 1901-02, by Daniel H. Burnham of D.H. Burnham & Company. Landmark. [21 stories] This towering wedge, laden with ornament, cleaves Broadway and Fifth Avenue. *Site of* St. Germain Hotel (also known as the Cumberland Hotel); Erie Railway Building.

E MADISON GREEN, No. 940
1982, by Philip Birnbaum Associates with David Kenneth Specter. [30 stories] More than 180 cantilevered balcony slabs overlook Broadway from this massive box. *Site of* Hotel Bartholdi.

23rd STREET

Franconi's Hippodrome. GSW.

W FIFTH AVENUE BUILDING, No. 1099
(Also known as the Toy Center South). 1908-09, by Maynicke & Franke. [14 stories] This severe white mass, with restrained ornamentation and a three-story arcade at top, is bent obliquely to conform to the angle of Broadway. The bridge connecting it to No. 1107 was built in 1967-68. *Site of* Fifth Avenue Hotel, 1856-59, by William Washburn; Franconi's Hippodrome, 1853; Madison Cottage (also known as Corporal Thompson's).

Sidewalk clock at the Fifth Avenue Building, 1988.

SIDEWALK CLOCK

1909, by Hecla Iron Works. Landmark. A generous, garland-wreathed face sits atop an elaborate fluted column.

Eternal Light Monument in Madison Square, 1979.

E MADISON SQUARE

[6.23 acres] Within the park are the Eternal Light Monument, 1924, by Thomas Hastings and Paul Wayland Bartlett; the Admiral David Glasgow Farragut Monument, 1880-81, by Augustus Saint-Gaudens, sculptor, and Stanford White, architect; *Skagerrak*, by Antoni H. Milkowski; statues of *William H. Seward* by Randolph Rogers; *Chester Alan Arthur* by George Edwin Bissell; and *Roscoe Conkling* by John Quincy Adams Ward. The *Statue of Liberty*'s arm, by Frédéric-Auguste Bartholdi, was here briefly. **Site of** Naval Memorial Arch and Colonnade (also known as the Dewey Arch), 1899; United States Arsenal (also known as the House of Refuge), 1807.

24th STREET

W ALBEMARLE BUILDING, No. 1107

(Also known as the Toy Center North). 1915. [16 stories] A white-brick tower whose façade forms a

Isaac Varian homestead. VM.

which induced the desire to tarry awhile," one chronicler recalled.[4] On its site, between Twenty-third and Twenty-fourth streets, the area's first sensational structure was built in 1853. Franconi's Hippodrome was a huge arena, covered by a great canopy, with room for 10,000 spectators. It featured chariot and horse races, trapeze and animal acts. "Very big and brilliant," was George Templeton Strong's review. "Much idiotic trumpery and foolery," he added.[5]

Franconi's only lasted two years. And the area was still rural enough in the 1850s—"apple trees drooping over the sidewalks, which were often covered with fallen blossoms"—to be suitable for a noble mortuary monument.[6] Major General William Jenkins Worth, a national hero who had fought in the War of 1812, the Indian wars, and the Mexican-American War, died in Texas in 1849 and was brought back to his native New York State. (Texas commemorated him with the name Fort Worth.) He was buried in Brooklyn while New York built a fifty-one-foot memorial obelisk at Madison Square. In 1857, Worth's remains were reburied under Broadway.

As the Worth Monument took form, the area's explosive growth was getting under way. In 1856, on the site of the Hippodrome, which faced both Broadway and Fifth Avenue, Amos Eno began building the Fifth Avenue Hotel, to accommodate 800 guests. Skeptics did not think fashionable New York would ever "live up there among the goats."[7] But "Eno's Folly" confounded them, thanks in part to a celebrated visit by the Prince of Wales in 1860. The Fifth Avenue Hotel also became a Republican Party stronghold, where "more state and national politics were brewed than in any other single spot in this country," and nine Presidents were spotted over time.[8] Besides the impressive guest register, there were other features to recommend the hotel. An 1866 guide book said that "all the rooms, besides being well lighted and ventilated, will have means of access by a perpendicular railway—intersecting each story."[9] In other words, an elevator; one of the earliest.

Across Twenty-fourth Street was the Albemarle Hotel of 1860, a "reserved and exclusive house of English flavor."[10] Next door was the luxurious

Fifth Avenue Hotel. NYI.

Albemarle Hotel and Hoffman House, ca. 1890. NYHS.

Hoffman House of 1864, whose clientele formed a " 'Who's Who' in sport, politics, the stage and Manhattan fast life," including wine agents, promoters, and "other bits of flotsam and jetsam from the pavement of Broadway."[11] The most famous and scandalous of its many paintings of scantily-clad subjects was *Nymphs and Satyr* by Adolphe Bouguereau, the "biggest single advertisement any hotel in this country—probably in the world—ever had."[12]

The builders of the Broadway Central Hotel at Bond Street, Elias S. Higgins and Henry Engelbert, were also responsible for the Grand Hotel, which was constructed in 1868 at Thirty-first Street, and was for several years the northernmost of New York's major hotels. Like its cousin downtown, the Grand had an elegantly detailed marble façade and a monumental mansard roof, reflecting a strong French influence.[13] Much gaudier, in design

grid with rosettes at each intersection. *Site of* Albemarle Hotel, 1859-60.

1115-17 BROADWAY

1912, by J.B. Snook's Sons. [12 stories] A plain tower, in brown brick. *Site of* Hoffman House, 1864, by John B. Snook, enlarged and expanded 1895, by Alfred Zucker.

E WORTH SQUARE

[0.07 acres]

Worth Monument, 1986 and 1988.

WORTH MONUMENT

1857, by James Goodwin Batterson. On the south face of this Quincy granite obelisk is a bronze bas-relief of Gen. William Jenkins Worth (who lies buried below). The elaborate fence posts are modeled on ceremonial swords.

25th STREET

W TOWNSEND BUILDING, No. 1123

1896-98, by Cyrus L.W. Eidlitz. [12 stories] Finely detailed architraves with pronounced window heads distinguish this rich, chamfer-cornered limestone façade. *Site of* Worth House.

Grand Hotel, 1987.

St. James Building, 1979.

ST. JAMES BUILDING, No. 1133

1896-97, by Bruce Price. [16 stories] A monumental three-story arcade runs along the top of this tower, with huge pediment-framed window bays projecting among the banded columns. There is also complex brickwork throughout, studded by rosette panels, and a great oculus over the entrance **Site of** St. James Hotel.

E   THOMAS CUSHMAN COMPANY BUILDING, No. 1122

1918-19, by Ely Jacques Kahn. [6 stories] There are streamlined touches to this simple façade, like ribbed spandrels. **Site of** New York Club.

LINCOLN TRUST COMPANY, No. 1124

1913. [3 stories] This façade is dominated by a single, three-story arch.

THEODORE B. STARR JEWELERS, No. 1126

ca. 1895. [5 stories] There are five-pointed stars in the second-floor capitals of this robust, red-brick Victorian façade.

1130 BROADWAY

1893. [7 stories] This has a large central bay framed by buff brick and ornamental masonry.

CROSS CHAMBERS BUILDING, No. 1132

(Also known as the Mark Cross store). 1901. [11 stories] A thin shaft, dominated by a single projecting bay and a copper balcony, that rests on garlanded brackets.

Hotel Imperial (left) and Union Dime Savings Bank (right), ca. 1909. NYHS.

and patronage, was the Gilsey House, at Twenty-ninth Street, which replaced the old Samler cottage. Stephen Decatur Hatch designed this mountainous hotel. (He later did the Union Dime Savings Institution, at Thirty-second Street, which was also ripely overstated. Daniel D. Badger, who fabricated the façade for Peter Gilsey's office building on lower Broadway, was responsible for the ironwork at Gilsey's hotel.) When it opened in 1871, the Gilsey House was painted a brilliant white and it earned its rank as "one of the most imposing of our metropolitan palace hotels."[14] Indeed, its clocktower dominates the streetscape to this day. The hotel attracted Oscar Wilde and "Diamond Jim" Brady, Congressmen, Army and Navy officers, coal operators, mine owners, and railroad magnates. Military men and mine promoters also patronized the Sturtevant House, across Twenty-ninth Street. Less celebrated hotels included the Coleman House, at Twenty-seventh Street, which offered "to the entomologist an abundant field for scientific research."[15]

The Victoria Hotel was built by Paran Stevens in 1872 at Twenty-seventh Street. This immense building was designed by Richard Morris Hunt "on the French plan of 'flats,' and rented in suites of apartments." It was called "the first of the monster 'Apartment Houses' erected in New York"—even though it was not the first apartment building as such.[16]

Where there were hotels, there were out-of-towners. And where there were out-of-towners, there was money to be made, not only by illicit activity but by the policeman who turned a blind eye to it. Shortly after being transferred into the district in 1876, Captain Alexander S. Williams ran into a friend on Broadway who asked why he was smiling. The police commander answered, "I've had nothing but chuck steak for a long time, and now I'm going to get a little of the tenderloin."[17] The name endured and became synonymous, as Stephen Crane saw it, with a "spirit that flings beer bottles, jumps debts and makes havoc for the unwary; also sings in a hoarse voice at 3 a.m."[18]

Broadway after dark looked something like this in 1882: "Moving rapidly through the throng . . . are a number of flashily-dressed women, generally young, but far from attractive. You would never mistake them for respectable women, and they do not intend that you shall. . . . Woe to the man who follows after one of these creatures. The next step is to some of the low dives which still occupy too many of the cellars along Broadway. Here bad or drugged liquors steal away the senses of the luckless victim, and robbery, or even worse violence, too often ends the adventure."[19] Those who were not lured by streetwalkers, might be roped into the dangerous dives known as "gambling hells," where visitors were fleeced without mercy.[20]

Those who preferred their pleasures slightly more sedate could patronize Delmonico's Restaurant, at Twenty-sixth Street, which "stood absolutely alone as the eating-house of the polite world." Its ballroom was the scene of "nearly all the grand banquets that have been given for a generation" and "no man ever attained eminence in the town without passing through."[21] There was a gentlemen's café overlooking Broadway and a dining room overlooking Madison Square. For a while, diners there had an unobstructed view of the Statue of Liberty—or, rather, its right arm—which came to Madison Square

Statue of Liberty arm in Madison Square. NYHS.

Delmonico's Restaurant, ca. 1888. NYHS.

212 FIFTH AVENUE, No. 1134-36

1912-13, by Schwartz & Gross. [20 stories] A façade with depth and rhythm, enhanced by articulated piers, window sills on brackets, and Gothic-inspired ornament. **Site of** Delmonico's Restaurant (also known as Café Martin), 1876.

26th STREET

W **1141-43 BROADWAY**

1926, by William S. Hohauser. [9 stories] There is an Art Deco roofline on this little brown-brick tower.

1145-47 BROADWAY

1875. [5 stories] The brickwork, window heads, and cornice remain in this old façade.

WALLACE & COMPANY BUILDING, No. 1149

1880. [4 stories] The façade of this small building is almost entirely rock-faced. **Near site of** Isaac Varian homestead.

1153 BROADWAY

1875. [4 stories] The upper two stories retain the original red bricks, window heads, and cornice.

1157 BROADWAY

(Also known as the Holland Brothers' Kinetoscope Parlor). 1874, by Thomas Wilson. [3 stories] Crisp, angular ornamentation adorns this building's oversized arched windows. Geometric designs extend to the ground-floor pilasters.

E **LOWELL BUILDING, No. 1140-46**

1914-15, by Maynicke & Franke. [16 stories] A striking, geometric white masonry composition with eleven-story bays between piers rotated 45 degrees. **Site of** Parker House.

VICTORIA BUILDING, No. 1148-50

1912, by Schwartz & Gross. [20 stories] This plain, white tower has Corinthian pilasters at top and

GILSEY HOUSE HOTEL
Views from 1979 and 1987.

bottom. *Site of* Victoria Hotel (also known as the French Flats, Stevens Flats House), 1870-72, by Richard Morris Hunt.

27th STREET

1161-75 Broadway, 1986.

w 1161-75 BROADWAY

ca. 1907. [5 stories] Expansive and powerfully horizontal windows are arrayed in equally forceful projecting vertical bays, making this a compelling design. *Site of* Coleman House Hotel.

BAUDOUINE BUILDING, No. 1181-83

1896, by Alfred Zucker. [11 stories] High above the street is a richly decorated, miniature Greek temple, with fluted Ionic columns, sculptural figures in the pediment, and antefixes. Elsewhere on the façade are lion's-head keystones.

e JOHNSTON BUILDING, No. 1170

1902-03, by Schickel & Ditmars. [13 stories] One of the most prominent turrets on Broadway, whose dome has an extravagant belvedere at top, anchors this richly ornamented limestone mass.

28th STREET

w 1185 BROADWAY

1920. [1 story] A nondescript taxpayer. *Site of* New Fifth Avenue Theater (also known as Keith & Proctor's Fifth Avenue Theater), 1891-92, by Francis Hatch Kimball; Gilsey's Apollo Hall (also known as the New Fifth Avenue Theater), 1868-69, by David & John Jardine, rebuilt 1873.

WALLACH BUILDING, No. 1203

1929, by Louis Shampan. [10 stories] A third-floor decorative course of complex and sensuous Art Deco forms enlivens this industrial-looking building. *Site of* Princess Building; San Francisco Minstrel Hall

in 1877 as part of an attention-getting and money-raising effort by its sculptor, Frédéric-Auguste Bartholdi.

The novelty of Bartholdi's gesture seemed fitting for the neighborhood. Entertainment, after all, was what the Tenderloin was about. Banvard's Museum and Theater, near Thirtieth Street, opened in 1867 as the first hall in New York built expressly as a museum. It had not only statues and paintings, but bird and animal specimens, "Japanese and Chinese curiosities," and a *tableau vivant* from Dante's *Inferno*.[22] The museum was acquired in 1879 by Augustin Daly and recreated as Daly's Theater. This was the most fashionable playhouse in New York and the highest priced (two dollars for top seats). It was said in the 1890s that Daly's " 'first night' audiences represent the wealth and culture of the metropolis."[23] The final Wallack theater, at Thirtieth Street, was opened by Lester Wallack in 1882. Although it was the "last word in theatrical construction," it never achieved the popularity of the Thirteenth Street house and Wallack retired in 1887, ending the family's thirty-five-year run on Broadway.[24] Auguring the future, Broadway was the setting for the first Kinetoscope parlor in 1894. To get a glimpse at the ninety-second spectacle, crowds lined up day and night outside 1157 Broadway, a building that still stands.[25] And it was the Tenderloin—not Times Square—that got some of the earliest electric skyline signs. One was mounted over Madison Square, on the St. Germain Hotel, in 1892. Its red, white, blue, and green bulbs said: "BUY HOMES ON LONG ISLAND. SWEPT BY OCEAN BREEZES."[26] The *New York Times* slogan, "All the News That's Fit to Print," made its debut in lights from that same point, before it got to the front page.[27]

The last great development on the Tenderloin was the Hotel Imperial, a project of the Goelet family. Built in phases, beginning in 1890, it was the "most sumptuous hotel Broadway had ever known" and it eventually stretched from Thirty-first to Thirty-second Street.[28] It had everything: McKim, Mead & White as architects, Edward A. Abbey for a muralist, plus the Caswell-Massey Apothecary, and a palm garden in green marble. In the closing years of the district's glory in the 1890s, Richard Harding Davis exclaimed: "One could wear a turban here, or a pith helmet, or a sealskin ulster down to his heels, and his passing would cause no comment. For everyone who visits New York, whether he be a Japanese prince, or a political exile from Erin, or the latest imported London pickpocket, finds his way sooner or later to this promenade of the tenderloin."[29]

By this time, however, the Tenderloin had been tamed and the "wild revelry and uproarious scenes" had "vanished with the resorts that tolerated them."[30] Business could raise its head. Fortunately, it did so with drama and beauty and even whimsy. The earliest office towers were appropriately hyperbolic. Alfred Zucker's Baudouine Building of 1896, at Twenty-eighth Street, even had a little Greek temple on the roof. But the real sensation was created by the architect Daniel H. Burnham of Chicago, who gave New York the Flatiron Building of 1902. Formally known as the Fuller Building, it captured the city's lofty ambitions and captivated the mercurial tourist. A contemporary critic said that while the building "was not improved in public

Baudouine Building and Johnston Building (foreground), 1988.

esteem by being called a flatiron," the "vilified Flatiron . . . does represent the commercial spirit of New York, whether people like their commercialism flung in their faces in that way or not."[31] By virtue of its brazenness, it quickly gained its place as one of New York's icons.

Meanwhile, the institution that gave life to the area, the Fifth Avenue Hotel, was closed in 1908 and torn down to make way for the Fifth Avenue Building, an imposing mass that was somewhat enlivened at street level by a great sidewalk clock. Elsewhere on the Tenderloin, the Gilsey House closed in 1911, to be converted into lofts for the garment trade that was filling the area; the Hoffman House was replaced by a twelve-story tower and the Victoria Hotel by the twenty-story Victoria Building in 1912. Wallack's Theater was torn down three years later, and Daly's was razed in 1920.

There was virtually no major construction for fifty years. What got built were mostly small-scale and plain structures, with the notable exception of the Wallach Building at Twenty-ninth Street, which had some wonderful

(also known as Herrmann's Theater, Shubert Princess Theater), 1873-75.

E HICKS BUILDING, No. 1178
(Also known as the Corn Exchange Bank). 1901, by Clinton & Russell. [5 stories] This small box has a handsomely detailed, recessed central bay.

POLAND SPRING BUILDING, No. 1180
1870. [5 stories] Large windows, framed by flat arches, dominate this old façade.

CENTURIAN BUILDING, No. 1182
1910, by Rouse & Goldstone. [16 stories] A sober, gray tower punctuated by big keystones; its ground floor is framed by two huge columns.

HOTEL BRESLIN, No. 1186
1903, by Clinton & Russell. [12 stories] The turreted, domed corner dominates this building, whose red-brick façade is divided by pronounced vertical window bays. *Site of* Sturtevant House Hotel, 1871.

29th STREET

W 1205 BROADWAY
[3 stories] A plain, buff-brick taxpayer. *Site of* Weber & Field's Imperial Music Hall, 1892.

PHILLIPS-JONES BUILDING, No. 1215-25
1920, by Louis Allen Abramson. [8 stories] A spartan building marked only by three-story pilasters at its base. *Site of* Banvard's Museum and Theater (also known as Daly's Theater, Wood's Museum and Menagerie), 1867.

E GILSEY HOUSE HOTEL, No. 1200
1869-71, by Stephen Decatur Hatch and Daniel D. Badger. Landmark. [8 stories] Notable for its chamfered corner, tower clock, and three-story mansard, the building unfolds like a great wave, revealing a marvelous roofscape, bays filled with pedimented windows, and columns throughout. *Site of* Casper Samler farmhouse (also known as the Anderson Cottage).

SHANLEY'S RESTAURANT, No. 1204-06
1885. [4 stories] Stripped of its cornice and other details, this building still has its old window heads and decorative courses.

FLATIRON BUILDING

*Under construction in 1901. NYHS. Other views from
1979 to 1987.*

30th STREET

w BIJOU BUILDING, No. 1237-39

(Also known as the Colonial Building). 1915, by Katz & Feiner. [16 stories] This plain, slender, brown-brick slab stretches to Sixth Avenue. *Site of* Bijou Theater, 1883-84, by John B. McElfatrick; Brighton Theater (also known as the Bijou Opera House), 1876-78.

PARKING LOT, No. 1251

Site of Peter Van Orden farmhouse.

E 1220 BROADWAY

1931, by Levy & Berger. [8 stories] There is some colorful Art Deco relief work in this industrial buff-brick box. *Site of* Wallack's Thirtieth Street Theater (also known as Palmer's Theater), 1882.

GRAND HOTEL, No. 1234

(Also known as the Clark Apartments, Hadson Hotel, New Grand Hotel). 1868, by Henry Engelbert. Landmark. [8 stories] This is a gloomily romantic marble ghost, filled with stunning details— a great mansard roof, shouldered architraves, incised keystones, and prominent quoins and pediments, one of which frames a scallop shell.

31st STREET

w DEMPSEY BUILDING, No. 1255-61

(Also known as the Stiner Building, Martin Building). 1909, by Townsend, Steinle & Haskell. [11 stories] This red-brick façade has masonry quoins, triple keystones, and splayed lintels.

BROWNING BUILDING, No. 1265-69

(Also known as Browning, King & Company). 1903, by John E. Nitchie. [8 stories] Three strong bays are topped by ornate arches with stone festoons, lions, and an eagle.

JOHN DAVID STORE, No. 1271-73

1928, by Starrett & Van Vleck. [7 stories] This plain, white-brick box has a striking Art Deco frieze composed of interlocking triangles. *Site of* Union Dime Savings Institution, 1875-76, by Stephen Decatur Hatch.

E 1250 BROADWAY

1967-69, by Shreve, Lamb & Harmon Associates. [40 stories] A 580-foot-tall shaft with dark windows and spandrels framed by vertical gray-white steel piers. *Site of* Hotel Imperial, 1889-90, by McKim, Mead & White, expanded 1902; the San Carlos, 1881, by Shaw & Anderson (incorporated into the Imperial); Winchester Hotel.

Wallach Building, 1988.

bursts of Art Deco ornamentation. As a district of small offices, faded hotels, and garment makers, the Tenderloin fell off almost everyone's map of places to go. The Hotel Imperial closed with a mass eviction in 1947, and the site lay fallow for two decades. The Grand Hotel became one of the largest single-room-occupancy residences on Broadway.[32] In 1966, across from the Flatiron, a devastating blaze took the lives of twelve firemen and left a lot that remained empty for more than a dozen years.

The Madison Green apartment tower that eventually went up at the site was too bulky, and blocked or ruined many vistas of the Flatiron Building. Similarly, the 1250 Broadway office tower at the Imperial site was out of keeping with the scale and nature of its surroundings.

Along the Tenderloin in the 1970s and '80s, Korean businesses predominated. Jewelry and perfumes were offered at the You Sung trading corporation in the Grand Hotel, while Dong Jin had belts, hosiery, scarves, and sunglasses at the Gilsey House. However, the spot occupied successively by the Madison Cottage, Hippodrome, and Fifth Avenue Hotel was still the heart of the area. The Fifth Avenue Building had become the Toy Center South, linked by sky bridge to the Toy Center North. They had more than 600 tenants, representing almost every major toy maker. Each winter, the Toy Fair would come to Madison Square, "bringing with it Smurfs, Chipmunks, Care Bears, Dream Date Barbie, video software for children, dolls for adults and 12,000 buyers from all over the United States and the world."[33]

That is what became of Satan's Circus.

View north in 1978 includes 1407 Broadway (left), One Astor Plaza (near the center), and 1250 Broadway (right).

New York City Department of City Planning

HERALD SQUARE
THE RIALTO
GARMENT CENTER

THIRTY-SECOND STREET TO FORTY-FIRST STREET

View north in 1988 includes 1407 Broadway (left), One Astor Plaza (center), and the McAlpin Hotel (right).

Broadway in this latitude has been the province over time of the first-nighter, the opera-lover, and finally, the bargain-hunter. With the exception of Macy's, however, there are almost no vestiges left of Broadway's colorful past. In the 1920s and '30s, the aesthetic jumble that had been the Rialto was transformed into the Garment Center, a skyscraping industrial quarter of showrooms and workrooms. The physical form of Broadway was reshaped with claustrophobic heaviness. Even the best of the Art Deco towers—the Bricken Casino, Bricken Textile, and Lefcourt Normandie buildings—were almost impossible to appreciate in the narrow canyon. And yet, though the garment trade deadened Broadway architecturally, it preserved the liveliness of the street, where buyers, manufacturers, and deliverymen overflowed the sidewalks in a bustle that always seemed to verge on anarchy.

Herald Building (left) and Broadway Tabernacle Congregational Church (center). NYHS.

Two centuries before it became Herald Square, the land at what is now the intersection of Broadway and Thirty-fourth Street belonged to Francisco Bastiane, a free black man, whose father was evidently a manumitted slave. Bastiane sold these fifteen acres in 1716 and the land passed to Peter Van Orden, whose farmhouse stood near the present crossing of Broadway and Thirty-first Street. His cousin, Jacobus Van Orden, had a much larger farm to the north, which ran along the west side of the Bloomingdale Road, from Thirty-third to Thirty-ninth Street.[1]

No significant building occurred along Broadway until 1857, when the abolition-minded Broadway Tabernacle congregation moved uptown from Worth Street and began constructing a somberly imposing Gothic church at Thirty-fourth Street. They were joined in 1864 by the Congregation Shaaray Tefila, which worshipped in a temporary synagogue at Thirty-sixth Street, sharing its quarters with the Seventy-first Regiment of the National Guard.[2] There was not much else to the area, which retained a small-town character through the 1870s. Across from the synagogue, a horse trainer would set up a tent every summer and fall, much to the delight and amusement of neighborhood boys.[3] On the same spot, the Coliseum was built in 1873, featuring wax-work cycloramas of London, Paris, and the Franco-Prussian War. That gave way to the New York Aquarium.

Two turning points came in 1879. Elevated railroad service along the Sixth Avenue line reached Broadway and Thirty-third Street, making the whole district much less remote. Also that year, at the Standard Theater near Thirty-second Street, Gilbert and Sullivan's *H.M.S. Pinafore* was introduced to New York audiences. The extraordinary success of that operetta spurred the development of a light-opera house called the Casino, which opened in 1882 at Thirty-ninth Street, pushing the theater district much farther northward. What attracted people to the Casino, besides the shows,

View toward the Flatiron Building in 1988 features the Bricken Casino Building (setback tower at center).

32nd STREET

GREELEY SQUARE

[0.14 acres] Within it is a statue of *Horace Greeley*, by Alexander Doyle.

Gimbel Brothers Department Store, 1986

w GIMBEL BROTHERS DEPARTMENT STORE, No. 1275-91

(Also known as A. & S. Plaza). 1908-10, by D.H. Burnham & Company; rebuilt and enlarged 1987-89, by RTKL Associates. [11 stories] In the rebuilding of this bulky, spartan, white brick mass, the façade of the lower seven floors was turned into an expanse of green glass. The copper-clad bridge to the Gimbels Annex was added in 1925, by Shreve & Lamb. *Site of* Standard Theater (also known as the Manhattan Theater), 1884-85, by John B. McElfatrick; Eagle Theater (also known as the Standard Theater), 1875.

Hotel Martinique (foreground) and McAlpin Hotel (background), 1979.

E HOTEL MARTINIQUE, No. 1260-66

1897-1900, by Henry J. Hardenbergh; expanded and enlarged 1907-11, by Hardenbergh. [17 stories] This richly ornamented white brick building is dominated by a huge mansard roof with masonry and copper dormers. There are also rich pediments, bold architraves, and big scallop shells on the façade.

Wilson Building, 1979.

WILSON BUILDING, No. 1270-80

1911-12, by Rouse & Goldstone. [12 stories] A
beautiful two-story arcade, under a large and
elegant cornice, tops this rusticated and round-
cornered tower.

33rd STREET

Saks & Company Store, 1945. GRAY.

W   SAKS & COMPANY STORE, No. 1311

(Also known as Herald Center, E.J. Korvette, Saks-
Herald Square, Saks-34th Street). 1901-02, by
Buchman & Fox; rebuilt 1967; rebuilt 1982-85, by
Copeland, Novak & Israel and Schuman,
Lichtenstein, Claman & Efron. [9 stories] In its
latest incarnation, this building has become a
polygonal box of dark blue reflective glass, with
thick strips of decorative chrome. ***Site of*** Parker's
Restaurant and Hotel.

were its novel amenities and eccentric architecture. Francis Hatch Kimball
concocted a kind of Moorish fantasy, with a domed turret outside and an interior filled with horseshoe arches, semi-spherical domes, low colonnades, and
latticework. The Casino was the first theater illuminated entirely by electricity and it had the first roof garden, a picturesque spot on a summer evening,
when most theaters were closed because of heat. It also gained notoriety as
the home of the *Florodora* showgirls, whose lives were a staple of popular
gossip, thanks to the scandals in which they were involved or implicated.[4]

Following the light opera of the Casino came the embodiment of opera
itself: the Metropolitan, founded by brash millionaires who could not, for all
their money, get into the few precious boxes that the old guard controlled at
the Academy of Music on Fourteenth Street. In response, they built the
world's largest auditorium, from Thirty-ninth to Fortieth Street, containing
122 boxes—more seats than even La Scala in Milan—and a stage exceeded
only by the opera houses of Paris and St. Petersburg.[5] Under the management of Henry E. Abbey, the Metropolitan Opera opened in October 1883
with a performance of Gounod's *Faust*.

The Met's somewhat utilitarian exterior earned it the nickname "yellow-
brick brewery" and it was clear that the architect, Josiah Cleveland Cady,
had no experience designing an auditorium, as 700 of the 3,778 seats offered
only obstructed or side views. However, aesthetics and acoustics took second
place to the patrons: Astors, Morgans, Vanderbilts, and Whitneys. As one

*The Casino, 1896.
MCNY.*

METROPOLITAN OPERA HOUSE
Exterior includes the Times Tower to the north. Inside is the tier of boxes called the Diamond Horseshoe. MET.

McAlpin Hotel, 1987; Frederick Dana Marsh mural from the McAlpin (below). Great American Salvage Company.

E   McALPIN HOTEL, No. 1300

1911-13, by F.M. Andrews & Company. [25 stories] In the form of an enormous, towering E, this brown brick building has a rusticated base and a highly ornamented, three-story arcade at top. *Site of* Alpine Apartment House, 1885-87, by David & John Jardine.

34th STREET

W   1313 BROADWAY

1903, by William H. Hume & Son. [5 stories] This is the holdout property that Macy's could not get, now masked by "World's Largest Store" billboards.

R.H. MACY & COMPANY STORE, No. 1317-29

1901-02, by DeLemos & Cordes; expanded 1923-24 and 1931. [10 stories] Within a red-brick mass, six great projecting bays are framed by four-story pilasters topped by medallions with Macy's trademark star. Above these bays are six great arches. The caryatids over the entrance on 34th Street are by J. Massey Rhind.

enthusiast noted, the audience, "such as New York alone of all American cities could furnish . . . constituted in itself a spectacle grander than any which could be put upon the stage."[6] In rebuilding the house after a fire in 1892, the boxes were reduced to a single tier known as the Diamond Horseshoe, after its bejeweled occupants, principally Caroline Astor. Her grandnephew described the scene as "A rich array of Luxury and Vice! But, spite of them, the music's very nice."[7]

The Met was at the heart of the Rialto. Within a week of its debut, the New Park Theater opened at Thirty-fifth Street. (Later renamed the Herald Square Theater, it was the first New York City playhouse to be controlled by the Shubert brothers of Syracuse, who took it over in 1900. Twelve years after that, it was one of the first big "photo play" theaters, under the management of Marcus Loew.[8]) In 1888, the Broadway Theater, one of the largest in the city, opened at Forty-first Street. The architect was John B. McElfatrick, who had recreated the Metropolitan interior after the fire and also designed the second Standard Theater. The Empire Theater, built for the producer Charles Frohman, opened at Fortieth Street in 1893. Another McElfatrick creation, it was "rich, quiet and restful" in its appointments and lasted an astonishing sixty years.[9] Also in 1893, with financing from the Goelet family, Henry E. Abbey opened a playhouse of his own at Thirty-eighth Street. Abbey's Theater was seen approvingly by its wealthy audience as a kind of adjunct to the Met, another place for society to show itself.[10] Just across the street was the Hotel Normandie, where Tchaikovsky stayed when he came to New York to open Carnegie Hall. All around the theaters and hotels, so many performers gathered or promenaded that a producer could cast a play simply by looking over the loiterers on the sidewalk.[11]

In this theatrical milieu, James Gordon Bennett Jr. began building the offices of the *New York Herald* in 1892. Although it seemed well out of the way for a newspaper—most were huddled together around City Hall Park—the trapezoidal parcel at Thirty-fifth Street was so visible that it offered a splendid showcase, where a building could make an oversize impression without scraping the sky.[12] Stanford White responded to this site with an adaptation of the Palazzo del Consiglio in Verona, "richly adorned with marble, with arcades of polished granite columns, press-rooms separated from Broadway only by plate-glass, and an enormous clock with a deep-toned bell."[13] On either side of the bell were two mechanical bronze blacksmiths, nicknamed *Stuff* and *Guff*, who would swing at it with their hammers as the hour tolled. Above them was a figure of *Minerva* and around them, on the eaves, were bronze owls that announced the time by winking their electric eyes. At midnight, crowds gathered at the sidewalk windows to watch the presses come to life. (The *Herald* occupied this commanding spot less than two decades before moving to Forty-first Street. The sculpture was removed and the building "irreparably mutilated," with the north half razed entirely.[14])

Bennett's newspaper gave the square its name, but Isidor and Nathan Straus gave it an identity. R.H. Macy & Company, which they owned, was doing business at the turn of the century in a jumble of buildings east of Sixth

Avenue, some of which still carry Macy's trademark star on their façades. The store needed a new home, but the Strauses did not want to build in the Union Square area, as the retail district had already shifted as far north as Twenty-third Street, leaving the future of Fourteenth Street in doubt.[15] They decided to bypass the Twenties and go to Herald Square, already a transportation hub, whose advantages were bound to increase with the coming of the new subway, which was under construction in 1900. Rival merchants from lower Sixth Avenue, who feared the effect of Macy's departure, bought the corner lot at Thirty-fourth Street and thwarted Macy's full assemblage of the Broadway blockfront, hoping to use this as leverage in obtaining certain concessions from the Strauses. Rather than capitulate, however, Macy's simply built around the holdout parcel (and later rented space there for its own enormous billboard). The one-million-square-foot store—its ornate façade ornamented with red, five-pointed stars—opened in November 1902. Among its features were a vacuum system for removing stale air, pneumatic tubes for moving cash, and escalators with flat steps, instead of inclined treads.[16]

Saks & Company of Washington, D.C., followed Macy's lead to Herald Square, with a high-quality, specialty apparel store. Saks actually managed to open first, since its building, between Thirty-third and Thirty-fourth streets, was much smaller.[17] The Gimbel Brothers, of Milwaukee and Philadelphia, opened their giant New York department store, extending from Thirty-second to Thirty-third Street, in 1910. The building, on the site of the Standard Theater, was designed by D.H. Burnham & Company, architects of Wanamaker's. In the wake of these successes from out of town, it appeared for a time that Marshall Field & Company of Chicago would open a New York branch at Thirty-sixth Street.[18]

Gimbel Brothers took control of Saks & Company in 1923 and built a Fifth Avenue branch, which became known for its luxury goods, while the

R.H. Macy & Company Store, 1988.

C HERALD SQUARE

[0.04 acres] Within it is the *James Gordon Bennett Memorial* (also known as the *Bell Ringers Monument*), 1939-40, designed by Aymar Embury II, with sculpture by Antonin Jean Paul Carles. A statue of *William Earl Dodge*, by John Quincy Adams Ward, was removed.

Broadway Tabernacle Congregational Church. NYI.

E MARBRIDGE BUILDING, No. 1302-28

1906-09, by Townsend, Steinle & Haskell. [11 stories] This chamfer-cornered, limestone mass has pediment-framed windows, crisply detailed architraves, and a rusticated base. *Site of* Broadway Tabernacle Congregational Church, 1857-59.

THOMAS F. CARR HOUSE, No. 1330

1881. [5 stories] The original detailing, including a mansard roof, has been removed.

New York Herald Building, 1895. NYHS.

R.H. MACY & COMPANY STORE

Views from 1979 to 1988 show the store as part of the Broadway street wall (this page), the 34th Street entrance (facing page) and the main floor on the Broadway side.

35th STREET

Johnson Building and Bennett Memorial, 1986.

W　**JOHNSON BUILDING, No. 1331-49**

1914, by Clinton & Russell. [12 stories] Prominent piers with limestone caps distinguish this otherwise dark, spartan, and utilitarian building in brown brick. *Site of* New Park Theater (also known as the Herald Square Theater), 1882-83; New York Aquarium, 1876; Coliseum, 1873. *Near site of* Jacobus Van Orden farmhouse.

E　**HERALD SQUARE BUILDING, No. 1332-50**

1928-30, by Clinton & Russell. [24 stories] A spare, buff brick tower with multiple setbacks and virtually no ornamentation. Its southern annex is a four-story limestone box. *Site of* New York Herald Building, 1892-94, by McKim, Mead & White, with statues of *Minerva* and *Stuff and Guff* by Antonin Jean Paul Carles; Congregation Shaaray Tefila synagogue and Armory of the 71st Regiment.

36th STREET

Hotel Marlborough. Advertisement from 1907.

W　**LEFCOURT MARLBORO BUILDING, No. 1359**

1923-25, by George & Edward Blum. [20 stories] Built for manufacturing, this chamfer-cornered buff

Sky bridge linking the Gimbel Brothers Department Store to its Annex, 1980.

older and unassuming Saks store on Broadway turned to moderately priced apparel.[19] The Gimbels building was linked by pedestrian bridges both to Saks-34th Street and to an annex on Thirty-second Street. The rivalry between Herald Square's two great stores—"Does Macy's Tell Gimbels?" the slogan asked—became part of the nation's popular lore, thanks to the movie *Miracle on Thirty-fourth Street.*

The early twentieth century was an expansive period for Herald Square, with the coming of the Hudson "tubes" (the commuter railroad now known as PATH) and the vast Pennsylvania Station. The Hotel Martinique, which had opened in 1900, was greatly expanded by 1910, to the designs of Henry J. Hardenbergh, architect of the Plaza and the Dakota. Among its deluxe features was a restaurant, modeled on the Apollo Room of the Louvre, with walnut pillars and wainscoting, gold silk tapestry, and panels depicting Louis XV, Voltaire, and the courtiers of Louis XIV.[20] The Martinique was followed in 1913 by the McAlpin Hotel, from Thirty-third to Thirty-fourth Street, whose 1,500 rooms made it the largest in the city. Its lounge was hung with tapestries, its main dining room decorated in gold, the men's café panelled in Circassian walnut, and the Marine Grill filled with glazed terra-cotta tiles by Frederick Dana Marsh.[21]

HOTEL MARTINIQUE
Views from 1979 and 1987.

brick tower has a hard, forbidding, industrial quality. *Site of* Marlborough Hotel, 1891, by Addison Hutton.

Greenwich Savings Bank, 1986.

E GREENWICH SAVINGS BANK, No. 1352-62

(Also known as the CrossLand Savings Bank). 1922-24, by York & Sawyer. Proposed landmark. [2 stories] A full-scale Roman temple whose Broadway portico has eight fluted columns, five feet in diameter and 40 feet tall, capped by Corinthian composite capitals. The elliptically shaped banking room has a 72-foot-high ceiling and a broad skylight.

FISCHEL BUILDING, No. 1364-70

1922, by Sommerfeld & Stecker. [16 stories] A severe, virtually unornamented, yellow brick tower with a restrained cornice and chamfered corner.

37th STREET

W LEFCOURT STATE BUILDING, No. 1375-85

1926-27, by Ely Jacques Kahn. [25 stories] A plain, yellow brick mass with unusual three-story Art Nouveau pilasters and lively zigzag coping.

BRICKEN BROADWAY BUILDING, No. 1385

1926, by Schwartz & Gross. [23 stories] Tall, tile-roofed porticoes, high above the street, are the most striking feature of this dark, imposing tower.

E NATIONAL TOWER BUILDING, No. 1372

1913-14, by George Keister. [12 stories] A buff brick façade topped by a bracketed cornice.

LEFCOURT NORMANDIE BUILDING, No. 1384-88

1926-28, by Bark & Djorup. [23 stories] A decagonal, three-story, Gothic tower, complete with cloud-piercing, gleaming gold finials, rises from the top of this otherwise drab skyscraper. *Site of* Hotel Normandie, 1887, by William H. Hume.

Greenwich Savings Bank, 1979.

The final burst of architectural extravagance in the area was the headquarters of the Greenwich Savings Bank, completed in 1924 at Thirty-sixth Street. Designed by York & Sawyer, it had forty-foot-high Corinthian columns on its three façades. Within its limestone walls was an enormous elliptical banking room, with a skylight and coffered ceiling more than seventy feet overhead.

From the late 1920s on, there would be little opulence in and around Herald Square; merely the stark functionalism—broken occasionally by some Art Deco exuberance—of industrial skyscrapers designed for the garment trade. These buildings were developed almost entirely by Abraham E. Lefcourt and Abraham Bricken. Lefcourt had begun his career in wholesale dry-goods but gave that up to concentrate on real estate. He played a large role in moving the industry away from Fifth Avenue toward the part of town where he owned property, "providing new and modern homes for the garment industry," he said, as well as amassing a fortune of some $100 million.[22] Lefcourt began on Broadway in 1923 with the Lefcourt Marlboro Building, replacing the Marlborough Hotel, at Thirty-sixth Street. After that came the Lefcourt Manhattan and Lefcourt State buildings. In 1926, he took title to the Normandie Hotel, outside of which he sold newspapers as a boy, and began the Lefcourt Normandie Building.

Bricken, a Russian immigrant who started in a tailor shop on Grand Street, followed Lefcourt in 1926 with the Bricken Broadway Building, at Thirty-eighth Street. The Broadway Theater was torn down in 1929 to make way for the Bricken Textile Building. This powerfully articulated, golden-brick Art Deco skyscraper by Ely Jacques Kahn offered its tenants large floors and unobstructed light from three sides, making it the "most popular building in the textile field."[23] (Decades later, it was still known as a first-class building and industry giants like Perry Ellis and Liz Claiborne had offices and showrooms there.) The next landmark theater to fall for a Bricken development was the Casino, which closed in 1930 as one of the southernmost playhouses in the city. Kahn designed its replacement, the Bricken Casino Building. While he could not outdo Kimball's theater, his tower was terrifically energetic, with a startling black-and-white brick scheme and sharply angled setbacks. Kahn's 1400 Broadway, which replaced the Knickerbocker Theater (formerly Abbey's), was a dull tower in comparison but notable as the "largest dress building in the world." Even today, a directory lists about 340 dress companies among the garment-related tenants.[24]

With the Depression came a temporary end to large-scale construction in the area. *Stuff* and *Guff* returned to Herald Square in 1940 as part of a freestanding monument to the Bennetts. However, little else of consequence was built until 1948, when construction began on 1407 Broadway, from Thirty-eighth to Thirty-ninth Street. Designed by Kahn & Jacobs, Ely Jacques Kahn's firm, the tower was an exciting hybrid of Art Deco and International

Lefcourt Normandie Building, 1979.

38th STREET

1407 Broadway, 1987.

w 1407 BROADWAY

1948-50, by Kahn & Jacobs. [40 stories] The façade is an unusual mixture of post-Deco jazziness and International Style refinement, meeting Broadway in a series of four different planes. It has light green brick, sliced through by wraparound bands—deep red mullions alternating with 6-over-6 windows.

E 1400 BROADWAY

1929-30, by Ely Jacques Kahn. [35 stories] Spartan and solid, this loft building demonstrates neither pretense nor imagination. *Site of* Abbey's Theater (also known as the Knickerbocker Theater), 1893, by John B. McElfatrick.

BRICKEN CASINO BUILDING, No. 1410

1930, by Ely Jacques Kahn. [33 stories] There is great delight to this two-toned, black-and-white, Jazz Age ziggurat. White brick piers and black brick spandrels meet in an interlocking pattern. Setbacks are cut on a bias, creating great variety in the upper floors. *Site of* The Casino, 1882, by Francis Hatch Kimball.

39th STREET

w WORLD APPAREL CENTER, No. 1411

1969, by Irwin S. Chanin. [40 stories] Alternating piers and vertical window bands compose the façade of this massive slab. *Site of* Metropolitan Opera House, 1883, by Josiah Cleveland Cady, rebuilt 1893, by John B. McElfatrick, remodeled 1903-05, by Carrère & Hastings.

Bust of Golda Meir outside the World Apparel Center.

GOLDA MEIR SQUARE

This triangular plaza—one of the few open spots in the Garment Center—includes a bust of *Golda Meir*, by Beatrice Goldfine.

E   LEFCOURT MANHATTAN BUILDING, No. 1412

(Also known as the Fashion Gallery Building). 1925-27, by George & Edward Blum; renovated 1989-90. [23 stories] This sober, brown brick tower has depth and detailing—arched windows at the upper setbacks and articulated piers with limestone caps. Huge chrome tubing has been added to the lower façade. *Site of* Oriental Hotel.

LEFCOURT MANHATTAN ANNEX, No. 1418

1929, by Victor Bark Jr. [6 stories] A simple buff brick façade with incised spandrel panels.

1430 BROADWAY

1956, by Emery Roth & Sons. [22 stories] Bands of light-colored brick alternate with ribbons of windows. *Site of* Empire Theater, 1892-93, by John B. McElfatrick & Sons, remodeled by Carrère & Hastings.

40th STREET

W   EMERSON BUILDING, No. 1431

1922-23, by F. & A. Ware. [12 stories] A simplified type of Gothic detailing distinguishes the top of this handsome, buff brick building, which has deeply recessed window bays. *Site of* Hotel Delavan.

1435 BROADWAY

1962. [6 stories] Ribbons of windows and white brick. *Site of* Martin Hotel.

1407 Broadway, 1986.

Style, with alternating bands of green brick and red mullions, and ranks as one of the best post-war buildings on Broadway.

After that, the area went into a forty-year decline. The Empire Theater closed in 1953 and New York lost "both a shrine and a symbol to those who recall the golden age of our theater," as the *New York Times* eulogized. Its proscenium had framed some of the century's greatest actors, the Barrymore clan among them, and *Life With Father*, which ran for eight years. While the legitimate theater had "survived many sinking spells" before, the *Times* warned that the "razing of the Empire will have implications darker than those born of any of its prior comas."[25]

Two years after the Empire was demolished, the Metropolitan Opera signed on to join a new cultural complex being planned uptown at Lincoln Square. That the Met wanted to leave the Garment Center was no surprise. In the 1920s, efforts were underway to build a new opera house as part of Rockefeller Center (which was called Metropolitan Square in its early development), leading the French writer Paul Morand to state flatly that the Met was "soon to be, very deservedly, demolished."[26] The opera withdrew from that project in 1929 and the infirmities of the house, in the eyes of its detractors, grew worse in the following decades—unmitigated by its grandeur. "Behind the proscenium and its golden curtain, the theater had nothing at all to recommend it," said Rudolf Bing, who took over as general manager in 1950. "Everything backstage was cramped and dirty and poor."[27] In April 1966, fifty-seven singers appeared in a program ending with the Final Trio from *Faust*, the opera that opened the house in 1883. Demolition began that year—

an effort to foreclose possible competition, critics said—and the Met was soon replaced by a banal behemoth of a skyscraper.[28]

Failure seemed endemic to Herald Square from the mid-1960s to the early '80s. Unprofitable for several years, Saks-34th Street closed in 1965. The building was stripped and reclad as an E.J. Korvette discount store, which opened in 1967 but only lasted thirteen years. The building was stripped and reclad again, reopening in 1985 as a mall called Herald Center, which was poorly conceived, poorly designed, and poorly patronized. Gimbels closed with brief notice in 1986, best remembered, if at all, for its bargain basement. Elsewhere on the Rialto, the Greenwich Savings Bank came close to collapse before it was taken over in 1981 by the Metropolitan Savings Bank.[29]

Certainly the unhappiest episode of Herald Square history began in 1973, when city officials started using the Martinique Hotel to house homeless families.[30] In time, it became one of the largest shelters in the city, where some 1,300 children lived at once. "It is difficult to do full justice to the sense of hopelessness one feels on entering," Jonathan Kozol wrote in *Rachel and Her Children*, his chronicle of homeless families. "It is a haunting experience. . . . Even the light seems dimmer here, the details harder to make out. . . . Something of Dickens' halls of chancery comes to my mind whenever I am wandering those floors."[31] When City Hall announced its retreat in 1988 from the policy of placing families in such surroundings, officials chose first to empty the infamous Martinique.

Bricken Textile Building, 1990.

BRICKEN TEXTILE BUILDING, No. 1441

(Also known as the W.T. Grant Building). 1929, by Ely Jacques Kahn. [33 stories] One of the Art Deco delights of the Garment Center. Luscious, contrasting yellow-orange and buff brick is arranged in horizontal bands and strong, prow-like projecting piers, which frame 6-over-6 windows and deep spandrel panels. *Site of* Broadway Theater, 1887-88, by John B. McElfatrick; Metropolitan Casino (also known as the Metropolitan Concert Hall, Metropolitan Skating Rink), 1880-81.

E W. O. R. BUILDING, No. 1440

1925, by Starrett & Van Vleck. [25 stories] This sober, brown brick tower has three-story pilasters at its base and a little arcade at top. *Site of* Holland Building.

Continental Building, 1988.

Saks & Company Store, reclad as Herald Center, 1988.

CONTINENTAL BUILDING, No. 1450

1930-31, by Ely Jacques Kahn. [43 stories] A white brick skyscraper with a large base and a slender, set-back shaft. *Site of* Hotel Vendome (also known as the Continental Hotel).

Gimbel Brothers Department Store, rebuilt as A. & S. Plaza, 1990.

Throughout the years, Macy's endured, as revealed in this sampling of commentary from 1939 to 1989: "A daily capacity of 137,000 customers, who may buy anything from diamonds to raspberries. . . . The souks of India and Morocco are no more fascinating than the stalls of Macy's. . . . The main floor is a giant bazaar with a touch of the carnival. Everything from auto tires to zithers. . . . Anything from an iguana to a painting by Joan Miró, from a set of Tom Swift books to fresh beluga caviar. . . . The paragon, the battlewagon of America's department store industry, probably the most famous retailer in the country."[32] Beginning in the mid-1970s, it was extensively refurbished in an attempt to lure younger and wealthier shoppers. In the midst of this makeover, however, one tradition was carefully maintained: the Thanksgiving Day Parade. The store went to extravagant lengths in this effort—104 feet in the case of Superman, the largest of the helium-filled balloons that are marched each November down Broadway, from Columbus Circle to Macy's.[33]

Although Herald Square had withstood earlier efforts to revivify it, the 1980s ended on something of an upbeat note. The Gimbels store had been rebuilt as A. & S. Plaza, a shopping center with a surprisingly large, light, and airy nine-level atrium, anchored by a branch of Brooklyn's Abraham & Straus department store. Two blocks away, after years of inattention, the Bennett monument was adopted by the *International Herald Tribune* (the Parisian descendant of the *Herald*) and restored in 1989. Once again, under *Minerva*'s watch, *Stuff* and *Guff* tolled the hours.

The Betty Boop balloon in the 1987 Macy's Thanksgiving Day Parade, as it moves through Duffy Square.

New York City Department of City Planning

TIMES SQUARE THEATER DISTRICT AUTOMOBILE ROW

FORTY-FIRST STREET TO FIFTY-EIGHTH STREET

View south in 1988 includes the Times Square Theater Center (foreground) and Times Tower (center).

Broadway underwent a convulsive growth in the 1980s that changed the Times Square area radically. Not all of the social and economic implications were clear as the decade ended, but it was obvious that the physical scale had completely changed, from a heterogeneous mix of old theaters and rag-tag commercial structures into a chilling canyon of hard-edged skyscrapers. Between 1982 and 1987, the Astor and Victoria theaters were razed to make way for the New York Marriott Marquis, the Loews State for One Broadway Place, the Strand for 1585 Broadway, the Pussycat for the Holiday Inn Crowne Plaza, and the Rivoli for 750 Seventh Avenue. The Palace and Broadway theaters were saved but incorporated into high-rises. As the building boom ended, it seemed that a lot of daylight had been lost in Times Square and that nighttime would never blaze as brightly again.

Andrew Hopper homestead, 1868. GSW.

The Great White Way was positively verdant until the last half of the nineteenth century. A large portion of it was owned by John Jacob Astor, who acquired what was then known as the Medcef Eden farm in 1803, for $25,000. (Its value increased two-thousand-fold in the next century and a quarter.) Eden's estate had been part of an even larger farm owned by Wolfert Webbers in the eighteenth century. This property stretched along both sides of the Bloomingdale Road, from Forty-first to Forty-ninth Street. Webbers lived with his wife Grietje near what is now Forty-fourth Street, not far from the spot where Generals George Washington and Israel Putnam met during the Americans' retreat from New York in September 1776.[1]

Another large parcel that had been in the Webbers family, running along the Bloomingdale Road from Forty-ninth to Fifty-third Street, was purchased in 1714 by Matthias Hopper. He passed it on to his son, Johannes, who built a charming, gambrel-roofed country house on the property in 1758 for *his* son, Andrew. More than a century later, the house still stood near Fiftieth Street, almost hidden behind melancholy willows. It was said that the "dignity of age became it well. The quaint carved mantles, the great yawning fire-places, and wide-arched hall retained the traditions of its better days."[2]

The Hopper house did not disappear until 1881, when William K. Vanderbilt replaced it with the American Horse Exchange, where some of the city's largest and most famous horse sales took place.[3] The exchange fit perfectly into the neighborhood, which was known by then as Long Acre Square, after the Long Acre in London, on which horse and harness dealers and coach builders were centered. The most prominent landmark of New York's Long Acre was the Brewster carriage factory, built in 1872 between Forty-seventh and Forty-eighth streets. In its vicinity, the "sound of the blacksmiths' ham-

View south in 1979 includes the Rivoli Theater (left) and the Astor and Gaiety theaters, under a "Dracula" billboard.

41st STREET

W **COMMERCIAL TRUST BUILDING, No. 1451-55**
ca. 1907; expanded. [7 stories] An original five-story window bay remains, with its geometric decorative border.

BROKAW BROTHERS BUILDING, No. 1457-63
(Also known as the Ninth Federal Building). 1915, by Rouse & Goldstone. [11 stories] A dour, brown brick tower. *Site of* Rossmore Hotel (also known as the Café de l'Opéra, Louis Martin's, Hotel Metropole), 1873, by John B. Snook.

The mural Times Tower *by Richard Haas on the Crossroads Building, 1979.*

INFORMATION CENTER, No. 1465
1986, by Prentice & Chan, Ohlhausen. [1 story] These are mobile trailers behind a false-front billboard painted with simplified Greek temples. *Site of* Crossroads Building (also known as the Heidelberg Building, Subway Central Building), 1910, by Henry Ives Cobb, with the *Times Tower* mural, by Richard Haas; Hotel Metropole. *Proposed site of* Times Square Center-South Tower, by John Burgee Architects with Philip Johnson.

E **WHITTAKER BUILDING, No. 1460**
(Also known as the Stevens Building). 1951, by Emery Roth & Sons. [15 stories] In a pleasingly modest box of International Style descent, white brick ribbons alternate with strips of three-pane windows. *Site of* Criterion Hotel (also known as the Calvert Hotel, Stuart House).

KNICKERBOCKER HOTEL, No. 1466
(Also known as the Newsweek Building). 1901-07, by Trowbridge & Livingston and Marvin & Davis, with Bruce Price; remodeled 1921. Landmark. [15 stories] A fantastic, almost sculptural evocation of the Gilded Age, this red-brick façade is laced with masonry ornament, ringed by deep cornices, and topped by a three-story copper mansard roof. Every window is bordered by quoins and many are topped by extravagantly ornamented pediments. *Site of* St. Cloud Hotel.

42nd STREET

Rialto Building, 1987; detail of the façade, 1986.

w   RIALTO BUILDING, No. 1481-83

1935, by Thomas W. Lamb and Rosario Candela. [4 stories] The undulating, Art Deco glass-brick façade has round columns and angular, projecting window bays above a band of deep blue glass panels. *Site of* Hammerstein's Victoria Theater and Paradise Roof Garden (also known as the Rialto Theater), 1898-99, by John B. McElfatrick & Son, rebuilt 1916, by Thomas W. Lamb; New York Tattersall. *Proposed site of* Times Square Center-Northwest Tower, by John Burgee Architects with Philip Johnson.

RIALTO THEATER

(Also known as the Cineplex Odeon Warner). 1935, by Thomas W. Lamb and Rosario Candela. [510 seats]

CHILDS RESTAURANT, No. 1485

1906, by Westervelt & Austin; remodeled, by Sweet & Shaw. [3 stories] Pilasters and garland-encircled oculi frame the horizontal windows in this surprisingly elegant little composition.

HOTEL LYRIC, No. 1491

ca. 1903. [4 stories] Traces of a cornice and one arched window remain on the 43rd Street façade. It is now covered by signs.

mer mingled with the tinkle of a horse-car bell. Stables abounded, and here and there a red flag indicated a horse auction . . .By night this district, now ablaze, was as dark as Egypt."[4] Even the southern end of the district, closer to the Rialto, was fairly sleepy. "Forty-second Street marks the end of Broadway as an interesting thoroughfare," it was stated in the 1890s, when the Rossmore and St. Cloud hotels were the "end of the world to the sport, the tipster and the chorus-lady."[5] One small hotel was destined for a kind of theatrical fame, however. At the Barrett House on Forty-third Street, Eugene O'Neill was born in 1888.

The foundations for the modern theater district were laid in 1895 by the Olympia, a multiple-theater complex so colossal as to be its own center of gravity. Built by the impresario Oscar Hammerstein and designed by John B. McElfatrick, the Olympia extended from Forty-fourth to Forty-fifth Street, and could accommodate 6,000 patrons. Within it were the Lyric Theater, the Concert Hall, and the Music Hall, which was decorated in Louis XIV style and had 124 boxes—more than any other amusement place in the world, Hammerstein claimed. The Olympia was besieged on opening night, as crowds, "with the strength of a dozen catapults, banged at the doors of the new castle of pleasure and sent them flying open."[6] Success was not long-lived, however. Although Hammerstein was credited as the "pioneer" who breached the Forty-second Street deadline, the real-estate press noted that "even he could not overcome the 'hoodoo' and the result spelt failure."[7] The Olympia was soon in foreclosure and its theaters were turned into separately managed houses. (In the glass-enclosed rooftop hall, Jardin de Paris, the first of Florenz Ziegfeld's *Follies* was staged in 1907.) Despite this debacle, Ham-

Oscar Hammerstein's Olympia, ca. 1895. NYHS.

Broadway Tabernacle Congregational Church. NYHS.

Times Tower, 1987.

C TIMES TOWER, No. 1475

(Also known as the Allied Chemical Building, One Times Square Plaza). 1903-05, by Cyrus L.W. Eidlitz and Andrew C. MacKenzie; rebuilt 1966-67, by Smith, Smith, Haines, Lundberg & Waehler. [24 stories] Only the shape remains of the original building, a Flatiron-like structure with a prow facing Times Square. It is otherwise clad in lifeless marble panels and festooned with huge electric signs. *Site of* Pabst Hotel.

TIMES SQUARE INFORMATION CENTER

[1 story] Two very large and colorful mosaic maps show points of interest citywide, current as of the early 1960s.

Long Acre Building, 1987.

E LONG ACRE BUILDING, No. 1472-78

1911-12, by Clinton & Russell. [12 stories] A red brick building with a turreted corner, dominant piers, and a distinct rooftop balustrade. *Site of* Shanley's Restaurant. *Proposed site of* Times Square Center-Northeast Tower, by John Burgee Architects with Philip Johnson.

TOFFENETTI'S RESTAURANT, No. 1482-90

(Also known as Nathan's Famous Restaurant). 1939-40, by Walker & Gillette and Skidmore, Owings & Merrill. [2 stories] Under the gaudy signage is a cool

merstein managed to cross the deadline again in 1899 with the Victoria Theater, on the north side of Forty-second Street. To admirers like Buster Keaton, Will Rogers, and George Jessel, the Victoria was the greatest of all vaudeville halls.[8]

Great and gaudy restaurants, the inevitable accompaniment to almost any theatrical quarter, began opening their doors at the turn of the century. Rector's Restaurant of 1899, next to the Barrett House, was known as the "American cathedral of froth and frivolity."[9] Churchill's Restaurant, which operated at Forty-sixth and Forty-ninth streets, styled itself "A Broadway Institution," and offered dining, ballroom dancing, and a twenty-act Cabaret Unique. The lone spiritual note in this indulgent atmosphere was provided by the Broadway Tabernacle Congregational Church, which moved in 1905 to its third Broadway home: a mountainous and vaguely French Gothic church, ten stories high, at Fifty-sixth Street.

Elsewhere on Broadway, stables and harness shops were giving way to dealers in horseless carriages. Their showrooms were known collectively as Automobile Row. In these "great halls of baronial aspect, on Oriental rugs and marble floors, America's most shining triumphs are displayed," Christopher Morley declared.[10] The Studebaker Building of 1902, which still stands

International Style building with a streamlined corner, handsome ribbon windows, and dark blue panels. *Site of* Fitzgerald Building and George M. Cohan's Theater, 1909-11.

NEW YORK THEATER
(Also known as the Big Apple Theater, Globe Theater).

43rd STREET

Paramount Building, 1978; Barrett House, 1884. NYHS.

w PARAMOUNT BUILDING, No. 1505
1925-27, by C.W. Rapp & George L. Rapp. Landmark. [33 stories] Eight great setbacks, several with big finials, culminate in a gigantic clock face and crowning globe. In contrast to this bold, buff brick tower, the entrance is delicately detailed. Originally, the Paramount Theater, by Rapp & Rapp, was in the base of the building. *Site of* Putnam Building (also known as the Longacre); Barrington Apartments.

c ARMED FORCES RECRUITING STATION
1950. [1 story] A glass and metal box.

E 1500 BROADWAY
1973, by Leo Kornblath. [33 stories] The sheer, dark brown glass façade rises from a six-story base. *Site of* Schrafft's Restaurant; Rector Hotel (also known as the Broadway Hotel, Claridge Hotel), 1909-10, by D.H. Burnham & Company; Rector's Restaurant, 1899; Barrett House (also known as the Broadway Hotel, Cadillac Hotel, Wallick's Hotel), 1883.

NATIONAL THEATER
(Also known as the Cineplex Odeon National). [2 theaters with 1,600 seats]

44th STREET

w ONE ASTOR PLAZA, No. 1515
(Also known as the W.T. Grant Building). 1968-70, by Kahn & Jacobs. [52 stories] Under its four great fins, which pierce the sky 745 feet above the street,

Studebaker Building, 1987.

at Forty-eighth Street, had an enormous elevator designed especially for autos, although Studebaker Brothers sold carriages, wagons, and harness well into the twentieth century.[11] Another extant building, the Pope Garage of 1905, at Fifty-fifth Street, housed Buick dealerships for more than fifty years. In 1909, the architect Francis Hatch Kimball elevated the aesthetics of Automobile Row with two gleaming white Gothic confections that harmonized with the nearby Tabernacle.[12] One was the A.T. Demarest carriage company building, on the corner of Fifty-seventh Street. Wrapped around it was the L-shaped building constructed for Peerless motors (one of the "Three P's" of luxury automobiles, along with Packard and Pierce-Arrow[13]). The two buildings were combined in 1916 for General Motors. A year later, the Ford Motor Company Building was constructed at Fifty-fourth Street, diagonally across from the spot where Henry Ford had opened his first showroom in 1905.[14] The United States Rubber Company Building, at Fifty-eighth Street, was completed in 1912 to designs by Carrère & Hastings and hailed as an "artistic addition to the automobile district."[15]

THE PEERLESS AND DEMAREST BUILDINGS

Views from 1979 and 1988 show a detail of the Peerless Building façade (left) and the Demarest Building roofline.

is a square shaft of alternating limestone and dark-gray glass. Through the curtain glass wall at the base can be glimpsed the lobby of the Minskoff Theater. *Site of* Astor Hotel, 1904, by Clinton & Russell. *Near site of* Wolfert Webbers farmhouse.
MINSKOFF THEATER
1973, by Robert Allan Jacobs. [1,620 seats]
LOEWS ASTOR PLAZA THEATER
[1,525 seats]

International Casino, as a Bond clothing store, 1979.

E   **INTERNATIONAL CASINO, No. 1514-26**
(Also known as the Bond Building, Criterion Center). 1935-36, by Eugene DeRosa, Thomas W. Lamb and Donald Deskey; remodeled 1988, by Bloch, Hesse & Shalat. [2 stories] Fantastic electric signage has always dominated this modest yellow, brown, and turquoise block-long building. *Site of* Oscar Hammerstein's Olympia, 1895, by John B. McElfatrick & Son: Music Hall (also known as the Moulin Rouge, New York Theater); Lyric Theater (also known as the Criterion, Vitagraph); and New York Roof Garden (also known as the Cherry Blossom Grove, Jardin de Paris); Armory of the Seventy-first Regiment.
CRITERION THEATER
1936, by Eugene DeRosa and Thomas W. Lamb; divided. [6 theaters with 3,030 seats]

45th STREET

W   **NEW YORK MARRIOTT MARQUIS HOTEL, No. 1535-47**
(Also known as the Portman Hotel). 1982-85, by John C. Portman Jr. [54 stories] In this utterly abstract and noncontextual structure, two gargantuan concrete monoliths enclose a semi-circular base that projects over Broadway, with a series of recessed horizontal masses above. *Site of* Gaiety Theater (also known as the Embassy 5, Minsky's Burlesque, Victoria), 1908-09, by Herts &

United States Rubber Company Building, 1990.

It was not as Automobile Row, however, that Broadway became known the world over; it was as the Great White Way. The birth of the modern theater district coincided with the growing use of electric illumination on building exteriors. Unlike gas jets, bulbs were almost impervious to weather, and they gave a steady, dazzling light—perfect for employment in a "conspiracy of commerce against night," as the writer Paul Morand described it.[16] Electric signs had grown as long as a city block by 1917, with a rooftop ex-

Times Square at night, 1923. NYHS.

travaganza from Forty-third to Forty-fourth Street, sporting three-story-high fountains and gigantic peacocks. It advertised Wrigley's chewing gum.[17]

"What a glorious garden of wonder this would be, to any one who was lucky enough to be unable to read," said the English novelist and social critic G.K. Chesterton, writing of Broadway in 1922. He ventured that an illiterate visitor, unaware of the imbecilic commercialism in the signs, might walk wonderingly "down that grove of fiery trees, under all that golden foliage and fruits like monstrous jewels."[18] In his 1927 book on nocturnal New York, Stephen Graham declared that one did not even have to see it to believe it. Broadway "has more light by night than it has by day," he said. "The blind are aware of some extra luminosity when they are taken along it."[19] It was the "apotheosis of electricity," to Odette Keun, a French visitor in the 1930s. "Bottles of beer appear on the firmament and transform themselves into dwarfs drinking; showers of gold peanuts fall from the skies; dragons breathing smoke become a film title; cigarettes are ignited; automobiles materialize."[20]

Inn-keeping in such an environment could not be—and was not—a sedate enterprise. The Astor Hotel, extending from Forty-fourth to Forty-fifth Street, was built by William Waldorf Astor in 1904 on a portion of the old Medcef Eden farm. The hotel was the "scene of more conventions, more banquets, more big social functions and more good times than any other hotel"— or, as Cecil Beaton said, it was "more like a terminal than a place in which to sleep."[21] Through the main entrance was a colonnade twenty-two feet high, in marble and gold. There were two banquet halls (one in Louis XV style), College Hall (Colonial), a women's lobby and reading room (Louis XIV), a

Astor Hotel. NYHS.

Tallant, remodeled 1949, by Edward Durell Stone; Astor Theater, 1906, by George Keister.

MARQUIS THEATER
1986, by John C. Portman Jr. [1,620 seats]

Loew Building, 1986; One Broadway Place, 1990.

E ONE BROADWAY PLACE, No. 1532-40
(Also known as the Metropolis Times Square mall). 1987-90, by Skidmore, Owings & Merrill and the Jerde Partnership. [44 stories] A relatively slender glass tower, with a dappled façade of cobalt blue and ice green, rises from a silvery base. An angular prow, topped by a high, trusswork finial, juts out above Broadway. *Site of* Loew Building and Loew's State Theater, 1919-21, by Thomas W. Lamb, divided 1968.

LOEWS THEATER.
Under construction.

1550 BROADWAY
(Also known as the M.&T. Bank). [4 stories] This is a red brick vestige of the nineteenth century, with a few remaining segmental-arched windows. It is now covered by signs.

46th STREET

CHURCHILL'S RESTAURANT, No. 1551
(Also known as Café Madrid, Howard Johnson's, Orpheum Dance Palace; includes the Gaiety Male Burlesk and New Paris Theater). 1895. [3 stories] There was once charm to this little building, which had arched windows and a tile roof. Only a few windows survive.

GLOBE THEATER, No. 1555*
(Also known as the Lunt-Fontanne Theater). 1909-10, by Carrère & Hastings; rebuilt 1957-58, by Roche & Roche. Exterior Landmark. [1,478 seats] *Broadway entrance is sealed off.

HORN & HARDART AUTOMAT, No. 1557-63

(Also known as Burger King). 1911, by Stuckert & Sloan; remodeled. [3 stories] Once, this building had a surprisingly elegant and classical façade, with delicate leaded windows. It was turned into a giant billboard.

CENTRAL THEATER, No. 1567

(Also known as the Forum 47th Street Theater, Holiday, Movieland, Trans-Lux Odeon). 1918, by Herbert J. Krapp. [868 seats]

MATHUSHEK & SON PIANO COMPANY BUILDING, No. 1569

[5 stories] Through the framework for giant signs, the semi-gabled roof can still be discerned on this rare nineteenth-century survivor.

Father Francis P. Duffy *in front of a Burger King, 1987.*

C   LONG ACRE SQUARE

(Also known as Duffy Square). [0.07 acres]. Within it are statues of *Father Francis P. Duffy,* by Charles Keck, and *George M. Cohan,* by Georg John Lober.

Times Square Theater Center and Father Duffy, *1979.*

TKTS (TIMES SQUARE THEATER CENTER)

1973, by Mayers & Schiff. [1 story] A red, trusswork frame supports canvas panels proclaiming "tkts" in huge orange letters.

Hunting Room (German Renaissance), a lounging room (Elizabethan), a barroom (Flemish), and a billiard room (Pompeiian). There were also Japanese, Chinese, and East Indian alcoves; an orangerie and palm garden; a grill room whose decorations amounted to a museum of native American relics; and a vast Roof Garden, concealed behind the enormous mansard roof, with pergolas, tempiettos, triumphal arches, fountains, arcades, and a bandshell.[22] The architects were Clinton & Russell, who designed a number of Astor projects, including the Long Acre Building at Forty-second Street.

The Astor Hotel had a near rival for grandeur. The Knickerbocker Hotel, another Astor enterprise, opened in 1906 at Forty-second Street. The lobby had marble pillars and brocade hangings. The main dining room had fountains and a beamed ceiling modeled on the Château de Fontainebleau. There were marble statues and tapestries depicting Julius Caesar's conquests. There was even gold service, for as many as forty-eight diners. The mirrored café gave into a barroom with oak paneling and a thirty-foot-long painting, *Old King Cole and His Fiddlers Three* by Maxfield Parrish, which was later moved to the Astors' St. Regis Hotel on Fifth Avenue. Upstairs, Enrico Caruso kept his own suite, chef, and servants. Downstairs, there were direct entrances from the subway to the hotel, furnished with settees and decorated with heraldic banners.[23] (Today, on the Grand Central Shuttle platform, there is still a door with a porthole window, marked "KNICKERBOCKER." The hotel itself was short-lived but the building was occupied for nearly two decades by *Newsweek*, another Astor holding.)

Between the openings of these two great hotels came the first pyrotechnical New Year's Eve in Times Square. The *New York Times* had just completed its headquarters on Forty-second Street and given its name to Long Acre Square. The newspaper decided to celebrate these events in festivities that coincided with the dawning of 1905. Within a few years, the New Year's ceremony around the tower had become a tradition, a "grand orgy after midnight, putting to blush the wildest capers of the Moulin Rouge, Maxim's, and other notorious places in Paris."[24]

Meanwhile, the *Times* had a new home of considerable beauty, modeled loosely on Giotto's Campanile in Florence. "Morning sun flushed its eastern wall, and sparkled on the cream-colored brick," Meyer Berger wrote, in his history of the newspaper. "Descending sun suffused the west wall with delicate crimson, and laid golden shafts across the publisher's desk on the twentieth floor. It flooded the news room on the seventeenth and made the composing room, on the sixteenth, a great hall of hulking shadows, spaced with gold."[25] The newspaper dubbed its new building the "City's Tallest Structure," asserting that height should be reckoned from the lowest basement. Since its basement pressrooms were built even deeper than the subway, Times Tower was 420 feet tall and edged out the Park Row Building, which everyone but the *Times* continued to believe was taller.[26] Despite the superlatives, the *Times* quickly outgrew its building and moved in 1913 to an annex on Forty-third Street, from which the newspaper is still published.

The *Times* and the theater district grew up together. A year and a half

KNICKERBOCKER HOTEL

Views from 1907 and 1986. NYHS, DD. Mural of Old
King Cole and His Fiddlers Three *by Maxfield Parrish.
Courtesy of the St. Regis-Sheraton Hotel.*

I. Miller Building, 1987.

E   I. MILLER BUILDING, No. 1552

1927-29, by Louis H. Friedland. [4 stories] This elegant limestone box was once the "Show Folks Shoe Shop Dedicated to Beavty in Footwear." Between two-story arched windows are small niches with statues of *Ethel Barrymore as Ophelia*, *Marilyn Miller as Sunny*, *Mary Pickford as Little Lord Fauntleroy* and *Rosa Ponselle as Norma*, by Alexander Stirling Calder.

ACTORS' EQUITY BUILDING, No. 1556-60

1924-26. [17 stories] Atop the plain cream brick façade is a Corinthian colonnade.

Lobby of the Embassy I Theater, 1988.

EMBASSY I THEATER

1925, by Thomas W. Lamb and Rambusch Studios, with murals by Arthur Crisp. Interior Landmark. [580 seats]

EMBASSY SUITES TIMES SQUARE HOTEL, No. 1564-66

1988-90, by Fox & Fowle. [43 stories] Despite its generously rounded corner and multi-colored

Rossmore Hotel and Times Tower, 1907. NYHS.

after Times Tower came the first new theater on Broadway since Hammerstein's Victoria. This was the Astor Theater, at Forty-fifth Street, on another part of the Medcef Eden farm. It was frequently leased to the producer and performer George M. Cohan. The Gaiety Theater, next door, was built especially for Cohan in 1909. A year later, he got a playhouse at Forty-third Street with his own name on it and murals depicting his show-business triumphs.[27] Today, all three theaters are gone, but a bronze statue of Cohan stands at Forty-sixth Street.

The Globe Theater opened in 1910 at Forty-sixth Street. Designed by Carrère & Hastings, it was a "comfortable, cozy little place, built on a fanshape plan that gives every seat a close view." A sliding ceiling could be opened in hot weather, allowing for year-round use of the auditorium.[28] In 1911, the Shuberts converted the old American Horse Exchange into a 1,800-seat theater. The auction ring was remade, with lattices and trellises, into something approximating a huge pergola, and the space was renamed the Winter Garden, "Broadway's Largest Temple of Folly." An innovative runway, thrust from the stage into the seating area, became known as the "bridge of thighs."[29]

The ultimate vaudeville hall, the Palace, opened at Forty-seventh Street in 1913. Created by Martin Beck, it quickly came under the control of E.F. Albee, and first captured the public's attention with performances by Ethel

Barrymore and Sarah Bernhardt. In time, the 1,700-seat theater came to be called the Valhalla of Vaudeville, the mecca of migrating minstrels, the home plate of show business.[30] "To play the Palace" meant the pinnacle of success and put a performer in the company of Fred and Adele Astaire, Bill "Bojangles" Robinson, Jack Benny, Fanny Brice, George Burns and Gracie Allen, W.C. Fields, the Marx Brothers, Ed Wynn, Eddie Cantor, Harry Houdini, Will Rogers, Sophie Tucker, and Odiva, the Plunging Samoan Nymph. Even in its architecture, the Palace exemplified the vaudeville house, with two balconies, level upon level of boxes, and a very high and wide proscenium arch over a large stage.[31]

As the last giant Broadway house built without the movies in mind, the Palace was in some ways instantly obsolete. Marcus Loew was already showing "photo plays" at the Herald Square Theater and within a month of the Palace opening, the Astor Theater began exhibiting *Quo Vadis*, the most ambitious moving picture that New York had yet seen—more than two hours long.[32] Several months later, the Criterion Theater (which had been the Lyric in Hammerstein's Olympia) became the first major Times Square playhouse devoted exclusively to movies.[33]

These efforts were quickly eclipsed by the Strand Theater, which opened in 1914 on the site of the Brewster carriage factory, at Forty-seventh Street. Although its façade was a rather restrained procession of three-story pilasters, inside was the "largest and most elaborate moving picture house in New York."[34] Its builder, Mitchel Mark, called it a " 'National Institution' which would stand for all time as the model of Moving Picture Palaces," and others said it was the "first modern 'cathedral of the motion picture.' "[35] It had 3,000 seats and a novel two-story rotunda and mezzanine promenade, encouraging people to pause and mingle. Its single balcony was a significant departure from the two-balcony auditorium of the day, and helped set a new style.[36] S. L. "Roxy" Rothafel was the director at the Strand, where live performances and musical concerts were interwoven with the picture show. Roxy was the social architect of the archetypal movie palace, as much as Thomas W. Lamb was the designer of the physical space, which he usually rendered in Neoclassical, Adamesque style. Both men were involved in Broadway's first great cinemas: the Strand, the Rialto, the Rivoli, and the Capitol.

The Rialto opened in 1916, taking the place of the Victoria Theater. It described itself as the "Temple of the Motion Picture—Shrine of Music and the Allied Arts," and its design evidenced a firm faith in the future of movies: the back of the auditorium was a solid wall, with no room for a center stage. (There were, however, small side stages flanking the screen.)[37]

Next came the 2,100-seat Rivoli Theater of 1917, the Parthenon of Times Square and "stateliest of Broadway's big film palaces."[38] Situated midway between Forty-ninth and Fiftieth streets, it had the façade of a Greek temple, with eight great Doric columns and a deeply sculptured pediment. "There is no building on Broadway, from the Battery to its northern end, that is more beautiful than the Rivoli Theater," exclaimed Adolph Zukor, the head of Paramount Pictures.[39]

Palace Theater Building, 1986; Embassy Suites, 1990.

ornamental panels and window trims, this dark gray tower is a somber addition to Times Square. ***Site of*** Palace Theater Building, 1912-13, by Kirchhoff & Rose.

PALACE THEATER

1912-13, by Kirchhoff & Rose; renovated 1965-66, by Ralph Alswang and John J. McNamara. Interior Landmark. [1,701 seats]

47th STREET

Site of 1585 Broadway, 1987; finished tower, 1990.

w 1585 BROADWAY

1988-90, by Gwathmey Siegel & Associates and Emery Roth & Sons. [42 stories] An exceptionally large building whose impact is mitigated by its placement far back from Broadway and by its cool, subtle façade, a finely articulated mix of silvery panels and blue glass in a notched and set-back tower. ***Site of*** Strand Theater (also known as the Cine Orleans, Cinerama, PentHouse, RKO Warner Twin), 1913-14, by Thomas W. Lamb, with George Keister and Otto Bauer; divided 1968; Brewster & Company Carriage Factory, 1872.

E THEATER ARTS BUILDING, No. 1576

1925. [3 stories] This is a delicate brick-and-tile "taxpayer" with oversized windows. ***Proposed site***

TWO CLASSIC THEATERS

View of the Palace Theater in 1988 (this page), as it was being prepared for renovation. View of the Strand Theater at night in 1917 (at top, facing page). NYHS. The Strand 70 years later, just before demolition began.

of Ramada Renaissance Times Square Hotel, by Mayers & Schiff Associates with Costas Kondylis.

Palais Royal and Theater Arts Building, 1987.

PALAIS ROYAL, No. 1578-90

(Also known as the Cotton Club, Latin Quarter, Princess Theater). 1912, by Shire & Kaufman. [2 stories] Large brick arches in Palladian form, with fan lights and side lights, march around all three sides of the hall.

48th STREET

Churchill's Restaurant, as Pussycat Cinema, 1979.

Churchill's Restaurant during demolition in 1986.

w HOLIDAY INN CROWNE PLAZA, No. 1603-07
1987-89, by the Alan Lapidus Group. [46 stories]

Rivoli Theater, 1979.

The biggest cinema of them all was the Capitol, at Fifty-first Street, which opened in 1919. The theater had walls of dark walnut, ceilings of gold, murals depicting *Youth*, *Song*, and *Chivalry*, and a wide and snowy marble staircase leading to the grand promenade. The auditorium, ornamented with silver leaf, had a dome sixty-four feet in diameter above its 5,300 seats. "One felt somehow very humble that all this pomp had been decreed for the edification of mortal man," said the New York *Sun*.[40]

Another half dozen theaters were built through the 1920s, with the result that more than 25,000 people could be seated at any given moment before one Broadway movie screen or other. "To Broadway first come all important motion pictures," Zukor declared. "If Broadway approves, the chances are that the rest of the country will also approve."[41]

Marcus Loew, who headed both the Loew's theater chain and Metro-Goldwyn-Mayer, opened the enormous State Theater, at Forty-fifth Street, in 1921. Designed by Lamb, it had a capacity of 3,400 and was reached through the base of the Loew Building, a small office tower. The Colony, at

Fifty-second Street, was opened by B.S. Moss in 1924 and, four years later, presented the debut of Mickey Mouse in *Steamboat Willie*. M-G-M opened the Embassy Theater, at Forty-sixth Street, in 1925. Designed by Lamb, the Embassy began as a high-society cinema, run by Gloria Gould, and later became America's first newsreel house.[42] Warner Brothers took over the Piccadilly Theater, near Fifty-second Street, in 1926 and renamed it the Warner. This was where the Vitaphone sound process was introduced to audiences, with a series of short subjects in 1926 and *The Jazz Singer* the next year.

It was left to Zukor to raise the theater district's architectural profile to skyline proportions, with the 372-foot Paramount Building of 1926, between Forty-third and Forty-fourth streets. With its setbacks, a great glass globe, and one of the largest clocks in New York, it became the Art Deco signature of Times Square. Inside was the 4,000-seat Paramount Theater, "like one of the sumptuous palaces described in old Arabian Nights tales" or a "blend of St. Peter's at Rome, the Parthenon, and the Valley of the Kings," with a Mighty Wurlitzer that was called the finest theater organ ever built.[43]

Closing out the era of the movie palace in richly excessive style was the Hollywood Theater at Fifty-first Street. This was Lamb's extravaganza for Warner Brothers and it opened in 1930. After entering through a modernistic lobby on Broadway, movie-goers proceeded through a vast baroque foyer, which was ringed by colossal marble columns and small balconies. In the auditorium, sculptural plasterwork, ornate chandeliers, and murals in the spirit of Fragonard and Watteau—their romantic depiction of seasonal themes included *Bird Nesting*, *Fruit Picking*, and *Tending the Yule Log*—made for a fantastic and opulent atmosphere. The Hollywood is the only one of the great movie palaces around Times Square to have survived into the 1990s intact.[44]

Opulence along Broadway was often suffused with show-business sentimentality. In 1927, Arthur Hammerstein built Hammerstein's Theater at Fifty-third Street as a tribute to his father, Oscar. It had stained-glass windows depicting scenes from Oscar's operas, and the overall Gothic design was meant to underscore its memorial character.[45] A more prominent display of

Detail of the recessed ceiling fixture in the Embassy I Theater, 1988.

From a round-edged base with a colossal entrance arch emerges an oddly shaped tower of magenta-tinted reflective glass and dull pink brick. ***Site of*** Churchill's Restaurant (also known as the Embassy 49 Theater, Pussycat Cinema, Trans-Lux West), 1910, by Herbert M. Baer, rebuilt 1937, by Eugene De Rosa; Philip Webbers house, 1792.

Holiday Inn Crowne Plaza, façade detail, 1990.

E STUDEBAKER BUILDING, No. 1600

(Also known as the National Screen Services Building). 1902, by James Brown Lord. [10 stories] This red brick, chamfer-cornered building is notable for the yawning arches at the ninth floor, framed by oversized medallions. The distinctive roofline cornice has been removed. ***Site of*** Central Market.

Circus Cinema, 1986.

CIRCUS CINEMA-WORLD THEATER, No. 1604

1927. [3 stories] A plain, white brick "taxpayer."

PARAMOUNT BUILDING

Views from 1986 to 1988 include the neighboring Times Tower, One Astor Plaza, and the Long Acre Building (this page), and a detail of the Broadway entrance.

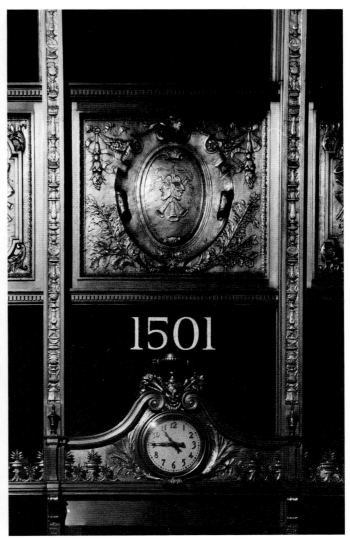

WARNER HOLLYWOOD THEATER

Views of the theater, now known as the Mark Hellinger,
include the auditorium (this page) and the grand foyer
(facing page), 1988.

49th STREET

Brill Building and Uris Building, 1987.

w   BRILL BUILDING, No. 1613-23

1931, by Victor Bark Jr. Proposed landmark. [10 stories] This squat and simple white brick box is embellished with delightful, geometric Art Deco spandrel panels. In a rooftop niche is a bust of the developer, Abraham E. Lefcourt; his son Alan is enshrined over the entrance. Originally, a Trans-Lux Theater, by Thomas W. Lamb and L.E. Dinslow, was in the base of the building. *Site of* Old Guard Armory.

750 Seventh Avenue, 1990.

E   750 SEVENTH AVENUE, No. 1612-26

1988-90, by Kevin Roche John Dinkeloo & Associates. [35 stories] Resembling an elongated step pyramid in glass, this black-and-gray tower culminates in a steeple-sharp peak. *Site of* Lindy's Restaurant; Rivoli Theater (also known as the United Artists Theater), 1917, by Thomas W. Lamb, divided 1981.

50th STREET

w   URIS BUILDING, No. 1633-49

(Also known as the Paramount Plaza Building). 1972, by Kahn & Jacobs. [48 stories] In its massiveness, darkness, and coldness—plus its

sentiment was at the I. Miller shoe store on Forty-sixth Street, where four statues by Alexander Stirling Calder—of Ethel Barrymore, Marilyn Miller, Mary Pickford, and Rosa Ponselle—were placed in gold-tiled niches in the façade.

Following these sentimental shrines came the more hard-edged, Deco-inspired buildings of the Thirties, whose kinetic, jazzy qualities seemed tailor-made for Times Square. The Brill Building of 1931, at Forty-ninth Street, had strongly geometric relief work and was animated by busts of the developer, Abraham E. Lefcourt, and his son, Alan. Known as Tin Pan Alley under one roof, the building bulged with music-publishing firms, artists' representatives, concert managers, publicists, dance bands, and booking agents.[46]

Although the Brill Building was starkly white, Art Deco buildings also came in rich colors. The second Rialto Theater, at Forty-second Street, had a glass-block and aluminum façade accented by cobalt-blue panels. Lindy's Restaurant—an all-night deli known for "creamy cheesecake and frothy gossip" and made famous by its chronicler, Damon Runyon—had a streamlined façade of black, red, and yellow.[47] Toffenetti's, at Forty-third Street, which billed itself as the "Cathedral of All Restaurants," had a sleekly curved, dark-blue skin. (It shared the building with the New York Theater, a newsreel house that replaced Cohan's Theater.) The International Casino, which replaced the old Olympia, was a brightly illuminated billboard of a building. Within it were the Casino nightclub and the "Theater of Tomorrow," B.S. Moss's New Criterion, which opened in 1936 with the enigmatic boast that "when television does come along, we are prepared."[48]

Besides a change in architecture, the 1930s brought changes in names and tenancies along Broadway. Moss's Colony cinema was turned into a legiti-

Rialto Building, 1986.

COMMEMORATIVE NICHES

At the I. Miller Building is a statue of Marilyn Miller as
Sunny, *by Alexander Stirling Calder; at the Brill
Building is a bust of Alan Lefcourt, the developer's son,
1987.*

windswept plaza with two deep holes—this overwhelming black building is far out of place. *Site of* Capitol Theater (also known as the Cinerama Theater), 1917-20, by Thomas W. Lamb, remodeled 1962.

Uris Theater, 1988.

URIS THEATER
(Also known as the Gershwin Theater). 1972, by Ralph Alswang. [1,870 seats]
CIRCLE IN THE SQUARE THEATER
1972, by Allen Sayles. [650 seats]

E AMERICAN HORSE EXCHANGE, No. 1632
1881-83, by David & John Jardine; rebuilt 1896, by A.V. Porter. [3 stories] The Winter Garden is in the shell of a building more than a century old. Outlines of the original arched windows and corner towers can be seen on the 50th Street and Seventh Avenue façades. *Site of* Andrew Hopper homestead, 1758.
WINTER GARDEN THEATER
1910-11, by William Albert Swasey; remodeled 1922-23, by Herbert J. Krapp. Interior Landmark. [1,516 seats]

1648-50 BROADWAY
1922, by the Bethlehem Engineering Corporation. [12 stories] A two-story Ionic colonnade stands atop this slender, white brick tower, whose entrance is framed by a massive arch.

51st STREET

W BROADWAY BLOCK BUILDING, No. 1651-57
(Also known as the Wilfred Building). 1928, by Schultze & Weaver; rebuilt and enlarged 1984, by the Gruzen Partnership. [6 stories] The 26-story Hotel Novotel sits atop this older building, whose Art Deco façade was removed in favor of flat, reddish-brown brickwork. *Site of* Albany Flats. *Near site of* John Hopper farmhouse.

Main stairway at the International Casino, 1988.

mate house in 1930 and renamed the Broadway. The Hollywood was turned into a legitimate house in 1934, and its Broadway entrance was soon sealed off. (Later renamed the Mark Hellinger, it was the home of *My Fair Lady*.) In 1935, the Palace stopped presenting live performers and soon Loew's State was the only theater in Times Square with regular vaudeville programs.[49] Churchill's Restaurant, at Forty-ninth Street, which had served for a time as the office of Irving Berlin, was transformed by Moss into a Trans-Lux Theater in 1937.

The Churchill's of the 1930s was Jack Dempsey's Broadway Bar, in the Brill Building. Upstairs was the Paradise nightclub, designed by Joseph Urban, and renowned as the home of "50 Girls 50—World's Most Beautiful Girls."[50] Other nightspots included the Roseland dance hall, the "downtown headquarters of hot music," next door to the Warner Theater.[51] Hammerstein's was converted in 1934 into Billy Rose's Music Hall—"honky tonk on a cosmic scale."[52] The Cotton Club moved from Harlem to Forty-eighth Street in 1936 and opened on Broadway in a lavish revue starring Cab Calloway, Bill Robinson, and 130 more performers.[53]

"It is the district of glorified dancing girls and millionaire playboys and, on a different plane, of dime-a-dance hostesses and pleasure-seeking clerks," the *W.P.A. Guide* said of Times Square in 1939.[54] "Broadway is not wicked, although wickedness may be conceived there," *Fortune* said that year. "Broadway is too loud and light and honky-tonk for wickedness."[55]

Both the International Casino and the Cotton Club closed in 1940. The casino was turned into a Bond clothing store, whose huge neon sign overlooked the square for almost five decades. The Cotton Club space was taken over in 1942 by the impresario Lou Walters, who created the long-running Latin Quarter nightclub. The décor was like the "inside of a box of Turkish

Delight" and Walters's daughter, Barbara, remembered "glorious shows, wonderful chorus girls, marvelous costumes."[56] Times Square was jumping. Five blocks downtown, at the Paramount, the big bands of Tommy Dorsey, Glenn Miller, and Benny Goodman lured the jitterbuggers, while Frank Sinatra's concerts in the 1940s caused riots among teenage bobby-soxers. CBS began broadcasting *Ed Sullivan's Toast of the Town* variety show in 1949 from its studio in Hammerstein's Theater. With a second CBS television studio a few yards to the west, the intersection of Broadway and Fifty-third Street came to be known as "Celebrity Corner."[57] A block away was Birdland, a cellar nightspot that featured "practically everybody of consequence in modern jazz."[58] From late 1951 to early 1952, Judy Garland's record-breaking engagement revived the Palace Theater. The old Globe Theater underwent a thorough remodeling and emerged in 1958, minus its Broadway entrance, as the Lunt-Fontanne.

There was still a certain innocence to the theater district—or, at least, a naïveté—after the war. Edward Durell Stone, that arch-establishment architect, showed a whimsical side in 1949 by remodeling the old Gaiety Theater with wall coverings made of movie-reel parts.[59] Next to the Winter Garden, patrons at Hawaii Kai dined among thatched-roof huts made of bamboo trunks, a stalactite-filled grotto, and a gurgling waterfall. Another waterfall—this one quite immense—was built atop the Bond store and flanked by two giant, semi-nude, neon-draped figures. These gave way in time to giant Pepsi bottles. (It was calculated that each bottle could hold 7,812 gallons of cola.[60]) Even the Mutual Life Insurance Company of New York, whose home office between Fifty-fifth and Fifty-sixth streets was opened in 1950, showed

Hawaii Kai Restaurant, 1988; Howard Johnson's Restaurant, 1979.

Hollywood Theater, 1988.

WARNER HOLLYWOOD THEATER, No. 1641*
(Also known as the 51st Street Theater, Mark Hellinger, Times Square Church, Warner Brothers Theater). 1929-30, by Thomas W. Lamb and Rambusch Studios. Exterior and Interior Landmark. [1,567 seats] *Broadway entrance is sealed off.

E SHERATON CITY SQUIRE HOTEL, No. 1652-66
1961, by Kahn & Jacobs. [22 stories] Two red-and-white brick slabs in a T shape sit above a garage with a forbidding metal grille. ***Site of*** Piccadilly Theater (also known as the Minsky's Oriental Theater, New Yorker, Republic, Warner), 1924, by Newton Schloss and Joseph Orlando; Roseland; Broadway Central Building (also known as the Healey & Company Coach Manufactory), 1892, by Henry J. Hardenbergh; Newport Flats.

52nd STREET

1675 Broadway, 1990.

W 1675 BROADWAY
1986-89, by Fox & Fowle. [35 stories] The façade is gray granite and the windows are green glass, but the overall massing of this slab—with projecting and set-back side walls—is creditably reminiscent of 30 Rockefeller Plaza. ***Site of*** Alvin Hotel (also known as the Hotel Lincoln); Saratoga Flats.

Broadway Theater, 1987.

B.S. MOSS'S COLONY THEATER, No. 1681-85

(Also known as the Broadway Theater, Cine Roma). 1923-24, by Eugene De Rosa and Rambusch Studios; renovated 1985-86. [1,778 seats].

E 1672-78 BROADWAY

1921, by Joseph Kleinberger. [9 stories] This rusticated masonry façade is topped by two-story pilasters with composite capitals and a delicate cornice.

810 SEVENTH AVENUE, No. 1680-88

1970, by Kahn & Jacobs. [41 stories] A dark gray glass shaft that stands awkwardly atop a 13-story base. *Site of* Broadway Rose Garden Theater (also known as the Metropolitan or Olympian Roller-Skating Rink), 1885, rebuilt 1914, by Koppe & Moore.

53rd STREET

Hammerstein's Theater entrance, 1987.

W HAMMERSTEIN'S THEATER BUILDING, No. 1697-99

(Also known as the Ed Sullivan Theater Building). 1925-27, by Herbert J. Krapp. [12 stories] Two Gothic niches and roofline finials bring a slightly fanciful edge to a very dark façade. *Site of* Irvington Flats.

that a giant corporation could be infected by White Way fancy. It installed a "weather star" on its roof, a mast that provided forecasts through a system of colored lights.

At the same time, however, Times Square was beginning its decline, as theater-goers and movie fans stayed home to watch television. In the mid-1950s, Meyer Berger detected the new edge to the neighborhood. "The first touch of blight is on it," he wrote. "It has begun to change from merely a light-flooded theater and restaurant center to a street of ever less pretentious and more or less rowdy carnival amusement places."[61] In 1957, the last vaudeville performance was given at the Palace and it became "just one more Broadway movie theater and a rather seedy one at that."[62] By the 1960s, the only people left who accepted the illusion of Times Square magic, Marya Mannes wrote, were "tourist transients who believe that Broadway is exciting, or rather who feel it must be. . . . It is on this ignorance that the predators feed, giving much of Broadway the shabby tawdriness of a boardwalk in a cheap resort."[63]

Times Tower was effectively destroyed between 1965 and 1966, stripped of every architectural detail except its "zipper"—the 360-foot-long electric bulletin board that girdles the building—and reclad as a marble shaft called the Allied Chemical Tower. This renovation was intended to provide the "key to a major transformation of the entire area," but had no such effect.[64] (The tower's old architectural features reappeared tantalizingly in 1979 as a ghost image across Forty-second Street, when Richard Haas painted a 130-foot-high *trompe-l'oeil* mural on the Crossroads Building.) The Capitol Theater, which had already been radically reduced in size, was demolished in 1967. Also that year, the Paramount Theater was converted to office space after undergoing an interior demolition that left the bobby-soxers' temple looking "like a murky corner of Hell."[65] The Astor Hotel almost defied the wreckers in 1967—a demolition project scheduled for five months ended up taking more than twice that time—but it finally succumbed. The pioneering Strand movie palace underwent the humiliation of subdivision into three theaters in 1968. General Motors, which had long been the dominant presence on Automobile Row, left Broadway that year for Fifth Avenue. The Latin Quarter closed in 1969 and so did the Broadway Tabernacle, after the congregation leased the property and moved its services to a nearby Catholic church.

One aspect of Broadway that was undimmed by time and undaunted by taste was the advertising spectacle, produced in the workshops of Artkraft Strauss, Van Wagner, and Douglas Leigh. In 1966, for example, a gin bottle about a half block long was installed atop the Bond building, pouring continuously into an awaiting glass. As if that were not enough overscaled debauchery in one spot, it was later joined by cigarette smokers with heads twenty-eight-feet high, from whose pursed lips 1,000 giant "smoke" rings puffed every hour.

On stage in the 1960s, perhaps the most widely watched performance was that of the Beatles, who made their American debut in 1964 on the Ed Sullivan show, broadcast from Hammerstein's Theater, while more than sixty

TIMES TOWER TRANSFORMED

Times Tower in 1907, 1979, and 1987. NYHS, DD, DD.

DAY AND NIGHT

Looking north from 46th Street in 1986 along the west side of Broadway (facing page) and the east side (this page).

HAMMERSTEIN'S THEATER

(Also known as CBS Radio Theater 4, CBS Studio 50, Ed Sullivan Theater, Manhattan Theater, Billy Rose's Music Hall). 1927, by Herbert J. Krapp; remodeled 1935, by William Lescaze. Interior Landmark. [1,265 seats]

HOTEL CUMBERLAND, No. 1701

(Also known as the Hotel Bryant). 1902, by Mulliken & Moeller. [12 stories] Both façades of this white brick building are dominated by heavily ornamented nine-story bays. *Site of* Hotel Bayard (also known as the Hotel Barnard). *Near site of* Cornelis Cosine farmhouse.

E 1700 BROADWAY

1969, by Emery Roth & Sons. [40 stories] This 533-foot-high building has a bronze curtain glass wall of some sophistication, using a Miesian device of small I-beams as mullions. *Site of* the Lansdale and the Canton, combined to form the Pocantico; the Windsor.

54th STREET

W LA PREMIERE, No. 1721

1977, by Philip Birnbaum. [32 stories] This is no more than a flat, buff brick shaft with balconies.

E FORD MOTOR COMPANY BUILDING, No. 1710

(Also known as the International Ladies Garment Workers Union offices). 1917, by Albert Kahn. [6 stories] Handsomely restrained, this rectilinear limestone façade has recessed window bays with elegant, fluted spandrel panels on which are bas-relief decorative plaques. *Site of* Clermont Flats.

Woodward Hotel, 1987.

WOODWARD HOTEL, No. 1724

1902-04, by George F. Pelham. [12 stories] Limestone pediments, bracketed balconies and cornice, and rusticated window surrounds stand out in this red brick façade. There is a fine corner turret whose copper cupola was removed.

police officers patrolled a "gaggle of giggling girls" outside on Broadway.[66] Another significant performance was that of Neil Simon's *Sweet Charity*, with which the Palace was reopened as a legitimate theater in 1966, having been taken over by the Nederlander family of Detroit, who sought to reverse years of unsympathetic alterations.[67]

At the time, the city was trying to encourage theater construction through zoning incentives. If the developer of an office building in Times Square added a legitimate theater to the project, he would get a substantial bonus of floor space in the tower. The Uris Building, which replaced the Capitol, ended up with 1.9 million square feet of space and two new legitimate theaters. Circle in the Square opened in 1972 with a revival of *Mourning Becomes Electra*, and went on to present *Uncle Vanya*, *Death of a Salesman*, and *Man and Superman*, among other plays. The Uris Theater (now the Gershwin) also opened in 1972, with *Via Galactica*, and later housed *Sweeney Todd*, *Pirates of Penzance*, and *Starlight Express*. One Astor Plaza was another recipient of the zoning bonus, generated in its case by the Minskoff Theater, which opened in 1973 with a revival of *Irene*. The tower also contains the 1,525-seat Loews Astor Plaza, the largest single-screen movie house left in Manhattan.[68]

Like the Allied Chemical Tower, One Astor Plaza was touted as the "first giant step in the inevitable emergence of New York's West Side."[69] It had little immediate effect, however. Generally, the 1970s and early '80s were years of decay for Broadway. The Trans-Lux became an X-rated showcase called the Pussycat Cinema in 1977, with a brazen marquee of red, swagged neon "curtains" and twinkling letters almost six feet high, set against blue and gold neon. The New York Theater became the Big Apple Cinema, and movies with titles like *Throbbin Hood* played on the site where George M. Cohan once presided. The Astor Theater was turned into a flea market and the Rivoli was divided in two. The Brill Building was almost still, after "song pluggers who used to lurk in every corner . . . wisely quit their stations."[70]

In 1973, plans were announced for a gigantic hotel from Forty-fifth to Forty-sixth Street that was supposed to be—as the Allied Chemical and One Astor Plaza towers were supposed to have been—a "revitalizing element" for Times Square.[71] It was badly stalled by the city's fiscal crisis. When the project resumed in 1982, it was inaugurated with one of the most bitterly contested demolitions in recent New York history. This storm centered on the Helen Hayes and Morosco theaters, on the side streets, but the wreckers also took out the Astor and Gaiety, on Broadway. The Marriott Marquis finally opened in 1985, with the "world's tallest atrium," thirty-seven stories high; two ballrooms; four restaurants and lounges, two of which revolved; 1,877 guest rooms; forty-seven meeting, banquet, and exhibit rooms; and the 1,620-seat Marquis Theater, which opened in 1986 and drew crowds with the musical *Me and My Girl*.[72]

The demolitions for the Marriott were followed by a sweeping move to give landmark status to most Broadway houses, which was accomplished by 1988 over the concerted protests of theater owners, who insisted that mass

NEW YORK MARRIOTT MARQUIS HOTEL

Views from 1988 show the atrium and the Marquis Theater.

55th STREET

w POPE GARAGE, No. 1731

(Also known as the Broadway Dance Center). 1905, by Townsend, Steinle & Haskell. [4 stories] High and wide segmental-arched bays distinguish the building, although they are missing the original ornament that gave them character.

The last car on Automobile Row, 1745 Broadway, 1985.

1745 BROADWAY

1905, by Raymond F. Almirall; rebuilt. [3 stories] Over time, the façade was simplified into a plain box with a curved corner. This was the site until 1985 of the last active showroom on Automobile Row.

Mutual Life Insurance Company Home Office, 1979.

E MUTUAL LIFE INSURANCE COMPANY HOME OFFICE, No. 1730-48

(Also known as the MONY Financial Services Building). 1950, by Shreve, Lamb & Harmon Associates; Weather Star by Artkraft Strauss; renovated 1987, by Kohn Pedersen Fox Conway. [25 stories] An unusual example of post-war Moderne, this sophisticated limestone tower would be at home around Rockefeller Center. Its Deco tendencies were underscored in a renovation of the lobby and entrance. *Site of* Sonoma Hotel; Rockingham; Ariston.

Demolition of the Strand Theater in 1987 afforded an unprecedented view of the Edison Hotel.

designation was akin to landmarking an industry, and would have dire economic and artistic consequences. Meanwhile, the old legitimate houses on Broadway were undergoing major transformations. The Shuberts' Winter Garden—which had been home to *West Side Story*, *Funny Girl*, *Mame*, and *Follies*—was taken over by the musical *Cats* in 1982 and filled with a "Red Grooms-esque collage of outsized rubbish . . . seen from a cat's eye perspective."[73] The Shuberts' Broadway Theater—where *Gypsy*, *Purlie*, *Candide*, and *Evita* had played—was completely renovated as a result of the development of an adjacent skyscraper. It reopened in 1986 and subsequently housed the hit musical version of *Les Misérables*. The Nederlanders' Palace—where *Applause* and *Woman of the Year* had achieved great success—closed for renovation in 1987 after 1,176 performances of *La Cage aux Folles*. The small office building from which E.F. Albee ruled vaudeville was razed and a forty-three-story Embassy Suites hotel was constructed adjacent to and above the auditorium, carried over the hall by four-story-high trusses.

New zoning incentives in the 1980s shifted development pressures from the East Side by allowing much denser buildings on the West Side for a fixed period of time. As developers rushed to meet that deadline, speculation and construction percolated madly. Soaring property values claimed, among other casualties, most of the remaining movie palaces: the Strand, the Rivoli, and the State. Another victim was Automobile Row. The last showroom, a Nissan dealership, moved to Eleventh Avenue in 1985.[74]

The developers made a point of saying that their skyscrapers would hew to Times Square's rhythms. For instance, the builders of One Broadway Place, on the site of Loew's State Theater, promised that a six-level mall in

Demolition of the Rivoli Theater, 1987.

the base of the forty-four-story tower would "bring the excitement and vigor of Times Square indoors."[75] Zoning guidelines required the installation of "super signs" on new buildings, going into some detail about size, illumination, and animation. Prodded by the Municipal Art Society and others who despaired that Times Square would become an utterly deadened business quarter, city planners came to embrace the "urban imagery of unparalleled brilliance and dynamism in which the signs themselves define the place."[76]

Even the massive Forty-second Street redevelopment plan was caught up in the belated effort to inject some of Broadway's old vibrancy into 600- and 700-foot office buildings. The government-backed project, first announced in 1981, involved four towers at Broadway, Seventh Avenue, and Forty-second Street; two of which, by the state's own reckoning, would "substantially exceed the bulk and densities" allowed under the zoning code.[77] The first designs, by John Burgee and Philip Johnson, were slabs with pseudo-mansard tops, identical in almost every way but their overall dimensions. Then, in 1989, after considerable criticism, the architects proposed buildings that differed from one another in shape, color, materials, and detailing. One of them even had a cylindrical electric sign rising more than twenty stories over the corner of Forty-third Street.

By the late 1980s, there were only scattered enclaves left of the old Times Square—that low-rise combination of shabbiness, sleaze, and sizzle, the "only part of the city whose very architecture seems to sleep with a hangover."[78] One such vestige was the block between Forty-fourth and Forty-fifth streets, where B.S. Moss's grandson converted the Bond store into a multiple-stage entertainment complex, evoking faintly the ghost of the Olympia.

56th STREET

Symphony House, 1987.

W   SYMPHONY HOUSE, No. 1755
1986, by Emery Roth & Sons. [43 stories] Massive in its east-west dimension, this pink brick slab rises from a red-granite office block. The regimented effect of more than 270 balconies on one façade is staggering. *Site of* Lozier Motor Company Showroom, 1905, by Francis Hatch Kimball.

FISK BUILDING, No. 1765-67
1921, by Carrère & Hastings and Shreve, Lamb & Blake. [26 stories] This red-brick building—240 feet wide—sweeps along 57th Street and is topped after several setbacks by a massive "temple" front with three-story Ionic pilasters. *Site of* Rutland Hotel.

E   CARNEGIE MEWS, No. 1756
1979. [37 stories] There is little character to this buff brick slab. *Site of* Broadway Tabernacle Congregational Church, 1903-05, by Barney & Chapman.

PEERLESS MOTOR CAR COMPANY BUILDING, No. 1758
(Joined to No. 1770 as the General Motors Building, also known as the Argonaut Building). 1909, by Francis Hatch Kimball. [9 stories] Glistening like vanilla frosting, this neo-Gothic façade has a three-story projecting bay. It is an L-shaped structure with frontages on Broadway and 57th Street, into which is tucked the Demarest Building.

A.T. DEMAREST MOTOR COMPANY BUILDING, No. 1770
(Joined to No. 1758 as the General Motors Building, also known as the Argonaut Building). 1909, by Francis Hatch Kimball. [9 stories] This neo-Gothic building is ringed with gabled buttresses and has a pair of lions at the base of its chamfered corner. It is distinguished from the Peerless Building by roofline gables.

DOWN TO THE GROUND AND BACK UP

Demolition of the Loew Building in 1987 proceeded from April (left), to May (top right), to July (bottom right and left on facing page). Plans for One Broadway Place, which replaced it, were by Skidmore, Owings & Merrill.

THE NEW TIMES SQUARE LANDSCAPE

View south in 1990, on this page, shows 1585 Broadway, the Crowne Plaza, Hotel Novotel, and 1675 Broadway (foreground). Views north in 1988 and 1990 show the addition of 750 Seventh Avenue (center) and One Broadway Place (right).

57th STREET

Colonnade Building, 1924. MCNY.

W   GENERAL MOTORS BUILDING, No. 1769-87

(Also known as Central Park Plaza). Colonnade Building, 1923, by William Welles Bosworth; expanded 1927-28, by Shreve & Lamb. [26 stories] Bosworth created the three-story Colonnade Building, which has Ionic columns as sturdy as tree trunks. On top of the Colonnade was placed the new tower, with stark, buff brick piers in a complex massing. *Site of* Thoroughfare Building, 1908.

E   SETAY BUILDING, No. 1776

(Also known as the Lazrus Building). 1927-29, by George & Edward Blum. [25 stories] This buff brick tower has strongly articulated piers, rising in a series of setbacks to a high, copper hip roof.

GOODRICH TIRES BUILDING, No. 1780-82

1909, by Howard Shaw and Waid & Willauer. [12 stories] A severely rectilinear central masonry bay dominates this façade.

UNITED STATES RUBBER COMPANY BUILDING, No. 1784-90

(Also known as the First Nationwide Savings Building, West Side Federal Savings Building). 1911-12, by Carrère & Hastings; renovated 1986-89. [20 stories] This overlooked gem of early skyscraper design meets the corner with a dramatically round edge, emphasized by the tremendous copper cornice. The white façade is characterized by strongly vertical bays and fine detailing.

Marriott Marquis (left), 1585 Broadway, Crowne Plaza, and One Broadway Place, 1990.

Another pocket of resistance was the block from Forty-sixth to Forty-seventh Street, where no building was higher than five stories and each had its share of honky-tonk. There was the Movieland cinema, the last incarnation of the Shuberts' Central Theater of 1918, which had housed the first professional collaboration of Richard Rodgers and Lorenz Hart and was later a Broadway showcase for Minskys' burlesque.[79] There was a game arcade and the long-abandoned Mathushek piano factory. There was an Automat-turned-Burger King. There was a cheap jewelry store in what had been the Broadway entrance to the Globe Theater. Finally, there was a Howard Johnson's in the old Churchill's Restaurant, with two burlesque houses upstairs—one gay, one straight—"burlesque" having come to mean something much more raw and explicit than it had in the Minskys' day.

Sex shows and pornography shops could still be found along Broadway in 1990, but they seemed to be near extinction. The suddenness of Broadway's transformation could be seen in two men's opinions as to what drew people to the area. In 1986, Al Kronish, founder of the Melody Burlesk at 1595 Broadway, was quoted as saying: "People who come to Times Square, they want *raunch.*"[80] Only a year later, David S. Solomon, developer of two new skyscrapers (in the place of the Strand and Rivoli theaters), was quoted as saying: "Investment bankers and lawyers don't want to work in an environment surrounded by flashing lights. They want museums and sidewalk cafés. What visitors want to see is the Champs-Elysées."[81]

Demolition of the Strand Theater in 1987, with the New York Marriott Marquis Hotel in the background.

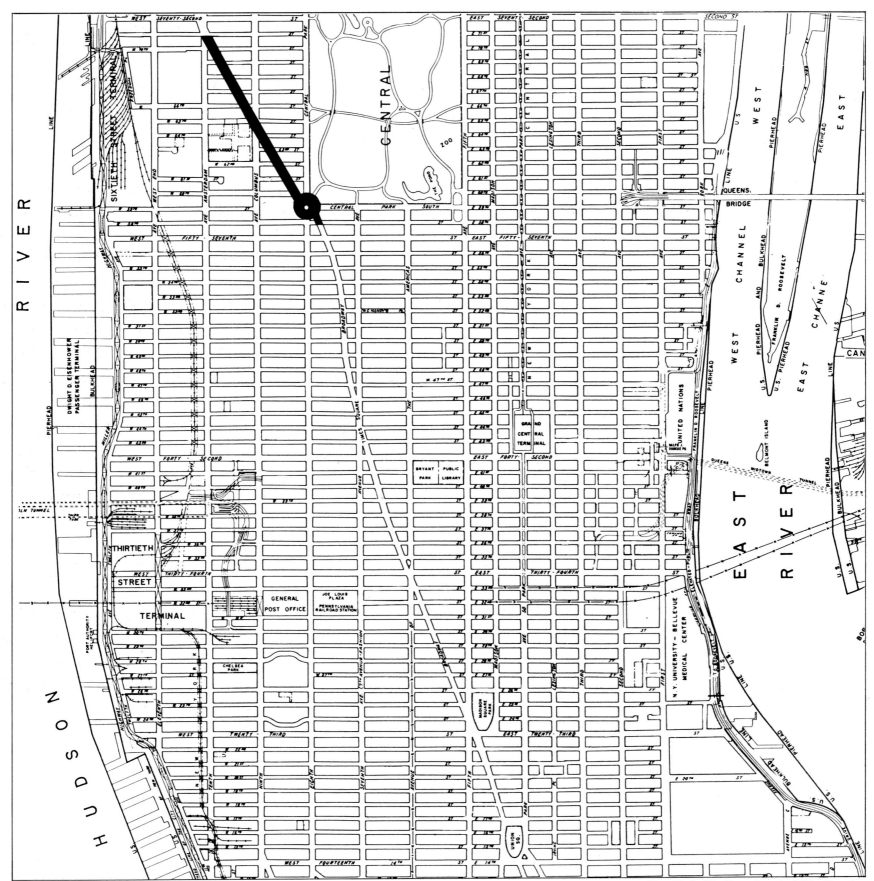

New York City Department of City Planning

COLUMBUS CIRCLE LINCOLN SQUARE

FIFTY-EIGHTH STREET TO SEVENTY-FIRST STREET

View of Columbus Circle in 1986 includes the Gallery of Modern Art and Columbus Memorial (center).

Broadway is transformed at Columbus Circle from a 100-foot-wide street to a 150-foot-wide boulevard, with islands of greenery along its spine. Apart from this generous, nineteenth-century layout, however, the area has a chilling modernity, as it was almost entirely recreated in the wake of the New York Coliseum and the Lincoln Center for the Performing Arts. In the thirteen blocks from Fifty-Eighth to Seventy-first streets are more than twenty buildings that were constructed after 1955. While Lincoln Center imparts solidity and character, the massive towers that it spawned seem to drain Broadway of neighborhood feeling, even though they added thousands of new neighbors. Indeed, the mix of cultural, commercial, and high-rise residential uses makes the area feel much more closely related to midtown Manhattan than to the rest of the Upper West Side.

Bloomingdale Church of 1816; Bloomingdale Church of 1885, pictured ca. 1905. NYHS.

A sprawling farm of some 300 acres covered most of this area in the eighteenth and early nineteenth centuries. Called "Little Bloomingdale," it stretched from Fifty-seventh to Sixty-ninth Street, and was owned by Etienne De Lancey, who lived on lower Broadway and also owned the "Bloomingdale" farm farther north. The property passed to his grandson, James Delancey, from whom it was confiscated because of his pro-British activities in the Revolutionary War, whereupon it was sold to John Somarindyck.[1]

North of that was the farm of Jacob Harsen, approximately from Sixty-ninth to Seventy-third Street. Harsen gave his name to the surrounding community—Harsenville—and founded the Bloomingdale Reformed Dutch Church in 1805, with Andrew Hopper, whose home at Fiftieth Street was a longtime landmark; Philip Webbers, whose family owned much of what would become Times Square; and James Striker, after whose family Stryker's Bay was named. In 1816, the congregation built a stout church, with a belfry, on the Bloomingdale Road, at what is now Sixty-eighth Street. Life during the 1820s was Arcadian, said a later pastor, with the church as the religious and social center of a bucolic community with some 2,000 people.[2] In the 1830s, however, the old families thinned out and their property was divided into the city blocks that had been decreed by the 1811 street plan. "Assessors and street commissioners, like an invading army, quartered themselves on the land," the pastor said. "Following in their track came a swarm of squatter sovereigns in the shape of newly arrived emigrants. These were utterly unsympathetic with the old church life of the hamlet." The fatal blow came in 1868, when the church was torn down by the city to make way for a much widened version of the Bloomingdale Road, known as the Boulevard. What this left, in the cemetery behind the church, were "dilapidated vaults, the

Lincoln Center for the Performing Arts and One Lincoln Plaza, seen through the Metropolitan Opera House, 1988.

UPPER WEST SIDE-CENTRAL PARK WEST HISTORIC DISTRICT

This designation covers every building on the east side of Broadway, from the Spencer Arms Hotel, at 69th Street, to No. 2080-94, at 72nd Street.

58th STREET

Gallery of Modern Art, 1980.

W   GALLERY OF MODERN ART, No. 1787-89
(Also known as the New York City Department of Cultural Affairs). 1964, by Edward Durell Stone. [10 stories] Atop curving, Y-shaped columns rests an almost windowless marble box edged with a kind of filigree work and punctured by two-story arched loggias at the top. *Site of* Grand Boulevard Hotel (also known as the New York American Building, New York Journal Building, Hotel Virginia).

240 Central Park South, 1987.

E   240 CENTRAL PARK SOUTH, No. 1800
1939-41, by Mayer & Whittlesey. [15 and 28 stories] Two yellow-brick towers with corner balconies are joined by a one-story base on Broadway composed of four curving storefronts.

COLUMBUS CIRCLE

National Maine Monument, 1981.

NATIONAL MAINE MONUMENT

1912-13, by Harold Van Buren Magonigle, with sculptures by Attilio Piccirilli, restored 1980. The allegories represent *Columbia Triumphant, Victory, Peace, Courage, Fortitude, Pacific Ocean, Atlantic Ocean, Justice, Warrior,* and *History.* A plaque on the park side, by Charles Keck, was cast from metal from the battleship *Maine.*

COLUMBUS MEMORIAL

1892, by Gaetano Russo; fountain added 1960, by Douglas Leigh. Statues portray *Christopher Columbus* and *Genius of Discovery* (also known as the *Genius of Geography*).

59th STREET-COLUMBUS CIRCLE I.R.T. STATION

1904, by Heins & LaFarge. Interior Landmark.

New York Coliseum and 10 Columbus Circle, 1987.

NEW YORK COLISEUM and 10 COLUMBUS CIRCLE BUILDING, No. 1819-29

1956, by Leon & Lionel Levy. [26 stories] This is a 1950s behemoth, L-shaped in elevation, with a buff-brick tower rising from a windowless, scaleless base.

1981-87 Broadway, with the Bel Canto at right, 1986.

broken headstones that marked the trampled graves, the goats that found sacrilegious pasturage above the dead."[3]

The "great Drive or Boulevard" had been outlined in 1866 by the Commissioners of Central Park, who, under Andrew Haswell Green, were charged with laying out the blocks west of the park. The thoroughfare was formally proposed in 1867, to take the place of the Bloomingdale Road.[4] It was to start at the Circle, a turnaround for horse-drawn vehicles at Fifty-ninth Street, and run about five miles, to 155th Street. It was to have center islands and broad sidewalks, lined by elm trees, shrubbery, and flowers. A contemporary noted that the road was "expected to be one of the later wonders of Manhattan, and land is held at fabulous prices along its entire length."[5] After construction began in 1868, the Tweed Ring turned the project into a "gigantic steal," all the way down to the price paid by taxpayers for the trees.[6] After the ring was broken up, the Boulevard was left unfinished for decades, plagued by dust, mud, and snow. Its main purpose seemed to be recreational. "The bicycle crowd has completely subjugated the street," Stephen Crane wrote. "The glittering wheels dominate it from end to end."[7]

Traveling north on the Boulevard in 1889, the bicyclists would first have passed several equestrian academies around the Circle, including Durland's at Sixtieth Street, which was ranked among the largest riding schools in the world.[8] Across from Durland's was a small apartment house, with a distinctive four-gabled roofline, that still stands. Next came Empire Park, a triangle north of Sixty-third Street, with a fountain in the center, and Lincoln Square, a vacant triangle at Sixty-sixth Street. At Sixty-seventh Street was a row of four-story brick buildings—still standing—that contained a saloon, undertaker, and bakery, as well as apartments. On the other side of the Boulevard was the enormous Armory of the Twenty-second Regiment, "in the general style of the fifteenth century," with loop-holes for cannon and muskets, a bastion for heavy guns, a machicolated parapet, and a sally-port and portcullis.[9] North of the Armory, on Sixty-eighth Street, was the new Bloomingdale church, which opened in 1886, dominating the local skyline with its spire. The rest of the Boulevard held vacant lots and shanties, with an occasional saddlery, blacksmith, horseshoe shed, coal yard, or grain loft.

In the 1890s and early 1900s, many of Times Square's characteristic institutions—hotels, theaters, and automobile dealerships—trickled northward. One of the earliest hotels was the Welden, a handsome little work by McKim, Mead & White, built in 1892 at Sixty-seventh Street. At Sixty-sixth Street stood the Hotel Marie Antoinette, built in 1895. Although it was fairly plain, in this part of town it amounted to what the *Tribune* called a "White Palace," boasting the "Charm and Refinement of Versailles" and residents like the impresario David Belasco.[10] (With the advent of the subway, the Marie Antoinette got a twelve-story northern wing. Its great mansard roof and flamboyant details made it an unlikely mate for the earlier building.) The Empire Hotel, whose rooftop domes overlooked Empire Park, catered to families as

First proposal for Columbus Center. Steve Rosenthal.

The giant governmental seals on the façade were designed by Paul Manship. **Site of** Pabst Grand Circle Hotel; Majestic Theater (also known as the Cosmopolitan Theater, International Theater), 1903, by John H. Duncan; renovated 1922, by Joseph Urban; Gotham National Bank Building (also known as the Manufacturers Trust Building), 1921, by Sommerfield & Steckler; Circle Theater, 1902-06. **Proposed site of** Columbus Center, by Skidmore, Owings & Merrill.

60th STREET

w **COVA BUILDING, No. 1841-43**
(Also known as the Columbus Circle Building). 1921, by B.H. & C.N. Whinston. [12 stories] Strongly articulated vertical bays, set among buff-brick piers, have delicately ornamented spandrel panels.

1845-47 Broadway, 1985.

1845-47 BROADWAY
(Also known as 15-17 Boulevard). 1889-90. [4 stories] At the roofline of this brick building are two big gables flanking two smaller gables.

Colonial Bank (right), Hotel Welden, and 22nd Regiment Armory (gabled tower). NYHS.

THE JERMYN, No. 1851-57

(Also known as the Hotel Midtown, New York Institute of Technology). 1904, by Mulliken & Moeller; rebuilt 1964, by Horace Ginsbern & Associates. [12 stories] A flat, dull, glass box in its current incarnation.

American Circle Building, 1946. GRAY.

E   GULF & WESTERN BUILDING, No. 1824-50

(Also known as 15 Columbus Circle, Paramount Communications Building). 1970, by Thomas E. Stanley. [44 stories] The gateway to the Upper West Side and Central Park West was marred by this 679-foot, black-and-silver striped shaft that is too tall, misshapen for its site, and wholly out of context. *Site of* American Circle Building; Durland's Riding Academy.

PARAMOUNT THEATER

1970, by Carson, Ludin & Shaw. [532 seats]

61st STREET

W   AMERICAN BIBLE SOCIETY BUILDING, No. 1865

1966, by Skidmore, Owings & Merrill. [12 stories] The deeply recessed horizontal window bays create a pattern like a titanic ladder back. *Site of* Packard Motor Car Showroom, 1906, by Albert Kahn.

CHEQUERS, No. 1871-77

1988-89, by Eli Attia. [25 stories] A pleasantly cool composition in charcoal-gray brick, its sawtooth tower rises from a base that is flush to the street wall.

CINEPLEX ODEON 62nd AND BROADWAY THEATER

1989. [300 seats]

well as transients, and, along with the Marie Antoinette, its restaurants achieved "gastronomic name and fame" in the 1890s.[11]

Seeking to divorce themselves from the sleepy connotations of the "Boulevard," property owners petitioned successfully in 1898 to have the street's name changed to Broadway.[12] Adorning this increasingly important thoroughfare were three major monuments sponsored by Carlo Barsotti, founder, editor, and publisher of *Il Progresso Italo-Americano*, the largest Italian newspaper in America. On the 400th anniversary of Columbus's voyage, the Columbus Monument was dedicated at the Circle, which was subsequently known by the explorer's name. Barsotti then led campaigns for the Verdi monument, at Seventy-fourth Street, which was dedicated in 1906, and the Dante monument, in Empire Park, which was unveiled in 1921.[13]

Arts and culture of one kind or another shaped the district throughout the twentieth century. Early on, a theater center grew up around Columbus Circle. In 1903, the Majestic Theater opened on the south side of the Circle, with *The Wizard of Oz*. It was followed by the Colonial, at Sixty-second Street; the Circle, at Sixtieth Street; and the Lincoln Square, at Sixty-fifth Street. Only the Colonial remained in the business of live productions for long. It was one of New York's most popular vaudeville houses and the setting in 1910 for Charles Chaplin's American debut, in a sketch called *The Wow-Wows*. ("Chaplin will do all right for America," was *Variety*'s opinion.[14]) Together with the theaters were the studio buildings that gave Lincoln Square a reputation as the chief artistic center in upper Manhattan. Foremost was the Lincoln Arcade, between Sixty-fifth and Sixty-sixth streets. Robert Henri's School of Art assembled there in 1909, with such students as Stuart Davis, Edward Hopper, and Rockwell Kent. George Bellows had a studio down the hall, which he shared with Eugene O'Neill. After a fire in 1931,

Hotel Welden, 1982; Hotel Marie Antoinette, ca. 1910. DWD, NYHS.

AN ITALIAN INFLUENCE

Christopher Columbus *overlooking Columbus Circle,
1979;* Dante Alighieri *in Dante Park, 1987.*

Technology Institute, Bible Society, and Chequers, 1988.

E   VACANT LOT, No. 1860

Site of 1860 Broadway, 1927, by Emery Roth.

62nd STREET

W   ONE HARKNESS PLAZA, No. 1887

1978, by Philip Birnbaum. [27 stories] With its silvery skin and pale green windows, this façade is a notch above standard "luxury" tower design, but the enclosed arcade is cold, uninviting, and little used. *Site of* Colonial Theater (also known as Hampden's Theater, Harkness Theater), 1904-05, by George Keister or John B. McElfatrick; remodeled 1972-73, by John J. McNamara.

EMPIRE HOTEL, No. 1889-95

1922, by Frederic I. Merrick. [13 stories] This plain, red-brick box is identifiable on the skyline by an enormous, anachronistic, neon rooftop sign. *Site of* the first Empire Hotel.

American Bible Society and 30 Lincoln Plaza, 1980.

E   30 LINCOLN PLAZA, No. 1884-96

1978, by Philip Birnbaum. [33 stories] Above a large base enclosing a sidewalk arcade is a huge, undulating wall of buff brick. The structure wraps around a much-used plaza, which features an attractive waterfall, meandering pool, and a well-tended lawn.

Lincoln Arcade, ca. 1948. GRAY.

the arcade was rebuilt and counted Alexander Archipenko and Thomas Hart Benton among its tenants.[15]

Like theaters and hotels, car dealerships moved up from the Forties and Fifties, until Automobile Row reached Seventieth Street in 1907, with the Winton Motor Company showroom.[16] That year, a rather elegant auto showroom and bank took the place of the Bloomingdale church at Sixty-Eighth Street. Also in 1907, the Goelet Garage opened at Sixty-fourth Street. Exceptionally handsome for its utilitarian purpose, it was later remodeled as the home of Bernarr MacFadden's publications.[17]

By far the most dominant force around Columbus Circle in the early twentieth century was William Randolph Hearst, publisher of the *Journal* and *American*, who hoped to turn the Circle into "Hearst Plaza," the hub of New York. His first acquisition, in 1895, was the old Virginia Hotel on Fifty-ninth Street, which served as offices for the *Journal*. Plans were drawn in 1904 showing a forty-story tower on that site for the *New York American* (the renamed *Morning Journal*), with a 555-foot-high clock tower. Nothing came of that scheme, but a little more than a decade later, Hearst began the American Circle Building on the site of Durland's Riding Academy. It was to have had thirty stories, but wartime steel shortages limited it to two floors. Within it was a mysterious chamber that did not come to light until the building's demolition in 1966: a "cameo Gothic cathedral," with vaulted ceilings, pointed arches, delicate stonework, and opulent chandeliers. There was spec-

GOELET GARAGE

Views from 1987 and 1988.

LINCOLN PLAZA CINEMAS
1981, by Drew Eberson. [3 theaters with 595 seats]

63rd STREET

w   EMPIRE PARK
(Also known as Dante Park). [0.14 acres] Statue of
Dante Alighieri by Ettore Ximenes (pedestal by
Warren & Wetmore).

LINCOLN CENTER FOR THE PERFORMING ARTS
1959-69, by Max Abramovitz, Pietro Belluschi,
Gordon Bunshaft, Wallace K. Harrison, Philip
Johnson, and Eero Saarinen.

Metropolitan Opera House, 1988.

METROPOLITAN OPERA HOUSE
1966, by Wallace K. Harrison. [3,788 seats] Its five
grand travertine and glass arches make this the most
recognizable of the Lincoln Center buildings. Foyer
paintings, *Le Triomphe de la Musique* and *Les
Sources de la Musique*, by Marc Chagall.

Philharmonic Hall, 1980.

PHILHARMONIC HALL, No. 1931-39
(Also known as Avery Fisher Hall). 1962, by Max
Abramovitz; rebuilt 1976, by Philip Johnson and John
Burgee, with Cyril Harris, acoustical engineer. [2,742
seats] Tapering, travertine-clad columns and broad
expanses of glass wrap around the auditorium house.

Winton Motor Carriage Garage, 1985.

ulation that Hearst built it as a private chapel for his mistress, the actress
Marion Davies.[18]

Ultimately, Hearst's most enduring contribution to the Circle was the
National Maine Monument, which started with a *Journal*-sponsored fundrais-
ing drive almost as soon as the battleship *Maine* was blown up in Havana
Harbor in 1898. The monument was designed for the prominent triangle on
Broadway between Forty-sixth and Forty-seventh streets, but a clerical
"oversight"—perhaps encouraged by Tammany leaders who had no use for
Hearst—foreclosed that site.[19] It was not until 1913 that the monument was
completed at the southwest corner of Central Park.

Despite Hearst's efforts as a developer, Columbus Circle and its environs

Colonial Bank at 68th Street, which also served as an automobile showroom, 1985.

NATIONAL MAINE MONUMENT
Views from 1981.

The curtain wall is deeply recessed at front, creating a vast loggia. Foyer sculpture, *Orpheus and Apollo*, by Richard Lippold. **Site of** Miller Building and Arcade Theater (also known as the Amsterdam Theater, New Comedy), 1913-14; Lincoln Square Court.

Juilliard School of Music, 1978.

JUILLIARD SCHOOL OF MUSIC, No. 1941-53

1968-69, by Pietro Belluschi, with Eduardo Catalano and Westermann & Miller. [5 stories] This horizontal travertine slab, punctured by a variety of windows, floats over Broadway at an oblique angle to the street. Plaza sculpture, *Three Times Three Interplay*, by Yaacov Agam. **Site of** Lincoln Square Arcade, ca. 1932; Lincoln Square Arcade (also known as the Broadway Arcade, Lincoln Arcade) and Lincoln Square Theater (also known as the Lincoln Theater), 1906 by John B. McElfatrick.

ALICE TULLY HALL

1968-69, by Pietro Belluschi, with Eduardo Catalano and Westermann & Miller. [1,096 seats] The entrance is tucked under a broad exterior stairway and elevated plaza.

E ONE LINCOLN PLAZA, No. 1900-16

(Also known as the ASCAP Building). 1971-72, by Philip Birnbaum. [42 stories] A dreadfully massive, broadly V-shaped skyscraper, with alternating tan and brown bays, rises from a large angular base with a sidewalk arcade.

64th STREET

E GOELET GARAGE, No. 1920-32

(Also known as the Lincoln Square Garage, MacFadden Building). 1906-07, by Frank M. Andrews. [6 stories] In this unusually handsome white-brick façade, generously horizontal window bays are topped by big broken pediments. Each spandrel panel is framed by brackets and ornamented with a garland-encrusted medallion.

Gotham National Bank Building, 1943. GRAY.

remained stubbornly resistant to progress. Except for the Gotham National Bank tower on the Circle and the new Empire Hotel, almost nothing of note was built during the 1920s and 1930s. Perhaps the most celebrated event in the period occurred in 1926 at the Hotel Welden, which had been converted to the Frank E. Campbell Funeral Chapel. Thousands of mourners had come to see the body of Rudolph Valentino and could not fit into the small chapel. A riot erupted, which the *Times* said was unprecedented for the number of people involved. Mounted police charged the crowd, "while women shrieked and yelled in terror and tried to scramble away from the horses' hoofs."[20]

One grand scheme for the neighborhood was something called the Palais de France, a sixty-five-story hotel, office building, exhibition hall, and French consular center, between Sixty-second and Sixty-third streets. This was overtaken almost as soon as it was announced by the 1929 stock market crash.[21] It was not until after World War II that two huge projects materialized, under Robert Moses, head of the Mayor's Slum Clearance Committee and the Triborough Bridge and Tunnel Authority. The Columbus Circle ur-

NEW YORK COLISEUM

Views from 1986 include two of the seals by Paul Manship: New York City (top right) and the Triborough Bridge and Tunnel Authority (bottom right).

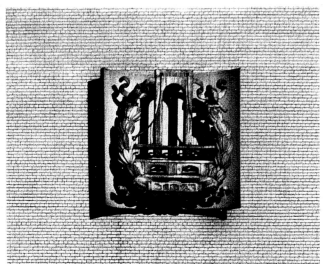

65th STREET

E LINCOLN SQUARE

(Also known as Richard Tucker Park). [0.05 acres] Within it is a bust of *Richard Tucker*, by Milton Hebald.

66th STREET

W EMPIRE BUILDING, No. 1965

1963, by H.I. Feldman. [5 stories] A silvery glass-and-metal box. *Site of* Hotel Marie Antoinette, 1895, by Julius Munckowitz, expanded 1902-03, by C.P.H. Gilbert (new wing also known as the Hotel Dauphin).

E COLONIAL BANK, No. 1960

(Also known as Bankers Trust Company, Bank Leumi). 1898, by Alfred H. Taylor; rebuilt 1962, by Oppenheimer, Brady & Lehrecke. [2 stories] Still visible at the edge of this cool, silver-and-black International Style box are remnants of the original façade including a pilaster with a foliate capital.

LINCOLN SQUARE BUILDING, No. 1966-68

1906, by Louis C. Maurer. [4 stories] A large cornice rises from two-story brick pilasters.

CINEMA STUDIO THEATER

Divided in 1979. [560 seats]

Hotel Welden and Lincoln Square Building, 1985.

VACANT LOT, No. 1972

Site of Hotel Welden (also known as the Campbell Funeral Chapel, Gutterman's Funeral Home, Hotel Tecumseh), 1890-92, by McKim, Mead & White.

SIMPSON BUILDING, No. 1974-78

1890. [4 stories] Arched windows and a deep cornice mark this chamfer-cornered brick building.

ban renewal area was created in 1951 and Moses built the nine-acre New York Coliseum exhibition hall, which extended from Fifty-eighth to Sixtieth Street. Opening in 1956 with three simultaneous shows—automobile, photographic, and philatelic—it was called "one of the wonders of the modern world" by Mayor Robert F. Wagner and drew 125,000 visitors on its first day.[22] The Coliseum sowed the seeds of gigantism, of Moses's "vision of a reborn West Side, marching north" into Lincoln Square, a blighted area inhabited by some 5,400 families.[23]

In the mid-1950s, Moses began talking with the architect Wallace K. Harrison about building an opera house between Sixty-third and Sixty-fourth streets, as part of the Lincoln Square urban renewal effort. The notion was well received by Charles M. Spofford, chairman of the Metropolitan Opera's executive committee, who had been championing a new house for some time. In 1955, the slum-clearance project was formally announced and the Met chose to make its move. Later that year, the New York Philharmonic also decided to relocate to Lincoln Square, having been told that its old home, Carnegie Hall, was going to be torn down. Under John D. Rockefeller III, Lincoln Center for the Performing Arts was formally established in 1956. Two years later, the design team—"six poets trying to write a poem," as Philip Johnson recalled it—began its work.[24] There were many passionate protests over the social and economic dislocations caused by the project, but Moses prevailed. In 1959, ground was broken by President Dwight D. Eisenhower.

Philharmonic Hall on Broadway, designed by Max Abramovitz, was the first of the buildings to open. At its debut, in 1962, Leonard Bernstein conducted the orchestra. Lincoln Center was the first true home for the 120-year-old Philharmonic, which had always been a tenant in its other quarters, beginning in 1842 at the Apollo Rooms on lower Broadway. Unhappily, the sound in its new hall was inconsistent, thin, harsh, and unnatural, not at all helped by acoustical baffles that were hung like clouds from the ceiling.[25] The interior was rebuilt in 1969 and the acoustical "clouds" removed, but the auditorium needed a further, radical alteration in 1976. Much of the funding for this came from Avery Fisher, who had made a fortune in high-fidelity components.

The Metropolitan Opera House, designed by Harrison, opened in 1966 with the world premier of Samuel Barber's *Antony and Cleopatra*, starring Leontyne Price and Justino Diaz. In attendance were 3,800 "tycoons, aristocrats, nabobs, bankers, moguls, potentates, fashion plates, grande dames and other assorted Great Society over-achievers," including Vanderbilts and Whitneys, descendants of the families who built the first Met.[26] Architecturally, the auditorium's gold-and-red conservatism disappointed critics, but Rudolf Bing, the general manager said: "The bulk of opera is nineteenth century. To put these works in an ultra-modern setting would be like mounting an old master in a new frame."[27]

Lincoln Center's final Broadway structure was built for the Juilliard School, which moved in 1969 from 122nd Street. Designed by Pietro Bel-

LINCOLN CENTER FOR THE PERFORMING ARTS
View from 1986.

PHILHARMONIC HALL
Views from 1988.

METROPOLITAN OPERA HOUSE
Views from 1988. DD, MET (right, facing page).

JUILLIARD SCHOOL OF MUSIC
View from 1986.

American Bible Society (left), One Harkness Plaza (right), 1987.

luschi, the building had a large auditorium, recital hall, drama workshop theater, and eighty-five practice rooms, which *Architectural Record* said were "fitted together with a sorcerer's skill in an arrangement as intricate as a Chinese puzzle."[28] It was, the *Times* marveled, the "Taj Mahal of conservatories, opulent, beautiful, and domineering—and big."[29] Within its complex shell was an independent theater on Broadway, Alice Tully Hall, a serene and tranquil auditorium that opened in 1969 and is the home of the Chamber Music Society of Lincoln Center, as well as the annual New York Film Festival.

There were other cultural enterprises along Broadway. The Gallery of Modern Art on Columbus Circle was designed by Edward Durell Stone for Huntington Hartford, heir to the A. & P. supermarket fortune, to house his "anti-abstract" and "anti-contemporary" collection. When it opened in 1964, its strangely filigreed façade and opulent interiors (including a Polynesian restaurant called the Gauguin Room) drew as much notice as the paintings.[30] After eleven years, the gallery closed, and the building is now headquarters of the city's Department of Cultural Affairs. The Colonial Theater was transformed in 1973 into the Harkness Theater, the first in the city devoted exclusively to dance, under the direction of the wealthy ballet patron, Rebekah Harkness.[31] It only lasted three years, but the Ballet Shop, in the Empire Hotel next door, is still in business.

Lincoln Center spurred corporate and institutional development, as well.

67th STREET

W 1981-87 BROADWAY

(Also known as 159-65 Boulevard). 1876 [4 stories] The buildings in this row are among the oldest existing structures on upper Broadway, distinguished by their strong unifying cornices and overall simplicity.

ALDEN THEATER

(Also known as the Regency Theater). 1933-34, by Leonard S. Henry; remodeled 1987, by David K. Mesbur and Peter Kofman. [450 seats]

THE BEL CANTO, No. 1991

1986-87, by John Harding. [26 stories] This thin, red-brick tower has chamfer-cut porches and a seven-story street wall enclosing a well-trafficked indoor public plaza.

1995 BROADWAY

1974, by Liebman & Liebman. [18 stories] A small, dark brown, steel-and-glass tower.

E ANSONIA POSTAL STATION, No. 1980-98

1955, by H.I. Feldman. [4 stories] A sprawling, white-brick structure. *Site of* Armory of the Twenty-Second Regiment, 1888-91, by Capt. John P. Leo.

68th STREET

W DORCHESTER TOWERS, No. 2001

1964-65, by S.J. Kessler & Sons. [20 and 34 stories] The impact of this white-brick building's huge volume is mitigated somewhat by the fact that most of the bulk was placed on the Amsterdam Avenue frontage.

The Copley under construction, 1986.

E THE COPLEY, No. 2000-10

1985-87, by Davis Brody & Associates. [29 stories] Soft-edged and handsome, if not too contextual, this

COLUMBUS CIRCLE

Views from 1979 to 1988 show the base of the Columbus Memorial and the top of the National Maine Monument (this page), the Gulf & Western Building, and the Columbus Memorial fountain.

Colonial Bank at 68th Street, 1979.

tower has ridged ribbons of buff brick alternating with gray window bands. ***Site of*** Colonial Bank, 1907 by Hoppin & Koen; Bloomingdale Reformed Dutch Church, 1884-85 by S.B. Reed; Bloomingdale Reformed Dutch Church and Cemetery, 1814-16.

Spencer Arms Hotel, 1988.

SPENCER ARMS HOTEL, No. 2016

(Also known as the Lincoln Plaza Hotel). 1903-07, by Mulliken & Moeller. [12 stories] Ornate, elegant, and elaborate, this building's red-brick façade is enveloped in decorative masonry trim and its six-story projecting bays are enhanced by gorgeous copper spandrel panels.

In 1966, the 150-year-old American Bible Society moved to new headquarters at Sixty-first Street, from which it continues to direct the distribution of Scripture worldwide. The Gulf & Western conglomerate (now Paramount Communications) consolidated its operations in 1970 at 15 Columbus Circle, a huge tower with an unusual subterranean movie theater, the Paramount, which is reached through a giant kiosk on Broadway. The American Society of Composers, Authors, and Publishers moved to One Lincoln Plaza, across from the Met, in the early 1970s. And the ABC television network, whose studios were scattered through the neighborhood, took over the old Winton showroom at Seventieth Street.

Lincoln Center also had a major effect on residential real estate, as did the developers Paul and Seymour Milstein, who built three enormous apartment buildings on Broadway with nearly 2,000 units among them. Dorchester Towers, extending from Sixty-eighth to Sixty-ninth Street, was constructed in 1964. Seven years later came One Lincoln Plaza, from Sixty-third to Sixty-fourth Street, which was so much larger than zoning rules allowed that the chairman of the City Planning Commission sued another government body for granting the variance. The Milsteins won that case and went on to build Thirty Lincoln Plaza, between Sixty-second and Sixty-third streets, despite planning commissioners' objections to its "alarming" density.[32] Across the street, the Harkness Theater was torn down to make way for One Harkness Plaza, an apartment tower that was completed in 1978. This was followed by the Copley condominium, on the site of the Bloomingdale church and graveyard; the Bel Canto, between Sixty-seventh and Sixty-eighth streets; Cheq-

30 Lincoln Plaza (left) and One Lincoln Plaza, seen from the courtyard side, 1980.

69th STREET

Nevada Towers (left) and One Sherman Square, 1979.

W **NEVADA TOWERS, No. 2021-35**

1977, by Philip Birnbaum. [28 stories] A strange, striped brown-brick polygonal tower. *Site of* the Nevada; Bloomingdale Reformed Dutch Church, ca. 1805.

Detail of the Seminole, 1979; the Ormonde, 1988.

E **THE SEMINOLE, No. 2020**

1895-96, by Ware & Styne-Harde. [7 stories] This building and the neighboring Ormonde form a lovely, orange-and-white ensemble. The two façades are tied together by decorative courses, arched windows, and pediments on small Ionic columns at the fifth story. Two lions guard the Seminole's entrance.

THE ORMONDE, No. 2022-30

(Also known as the Embassy Hotel, Embassy Tower). 1899-1900, by Robert Maynicke; enlarged 1908. [12 stories] It rises five stories higher than the Seminole and turns the corner with a major turret. There is a two-story arcade at the top and an ample cornice.

The Copley, 1988.

uers, at Sixty-second Street; and the Coronado, on the site of the Winton showroom.

A quarter century of intense development led to a tremendous showdown at the end of the 1980s over a plan to replace the Coliseum with a two-towered office, apartment, and shopping complex called Columbus Center, developed by Mortimer B. Zuckerman. Critics, led by the Municipal Art Society, captured the public imagination with the specter of the building's shadow falling in a huge swath over Central Park. In court, they argued that the city had

70th STREET

W   SHERMAN SQUARE (WAR MEMORIAL)
[Traffic triangle]

Sherman Square Hotel, 1953. GRAY.

ONE SHERMAN SQUARE, No. 2039-49

1971, by S.J. Kessler. [42 stories] Colossally out of
scale and character with the neighborhood, this
yellow and tan brick behemoth has almost 150
balconies over Broadway. *Site of* Sherman Square
Hotel; Jacob Harsen homestead.

The Coronado, 1990.

E   THE CORONADO, No. 2040-52

1988-90, by Schuman, Lichtenstein, Claman &
Efron. [21 stories] The turreted corner of this
contextual red-brick tower echoes that of the
Ormonde across the street, and its setback massing
complements the Alamac next door. *Site of* Winton
Motor Carriage Garage (also known as ABC Studios,
Studebaker Garage), 1906 by Charles A. Reid.

ALAMAC HOTEL, No. 2054-62

1922-25, by Maynicke & Franke. [19 stories] A
plain, dark-brown brick façade is topped by an
ornamented pavilion projecting from the setbacks of
the upper floors. *Site of* Church of the Blessed
Sacrament school.

Rendering of the revised proposal for Columbus Center, by Skidmore, Owings & Merrill.

effectively and improperly required the project to be twenty percent bigger
than zoning allowed. The opponents' legal victory in 1987 spelled the end to
a 925-foot-high scheme by the architect Moshe Safdie. In 1989, Zuckerman
unveiled a 752-foot-high plan by Skidmore, Owings & Merrill, which received
a qualified endorsement from some—but not all—of the original opponents to
the project.[33] Elsewhere along Broadway, even after the real-estate market
started unraveling in the late 1980s, several blocks looked like prime construction sites, as they were either vacant or filled with three-, four-, and
five-story buildings. It appeared that community-versus-developer battles
over the future of Lincoln Square were far from over.

*A night view toward Broadway from Lincoln Center in
1988, across the reflecting pool and the* Reclining Figure
by Henry Moore, with Philharmonic Hall at left.

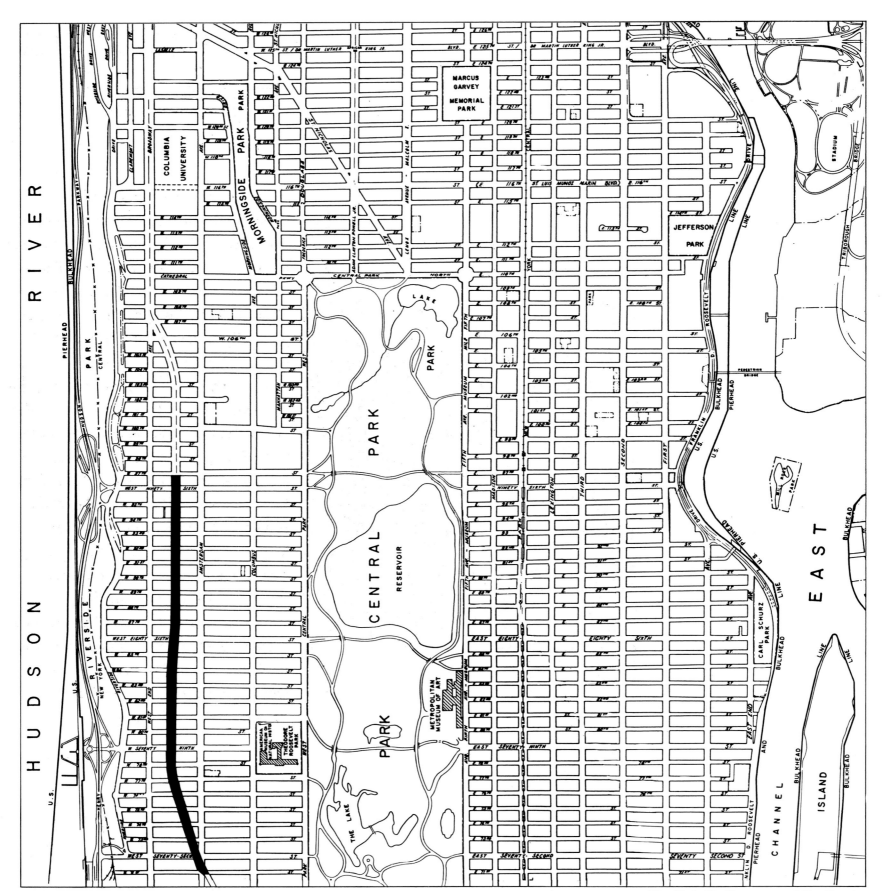

New York City Department of City Planning

UPPER WEST SIDE

SEVENTY-FIRST STREET TO NINETY-SEVENTH STREET

Hotel Euclid Hall, 1985.

Broadway becomes an imposing residential boulevard north of Seventy-first Street, shabby and madcap in some places, quite stately in others. This is the core of the Upper West Side, although that designation is now used generally to mean anything west of Central Park. Giving Broadway its primary aesthetic identity are the great apartment hotels that were built before World War I, with designs borrowed from Paris, Florence, or Vienna, and translated into a peculiarly New York form and scale. There are also plain brown-brick boxes from the 1920s, larger red-brick boxes from the 1980s, and an odd lot of small commercial buildings. Despite its density, Broadway maintains a civilized feeling, thanks to its generous dimension, the uniformity of its building line, its shifting axis, and to the chain of greenery along its spine.

The thoroughfare that is now Broadway was the main artery of this district from the beginning. The Bloomingdale Road was opened in 1703 as far as Nicholas De Peyster's barn, approximately at 115th Street. Broadway follows the course of the old country highway until Eighty-seventh Street, at which point the ancient roadbed veers easterly and travels between Broadway and Amsterdam Avenue. (Its course is still discernible in some places, like the angled alleyway, about eight feet below grade, that runs north from Ninety-seventh Street, taking an oblique slice out of the Borchardt apartment house.)

Besides being the name of the district and the highway, Bloomingdale was also the name of Etienne De Lancey's 300-acre upper farm, which ran from Seventy-eighth to Eighty-ninth Street. His "Country House at Bloomendall," mentioned as early as 1729, may have been located approximately where the Apthorp apartment building stands today.[1] De Lancey's property ended up in the hands of Charles Ward Apthorp, who already owned a large farm from Eighty-ninth to Ninety-sixth Street. Apthorp's daughter, Charlotte, married John Cornelius Vanden Heuvel, the former Dutch governor of Guyana, who built a country estate on his father-in-law's land in about 1792.[2] The mansion, between Seventy-eighth and Seventy-ninth streets, "was remarkable for its magnificence among the many beautiful places" in the area. Its ample and handsome porch had four columns of white cedar that had grown on the property.[3]

Directly south of the De Lancey estate was the farm of Teunis Somarindyck. In the late 1700s, three decades before he became king of the French, Louis Philippe, the exiled duc d'Orléans, was said to have taught school in the Somarindyck house, near Seventy-fifth Street.[4] Six hundred feet to the south was the country villa "Chevilly," where Madame d'Auliffe, who had been *dame d'honneur* to Marie Antoinette, entertained other refugees from the Reign of Terror.[5]

In the early nineteenth century, the district gained a reputation as a pleasant and healthful suburban retreat. The Vanden Heuvel estate was converted by William Burnham to a resort called the Mansion House in 1831. "The rear grounds and gravelled walk to the Hudson River, skirted on either

Vanden Heuvel Mansion, subway kiosk (left), and First Baptist Church (right). NYHS.

View south in 1979 includes the Colorado, Hotel Belleclaire, 233 West 77th Street, and the Apthorp.

71st STREET

72nd STREET I.R.T. CONTROL HOUSE AND STATION
1904, by Heins & LaFarge; interior rebuilt 1989. Interior Landmark. [1 story]

Capitals of Christ Church and Lester Building, 1983.

W **LESTER BUILDING, No. 2061-65**
1925, by Very, Brown & Behr. [8 stories] *Site of* Christ Church, 1889-91 by Charles Coolidge Haight.

2067 BROADWAY
1922, by Rosario Candela. [7 stories]

COLONIAL CLUB, No. 2069
(Also known as the Lincoln Trust Building). 1890-94, by Henry F. Kilburn. [6 stories]

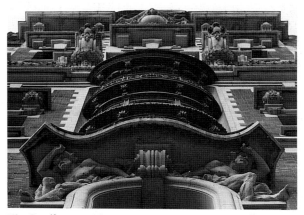

The Dorilton, 1982.

E **THE DORILTON, No. 2068**
1900-02, by Janes & Leo. Landmark. [12 stories]

2080-94 BROADWAY
1938, by Arthur Weiser. [2 stories]

72nd STREET

Embassy Theater Building, 1986.

w THE ALEXANDRIA, No. 2081-89

1989-90, by Frank Williams & Associates and
Skidmore, Owings & Merrill. [25 stories] **Site of**
Embassy Theater Building and Embassy Seventy-
second Street Twin Theater, 1938, by Peter
Copeland and Schwartz & Gross; Hotel St. Andrew,
1893 by Andrew Craig.

WOOD DOLSON BUILDING, No. 2091

1922, by F. & A. Ware and John D. Boyd.
[3 stories]

RUTGERS BUILDING, No. 2095-99

1924-26, by Henry Otis Chapman. [5 stories] **Site of**
Rutgers Riverside Presbyterian Church, 1889-90, by
R.H. Robertson; Rutgers Presbyterian Chapel,
1888.

Giuseppe Verdi and the Central Savings Bank, 1979.

E VERDI SQUARE

(Also known as Sherman Square, Needle Park).
Scenic Landmark. [0.05 acres] Monument to
Giuseppe Verdi, with statues of *Aida*, *Falstaff*,
Otello, and *Leonora*, by Pasquale Civiletti.

Dr. Valentine Mott summer house, 1853. NYHS.

side by forest trees, &c. make it fascinating," a contemporary writer declared, and on summer afternoons, women and children sauntered leisurely
through the verdant acreage.[6] Dr. Valentine Mott, head of New York University's Medical College on lower Broadway and one of the foremost physicians
and surgeons of his day, built a Greek Revival summer house near Ninety-
third Street in 1835, its overscaled porch framed by huge Ionic columns.[7]
Edgar Allan Poe and his wife, Virginia, spent the summers of 1844 and 1845
in the Brennan cottage, near Eighty-fourth Street. There, Poe wrote *The
Raven.*[8]

Bloomingdale in 1851 was a "remarkably neat village [that] consists
chiefly of country seats, and contains some 400 inhabitants."[9] A ride along
the Bloomingdale Road was a pleasure—"the country on either side of it was
so fresh and rural, the houses so charming, whether they were the villas of
millionaires or quiet two story cottages"—and it afforded lovely glimpses of
the Hudson, "sometimes at the foot of a narrow lane, where the water was
but a point of lightness closing the vista, sometimes a broad expanse showing
a large and noble view of the grand river."[10] One of the favorite destinations
of visitors to Bloomingdale was the Kelly villa at Seventy-fifth Street, near
the old Somarindyck house, where many dances and lawn parties were held.[11]

The end of this suburban period was heralded by the widening of the
road into the Boulevard, beginning in 1868, which transformed the country
highway into something more urban, lined with livery and boarding stables,
greenhouses and gardens, shanties and saloons. William Backhouse Astor,
the son of John Jacob Astor, picked up a large tract of land along the road at
a farm auction in 1860, and the family went on to acquire the Vanden Heuvel
property in 1879 and the Kelly property in 1884.[12] The Astors did not build
on them for another twenty years, however.

Before the century turned, churches were, by far, the most prominent
buildings on the Boulevard. In 1889, Christ Church was under construction
at Seventy-first Street. This was a new home for the city's oldest independent

Kelly family villa at 75th Street, 1896. NYHS.

Episcopal congregation, which had been on Fifth Avenue. At Seventy-third Street, the Rutgers Riverside Presbyterian Church, by R.H. Robertson, was also under construction in 1889. This congregation—named for its benefactor, Colonel Henry Rutgers, and in existence since 1798—moved uptown from Madison Avenue. The First Baptist Church, at Seventy-ninth Street, opened in 1893, after the congregation—already 148 years old and known as the "Mother of Churches"—moved from Park Avenue.[13] Other houses of worship nearby were the Roman Catholic Church of the Blessed Sacrament, at Seventy-first Street; the Manhattan Congregational Church, at Seventy-sixth Street; and the Evangelical Lutheran Church of the Advent, at Ninety-third Street, which is still standing, as is the First Baptist.

On the social front in the 1890s, the Hotel St. Andrew, at Seventy-second

Colonial Club, 1986.

73rd STREET

Rutgers Church (left) and the Ansonia Hotel. MCNY.

w **ANSONIA HOTEL, No. 2101-15**
1899-1904, by Paul E.M. Duboy. Landmark.
[17 stories]

Central Savings Bank, 1979.

E **CENTRAL SAVINGS BANK, No. 2100-14**
(Also known as the Apple Bank for Savings, Harlem Savings Bank). 1926-28, by York & Sawyer; ironwork by Samuel Yellin. Landmark. [6 stories]

74th STREET

w **2121-27 BROADWAY**
1907. [4 stories]

2131 BROADWAY
1929, by Charles E. Birge. [2 stories]

THE ELDORADO, No. 2135-37
(Also known as 307-09 Boulevard). ca. 1887.
[5 stories]

E **HOTEL KIMBERLEY, No. 2120-22**
(Also known as the Fitzgerald). 1921, by Sugarman & Hess and William E. Bloodgood. [15 stories]

EARLY CHURCHES

Views of First Baptist Church from 1986 and 1988 (left and bottom right); Christ Church in 1911. DD, NYHS.

Street, boasted the Versailles Garden Grill and the Art Den. Across the street, the Colonial Club opened its new home in 1894. The clubhouse, which is still standing, had a billiard room, ballroom, and main dining room overlooking the Boulevard, with a smoking room, library, and women's dining room in the turreted corner, plus bowling alleys in the basement. Founded in 1889 to preserve colonial relics and memories, the club's most significant feature may have been that some rooms were open at all times to the wives and daughters of members—a liberal innovation for the period.[14]

In 1897, the Board of Rapid Transit Railroad Commissioners proposed a subway plan that carried profound implications for Broadway. Because it came at a time when the middle class had reconciled itself to apartment life, the subway almost preordained large-scale construction.[15] The railroad was to have stations for express and local trains at Seventy-second and Ninety-sixth streets, with three smaller local stations at Seventy-ninth, Eighty-sixth, and Ninety-first streets.[16] The location of the earliest apartment houses was an above-ground reflection of the subterranean station layout, for the largest buildings tended to be closest to subway stops: the Dorilton and Ansonia near Seventy-second Street, the Apthorp at Seventy-ninth Street, the Bretton Hall and Belnord at Eighty-sixth Street.

The first of these apartment buildings was also the grandest and most delirious: the Ansonia Hotel, extending from Seventy-third to Seventy-fourth Street, which was begun in 1899. Because of subtle course changes in the road, the Ansonia is visible for a great distance, looking, Saul Bellow wrote in *Seize the Day*, "like a baroque palace from Prague or Munich enlarged a hundred times, with towers, domes, huge swells and bubbles of metal gone green from exposure, iron fretwork and festoons."[17] The architect was Paul E.M. Duboy and the developer was William Earl Dodge Stokes. Their creation was a musical, theatrical place. Its more than 300 suites had virtually soundproof walls (perfect for rehearsing), its restaurant featured dancing every night, and its café had a string orchestra. Tenants and guests included Leopold Auer, Billie Burke and Florenz Ziegfeld, Feodor Chaliapin, Mischa Elman, Giulio Gatti-Casazza, Moss Hart, Sol Hurok, Lauritz Melchior, Yehudi Menuhin, Ezio Pinza, Zasu Pitts, Lily Pons, Igor Stravinsky, and Arturo Toscanini. Many years later, in designating the Ansonia a landmark, the city found that its Beaux-Arts exterior "has a joyous quality befitting its musical associations" and that it "continues to provide a vital service to the music world."[18]

Another madly overblown Beaux-Arts composition was the Dorilton, at Seventy-first Street, begun in 1900 to designs by Janes & Leo. "The sight of it makes strong men swear and weak women shrink affrighted," the *Architectural Record* commented.[19] (It is now, deservedly, an official landmark.) Marble, bronze, and leaded glass decorated the main hall, in the style of Louis XVI. There were four apartments to a floor, containing five to nine rooms. The dining rooms had beamed ceilings and wainscoting, the conservatories had glass doors, the bathrooms were paneled in mirrors, and the kitchens had refrigerators. Electricity was "furnished free at all hours."[20]

BEACON HOTEL, No. 2124-34

1927-29, by Walter W. Ahlschlager. [24 stories] *Site of* the St. Helene, 1901, by John H. Duncan; Dakota Stables.

BEACON THEATER

1927-29, by Walter W. Ahlschlager; interiors by Rambusch Studios; murals by Valdemar Kjoldgaard; organ by Wurlitzer. Interior Landmark. [2,660 seats]

75th STREET

W **THE ASTOR APARTMENTS, No. 2141-57**

1902, by Clinton & Russell; expanded 1913, by Peabody, Wilson & Brown. [8 and 12 stories] *Site of* the Kelly villa; Teunis Somarindyck house.

E **MAJESTIC TOWERS, No. 2140-46**

1924, by Schwartz & Gross. [15 stories]

AEON GARAGE, No. 2148-56

1914, by Walter Haefell. [5 stories]

76th STREET

W **THE COLORADO, No. 2161-69**

1925, by Robert T. Lyons. [15 stories]

Hotel Belleclaire, 1986; Manhattan Towers Hotel, 1979.

HOTEL BELLECLAIRE, No. 2171

1901-03, by Emery Roth. Landmark. [10 stories]

E **SPEEDOMETER BUILDING, No. 2160**

1907, by Townsend & Oppenheimer. [4 stories]

MANHATTAN TOWERS HOTEL, No. 2162-68

(Also known as the Opera). 1928-30, by Tillion & Tillion. [24 stories] *Site of* Manhattan Congregational Church, 1900-01, by C.W. & A.A. Stoughton.

MANHATTAN CONGREGATIONAL CHURCH

(Also known as the Promenade Theater). 1928-30; remodeled in 1969. [399 seats]

ANSONIA HOTEL

Views from 1978 to 1986.

THE DORILTON
Views from 1979 to 1990.

THE WELLSMORE, No. 2170-78
(Also known as the Benjamin Franklin). 1909-11, by Janes & Leo. [12 stories]

77th STREET

w   233 WEST 77th STREET, No. 2181-89
1922, by Sugarman & Hess and A.G. Berger. [14 stories]

THE CURLEW, No. 2193-99
ca. 1892. [5 stories]

E   77th STREET MARKET, No. 2182-86
(Also known as the 77th Street Theater). 1905, by George F. Pelham; converted 1914-15, by Thomas W. Lamb; rebuilt as a supermarket. [2 stories]

2194-96 BROADWAY
1901, by M.C. Merrit. [2 stories]

78th STREET

Details of the Apthorp Apartments, 1979.

w   APTHORP APARTMENTS, No. 2201-17
1906-08, by Clinton & Russell. Landmark. [12 stories] *Site of* John Cornelius Vanden Heuvel Mansion (also known as Burnham's Hotel or Mansion House), ca. 1792; possible location of Etienne De Lancey's country home.

E   THE SANFORD and THE REXFORD, No. 2200-18
1913, by Schwartz & Gross. [12 stories]

79th STREET

79th STREET I.R.T. STATION
1904, by Heins & LaFarge. Interior Landmark.

w   FIRST BAPTIST CHURCH, No. 2221
1890-93, by George Keister.

The next significant building, begun in 1901, was the Hotel Belleclaire, at Seventy-seventh Street, a premier commission for the young architect Emery Roth. The hotel was known for its Flemish-style men's café (which had a stock-exchange ticker), its Mission-style library, its Moorish-style private dining room—and for having summarily ejected Maxim Gorky, for staying there openly with his mistress.[21] The Belleclaire's interior eclecticism was reflected in the façade, a mixture of Art Nouveau and Vienna Secession styles that is regarded today as a "fascinating stylistic anomaly," worthy of landmark status.[22]

Roth was one of several architects who transformed upper Broadway as the subway was being planned and built. His first major commission was the Saxony, which was begun in 1899 at Eighty-second Street, and he later designed the Myron Arms and the Manhill. Another active architect was Harry Mulliken, whose hotels on Broadway included the Cumberland, Spencer Arms, Thomas Jefferson, and, above all, the Bretton Hall of 1902, between Eighty-fifth and Eighty-sixth streets, which claimed to be the largest uptown hotel, with "all the comforts of New York City's *best* Hotels at one-third less price."[23] The prolific firm of Neville & Bagge, which dominated Hamilton Heights, produced some of the Upper West Side's most exuberant early hotels and apartment houses: the Hotel Bonta of 1900, at Ninety-fourth Street; the Cornwall of 1910, at Ninetieth Street; and the Roxborough of 1910, at Ninety-second Street.

The Astors began developing their local holdings in 1902, when William Waldorf Astor—the builder of the Astor Hotel and a grandson of William Backhouse Astor—commenced work on the Astor Apartments, at the site of the Somarindyck and Kelly homes. The eight-story structure was designed by Clinton & Russell, which was also responsible for the Astor Hotel. In 1906, that firm designed the Astors' single greatest building in the neighborhood:

Detail of the Hotel Belleclaire, 1979.

EARLY APARTMENT BUILDINGS AND HOTELS

Clockwise from upper left: the Saxony, 1988; the Cornwall, 1987; Hotel Bonta, 1988; Hotel Bretton Hall, 1988.

First Baptist Church, 1986 and 1988.

BROADWAY STUDIO BUILDING, No. 2231-39

(Also known as the New York School of Fine and Applied Art). 1905-06, by William W. Howe. [5 stories]

E   OLIVER A. OLSON STORE, No. 2222

ca. 1907, by George F. Pelham. [2 stories]

KRESGE'S STORE, No. 2228

1906, by George F. Pelham. [2 stories]

80th STREET

Centre Hotel, 1979.

W   CENTRE HOTEL, No. 2241-47

(Also known as 411-17 Boulevard, Hotel Brent, Calvin Apartments, Zabar's). 1882; rebuilt 1920, by B.H. & C.N. Whinston. [4 stories]

2249 BROADWAY

(Also known as 419 Boulevard, Zabar's). ca. 1890. [5 stories]

2251-59 BROADWAY

1905, by Charles Volz. [3 stories]

the Apthorp Apartments, on the Vanden Heuvel site. (William Waldorf Astor's mother, née Charlotte Augusta Gibbes, was the daughter of Susan Vanden Heuvel, whose mother was Charlotte Apthorp.[24]) Deemed an outstanding example of the Italian Renaissance style by the Landmarks Preservation Commission, the Apthorp's plan is that of a hollow square, with a central courtyard reached through portes-cochère on Broadway and West End Avenue. There are four entrances to the building, one at each corner of the court. In this layout, each landing has only two or three apartments, contributing a sense of intimacy to an otherwise vast building. Interior decorations show the qualities of the exterior—sumptuous but restrained.

The Apthorp was exceeded in size by the Belnord, which covers the block from Eighty-sixth to Eighty-seventh Street, and was begun in 1908. Although it had only 175 units, the population was more than a thousand, and it was said to be the largest apartment house in the world.[25] The Belnord was built on a hollow-square plan, with a half-acre courtyard, beneath which was a sub-courtyard illuminated by skylights and gratings. This allowed underground deliveries, out of sight of tenants and pedestrians. Another considerate aspect of the layout was that parlors, dining rooms, and kitchens were placed on the street side, while bedrooms and servants' quarters looked out on the quiet courtyard. The decorative scheme was in the style of Louis XVI, featuring wainscoting, painted woodwork, and walls covered in "harmoniously tinted" silks.[26]

The second spate of Astor development was led by Vincent Astor, who had come into a fortune at a young age after the death of his father, John Jacob Astor IV, aboard the *Titanic*. In 1914, Vincent began the Astor Court, between Eighty-ninth and Ninetieth streets, a massive building with a verdant interior yard. It was designed by Charles A. Platt, who was also the architect of the Astor Building at Broadway and Vesey Street. Vincent declared that his desire was "in every way to attempt to aid mankind" and, in 1915, he built a subsidized shopping center for the middle and lower classes, the Ninety-fifth Street Market.[27] Intended to recall a Florentine marketplace, it was wrapped by a generous arcade, under a frieze depicting cattle, sheep, pigs, chickens, ducks, fish, vegetables, and fruits.[28]

From the early twentieth century to the present, upper Broadway had so many stores, services, and diversions that one did not have to go far from home to find virtually every necessity of life, and a few indulgences, too. Frequently, commercial establishments would be grouped in two-story "taxpayers," modest structures that were not too expensive to build or operate but generated enough income to pay property taxes. One of these, between Eighty-sixth and Eighty-seventh streets, might be considered typical. Built in 1909, with a few Spanish Colonial flourishes, it endured until the mid-1980s, at which time it housed a clothier, cobbler, pharmacist, jeweler, stationer, optician, cafeteria, cookie shop, dance studio, pizza parlor, supermarket, and liquor store. In another taxpayer at Seventy-ninth Street was the neighborhood department store, Oliver A. Olson, which was described in the mid-1920s as ranking high among New York merchants.[29] Across from Olson, in

APTHORP APARTMENTS
Views from 1986 and 1988.

THE BELNORD
Exterior view from 1988; interior is undated.
DD, MCNY.

95th Street Market. MCNY.

the Broadway Studio Building at Eightieth Street, was the New York School of Fine and Applied Art, founded by Frank A. Parsons in 1896 (and now known as the Parsons School). Its design courses covered interiors, furniture, costumes, and graphics, and the school was noted for its reference library on the decorative arts.[30]

For amusement, one could find a string of vaudeville and movie theaters on Broadway, none more than five blocks away from the next. They were descended in part from the tradition of open-air shows, in which vacant Broadway lots were transformed into "retreats," featuring refreshments and a concert or movie.[31]

Between Ninety-sixth and Ninety-seventh streets, the movie pioneer William Fox (whose name endures in 20th Century-Fox) developed the single greatest theatrical complex on the Upper West Side before Lincoln Center. He began in 1911 with the "first modern house to be erected as a home for motion pictures"—the Riverside Theater, above which was a large Roof Garden.[32] These were followed three years later by the Riviera Theater and Japanese Garden, the latter being decorated in a cinematically Oriental style, with boxes in the form of pagodas and light fixtures in the form of lanterns.[33] Together, these four houses could seat more than 6,600 patrons and, like so many movie palaces, they were designed by Thomas W. Lamb.

Lamb designed the Keith's Eighty-first Street Theater, a 2,015-seat vaudeville and movie house that opened in 1913 where an open-air show had been; the Standard Theater of 1914, at Ninetieth Street; and the Loew's Eighty-third Street Theater of 1921, which was a 2,634-seat movie palace.[34] Lamb was also involved in the conversion of an old market and garage into the Seventy-seventh Street Theater in 1915. Other conversions included a Christian Science chapel at Eighty-second Street, which was remodeled as the Schuyler Theater in 1912, and a portion of the Astor market, which was remade into the Symphony Theater in 1918.

E THE HADRIAN, No. 2240-46
(Also known as the Hotel Varuna). 1902, by John H. Duncan. [10 stories]

THE BROADWAY, No. 2248-50
1986-87. [20 stories]

Keith's 81st Street Theater. GRAY.

KEITH'S 81st STREET THEATER
(Also known as CBS-TV Studio, Conran's store, Reeves Teletape Studios). 1913, by Thomas W. Lamb; murals by Arthur Brounet; rebuilt 1986-87, by Beyer Blinder Belle. [3 stories]

81st STREET

W THE FORRES, No. 2261-71
ca. 1900. [7 stories]

THE SAXONY, No. 2273-79
1899-1900, by Emery Roth. [7 stories]

E 2260-68 BROADWAY
1912, by Gaetan Ajello. [12 stories]

2270-76 Broadway, 1988.

2270-76 BROADWAY
(Also known as 438-44 Boulevard). 1885-88, by John Averit Webster. [5 stories]

82nd STREET

w LANSING BUILDING-CHRISTIAN SCIENCE CHAPEL, No. 2281-99
(Also known as the Schuyler Theater) ca. 1898; rebuilt 1912, by Harrison G. Wiseman; rebuilt as a supermarket. [2 stories]

E THE MYRON ARMS, No. 2280-84
1922, by Emery Roth. [14 stories]

THE JEROME PALACE, No. 2290-96
(Also known as the Manhill). 1923, by Emery Roth. [14 stories]

83rd STREET

w THE AMIDON, No. 2301
1892. [7 stories]

WEST SIDE REPUBLICAN CLUB, No. 2307
1897, by J.A. Schweinfurth. [3 stories]

BROADWAY FASHION BUILDING, No. 2309-15
1930-31, by Sugarman & Berger. Proposed landmark. [4 stories]

E THE BROMLEY, No. 2300-08
1986-87, by Philip Birnbaum Associates. [23 stories] *Site of* Loew's 83rd Street Theater, 1920-21, by Thomas W. Lamb.

LOEWS 84th STREET SIXPLEX, No. 2310
1984-85 by Held & Rubin. [6 theaters with 2,975 seats]

84th STREET

w THE ALAMEDA, No. 2321-27
1914, by Gaetan Ajello. [12 stories]

THE TOWERS, No. 2333-39
1920, by Gronenberg & Leuchtag. [14 stories]

E EAGLE COURT APARTMENTS, No. 2320-24
1914; rebuilt 1984, by Avinash K. Malhotra. [6 stories] *Near site of* the Brennan house (also known as the Edgar Allan Poe cottage).

85th STREET

w HOTEL EUCLID HALL, No. 2341-49
1900-02, by Hill & Turner. [7 stories]

E HOTEL BRETTON HALL, No. 2350
1902, by Harry B. Mulliken. [12 stories]

Riviera Theater, 1954. GRAY.

Escalating commercial pressure in the 1920s propelled the churches to make more lucrative use of their Broadway frontages. In 1922, the Church of the Blessed Sacrament sold its corner property, on which its school had stood, and the Hotel Alamac was built in its place.[35] Christ Church sold the Broadway portion of its sanctuary in 1925, whereupon the building was truncated, with the bell tower and the eastern part of the nave being replaced by an eight-story office building.[36] Under the Reverend Danie Russell, the Rutgers congregation leased its corner lot to a bank, which tore down the Robertson church and built a small office building on Broadway, joined to a new parish house and sanctuary in mid-block. Critics decried the "shocking mixture of church and bank," but Russell answered: "It is no more than a question of putting real estate values, which are lying idle, to work for the kingdom of God."[37] The Manhattan Congregational Church was torn down in 1928 for the Manhattan Towers Hotel, a mixed-use building that included a Congregational sanctuary in its base. The religious function was announced architecturally by a cross at the summit of the tower and large Gothic arches along the Broadway façade.

The other major mixed-use development—and, like Manhattan Towers, one of the tallest buildings in the vicinity—was the twenty-four-story Beacon Hotel and Theater, completed in 1929 at Seventy-fifth Street. Named for an airplane beacon on its roof, the hotel catered "especially to New Yorkers who favor the atmosphere of the upper Broadway section, with its many social activities, beautiful restaurants, and many high grade moving picture palaces"—one of which was under the same roof.[38] The Beacon Theater opened Christmas Eve 1929 with an overflow crowd of 3,000. The feature on screen was *Tiger Rose*, an "All Talking Sensation," but the real attraction was the auditorium itself, whose Greco-Baghdad décor was said to be "representative of New York, which has drawn to itself all that is most gorgeous from the four corners of the earth."[39] There were thirty-foot-high martial Greek figures,

EATING IN, DINING OUT

Food stores and restaurants have always lined upper Broadway. Views from 1979 show a kosher butcher, Chinese restaurant, and all-night grocery store.

86th STREET

W **THE BOULEVARD, No. 2361-79**

1987-89, by Schuman, Lichtenstein, Claman & Efron, with Alexander Cooper & Partners. [21 stories] *Site of* 2361-79 Broadway, 1909, by John R. Hinchman and Walker & Hazzard.

E **THE BELNORD, No. 2360**

1908-09, by H. Hobart Weekes. Landmark. [12 stories]

87th STREET

W **THE FIFE ARMS, No. 2381-87**

1901, by George F. Pelham. [7 stories]

THE METROPOLITAN, No. 2389-95

(Also known as the Central Apartment Hotel). ca. 1895. [8 stories]

E **THE MONTANA, No. 2380-98**

1984, by the Gruzen Partnership. [26 stories]

88th STREET

W **255 WEST 88th STREET, No. 2401-07**

1924, by Rouse & Goldstone. [14 stories]

THE SAVANNAH, No. 2409-15

1987, by Schuman, Lichtenstein, Claman & Efron. [18 stories] *Site of* Adelphi Theater (also known as the New Yorker Theater, Yorktown Theater), 1914, by Rouse & Goldstone; renovated 1933, by Boak & Paris.

E **THE BUCHOVA, No. 2400-06**

1915, by George F. Pelham. [12 stories]

THE BELLGUARD, No. 2408-14

1915, by George F. Pelham. [12 stories]

89th STREET

W **THE ADMASTON, No. 2421-29**

1910, by George & Edward Blum. [12 stories]

THE NEW WEST, No. 2431-39

1987, by Philip Birnbaum & Associates. [23 stories] *Site of* Standard Theater (also known as Stoddard Theater), 1914-15, by Thomas W. Lamb; rebuilt as a supermarket.

E **ASTOR COURT, No. 2420-34**

1914-16 by Charles A. Platt. [12 stories]

crouching lions in relief, hugely fluted columns, a plaster drape over the proscenium, and murals depicting Oriental caravans.

In such a theatrical neighborhood, even a large financial institution could assume period costume: that of a Florentine palazzo. The headquarters of the Central Savings Bank, between Seventy-third and Seventy-fourth streets, was built in 1928 and designed by York & Sawyer to look as if it had been on the Upper West Side since the days of the Medici. Enclosed by its massively rusticated walls was a cavernous, barrel-vaulted banking room.

The Central Savings Bank was the last structure erected on such a generously grand scale. Succeeding developments were either starkly functional or sleekly streamlined affairs: the Broadway Fashion Building, at Eighty-fourth Street, an Art Deco masterpiece completed in 1931; the Thalia Theater, which was carved out of the Astor market in 1932; and the Embassy Theater, built in 1938 as part of a taxpayer on the site of the St. Andrew Hotel.

Except for these three buildings, very little was constructed on Broadway for the fifty years following the Great Depression. Physical and social deterioration seemed to go hand in hand in some places. By the mid-1960s, Verdi Square had become an "abominable arena" called Needle Park, after the drug trade that flourished there, and it "surpassed Times Square as a sex wilderness."[40] Across the street, the Ansonia had fallen apart. The lobby was "something out of a George Price cartoon" or the "vestibule of a skid row hotel," Paul Goldberger wrote. "Its elevators could be in a factory, and its corridors look like bowling alleys from the wrong side of the tracks."[41] In the 1970s and '80s, the Ansonia was the setting of prolonged legal warfare between the residents and the owners, rivaled only by the Belnord, where perhaps the "longest and most bitter landlord-tenant battle in the city" was

Broadway Fashion Building, 1986.

BEACON THEATER
View from 1988.

CENTRAL SAVINGS BANK

Views from 1988.

90th STREET

w **THE CORNWALL, No. 2441-49**
1909-10, by Neville & Bagge. [12 stories]

THE VERSAILLES, No. 2451-59
ca. 1900. [6 stories]

E **HAROLDON COURT, No. 2440-46**
1921, by Rouse & Goldstone. [13 stories]

GREYSTONE HOTEL, No. 2448-56
1922-23, by Schwartz & Gross. [14 stories]

91st STREET

w **2461 BROADWAY**
1896. [5 stories]

E **THE DE SOTO, No. 2460-66**
1917, by Schwartz & Gross. [13 stories]

ST. JAMES COURT, No. 2468
1900. [7 stories]

92nd STREET

The Roxborough, 1985.

w **THE ROXBOROUGH, No. 2481-87**
1910, by Neville & Bagge. [12 stories]

E **THE CLAYTON, No. 2478-88**
1922, by Rosario Candela. [15 stories]

2500 BROADWAY
1925, by J.M. Felson. [15 stories]

93rd STREET

w **2501 BROADWAY**
ca. 1900. [5 stories] *Site of* Dr. Valentine Mott
summer house, 1835.

Two-story Embassy Theater Building (left) and the 72nd Street I.R.T. Control House, 1986.

waged for more than a quarter-century.[42] Other once-elegant hotels, like the Beacon and the Belleclaire, were turned into single-room-occupancy dwellings. With 460 units, the Bretton Hall was the largest "S.R.O." on Broadway.[43]

The story of this period was not, however, entirely about declining fortunes. "It was a kind of golden age for the Upper West Side," Peter Salwen wrote in his history of the neighborhood, "though (as always with golden ages) hardly anyone noticed at the time."[44] In the late 1950s, the Thalia had begun showing Hollywood classics, and in 1960, the old Adelphi Theater at Eighty-ninth Street became a revival house called the New Yorker. Broadway could boast what Kate Simon called a "gorgeous array of movie history, a chain of jewels linked in double-feature."[45] Next door to the New Yorker Theater, Peter Martin opened the New Yorker Bookshop in the mid-1960s. Offering many titles in politics, psychology, and poetry, it became a literary landmark. Neighboring booksellers on Broadway included Bloomsday (later Shakespeare & Company), Dolphin, Gryphon, and, in the Astor market, the Pomander Bookshop.

The Continental Baths, a gay establishment in the basement of the Ansonia, featured all kinds of performances in the late 1960s and early 1970s—some of them, like Bette Midler's concerts, the stuff of entertainment legend. "Those tubs became the showplace of the nation," she said.[46] The Congregational sanctuary in the Manhattan Towers Hotel, which had been used by the Mormons for eight years, was turned into the off-Broadway Promenade Theater, which debuted in 1969 with a musical by the name of *Promenade*. The television shows *Sesame Street* and *Search for Tomorrow* were taped at the Eighty-first Street Theater, which had been converted into a studio. In 1978, the Symphony Theater became Symphony Space, an unorthodox neighborhood cultural center offering musical concerts and literary readings, drama, dance, and film. The Beacon remained a movie house until the mid-

1970s, when it was turned into an all-purpose performing arts center and concert hall. It was designated a landmark in 1979, in part because its architecture still offered a "sense of the fantasy and drama of the theater."[47]

Foremost among the retailers, Zabar's mirrored—and even foretold—neighborhood demographic changes, as it ballooned from a delicatessen into an enormous gourmet food and kitchenware center. Founded by Louis and Lillian Zabar in the 1930s, it had expanded to four locations by the 1940s but contracted after 1950 to a single storefront in the Centre Hotel at Eightieth Street. In the mid-1960s, the store was growing again and gaining a national reputation. Every week in the late 1970s, Zabar's sold 12,000 pounds of cheese, 10,000 croissants and brioches, 6,000 pounds of coffee, and 1,000 pounds of smoked salmon.[48]

In spite of its rebounding commercial life, Broadway as a physical entity remained frozen in its pre-Depression state through the 1970s. It was a measure of local stasis that the blockfront at Ninety-sixth Street stood largely vacant, except for a community garden, for fifteen years after the Riviera and Riverside theaters were razed in 1976. Finally, in 1981, after several false starts by other developers, William Zeckendorf Jr. began a huge condominium apartment tower called the Columbia. This project has been credited—and blamed—for triggering the wave of luxury high-rise construction in the mid-1980s.[49] The Columbia was followed in 1983 by the twin-towered Montana, between Eighty-seventh and Eighty-eighth streets, the first new luxury rental building above West Seventy-second Street in decades.

Concerted redevelopment began in 1985. Theaters and taxpayers were particularly vulnerable because they occupied large parcels under single ownership, and had no resident tenants. The Embassy Theater was torn down to

Keith's 81st Street Theater, 1985.

250 WEST 94th STREET, No. 2511-19
1924-25, by Sugarman & Berger. [14 stories]

Evangelical Lutheran Church of the Advent, 1988.

E **EVANGELICAL LUTHERAN CHURCH OF THE ADVENT, No. 2502**
1900, by William A. Potter.

HOTEL NARRAGANSETT, No. 2508
(Also known as the Bonta-Narragansett). 1902, by George Hill. [12 stories]

HOTEL BONTA, No. 2512
(Also known as the Bingham, Bonta-Narragansett). 1900, by Neville & Bagge. [7 stories]

94th STREET

95th Street Market, 1987.

W **95th STREET MARKET, No. 2525**
(Also known as the Astor Market). 1915, by Tracy & Swartwout; rebuilt. [2 stories] Thalia Theater, 1931-32, by Schlanger & Irrera.
CRYSTAL CARNIVAL SKATING PALACE
(Also known as the Symphony Theater, Symphony Space). 1917, by William H. Gompert. [1,411 seats]

E HOTEL APTHORP, No. 2520-24

(Also known as the Hotel Monterey, West Side Studios). 1914, by Schwartz & Gross. [12 stories]

HOTEL NEWTON, No. 2528

1902, by Ross & McNeil. [9 stories]

THE BONNYVIEW, No. 2532-36

(Also known as 700-04 Boulevard). 1885. [5 stories]

95th STREET

W THE TUILERIES, No. 2541-47

ca. 1900. [7 stories]

CASINO, No. 2551-55

(Also known as the Club Broadway, 96th Street Theater). 1904, by Rouse & Sloan. [2 stories]

E PRINCETON HOUSE, No. 2540-46

1986-87, by Schuman, Lichtenstein, Claman & Efron. [17 stories]

96th STREET

Broadway Mall Center, 1987.

BROADWAY MALL CENTER

(Also known as a comfort station). 1927, by Charles B. Meyers; remodeled. [1 story]

W THE COLUMBIA, No. 2561-79

1981-83, by Liebman Williams Ellis Architects. [36 stories] *Site of* Riviera Theater and Japanese Garden Theater, 1914, by Thomas W. Lamb, with D'Oench & Yost; Riverside Theater and Roof Garden, 1911, by Thomas W. Lamb, with John H. Duncan.

E THE WOLLASTON, No. 2558-66

1900. [7 stories]

THE WILMINGTON, No. 2568-74

ca. 1898. [7 stories]

The Colonial Club, Alexandria, and Ansonia, 1990.

make way for the Alexandria apartments. The façade of the Eighty-first Street Theater was preserved, but the auditorium itself was demolished for a residential tower called the Broadway. Loew's Eighty-third Street Theater was replaced by the Bromley condominium. The Eighty-sixth Street taxpayer made way for the Boulevard apartment house. The New Yorker Theater was demolished for the Savannah cooperative. The old Standard Theater, which had been a supermarket since the 1950s, was torn down for the New West apartment building.

These towers generally reflected 1984 zoning rules that were meant to encourage contextual architecture, primarily through the maintenance on Broadway of a uniform "street wall"—that is, the sheer rise of buildings from the sidewalk. The Bromley illustrated the strengths and defects of this approach. Its street wall did indeed fit the existing shape of Broadway, yet the piling of bulk above the street-wall line tended to defeat the goal of contextualism.

In cost (a quarter of a million dollars for a studio apartment), the Bromley and its kin were not at all contextual. Many Upper West Siders looked with alarm in the mid-1980s at such prices, fearing that their heterogeneous, frayed-at-the-edge neighborhood would become another Upper East Side—fancy, precious, and unaffordable. By 1990, however, with the end of a tax-benefit program that had stimulated much of the new construction, development had slowed considerably. It seemed that worries of rampant gentrification had been inflated, as had been any hopes that some of Broadway's tenacious squalor might also be reversed in the process.

STRYKER'S BAY MORNINGSIDE HEIGHTS

NINETY-SEVENTH STREET TO LASALLE STREET

Broadway is utterly transformed as it moves through the Stryker's Bay neighborhood in the Nineties—a mix of old-time elegance and contemporary decrepitude—and heads into a half-mile stretch where it is lined by educational and religious institutions. The most prominent of these is Columbia University, around which the others, some of them affiliates, have gathered. Columbia's campus runs for six blocks on the east side of the street, with Barnard College across Broadway and Teachers College across 120th Street. They are followed by the Union Theological Seminary and Manhattan School of Music on the west, and the Jewish Theological Seminary on the east. Together, these large and small campuses give Broadway a cultural patina and help create an urban version of college-town atmosphere, complete with pseudo-Gothic towers, wrought-iron gates framed by Neoclassical statuary, and ersatz Colonial façades.

Morningside Heights, seen from the elevated 125th Street I.R.T station, 1987.

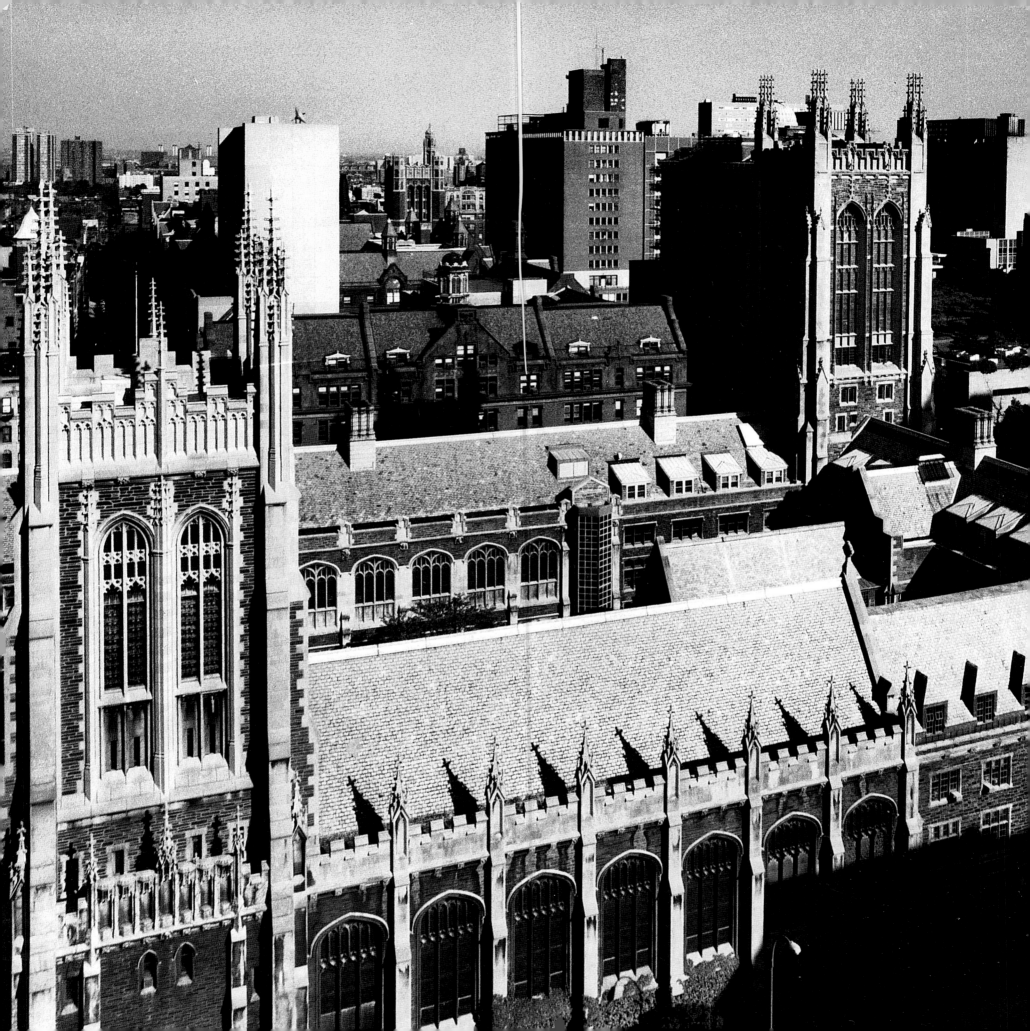

In colonial times, the promontory along the Hudson River, west of the town of Harlem, was known as Harlem Heights. Upon it, in the early 1700s, was the 266-acre estate of Thomas De Key, extending from 107th to 124th Street—"a Plantation with a very good stone House, Barn, and Orchard, containing about four or five Hundred Apple Trees, and a Pair Orchard, with a great many fine Grafted Pairs. . . . very well Timber'd and Watered; it has a very fine Brook very convenient for a Fish Pond."[1] South of that was the plantation of Theunis Eidesse Van Huyse, one portion of which was acquired by Charles Ward Apthorp and sold to Gerrit Striker in 1764. This farm included a cove on the Hudson River, almost exactly at the foot of Ninety-sixth Street, which came to be known as (and spelled) Stryker's Bay.

One of the more crucial early skirmishes of the Revolution was fought in September 1776 in a buckwheat field roughly where Barnard College stands today. While the Americans were retreating from New York, they paused long enough to rout a superior British force on Harlem Heights. This so boosted their morale that General George Clinton said, "I consider our success in this small affair, at this time, almost equal to a victory."[2] On the Broadway façade of Columbia's Mathematics Hall is a marker depicting the American commanders who were mortally wounded in that battle.

After the Revolutionary War, part of the old Van Huyse estate, from Ninety-ninth to 107th Street, was purchased by Herman Le Roy, one of the first wardens of Grace Church and a president of the Bank of New York. In 1785, Nicholas De Peyster bought the west half of the De Key farm and James De Peyster bought the east half. Part of the irregular boundary between their properties ran along a country road called De Peyster's Lane, the outline of which is still preserved by the sharply angled lots of three small buildings on the west side of Broadway, between 111th and 112th streets. In the 1790s, the Bloomingdale Road was extended from Nicholas De Peyster's barn, at 115th Street and Riverside Drive, to meet the "high Road to Kings Bridge"

Major Andrew Leitch, wounded at Harlem Heights, depicted in a tablet at Columbia, 1987.

Union Theological Seminary, with the John Crosby Brown Memorial Tower on Broadway (right), 1987.

97th STREET

w **UNTER DEN LINDEN BUILDING, No. 2581-87**
1899. [2 stories]

240 WEST 98th STREET, No. 2589-95
1920-21, by Schwartz & Gross. [14 stories]

e **THE POWELLTON, No. 2576-84**
1901, by William H. Boylan. [7 stories]

THE BORCHARDT, No. 2586-98
1910, by Rouse & Goldstone. [12 stories]

98th STREET

w **THE WILLIAM, No. 2601-07**
(Also known as the Elmhurst). ca. 1900. [7 stories]

The William, Arragon, and Navarre, 1987.

THE ARRAGON and THE NAVARRE, No. 2609-15
(Also known as the Clinton Residential Club). 1900. [7 stories]

e **THE GRAMONT, No. 2600-10**
1910, by George & Edward Blum. [12 stories]

THE MARION, No. 2612-14
1905, by Horgan & Slattery. [9 stories]

LA RIVIERA, No. 2616
1900. [8 stories]

99th STREET

w **THE KARLSRUHE, No. 2621-23**
(Also known as the Colonial). 1890. [7 stories]

RIVERVIEW THEATER, No. 2633-35
(Also known as the Carlton Theater, Carlton Terrace Ballroom, Keystone Theater). 1912-13, by

Henry B. Herts; remodeled 1932, by Raymond Irrera; rebuilt as a supermarket. [1 story]

CARLTON TERRACE HOTEL, No. 2637-39
(Also known as the Hotel Whitehall). 1922-23, by Charles B. Meyers. [15 stories]

E **TRAFALGAR TOWER, No. 2618-22**
1930, by George G. Miller. [20 stories] ***Near site of*** St. Michael's Church, 1806.

MIDTOWN THEATER, No. 2626
(Also known as the Metro Theater). 1932-33, by Boak & Paris; divided. Landmark. [2 theaters with 525 seats]

The Allenhurst, 1979.

THE ALLENHURST, No. 2636
(Also known as the Midway Hotel). 1912, by Rouse & Goldstone. [12 stories]

100th STREET

W **HENRY GRIMM BUILDING, No. 2641**
(Also known as the Boulevard House). 1871; expanded 1900; remodeled 1920. [3 stories]

THE BEN-HUR, No. 2645
1899. [7 stories]

THE LINLAUGH, No. 2649
ca. 1900. [7 stories]

THE BROADWAY, No. 2651-57
ca. 1900. [7 stories]

E **THE WALTER ARMS, No. 2648-58**
1925, by Emery Roth. [15 stories]

101st STREET

W **THE DARLINGTON, No. 2659-67**
1901, by Neville & Bagge. [7 stories]

THE MAGNOLIA, No. 2669-75
ca. 1900. [6 stories]

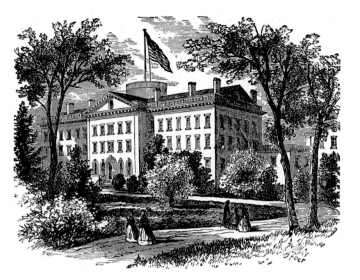

Bloomingdale Asylum for the Insane. NYI.

at a junction near the present St. Nicholas Avenue and 147th Street.[3] (Between 103rd and 108th streets, the old Bloomingdale roadbed crosses from the east to the west side of Broadway; near 125th Street, it recrosses to the east side.)

The first landmark in the area was St. Michael's Church, a "comely neat structure of wood with a spire and belfry" that was begun in 1806 on the Bloomingdale Road, at Ninety-ninth Street.[4] At the time, St. Michael's was the only Episcopal parish between the Bowery and Yonkers. Although the original church burned in 1853, the congregation remains on virtually the same site, in a church that fronts on Amsterdam Avenue.

In 1818, the Bloomingdale Asylum for the Insane was begun. Founded at the New York Hospital in 1807, the asylum was moved from crowded lower Broadway to this remote location, "one of the most beautiful and healthy spots on New York island."[5] Its grounds stretched from 116th to 120th Street, with winding avenues, cedar hedges, fir trees, and flowers—"so many objects to please the eye, and relieve the melancholy mind from its sad musings."[6] To give the "appearance of a palace rather than a jail," the quarters were "spacious and exquisitely furnished with every comfort . . . calculated to awaken lofty and pleasant sentiments." As many as 335 patients were treated annually, and the "appearance of the largest liberty is granted to all except the most violent."[7] One of the Bloomingdale Asylum buildings still stands: a red-brick and pitch-roofed structure near Low Library, on the Columbia campus.[8]

Another remnant of Bloomingdale days is the Henry Grimm Building of 1871, at 100th Street. This clapboard Italianate residence, with a ground-floor saloon, was one of the first structures built on the Boulevard, after that public drive from Fifty-ninth to 155th Street was created in the late 1860s. The structure is also one of perhaps only two surviving wood-frame buildings on the West Side, according to a study by Mark P. Shiff and Peter H. Wollenberg. Grimm was able to build in wood because the municipal prohibition against it had not yet been extended north of Eighty-sixth Street. A dabbler in real estate, Grimm may have bought his lot with the hope that construction of the Boulevard would increase traffic and development nearby.[9] Yet, the neighborhood remained suburban enough through the 1880s to attract Isidor and Ida Straus, who moved into a mansard-roofed country villa at 105th Street, not long before Isidor and his brother took control of Macy's. "With its ample lawns and large trees [it] contributed an atmosphere of old-time Bloomingdale," the *Times* said about the villa in its latter days, and in springtime, a "wealth of wisteria vines . . . covered the old wooden house with a mass of purple blooms."[10]

Even as the Strauses enjoyed pastoral life, Columbia College was being forced into a decision that would profoundly affect Harlem Heights. Plagued by overcrowding and noise on its campus at Madison Avenue and Forty-ninth Street, Columbia might have left the city to find a larger site or divided itself to fit smaller parcels. However, its attention was drawn to the Bloomingdale Asylum, "four undivided city blocks about eighteen acres in extent, nobly situated on the crown of the Island."[11] Columbia purchased the grounds in 1892. (The asylum went to White Plains in 1894 and is now known as the New York Hospital-Cornell Medical Center Westchester Division.) Many in the Columbia community greeted the college's uptown move with "considerable alarm, for the region was about as remote and inaccessible as Mt. Kisco."[12] There was an appeal to that distance, however—"it has been preserved from the evils of slums and tenement houses"—as well as a certain romance, which was exploited by the architect Charles Follen McKim, who envisioned the university as a city on a hill overlooking New York.[13] The name of this hill, agreed the representatives of the major institutions located there, should be Morningside Heights, and so it was rechristened.[14]

Henry Grimm Building, 1979.

E THE CHEPSTOW, No. 2660-70
(Also known as the Thomas Jefferson). 1906, by Mulliken & Moeller. [10 stories]

THE KENT, No. 2672
1900. [7 stories]

102nd STREET

W BROADMOOR HOTEL, No. 2681-87
1926-27, by George F. Pelham. [16 stories]

HOTEL LANGHAM, No. 2689-93
(Also known as the Marseilles Hotel). 1902-05, by Harry Allan Jacobs. Proposed landmark. [10 stories]

E 2680-84 BROADWAY
(Also known as 860-64 Boulevard). ca. 1897. [5 stories]

2686-90 BROADWAY
(Also known as 866-70 Boulevard, Malibu Studios Hotel). ca. 1897. [5 stories]

103rd STREET

W THE FRIESLAND, No. 2701-07
ca. 1900. [8 stories]

2709-17 BROADWAY
ca. 1898. [7 stories]

E B.K. BIMBERG'S BROADWAY THEATER, No. 2704
(Also known as the Columbia Theater, Edison, Essex, Nuevo Edison). 1913, by Edward S. Casey. [600 seats]

THE GRAFTON, No. 2708
[5 stories]

HORN & HARDART AUTOMAT, No. 2710-14
1930, by F.P. Platt & Brothers. [2 stories]

104th STREET

W THE ARMSTEAD, No. 2721-27
1925, by Gronenberg & Leuchtag. [15 stories]

THE RUREMONT, No. 2731
ca. 1900. [7 stories]

THE ELIZABETH, No. 2733-37
ca. 1900, by S.B. Ogden & Company. [6 stories]

COLUMBIA UNIVERSITY

View of the campus from Broadway and 116th Street, ca. 1910, showing the School of Engineering (left), School of Mines (center), and Low Library (right). NYHS. Views from 1979 to 1988 show the Class of 1900 Pylon, with the statue Scientia; *the School of Engineering (bottom right, this page); Havemeyer Hall (top of the facing page); detail of a torchère at Havemeyer; and a classroom in Havemeyer.*

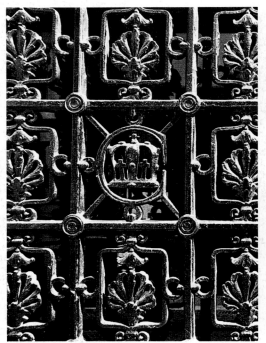

COLUMBIA UNIVERSITY

Views from 1987 and 1988 show Earl Hall Center (at top of facing page); grillwork on the School of Journalism; statue of Thomas Jefferson in front of Journalism; the School of Mines (at left, this page); and the Rutherfurd Astronomical Observatory atop Pupin Physics Laboratories.

BARNARD COLLEGE

Views from 1979 and 1987 show the Barnard Greek Games statue and the entrance to Brinckerhoff Hall, above; Adele Lehman Hall and Wollman Library, below.

The first cornerstone of the university, that of Low Library, was laid in 1895. By 1897, six Columbia buildings were complete, two of them on Broadway: Havemeyer Hall, dedicated then, as it is now, to the study of chemistry, and the School of Engineering, which is now Mathematics Hall. The center of religious and social services, Earl Hall, opened in 1902, followed in two years by the School of Mines, which is now Lewisohn Hall. The Furnald Hall dormitory was begun in 1912, as was the School of Journalism next door, built with money from Joseph Pulitzer, publisher of the *New York World*, who endowed the school itself. Columbia's monumental Broadway entrance at 116th Street was built one pylon at a time, in 1916 and 1925. The School of Business, now Dodge Hall, was completed in 1924. The Chandler Laboratories, appended to Havemeyer, were finished in 1926. Pupin Physics Laboratories opened in 1927, topped by the Rutherfurd Astronomical Observatory, a copper-domed installation with a thirteen-inch refracting telescope.

The Barnard College for women, an independent affiliate of Columbia, moved in 1897 from Madison Avenue and Forty-fourth Street, where it had been founded in 1889. In its early years on Broadway, Barnard consisted of a U-shaped group of three buildings around a courtyard at 119th Street. On Broadway was Brinckerhoff Hall, containing the college theater, gymnasium, and lecture rooms. As the campus expanded southward, Barnard Hall was built in 1917, with three gymnasium floors, a swimming pool, library, and dining rooms.

The other major member of the Columbia family on this part of Broadway is Teachers College, which moved uptown from University Place. Its

Horace Mann School at Teachers College, 1979 and 1988.

E   BROADWAY VIEW HOTEL, No. 2720-24
(Also known as the Regent Hotel). 1922-23, by Carrère & Hastings, with Shreve, Lamb & Blake. [17 stories] *Site of* Hope Baptist Church (also known as the Boulevard Baptist Church, Metropolitan Tabernacle Church), 1890-94, by Henry F. Kilburn.

THE OVERDENE, No. 2730-38
1915, by Gaetan Ajello. [14 stories]

105th STREET

W   THE CLEBOURNE, No. 2741-47
1912, by Schwartz & Gross. [12 stories] *Site of* Isidor Straus house.

THE WESTBOURNE, No. 2749
ca. 1900. [7 stories]

THE LANCASTER, No. 2753
ca. 1900. [7 stories]

E   2750-56 BROADWAY
ca. 1900. [5 stories]

DUKE ELLINGTON BOULEVARD

Memory at Straus Park, 1985.

W   BLOOMINGDALE SQUARE
(Also known as Schuyler Square, Straus Park). [0.07 acres] The *Straus Memorial*, which includes the statue *Memory*, is by Augustus Lukeman; the fountain and exedra by Evarts Tracy.

E   225 WEST 106th STREET, No. 2760-68
1927, by Boak & Paris. [15 stories]

OLYMPIA THEATER, No. 2766-70
1913, by V. Hugo Koehler; divided 1980 and 1981; remodeled in 1987. [2 theaters with 900 seats]

107th STREET

W THE TROUVILLE, No. 2783-85
(Also known as the Luana). 1899, by Henry
Andersen. [7 stories]

CHARLETON APARTMENTS, No. 2789-99
1923-24, by Rosario Candela. [15 stories]

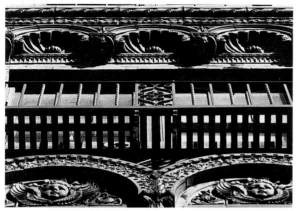

245 West 107th Street, 1979.

E 245 WEST 107th STREET, No. 2780-86
1928, by Sugarman & Berger. [16 stories]

SHERWOOD HOUSE, No. 2794
ca. 1900. [5 stories]

108th STREET

W THE MANHASSET, No. 2801-21
1904, by Janes & Leo. [11 stories]

E THE MANCHESTER, No. 2800-08
1909-10, by Neville & Bagge. [12 stories]

109th STREET

E LION PALACE MUSIC HALL, No. 2828-34
(Also known as the Nemo Theater). ca. 1900, by
James W. Cole; rebuilt 1910, by Thomas W. Lamb;
rebuilt as a supermarket. [2 stories]

CATHEDRAL PARKWAY

**W 110th STREET-CATHEDRAL PARKWAY
I.R.T. STATION**
1904, by Heins & LaFarge. Interior Landmark.

HENDRIK HUDSON ADDITION, No. 2841-47
(Also known as the College Residence Hall).
1907-08, by William L. Rouse. [12 stories]

2851-59 BROADWAY
1925, by J.M. Felson. [15 stories]

Claremont Hall, 1987; Hotel Langham, 1987.

Main Hall opened in 1894, facing 120th Street. On Broadway is the former Horace Mann School, established in connection with the college in 1887, "not merely a model school, but a laboratory for the practical trial and demonstration of new educational methods."[15] The school operated both in Manhattan and the Bronx for several decades, but vacated its Broadway building in 1946.

Between waves of institutional development came apartment and hotel construction, fueled by the building of the subway. Before rapid transit, the typical multiple dwelling was a seven-story tenement. That changed in 1902, when work was begun on the lavish, ten-story Hotel Langham, near what would soon be the 103rd Street underground railroad station. Akin to the Marie Antoinette, Ansonia, and Belleclaire, the mansard-topped Langham was later judged to have "advanced Broadway's case as America's leading Parisian boulevard."[16] (It is known today as the Marseilles Hotel.) Another great mansard roof was added to the skyline in 1904, when the Manhasset was built, from 108th to 109th Street. It was designed by Janes & Leo, and is halfway in time and style between the bulbous Dorilton and the suave Benjamin Franklin, which they also designed. The Hendrik Hudson, at Cathedral Parkway, had ten-room apartments, a billiard parlor and café especially for the tenants, and a children's playground on the roof, overlooking the Hudson River, "providing health and diversion for the little folks."[17] This appeal to health consciousness was a clever way to overcome the area's prime liability: its distance from mid-Manhattan. The promoters of the Washington Irving, at 112th Street, said the "invigorating air from the river and the cliffs is no small factor in making this locality very desirable."[18]

By the time the Washington Irving opened, the Strauses' home was the last country place left in the vicinity, "crowded up against the side of a great

The Manhasset, 1985; the Hendrik Hudson Addition, 1987.

2840-46 Broadway, 1987.

E **2840-46 BROADWAY**

1911, by Townsend, Steinle & Haskell. [2 stories]

111th STREET

E **THE ROCKFALL, No. 2860-66**

1909, by George & Edward Blum. [10 stories]

THE WASHINGTON IRVING, No. 2868-76

(Also known as the Devonshire). 1908, by Neville & Bagge. [10 stories]

112th STREET

W **CLAREMONT HALL, No. 2881**

1901, by George F. Pelham. [7 stories]

THE VIKINGS, No. 2889-97

(Also known as the Allerton). 1910, by Neville & Bagge. [12 stories]

E **THE OSTEND, No. 2880**

(Also known as McBain Hall, Oxford Residential Club, University Court). 1900, by Neville & Bagge. [7 stories]

THE YORKSHIRE, No. 2892-98

(Also known as Armstrong Hall). 1908, by Neville & Bagge. [8 stories]

113th STREET

W **THE FOREST CHAMBERS, No. 2901-13**

1909, by George & Edward Blum. [12 stories]

E **GARAGE, No. 2906-08**

1909-10, by Thomas W. Lamb. [4 stories]

ST. LUKE'S HOME FOR AGED WOMEN, No. 2910-14

(Also known as Frank S. Hogan Hall). 1898; rebuilt, by R.M. Kliment & Frances Halsband. [7 stories]

apartment house . . . lost amid such surroundings."[19] In 1912, Isidor and Ida perished aboard the *Titanic*. Almost immediately, their property was redeveloped with a twelve-story apartment building called the Clebourne. Bloomingdale Square, a block north of the Straus home, was renamed in their honor and given a fountain, with a melancholy allegorical figure of *Memory*.

In this neighborhood, as in other parts of the city, Broadway developed in the early twentieth century as the center of entertainment. Amid the groggeries and beer gardens around 110th Street, a notorious section known as "Little Coney Island," the Lion Palace Music Hall was built in about 1900 and later converted by William Fox into the Nemo Theater. The Olympia Theater opened at 107th Street in 1913 and, although remodeled many times since, has always operated under that name, making it a kind of theatrical landmark in age and continuity.[20] Other theaters that opened in 1913 were the Carlton, at 100th Street, and B.K. Bimberg's Broadway Theater, at 103rd Street. Also in 1913, Adolphus Busch of the Anheuser-Busch Brewing Association opened a summer beer garden at Ninety-eighth Street.[21] This was directly north of a little commercial building called the Unter den Linden, which still stands.

Two important schools were constructed in 1910 on either side of 122nd Street. To the south was the nondenominational Union Theological Seminary, which had been founded in 1836 and moved uptown from Park Avenue. The seminary chose Gothic architecture for its campus in the belief that the "buildings should become an element in the education" of its students and in the hope that "ecclesiastical architecture in many a parish would be bettered through the influence" of Union alumni who had studied in this setting.[22] The school's interconnected buildings surround a picturesque quadrangle almost two blocks long. At the southeast corner is the landmark John Crosby Brown

114th STREET

w   BROADWAY PRESBYTERIAN CHURCH and PARISH HOUSE, No. 2921
1911-12, by Louis E. Jallade.

THE LUXOR, No. 2931-35
1910, by Gaetan Ajello. [12 stories]

E   COLUMBIA UNIVERSITY
1892-94, by Charles Follen McKim of McKim, Mead & White. *Site of* Bloomingdale Asylum for the Insane, 1818-21.

CARMAN HALL
1959, by Shreve, Lamb & Harmon. [13 stories]

FERRIS BOOTH HALL, No. 2926
1959-60, by Shreve, Lamb & Harmon. [4 stories]

FURNALD HALL, No. 2940
1912-13, by McKim, Mead & White. [10 stories]

SCHOOL OF JOURNALISM, No. 2950
1912-13, by McKim, Mead & White. [6 stories] Statue of *Thomas Jefferson* by William Ordway Partridge.

116th STREET GATEWAY
1916 and 1925, by McKim, Mead & White. Statues *Letters* and *Scientia* by Charles Keck.

SCHOOL OF BUSINESS
(Also known as Dodge Hall). 1922-24, by McKim, Mead & White. [7 stories] Includes the McMillin Academic Theater (also known as the Kathryn Bache Miller Theater). *Site of* Bloomingdale Insane Asylum Doctors' Residence (also known as Old South Hall).

SCHOOL OF MINES, No. 2970
(Also known as Lewisohn Hall). 1904, by Arnold W. Brunner. [5 stories] Statue of the *Great God Pan* by George Grey Barnard.

CLASS OF 1891 MEMORIAL GATEWAY
1916, by McKim, Mead & White.

EARL HALL CENTER, No. 2980
1901-02, by McKim, Mead & White. [3 stories]

SCHOOL OF ENGINEERING, No. 2990
(Also known as Mathematics Hall). 1896, by McKim, Mead & White. [5 stories] The *Battle of Harlem Heights* marker is by James Edward Kelly.

HAVEMEYER HALL and HAVEMEYER EXTENSION, No. 3000-12
1896, by McKim, Mead & White; expanded 1989, by Davis, Brody & Associates. [5 stories]

CHANDLER LABORATORIES-HARRIS HALL, No. 3010
1925-26, by McKim, Mead & White. [10 stories]

MARCELLUS HARTLEY DODGE PHYSICAL FITNESS CENTER, No. 3020
1974, by the Eggers Partnership. [3 stories]

Jewish Theological Seminary (right foreground) and the Morningside Gardens Houses, 1987.

Memorial Tower, within which is the Memorial Entrance Hall, whose spidery, fan-vaulted ceiling springs up through a wide and winding marble staircase.

North of the seminary was the Institute of Musical Art, which opened in 1910 and was directed by Frank Damrosch. Two decades later, the institute was joined by the Juilliard Graduate School, and the two were combined in 1946 as the Juilliard School of Music.[23] (In 1969, Juilliard relocated to Lincoln Center, and its small complex was taken over by the Manhattan School of Music, which moved from East 105th Street.)

There was one final wave of private development in the 1920s, during which ten large apartment houses and hotels were built, most of them fifteen stories tall, massive in bulk and spare in ornamentation. The Broadway View Hotel of 1923, at 104th Street, made room in its lower floors for the fundamentalist congregation whose church it had replaced. As a consequence, card-playing and dancing were forbidden in the hotel, and guests were closely scrutinized.[24]

With the Depression came far fewer and more modest buildings, but there were a couple of bursts of Art Deco exuberance in the early 1930s: the Midtown Theater, near Ninety-ninth Street, and the Horn & Hardart Automat, at 104th Street.

The last institution to build a campus in Morningside Heights was the Jewish Theological Seminary of America, founded in 1886, which describes itself as the academic and spiritual center of Conservative Judaism. It moved in 1930 to a red-brick, Neo-Colonial quadrangle between 122nd and 123rd

Midtown Theater, 1985.

streets. The most prominent structure, straddling the entrance arch, is the Jacob H. Schiff Building, which housed the library stacks until April 1966, when a fire consumed some 70,000 books in the tower.

Nothing was built on the scale of the seminary for another twenty-five years. When work crews appeared in the neighborhood, it was usually to divide spacious old apartments into single-room dwellings for the poor.[25] The response to this housing crisis came in the mid-1950s, with the construction of three projects on the east side of Broadway, with room for nearly 4,200 families. This $68.5 million effort was described by the *Times* in 1957 as the "biggest face-lifting job under way in the city . . . eradicating slum furrows from the Morningside Heights-Manhattanville area."[26] The southernmost project was a 972-unit, middle-income cooperative called Morningside Gardens, between 123rd and Lasalle streets. Built by a consortium including Columbia, Barnard, Teachers College, Juilliard, and the two seminaries, it opened in 1957. Morningside Gardens was situated directly across the street from the lower-income General Ulysses S. Grant Houses in an "open effort to prevent economic stratification."[27]

From the 1950s through the 1980s, Columbia and Barnard filled in the Broadway frontage of their campuses with seven new structures. Barnard built Adele Lehman Hall, which contains the Wollman Library; Helen Reid Hall, a dormitory; the Millicent McIntosh Center for student activities; and, finally, Centennial Hall of 1988, an eighteen-story dormitory that not only reshaped the skyline but represented Barnard's "transition from a commuter college to an almost fully residential college."[28] Columbia filled in the south-

PUPIN PHYSICS LABORATORIES-RUTHERFURD ASTRONOMICAL OBSERVATORY, No. 3030
1924-27, by McKim, Mead & White. [15 stories]

115th STREET

w THE REGNOR, No. 2941-47
(Also known as Gaynor Court). 1911, by Gaetan Ajello. [12 stories]

THE REXOR, No. 2949-59
1911, by Gaetan Ajello. [12 stories]

116th STREET

e 116th STREET-COLUMBIA UNIVERSITY I.R.T. STATION
1904, by Heins & LaFarge. Interior Landmark.

BARNARD COLLEGE

HELEN REID HALL, No. 2961
1961, by R.B. O'Connor and W.H. Kilham Jr. [8 stories]

CENTENNIAL HALL
1987-88, by James Stewart Polshek & Partners. [18 stories]

BARNARD HALL, No. 3005
1917, by Brunner & Tryon. [5 stories] Statue of the *Barnard Greek Games* by Chester Beach.

HELEN HARTLEY "BAB" JENKINS GEER MEMORIAL GATE
1920.

ADELE LEHMAN HALL-WOLLMAN LIBRARY, No. 3009
1959, by O'Connor & Kilham. [5 stories]

MILLICENT McINTOSH CENTER, No. 3019
1969, by Vincent G. Kling & Associates. [2 stories]

BRINCKERHOFF HALL, No. 3025
1896, by Lamb & Rich. [5 stories] Includes the Minor Latham Playhouse.

REINHOLD NIEBUHR PLACE

w UNION THEOLOGICAL SEMINARY
1908-10, by Allen & Collens of Boston; remodeled 1952, by Collens, Willis & Beckonert.

JOHN CROSBY BROWN MEMORIAL TOWER, No. 3041
Landmark. [10 stories]

BURKE LIBRARY, No. 3041
[5 stories]

HASTINGS HALL DORMITORY, No. 3079
[7 stories]

UNION THEOLOGICAL SEMINARY

Views from 1987 and 1988 show the quadrangle (this page) and the John Crosby Brown Memorial Tower (facing page), including its rotunda.

**E TEACHERS COLLEGE:
HORACE MANN SCHOOL, No. 3032**

(Also known as Horace Mann Hall). 1901, by
Howells & Stokes and Edgar H. Josselyn. [6 stories]

121st STREET

E REED HOUSE, No. 3060-62

(Also known as Goldsmith Hall of the Jewish
Theological Seminary). 1905-06, by Neville & Bagge.
[7 stories]

CASTLE COURT, No. 3074-78

(Also known as the Roxbury). 1905-06, by Neville &
Bagge. [6 stories]

SEMINARY ROW

**W MANHATTAN SCHOOL OF MUSIC
(FORMER JUILLIARD SCHOOL OF MUSIC)**

INSTITUTE OF MUSICAL ART, No. 3083-85

1910-11, by Donn Barber. [5 stories]

MITZI NEWHOUSE PAVILION

1970, by MacFadyen & Knowles. [2 stories]

GRADUATE SCHOOL AND AUDITORIUM

1931, by Shreve, Lamb & Harmon. [8 stories]

FAIRVIEW COURT, No. 3117-29

1911, by Harold L. Young. [6 stories]

3133-37 BROADWAY

1895. [5 stories]

E JEWISH THEOLOGICAL SEMINARY

1930, by William Gehron of Gehron, Ross, Alley,
with David Levy.

JACOB I. SCHIFF BUILDING, No. 3080

LOUIS BRUSH BUILDING

[8 stories]

123rd STREET

E MORNINGSIDE GARDENS HOUSES

1957, by Harrison & Abramovitz.

MORNINGSIDE GARAGE, No. 3100
[2 stories]

549 WEST 123rd STREET
[22 stories] *Site of* Fort Laight, 1814, by General
Joseph Swift.

100 LASALLE STREET
[22 stories]

B.K. Bimberg's Broadway Theater, as the Nuevo Edison Spanish-language cinema, 1985.

west corner of its campus with the Carman Hall dormitory and Ferris Booth Hall student center. The last open spot on Broadway was taken in 1974 by the Marcellus Hartley Dodge Physical Fitness Center. This was the gymnasium that Columbia wanted to build in Morningside Park until protests from its Harlem neighbors and tumultuous student uprisings convulsed the campus in 1968, bringing a punishing police response and leaving the university traumatized for years—and the gym unbuilt.[29]

In the 1960s, as described by Kate Simon, a walk down Broadway took one "past the saloons and Chinese restaurants, past a Latin American club, an Israeli club and metallic pancake parlors, past the supermarkets made of gutted movie houses, past Wurstgeschaften and cafeterias of the old and lonely."[30] The walk would also take one past large single-room-occupancy hotels, including the old Broadway View, which had been renamed the Regent.

That world began to change in the 1980s. Big Broadway apartment houses were converted to cooperatives, at prices that would have been incredible a decade earlier. The Gramont at Ninety-eighth Street, for example, called itself a "PreWar Classic" (not specifying World War I) and offered a three-bedroom apartment for "only" $608,000.[31] Elsewhere along Broadway, the Midtown Theater, which had been showing pornographic movies, was rehabilitated in 1982 as the Metro, and later made an official landmark. Another conversion involved the old Bimberg's Broadway Theater, which for many years had been the Nuevo Edison, one of the few Spanish-language cinemas in New York, where Cantinflas movies drew large crowds. In 1987, it was renamed the Columbia and turned into a first-run, English-language theater—a change that spoke volumes about the neighborhood's metamorphosis.[32]

Broadway Barber Shop, 2713 Broadway, 1987.

New York City Department of City Planning

HARLEM MANHATTANVILLE HAMILTON HEIGHTS

LASALLE STREET TO 168TH STREET

Audubon Park Apartments and the Chapel of the Intercession, 1987.

Broadway, through much of the city, has been shaped by forces that were intertwined, multi-layered, and spread over time. In these two miles, however, the force was simpler, quicker, and more dramatic: the I.R.T. There are few places in Manhattan where the impact of transportation is so clear and unequivocal as in this realm of six-story red- and white-brick apartment buildings, most of which were built within five years after the arrival of the subway in 1904. They have an astonishing overall uniformity, notwithstanding the individual touches—some quite refined—that each was given. What breaks up this well-ordered but monotonous procession are the enormous contemporary housing projects in the 130s, Trinity Cemetery and Audubon Terrace in the 150s, and the mountainous, ever-evolving Columbia-Presbyterian Medical Center in the 160s.

An Astor family vault at Trinity Church Cemetery, 1988.

These rugged heights over the Hudson River were called Penadnic by the Rechgawawanc people who first dwelled in the area. Early European occupants knew them as Jochem Pieter's Hills, after the settler Jochem Pietersen Kuyter.[1] They were eventually named in honor of Alexander Hamilton, whose country estate was created from one of the fourteen lots into which the hills were divided in 1691. North of Hamilton's property was Carmansville, a mid-nineteenth-century hamlet named after its developer, Richard F. Carman. North of Carmansville was Minniesland, the estate of John James Audubon, which he purchased in 1840.

In the deep valley between Harlem Heights and Hamilton Heights was Manhattanville—a "flourishing little town, pleasantly situated near the banks of the Hudson"—which grew up in the early nineteenth century.[2] It had a school, public house, and market; an Episcopal church and Friends' meeting-house; ferry service to New Jersey and a daily stage to New York City.

The first big institutional developer on the heights was the Parish of Trinity Church, which bought twenty-three acres from Carman to establish Trinity Church Cemetery in 1843. The burial ground, 153rd to 155th Street, could be reached from the city by the Manhattanville stage or the steamboat *Boston*.[3] After burials south of Eighty-sixth Street were almost totally banned, Trinity became not only the largest graveyard in Manhattan but the only active one. There is great drama to this dense and beautiful city of the dead, as it stretches up the steep hillside, each terrace in the bosky landscape marked by rows of vault façades. In the late 1860s, the cemetery was "much injured by the laying out of the Public Drive [the Boulevard], which passes through it, ruining many of the vaults."[4] To connect the two divisions, a suspension bridge with Gothic towers was built across the Boulevard in 1871 and the cemetery managed to retain its allure for the "living capitalists, conscious of coming doom, [who] have here erected granite or marble structures for their last earthly homes"—the Astors being the foremost members of this society.[5]

With large tracts of open land, Hamilton Heights and Washington Heights, to the north, attracted much institutional development. The Academy of the Holy Infancy began building at 131st Street in 1853 and was chartered ten years later as Manhattan College, "one of the leading secular educa-

View south in 1979 includes the Alexander Hamilton,
Windsor Court and Crystal Court (finials), and the Georgia.

LASALLE STREET

E **GENERAL ULYSSES S. GRANT HOUSES**
1956-57, by Eggers & Higgins.

3150 BROADWAY
[22 stories]

3170 BROADWAY
[22 stories]

DR. MARTIN LUTHER KING JR. BOULEVARD

I.R.T. MANHATTAN VALLEY VIADUCT
1900-04, by William Barclay Parsons, chief engineer. Landmark.

E **THE MARCELLUS, No. 3200**
1906-07, by Neville & Bagge. [6 stories]

THE LUCIAN, No. 3210
1906-07, by Neville & Bagge. [6 stories]

126th STREET

E **MANHATTANVILLE HOUSES**
1960-61, by William Lescaze.

545-555 WEST 126th STREET
[20 stories]

3240-50 BROADWAY
[20 stories]

131st STREET

Warren-Nash Motor Corporation Garage, 1987.

E **WARREN-NASH MOTOR CORPORATION GARAGE, No. 3280-90**
ca. 1930. [8 stories] *Near site of* Academy of the Holy Infancy (also known as Manhattan College), 1863.

TRINITY CHURCH CEMETERY

Views from 1988 include the Fraser, Smith, Coddington, and Lawrence family vaults (left, facing page) and the graves of C.S. Watkins and Richard Sands (this page).

133rd STREET

w RIVERSIDE PARK COMMUNITY APARTMENTS, No. 3333
1976, by Max Wechsler Associates, Richard Dattner & Associates, Henri A. LeGendre & Associates. [35 stories]

134th STREET

E CLAREMONT THEATER, No. 3338
1914, by Gaetan Ajello; partially demolished. [3 stories]

135th STREET

w THE KATHMERE, No. 3341-49
1905-06, by George F. Pelham. [6 stories]

THE WILLIAM HENRY, No. 3351-59
1906, by Schwartz & Gross. [6 stories]

E THE ST. EVONA, No. 3340-46
1909, by Townsend, Steinle & Haskell. [7 stories]

THE HUDSON-FULTON, No. 3348-58
1909, by Neville & Bagge. [7 stories]

136th STREET

The Saxonia, 1987.

w THE SAXONIA, No. 3361-73
1906-07, by Neville & Bagge. [6 stories]

LESLIE COURT, No. 3375-79
1907, by Emery Roth. [6 stories]

E *Site of* Hebrew Benevolent Orphan Asylum, 1883-84 by William H. Hume.

Colored Orphan Asylum. NYI.

tional institutions of the Catholic Church."[6] (It is now located at 242nd Street in the Bronx.) The Colored Orphan Asylum moved to the area during the Civil War to get as far away from the city as possible. Founded in 1836 as the first benevolent institution in New York City for African-Americans, the asylum was savagely attacked during the Draft Riots of 1863, when a mob stormed its Fifth Avenue home and set it ablaze while 233 children were inside.[7] They escaped safely, but the managers decided to move their young charges to the Fields Mansion at 151st Street. Five years later, the asylum opened its own campus, between 143rd and 144th streets, with room for 300 children. Set among pretty lawns, its picturesque buildings had dormitories, classrooms and sewing rooms, a chapel, observatory, and veranda. "One cannot visit this peerless place, and contemplate its saintly charities, without

Row houses at 3470-78 Broadway, 1987.

feeling himself improved and drawn perceptibly nearer to Heaven," said the Reverend J.F. Richmond.[8]

The Fields Mansion, in 1879, became home to the Hebrew Sheltering Guardian Society for Jewish infants, orphans, and deserted children. Five years later, the Hebrew Orphan Asylum opened an enormous structure for 1,000 children, east of the Boulevard, between 136th and 138th streets. Following these benevolent Jewish organizations came the Montefiore Home for Chronic Invalids, forerunner of the Montefiore Medical Center. Its 140-bed hospital, between 138th and 139th streets, was opened in 1889. This was built on the pavilion plan, so that contagion could be isolated and the sexes segregated. Montefiore was supported largely by the Jewish community, although it accepted patients without regard to religion, who "by reason of incurable disease, are unable to obtain treatment at other institutions."[9]

Through the 1890s, there were few dwellings in the district, except for an incongruous group of bay-front, brownstone row houses at 142nd Street and a cluster of limestone row houses on either side of 152nd Street. As the twentieth century began, great expanses of land were still available—enough to accommodate the American League Ball Park, which was built in 1903 between 165th and 168th streets. From home plate to the Broadway fence, the hilltop park measured 460 feet. Pine and spruce grandstands went up along 165th Street and Fort Washington Avenue. On opening day, more than 16,000 fans came to watch "Wee Willie" Keeler lead New York to a six-to-two victory over Washington. Before moving to the Polo Grounds in 1912, the New York team was already in pinstripes. Although the players were best known as the Hilltoppers or Highlanders, they also had a new name: the Yankees.[10]

While the Yankees played, the rapid-transit railroad advanced. It was

Row houses at 3680-90 Broadway, 1987.

HAMILTON PLACE

E   MONTEFIORE PARK
[0.34 acres]

137th STREET

W   CROMWELL APARTMENTS, No. 3381-89
1906-07, by Emery Roth. [6 stories]

ROYAL ARMS, No. 3393-99
1906, by Thain & Thain. [6 stories]

138th STREET

W   3401-19 BROADWAY
1906, by Neville & Bagge. [6 stories]

Montefiore Home. King's Handbook.

E   GOTHAM THEATER, No. 3408-18
(Also known as the Delmar Theater). 1921-22, by Herbert J. Krapp; rebuilt as a supermarket. [3 stories] *Site of* Montefiore Home for Chronic Invalids, 1884-87, by Buchman & Brunner & Tryon.

139th STREET

W   PALISADE COURT, No. 3421
1905, by Neville & Bagge. [6 stories]

THE ROYALTY, No. 3431-35
1906, by Neville & Bagge. [6 stories]

E   THE SULGRAVE, No. 3420-28
1905-06, by George F. Pelham. [6 stories]

THE WESTBOURNE COURT, No. 3430-38
1909, by Neville & Bagge. [7 stories]

140th STREET

W   ELLERSLIE COURTS, No. 3441-59
1907-08, by Neville & Bagge. [6 stories]

I.R.T. MANHATTAN VALLEY VIADUCT
Views from 1979 and 1987.

Knowlton Court, 1987.

carried across the deep valley from 122nd to 135th Street on a dramatic, 2,174-foot-long viaduct, with a soaring arch high above 125th Street. (This landmark is the "most imposing and visually impressive above-ground engineering structure of the I.R.T."[11]) The subway reached 157th Street in 1904 and 215th Street in 1906. In its wake came a breathtaking surge of development known as the "Subway Boom," which transformed a "practically vacant and unimproved stretch into a nearly finished part of our great city in the short period of less than three years."[12] In the thirty blocks from 133rd to 163rd Street, where there had been a dozen row houses in 1898, sixty-three apartment buildings were existing or under construction by 1908. Broadway "paused to dream a bourgeois dream"—it built "rows of six-story brownstone flats, opened drug stores at convenient corners, induced greengrocers and delicatessen gentlemen to come and minister to its needs, and prepared to cultivate domesticity."[13]

Particularly busy were the architects George F. Pelham, Schwartz & Gross, and Emery Roth, whose work was noted for being influenced by the Vienna Secession style. Far ahead of them, however, were Thomas P. Neville and George A. Bagge, architects of three dozen buildings on Broadway. Neville & Bagge was later described as a firm "distinguished more by its ability to maximize rentable space than by any other notable characteristic."[14] That is true enough, but they can also be credited with giving a decent, middle-class air to the tenement form, with variations that were exuberant (3401

E **WINGATE HOTEL, No. 3440-48**
1905, by Schwartz & Gross. [7 stories]

THE ROCKCLYFFE, No. 3450-56
1905, by Schwartz & Gross. [7 stories]

141st STREET

W **GARNET HALL, No. 3465-71**
1909, by Sommerfeld & Steckler. [6 stories]

COLONIAL COURT, No. 3473-77
1907, by Moore & Landsiedel. [6 stories]

E **THE WOODMERE, No. 3458-68**
1909, by Schwartz & Gross. [10 stories]

ROW HOUSES, No. 3470-78
(Also known as 2312-20 Boulevard). 1892, by John C. Burne. [4 stories]

142nd STREET

W **3481-83 BROADWAY**
1905, by Neville & Bagge. [6 stories]

3485 BROADWAY
1905, by C.B. Brun. [6 stories]

THE SARSFIELD, No. 3489-95
1911, by Neville & Bagge. [10 stories]

E **THE CASTLETON, No. 3480-86**
1906, by Neville & Bagge. [6 stories]

THE SAGUENAY, No. 3488-96
1906, by Neville & Bagge. [6 stories]

143rd STREET

W **GREYLOCH DWELLINGS, No. 3501-09**
1909, by George F. Pelham. [6 stories]

DALLAS COURT, No. 3511-15
1909, by George F. Pelham. [6 stories]

E **WASHINGTON COURT, No. 3504-18**
1906-08, by Neville & Bagge. [6 stories] *Site of* Colored Orphan Asylum, 1867-68.

144th STREET

W **RAFFORD HALL, No. 3519-29**
1907, George F. Pelham. [6 stories]

E **BLERVIE HALL, No. 3520-32**
1908, by George F. Pelham. [6 stories]

AUDUBON THEATER

Views from 1979 to 1987.

B.S. Moss's Hamilton Theater, 1987.

Broadway, at 138th Street), refined (Ellerslie Courts, at 140th Street), or delicate (Knowlton Court, at 158th Street). Their Washington Court of 1908, twin structures with French Gothic ornamentation, took the place of the Colored Orphan Asylum, which had departed for Mount St. Vincent in the northwest Bronx.[15]

By and large, most Broadway apartment buildings above 125th Street followed a kind of "Subway Boom" style—red brick with limestone bays and quoins, windows with heavy keystones and splayed lintels. Many had prominent cornices, some had unusual recessed fire escapes. With such a uniform product, competitors could only distinguish themselves by using marketing techniques. One way to set a building apart from its neighbors was to give it a name, and the developers on Hamilton Heights seemed to have a penchant for vaguely Anglo-Saxon nomenclature. Another way to promote local real estate was to stress the advantage of living five miles from midtown. The builders of the Audubon Park Apartments described 156th Street as "Manhattan's only Section of Natural Beauty—adds the Charm of Country to the City Home."[16] This is not to say that conditions were idyllic. In 1909, Montefiore officials noted that neighbors were greatly annoyed to see patients in the street and to hear the "moaning and outbursts of physical pain among our sufferers."[17] The hospital moved to Gun Hill Road in the Bronx in 1913.

As was the case elsewhere, Broadway became the neighborhood entertainment center. The pioneer, once again, was William Fox, who opened the 2,368-seat Audubon Theater and Ballroom, between 165th and 166th streets, in 1912. The builder—whose film company was eventually merged with 20th Century Pictures—is slyly commemorated with fox-head medallions on the façade. The Audubon was the major uptown outlet on the Fox circuit, pres-

145th STREET

W THE MECKLENBURG, No. 3551-59
1906, by Neville & Bagge. [6 stories]

E THE RUDSONA, No. 3542
1907, by Neville & Bagge. [6 stories]

146th STREET

W THE NORTHCLIFF, No. 3561-69
1914, by Schwartz & Gross. [10 stories]

E B.S. MOSS'S HAMILTON THEATER, No. 3560-68
1912-13, by Thomas W. Lamb; rebuilt. [3 stories]

DOUGLAS COURT, No. 3570-78
ca. 1907. [6 stories]

147th STREET

W BUNNY THEATER, No. 3589
(Also known as the Dorset Theater, Nova, Tapia). 1913, by George F. Pelham. [702 seats]

E THE EDWIN, No. 3580-86
1908, by Clarence True. [6 stories]

THE HUDSON VIEW, No. 3590-98
1905, by Neville & Bagge. [6 stories]

148th STREET

W 3601-05 BROADWAY
1900, by Buchman & Fox. [7 stories]

THE RIVERVIEW, No. 3607-11
1902, by Buchman & Fox. [7 stories]

E THE ST. CHARLES, No. 3600
1904, by George F. Pelham. [5 stories]

THE RICHARD, No. 3604
1898, by John P. Leo. [5 stories]

THE CHARLES, No. 3610
1898, by John P. Leo. [5 stories]

THE WALLACE, No. 3618
1907-08, by George F. Pelham. [6 stories]

149th STREET

W ETHELBERT COURT, No. 3621-29
1910, by Moore & Landsiedel. [6 stories]

THE ONGIARA, No. 3631-37
1910, by Neville & Bagge. [6 stories]

The Panama (left) and Mansfield (right), 1987.

ᴇ **THE MANSFIELD, No. 3620-30**
1907, by John Hauser. [6 stories]

150th STREET

ᴡ **THE SOUTHOLD, No. 3641-47**
1913, by Mulliken & Moeller. [10 stories] *Site of* Hebrew Sheltering Guardian Society Orphan Asylum, 1892, by John H. Duncan; Fields Mansion.

THE NORTHOLD, No. 3649-55
1913, by Mulliken & Moeller. [10 stories]

ᴇ **THE PANAMA, No. 3640-52**
1906, by Neville & Bagge. [6 stories]

151st STREET

ᴡ **THE WASHINGTON IRVING, No. 3661-69**
1908, by Neville & Bagge. [6 stories]

THE PAVONAZZA, No. 3671-73
1909, by B. Levatan. [6 stories]

ᴇ **KENSINGTON COURT, No. 3660-66**
1909, by Gross & Kleinberger. [6 stories]

ROW HOUSE, No. 3672
(Also known as 2534 Boulevard). ca. 1895. [4 stories]

152nd STREET

ᴡ **THE ST. REGIS, No. 3675-77**
1909, by Young & Gronenberg. [6 stories]

HALIDON COURT, No. 3679-81
1910, by Emery Roth. [6 stories]

ᴇ **ROW HOUSES, No. 3680-90**
(Also known as 2540-50 Boulevard). 1895. [4 stories]

enting vaudeville shows and movies. The architect was the ubiquitous Thomas W. Lamb, who was also responsible for the Hamilton, which opened in 1913 at 146th Street. Built by B.S. Moss, it is marked by sweeping arches and mirthful terminal figures of nude women. Equally striking are the rabbit heads on the Bunny Theater, between 147th and 148th streets, which was named for the comedian John Bunny. It opened in 1913 and is still in use, making it one of the oldest continuously operated theaters in New York City.[18] One of the shortest-lived was the Gotham Theater, which opened in 1922 on the site of Montefiore hospital and lasted three decades before it became a supermarket. The Gotham was designed by Herbert J. Krapp, best known for his legitimate playhouses in the theater district, who also designed the Rio Theater of 1920, at 160th Street.

Popular as the theaters may have been, Archer M. Huntington—a scholar, art patron, and philanthropist—envisioned a much nobler cultural legacy for Hamilton and Washington heights. At the time of the Subway Boom, he began buying up the old Audubon estate, then known as Audubon Park. What resulted was Audubon Terrace, the setting for the Washington Heights Museum Group, "one of the foremost cultural centers in New York City and among the first of its kind in the country."[19] Huntington's cousin, Charles Pratt Huntington, designed much of the terrace, and his wife, Anna Hyatt Huntington, executed much of the sculpture. The first institutions to open there were the Hispanic Society of America and the American Numismatic Society.

The American Geographical Society was the first building in the complex on Broadway. The society, which had been founded in 1852, moved its headquarters and library from West Eighty-first Street in 1911. Besides its scholarly work, the organization helped negotiate boundary disputes, sponsored arctic and antarctic expeditions, and welcomed visitors like Richard E. Byrd, Sir Edmund P. Hilary, Charles A. Lindbergh, and Woodrow Wilson. In the

Bunny Theater, 1987.

AUDUBON TERRACE

Views from 1986 and 1987 show the entrance to the American Geographical Society (left) and one of the main doors to the Museum of the American Indian-Heye Foundation.

TRINITY STUDIO, No. 3696
1910, by Emery Roth. [6 stories]

153rd STREET

TRINITY CHURCH CEMETERY
1842-43; wall and gates, 1876, by Vaux & Radford; landscaped 1881, by Vaux & Company. *Site of* Suspension Bridge, 1871, by Vaux, Withers & Company.

E **CHAPEL OF THE INTERCESSION**
(Also known as the Church of the Intercession). 1911-14, by Bertram Grosvenor Goodhue. Landmark.

155th STREET

W **AUDUBON TERRACE-WASHINGTON HEIGHTS MUSEUM GROUP**
Master plan by Charles Pratt Huntington. Major statues by Anna Vaughn Hyatt Huntington. Historic District. *Site of* Audubon Park.

MUSEUM OF THE AMERICAN INDIAN-HEYE FOUNDATION, No. 3745
1916-22, by Charles Pratt Huntington. [5 stories]

AMERICAN GEOGRAPHICAL SOCIETY, No. 3755
(Also known as Boricua College). 1909-11, by Charles Pratt Huntington. [5 stories]

E **AUDUBON PARK APARTMENTS, No. 3750**
1905-6, by Schwartz & Gross. [6 stories]

156th STREET

W **HISPANIA HALL, No. 3761**
1909, by George F. Pelham. [6 stories]

AUDUBON HALL, No. 3765-79
1909, by George F. Pelham. [6 stories]

E **ROBERT FULTON COURT, No. 3760-68**
1909, by Neville & Bagge. [6 stories]

THE COLUMBUS, No. 3770-76
1909, by Neville & Bagge. [10 stories]

158th STREET

W *Site of* Church of the Intercession, ca. 1872.

E **KNOWLTON COURT SOUTH, No. 3800**
1907-08, by Neville & Bagge. [6 stories]

1960s, its cartographers were engaged in classified work for the space program.

Across the terrace, the Museum of the American Indian-Heye Foundation opened in 1922. Founded by George Gustav Heye, it is "devoted to the collection, preservation, study, and exhibition of all things connected with the anthropology of the aboriginal peoples of North, Central, and South America."[20] As such, it is unrivaled. On display at Audubon Terrace are garments, costumes, masks, jewelry, religious artifacts, tools, weapons, vessels, and household craftwork—objects as big as a sixty-foot whaling canoe from the Northwest, as small as three-inch shrunken heads made by the Jivaro Indians of Ecuador.

Catercorner from Audubon Terrace—and seeming to spring from the same boundless optimism about the neighborhood's future—is the cathedral-like Chapel of the Intercession, which was built in 1912 with room for 970 worshippers. The church had been part of Carmansville since 1847, and was located at Broadway and 158th Street for several decades. In the 1900s, however, the rapidly growing congregation far exceeded its accommodations and

American Geographical Society—now Boricua College—at Audubon Terrace, 1978.

Columbia-Presbyterian Medical Center, 1988.

it was taken over by Trinity Parish, which built the enormous sanctuary, plus a vicarage and parish house, in Trinity Cemetery. The architect, Bertram Grosvenor Goodhue (who is buried in the chapel), created a "very free combination of handsome Gothic design elements," according to the landmark citation.[21]

In 1921, the old American League ballfield was acquired by a partnership of the Presbyterian Hospital, on Park Avenue, and Columbia's College of Physicians and Surgeons, on Tenth Avenue. They planned nothing less than the world's greatest medical complex, and within seven years, the first six units of the Columbia-Presbyterian Medical Center had been built, dominating the local landscape like Mount Shasta, the *Times* said. "Ride or walk for miles in the upper city streets and avenues, then look up again and there it is, still looming on the horizon."[22] Another contemporary observer said that the Medical Center's "connection with pain, its significance as a temple of suffering will appal you, so huge is this area, so inclusive its field of action."[23] (In the late 1980s, there were some 45,000 admissions annually to its inpatient facilities.) On Broadway is Babies Hospital, the nation's oldest hospital for children and infants. Founded in 1887, it moved from Lexington Avenue to the Medical Center in 1929. It was noted for its temperature-controlled ward for premature babies, its solariums, and its milk-formula laboratory, as well as for being "open to all classes, creeds and nationalities," where "rich child and poor juggle blocks and spatter sand in convalescent happiness."[24]

Outside the institutions, Broadway in the 1930s was a "long, unending monotone of delicatessen stores, dry cleaners, and millinery shops; of low, squat, colorless buildings, baby-carriage laden sidewalks, and neighborhood

KNOWLTON COURT NORTH, No. 3810
1907-08, by Neville & Bagge. [7 stories]

FORT WASHINGTON AVENUE

W **RIO THEATER, No. 3837**
1920, by Herbert J. Krapp; rebuilt as a supermarket. [2 stories]

159th STREET

E **THE WASHINGTON HEIGHTS, No. 3820-26**
1905-06, by Neville & Bagge. [6 stories]

THE GEORGIA, No. 3828-34
1909, by George F. Pelham. [6 stories]

160th STREET

W **THE LETCHWORTH, No. 3841-49**
1912, by Neville & Bagge. [10 stories]

THE HAMPSTEAD, No. 3851-59
1912, by Neville & Bagge. [10 stories]

E **CRYSTAL COURT, No. 3840-46**
ca. 1905. [6 stories]

WINDSOR COURT, No. 3850-58
ca. 1905. [6 stories]

161st STREET

W **THE ALFREDO, No. 3875**
1908, by Schwartz & Gross. [6 stories]

E **THE ALEXANDER HAMILTON, No. 3860-66**
1906, by Neville & Bagge. [6 stories]

THE BRIARCLIFF, No. 3868-74
1908-09, by Gross & Kleinberger. [6 stories]

162nd STREET

W **THE NEWCASTLE, No. 3879**
1911, by Schwartz & Gross. [6 stories]

BALMORAL COURT, No. 3885-95
1909, by Schwartz & Gross. [6 stories]

E **CAROLYN COURT, No. 3880-88**
1909, by Gross & Kleinberger. [6 stories]

ROSBERT HALL, No. 3890-98
1909, by Gross & Kleinberger. [6 stories]

CHAPEL OF THE INTERCESSION
Views from 1987 and 1988.

163rd STREET

w **CHARLESTON COURT, No. 3905**
1909, by Schwartz & Gross. [6 stories]

RICHMOND COURT, No. 3915
1909, by Schwartz & Gross. [6 stories] *Site of* Deaf and Dumb Asylum out buildings.

E **THE MEDFORD, No. 3900-08**
1910. [6 stories]

THE BARRYHOLM, No. 3910-18
1910. [6 stories]

164th STREET

w **THE WILTON, No. 3921-29**
1909, by Neville & Bagge. [6 stories]

HAMLET COURT, No. 3931-39
1909, by Neville & Bagge. [6 stories]

E **PRINCESS COURT, No. 3920**
ca. 1905. [6 stories]

BRACKLYN COURT, No. 3926-36
1909, by Neville & Bagge. [10 stories]

165th STREET

w **COLUMBIA-PRESBYTERIAN MEDICAL CENTER**
1925-29, by James Gamble Rogers Inc. *Site of* American League Baseball Park.

BABIES HOSPITAL ADDITION
1966 and 1968, by Rogers, Butler, Burgun. [12 stories]

BABIES HOSPITAL, No. 3959
1928-29, by Henry Colden Pelton. [12 stories]

MEDICAL CENTER CONCOURSE
1988-90, by Skidmore, Owings & Merrill.

NEW YORK CITY DISTRICT HEALTH CENTER
[8 stories]

E **AUDUBON THEATER and BALLROOM, No. 3950**
(Also known as the Beverly Hills Theater, San Juan). 1912, by Thomas W. Lamb; interiors by Rambusch Studios. *Proposed site of* Audubon Research Building, by Perkins & Will and Bond, Ryder & Associates.

166th STREET

E **MITCHEL SQUARE**
[0.77 acres] *Washington Heights-Inwood War Memorial*, by Gertrude Vanderbilt Whitney (pedestal by Delano & Aldrich).

hausfraus."[25] Frozen by the Depression and the war, the neighborhood was slow to recover—and, in some ways, never did. In the 1950s, most of its movie theaters were converted to supermarkets, although the Audubon continued in operation as the San Juan. Its enduring infamy came in 1965, when the African-American nationalist leader Malcolm X was assassinated in the ballroom as he addressed a rally of hundreds of his followers.

In a broad social and geographic sense, Hamilton Heights was part of Harlem and, like the community to the east, it was abandoned by private builders. What little construction occurred in recent decades was publicly subsidized and enormous in scale. The twenty-one-story General Ulysses S. Grant Houses, extending from Lasalle to 125th Street, were the tallest public project in the city when they opened in 1956. Today, they have a population of 5,000. Ironically, of the first five families to move to the Grant Houses, three had been displaced by the slum clearance for Manhattanville Houses, from 126th to 131st Street. That project, begun in 1957, now has a population of more than 3,200.[26] One last monumental housing effort was the Riverside Park Community Apartments of 1976, from 133rd to 135th Street. With 1,200 apartments under one roof, it was called the largest residential structure in the United States.[27]

Between the projects and the medical center, the genteel institutions of Audubon Terrace were looking more and more out of place. Through lean and tenuous years, however, their unity was unbroken until 1978, when the American Geographical Society departed. On the edge of bankruptcy, it accepted an invitation from the University of Wisconsin and, in 1978, moved books, maps, atlases, and globes to Milwaukee.[28] Two years later, it was replaced by Boricua College, a private, bilingual school founded in 1974, principally to serve Puerto Rican and other Hispanic students. In the 1980s, the Museum of the American Indian was also taking steps to vacate Audubon Terrace, in the belief that its "location and cramped quarters have deterred visitors and led to a neglect of the thousands of artifacts."[29]

Not all the signs in the neighborhood were despairing. Babies Hospital, which had been considerably enlarged in the 1960s, opened another addition in 1987, with six new operating rooms. Presbyterian Hospital itself was embarked on a $496 million modernization and construction effort. On a very small scale, a sweet Christmas tradition was upheld at Trinity Cemetery, where a lantern-lit commemorative procession made its way once every December to the grave of Clement Clarke Moore, the author of *A Visit from St. Nicholas*.

Yet, the neighborhood was living in anguish. By the end of the 1980s, the police could round up nearly forty drug dealers in a single raid on Broadway, from crack dens operating on the spot where the old orphan asylum once provided its "saintly charities" to the city's poorest children. Everything north of Trinity Cemetery was in the 34th Precinct, headquartered at Broadway and 183rd Street, which had the unwanted distinction of being the city's deadliest precinct, with a homicide every eighty-eight hours.[30] Broadway's old bourgeois dream was taking on nightmarish overtones.

Riverside Park Community Apartments, 1978.

WASHINGTON HEIGHTS INWOOD MARBLE HILL

168TH STREET TO 230TH STREET

Street sign at Fort Tryon Park, 1979.

Broadway loses much of its cosmopolitan quality as it winds under the thick canopy of Fort Tryon Park, then passes by gas stations and a junior high school, a funeral parlor and auto-body shops, an American Legion hall and a saloon called the Hedgehog Inn. For the first time since its journey began at Bowling Green, the street appears to be meandering, rather than surging through the city. Geography and topography conspire to make these oddly shaped and often quite verdant blocks seem very remote from what preceded them. Broadway conveys the sense of being the modern descendant of an old country highway—which is exactly what it is, complete with a few relics like an eighteenth-century farmhouse and a nineteenth-century gatehouse. Even in the 1980s, residents of the Inwood area at the top of the island were known to refer to their neighborhood as "upstate Manhattan."

H aving traveled a straight line since 108th Street (where it departed for the last time from the route of the Bloomingdale Road), Broadway swerves sharply again at 168th Street. For the next sixty blocks, it follows the twisting, turning course of a seventeenth-century highway that was first known as the King's Way and later as the Kingsbridge Road, after the construction in 1693 of the King's Bridge across the Spuyten Duyvil Creek. The road preserved in part the route of the Weckquaesgeek path whose southernmost end formed the oldest portion of Broadway. On the west side of the trail, between what would become 176th and 181st streets, a sizable area was already under cultivation before the Europeans arrived. The white settlers called this the Great Maize Land and, with no title to it, allotted the parcel in 1691 to Joost Van Oblinus, the magistrate of New Harlem.[1]

The Oblinus farm was large but not nearly as expansive as the Dyckman farm, which covered 300 acres at the end of Manhattan Island, almost everything north of the present Dyckman Street. Jan Dyckman and his partner, Jan Nagel, began assembling the property in 1677. At first, they leased the land to tenant farmers for one hen a year, agreeing to furnish apple and pear trees to their lessees. Then Dyckman moved to the farm, settling on the bank of the Harlem River. His grandson, William, built an upland house, near 208th Street. The family sided with the Americans in the Revolutionary War and fled Manhattan after it was occupied by British troops. When they returned, they found their house in ruins.[2]

Sometime soon after 1783, William Dyckman began a new dwelling, the pleasant Dutch Colonial farmhouse, with a blanketing gambrel roof, that still stands at 204th Street. He probably incorporated as much material as he could salvage from the earlier structure. During the rebuilding, the family lived in an old shed that was eventually incorporated as the south wing of the new house, and used as a summer kitchen or bake house.[3] The great porch facing Broadway was probably added in the early nineteenth century by William's son, Jacobus. The house stayed in the family until 1871, passed down to Isaac Michael Dyckman.

Between the Dyckman and Oblinus farms was the Blue Bell Tavern, at what is now 181st Street. At least as early as 1753, it was offering "very comfortable" lodging and food, and was the best known of the several road houses that dotted the Kingsbridge highway.[4] In 1773, Caleb Hyatt built a tavern near what is now 225th Street, where President Washington stopped on his way to and from a tour of New England in the fall of 1789.

Following the road houses came the country estates. In 1851, John Seaman bought a twenty-five-acre hillside parcel, between 214th and 217th streets, that included well-known marble quarries on the Kingsbridge Road.[5] These were used by his brother, Valentine, to build a marble house and, at the base of the hill, a monumental entry arch, thirty-five feet high and twenty feet deep. A winding road led from there to the home, through grounds "laid out with charming walks and shrubbery, and adorned with arbors and statuary."[6] The marble arch, which still stands, probably doubled as a gatekeeper's house, and had stairs, windows, and plaster walls within.[7]

4720-28 Broadway and Fort Tryon Park, 1985.

168th STREET

w **THE CARROLLTON, No. 4001-09**
1909, by L.A. Goldstone. [6 stories]

THE COURTWOOD, No. 4015
1909, by L.A. Goldstone. [6 stories]

169th STREET

w **UPTOWN THEATER, No. 4037**
1925-26, by Eugene De Rosa; rebuilt as a supermarket. [1 story]

171st STREET

w **HERBEN HALL, No. 4061-67**
1916, by Neville & Bagge. [6 stories]

MANTIER COURT, No. 4069-75
1916, by Neville & Bagge. [6 stories]

172nd STREET

w **ABBEY HALL, No. 4079-85**
1915. [6 stories]

E **4080-84 BROADWAY**
1936, by Miller & Goldhammer. [6 stories]

173rd STREET

w **TEMPLE APARTMENTS, No. 4101**
1925-26, by Donn Barber. [12 stories]

BROADWAY TEMPLE UNITED METHODIST CHURCH, No. 4111
(Also known as Iglesia Metodista Unida Broadway Temple). 1952, by Shreve, Lamb & Harmon.

TEMPLE APARTMENTS, No. 4117
1925-26, by Donn Barber. [12 stories]

174th STREET

w **WRIGHT HALL, No. 4119-27**
1920. [6 stories]

4133-39 BROADWAY
1920. [6 stories]

175th STREET

E **LOEW'S 175th STREET THEATER, No. 4140**
(Also known as the United Church-Science of Living Institute). 1928-30, by Thomas W. Lamb and Rambusch Studios. [3,600 seats]

DYCKMAN HOUSE
Views from 1979 and 1985.

176th STREET

w **SHIRBAR ARMS, No. 4161-69**
1930. [6 stories]

177th STREET

w **THE MARTLETON, No. 4181-89**
1909, by George F. Pelham. [6 stories]

THE FLORIAN, No. 4191-99
1909, by George F. Pelham. [6 stories]

E **THE CONTINENTAL, No. 4180-84**
1909, by Neville & Bagge. [6 stories]

CHEMICAL BANK BRANCH, No. 4186
(Also known as the Dominican Bank). 1930. [1 story]

178th STREET

GEORGE WASHINGTON BRIDGE BUS STATION, No. 4211
1963, by Pier Luigi Nervi and the Port of New York Authority. [3 stories]

179th STREET

w **HEATERDELL COURT, No. 4221-29**
1909, by Schwartz & Gross. [6 stories]

THE RAVENWOOD, No. 4231-37
1909, by Schwartz & Gross. [6 stories]

E **IVY COURT, No. 4220-28**
1910. [5 stories]

4230 BROADWAY
1905. [3 stories]

THE SWAMPSCOTT, No. 4232-38
1909, by A.B. Kight. [6 stories]

180th STREET

w **HAVEN COURT, No. 4241**
1908, by Neville & Bagge. [6 stories]

NATIONAL CITY BANK BRANCH, No. 4249
(Also known as Citibank). [2 stories]

HARLEM SAVINGS BANK BRANCH, No. 4255
(Also knows as Apple Bank for Savings). [1 story]
Site of Holyrood Protestant Episcopal Church (also known as the Garfield Theater), 1893, rebuilt in 1911.

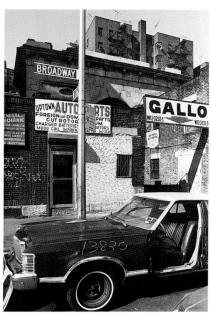

Marble Gate to the Seaman-Drake estate early in the century and in 1987. NYHS, DD.

Other notable arrivals in this rural colony included James Gordon Bennett, the founder of the *New York Herald*, who bought an estate in the mid-1850s and made his country home at about 184th Street, west of the Kingsbridge Road. William B. Isham bought an estate south of the Seamans' in 1864. Five years later, the political boss William M. Tweed acquired a striking home, known as the "Castle," north of 192nd Street. It is said that his interest in developing the Boulevard as a major uptown thoroughfare can be traced to his ownership of this remote site.[8]

The second half of the nineteenth century saw the slow progress of an extraordinary engineering project that literally recreated the map of upper Manhattan. The sinuous and narrow Spuyten Duyvil Creek had always been practically unnavigable, preventing passage from the Hudson River to the Harlem River and Long Island Sound. A new waterway along the line of Dyckman's Canal, at 222nd Street, was authorized by the Common Council in 1840 and by the Congress in 1874 but work was not begun in earnest until 1888.[9] The Harlem Ship Canal finally opened in 1895, as did the Ship Canal Bridge, which carried the Kingsbridge Road over the water. The effect of this channeling work was to turn the Marble Hill neighborhood into a small island, which it remained until 1913, when the remaining loop of the Spuyten Duyvil was drained and filled, fusing this cast-off chunk of Manhattan to the Bronx.[10] (Despite the change in physical geography, and despite a spirited effort by the Bronx Borough President in 1939 to claim the area by planting the Bronx flag in its soil, Marble Hill is administered to this day as part of the Borough of Manhattan.[11])

The early twentieth century was not marked in this area by the intense development that transformed neighborhoods to the south. There was no Subway Boom because there was no subway. Broadway and the Interborough Rapid Transit system parted ways at 168th Street. The railroad tracks did not near Broadway again until an elevated station at 215th Street.

Instead of apartment houses, Broadway saw the building of a new country estate in the early 1900s, when the Chicago millionaire C.K.G. Billings assembled several smaller properties, including the old Castle, into a large parcel north of 190th Street. As late as 1911, Stephen Jenkins said: "There are still several estates on the west side of the road, and the green lawns and fine trees make a scene of great beauty. As in the days of old, a number of the mansions have been converted into road-houses where the autoist may refresh himself. But the doom of these places is near at hand."[12] Indeed, he virtually predicted the demolition of the Dyckman House and noted that the land under the Holyrood Chapel, a rustic-looking church at 181st Street, had become so valuable that the congregation sold it only eighteen years after building there. The sanctuary was turned into the Garfield Theater, a movie and vaudeville house.[13]

Fighting the development trend, two of Isaac Michael Dyckman's daughters, Mary Alice Dean and Fannie Fredericka Welch, purchased their family's dilapidated old homestead in 1915. They restored it, surrounded it with a landscaped park, and filled it with period furniture, curios, relics, and ephemera. Then they gave it to New York City. Four years earlier, William B. Isham's daughter, Julia Isham Taylor, had given his estate for use as a public park. The Isham house was still standing in the 1920s, "set in the midst of a charming lawn, with a delightful view of Inwood Hill and the Hudson at the mouth of the Ship Canal. Tea may be obtained, served on the veranda."[14] In 1917, John D. Rockefeller Jr. purchased the Billings estate and offered it to

View of the Harlem River Ship Canal from Broadway, with Manhattan at left, 1987.

E **THE BROCKTON, No. 4242-46**
1910, by A.B. Kight. [6 stories]

HEIGHTS THEATER STOREFRONT, No. 4252
1910. [2 stories]

181st STREET

W **B.S. MOSS'S COLISEUM THEATER, No. 4261**
1920, by De Rosa & Pereira; divided. [3,500 seats]
Site of Blue Bell taverns.

THIRTY-FOURTH POLICE PRECINCT STATION, No. 4295
1985. [2 stories]

THE CYRIL, No. 4305
1915. [5 stories]

E **THE ELMSFORD, No. 4260-78**
1909, by George F. Pelham. [6 stories]

183rd STREET

E **4300-08 BROADWAY**
1940, by Charles Kreymborg. [6 stories]

185th STREET

E **PRIMARY SCHOOL 48, No. 4360-74**
1990–92, School Construction Authority. [4 stories]
Site of Coliseum Garage (also known as the Normandy Garage), 1922, by Charles B. Meyers.

187th STREET

W **MOUNT SINAI JEWISH CENTER OF CONGREGATION MOUNT SINAI ANSHE EMETH, No. 4381**
1959. [2 stories] *Site of* St. Elizabeth Roman Catholic Church and Rectory.

4389-99 BROADWAY
[6 stories]

E **4380-86 BROADWAY**
1927, by Charles Kreymborg & Son. [6 stories]

4410 BROADWAY
1938, by H. Herbert Lillien. [6 stories]

4420 BROADWAY
1938, by H. Herbert Lillien. [6 stories]

GORMAN MEMORIAL PARK
[1.89 acres]

189th STREET

w   **ABBEY TOWERS, No. 4411-23**
1926, by Cohen & Siegel. [7 stories]

190th STREET

w   **THE ROSEFIELD, No. 4441-43**
[6 stories]

LA JOAN, No. 4447-55
[6 stories]

FAIRVIEW AVENUE

E   **4460-66 BROADWAY**
1928, by Charles Kreymborg & Son. [7 stories]

CHABAN HALL, No. 4500
1925, by David S. Lang. [6 stories]

192nd STREET

w   **FORT TRYON APARTMENTS, No. 4489–4523**
1948, by H.I. Feldman. [7 stories]

GAS STATION, No. 4525
[1 story]

193rd STREET

E   **THE RADCLIFFE, No. 4520-28**
1925, by David S. Lang. [6 stories]

THE BROADWAY ARMS, No. 4530-36
1930. [6 stories]

BENNETT AVENUE

w   **FORT TRYON PARK**
[66.62 acres] Scenic Landmark. *Site of* C.K.G.
Billings estate, 1901-05; Black Horse Inn, 1805.

NAGLE AVENUE

E   **4580 BROADWAY**
1937, by H.I. Feldman. [6 stories]

196th STREET

E   **INTERMEDIATE SCHOOL 218, No. 4600**
[4 stories] 1989-91, by Richard Dattner Architects.
Site of Jewish Memorial Hospital-Tosk Clinic,
1933-37, by Charles B. Meyers.

the city for parkland, as part of a deal that would enable him to develop the Rockefeller University. (The city did not accept until 1931, after Rockefeller paid for building the park, which he called Fort Tryon.[15]) The last large part of the Dyckman tract, twenty-eight acres at the tip of Manhattan, was kept relatively open, after being purchased in 1922 by George Fisher Baker to create Baker Field, Columbia's athletic grounds. Another open spot was the triangle bounded by Broadway, Nagel Avenue, and Ellwood Street, which was a truck farm run by the Zerrenner family.[16]

Although portions of Broadway were still under cultivation in the 1920s, Washington Heights went through a spell of deliciously overinflated thinking. It began with B.S. Moss's Coliseum Theater of 1920, at 181st Street, which boasted that it was the third-largest theater in the United States. It culminated in 1928, when work was begun on the Loew's 175th Street Theater, designed by Thomas W. Lamb in Byzantine-Romanesque-Indo-Hindu-Sino-Moorish-Persian-Eclectic-Rococo-Deco style. Even its publicity could almost induce heart palpitations: Oriental palace of Jewels! Worth going miles to see! Times Square Entertainment Brought Nearer Home![17] It opened in 1930 with *Their Own Desire* (starring Norma Shearer) and, direct from the Capitol Theater, the musical comedy stars Shaw and Lee.

Both of these projects would have paled, however, if the Reverend Dr. Christian F. Reisner, pastor of the Broadway Temple Methodist Church, had fulfilled his vision. In 1923, he announced plans for a 725-foot-high "cathedral-like apartment house and church topped with a cross visible for 100 miles by

Broadway Temple as envisioned and, in 1988, as built. New York, The Wonder City, DD.

B.S. MOSS'S COLISEUM THEATER

Views from 1979 include the marquee from its time as an R.K.O. cinema.

LOEW'S 175TH STREET THEATER

Views from 1978 and 1988.

CONGREGATION OHAV SHOLAUM SYNAGOGUE, No. 4624-26
1950. [2 stories]

SHERMAN AVENUE

E **PACKARD MOTOR CAR GARAGE, No. 4650**
(Also known as the Pilot Garage). 1926, by Albert Kahn. [1 story]

DONGAN PLACE

E **TRYON GARDENS, No. 4690 and 4700**
1936, by Sugarman & Berger. [6 stories]

ARDEN STREET

E **4720-28 BROADWAY**
1935, by Horace Ginsbern. [6 stories]

THAYER TOWERS, No. 4730-34
1929, by Springsteen & Goldhammer. [6 stories]

THAYER STREET

E **4740-46 BROADWAY**
1924, by Charles Kreymborg & Son. [6 stories]

RIVERSIDE DRIVE

W **INWOOD PLAZA**
[Traffic triangle] *Site of* Mount Washington Presbyterian Church, 1844, enlarged 1856.

DYCKMAN STREET

W **BROADDYKE APARTMENTS, No. 4761-79**
1927, by Franklin, Bates & Heindsman. [6 stories]

E **NEW YORK PUBLIC LIBRARY-INWOOD BRANCH, No. 4790**
1950, by Tachau & Vought. [2 stories]

JUNIOR HIGH SCHOOL 52, No. 4808
[3 stories] *Site of* Grammar School 52.

CUMMING STREET

W **GEORGE WASHINGTON COURT, No. 4791-97**
1924, by Matthew W. Del Gaudio. [6 stories]

ACADEMY STREET

W **HAWTHORNE GARDENS, No. 4861-79**
1928, by Allan B. Bates and Theodore E. Heindsman. [6 stories]

Church of the Good Shepherd, 1988.

aeroplane."[18] A "city in itself," the Broadway Temple project was to have a central tower, flanked by twelve-story residential wings on 173rd and 174th streets, with more than 450 apartments and hotel rooms, an auditorium for several thousand people, a community hall, a Sunday School, a gymnasium and swimming pool.[19] The two wings actually were built in the mid-1920s but overreaching ambition and the Great Depression conspired against the tower that was to have soared skyward between them.

In spite of the Depression, there was something of a Subway Boom in the mid- to late 1930s. The Independent rapid transit line reached upper Broadway in 1932, running from Dyckman to 207th Street. Jewish Memorial Hospital was begun in 1933, on the site of the Zerrenners' farm, and the Church of the Good Shepherd was built in 1935 at Isham Street. There followed several minor masterpieces of Art Deco or modernist styling, including 4720–28 Broadway of 1935, at Arden Street; Tryon Gardens of 1936, at Dongan Place; and 4080–84 Broadway of 1936, at 172nd Street.

When construction resumed after World War II, it picked up along modernist lines, with the handsome Fort Tryon Apartments of 1948, north of 192nd Street, and the Broadway Temple sanctuary of 1952, which filled the space between the north and south wings, however modestly.[20] Two other religious properties were developed in the 1950s: the synagogue of Congregation Ohav Sholaum, next door to Jewish Memorial Hospital, whose members

TOUCHES OF DECO AND MODERNE

Clockwise from the upper left: Tryon Gardens, 1987; Jewish Memorial Hospital, Tosk Clinic, 1985; 4080-84 Broadway, 1979; and 4720-28 Broadway, 1987.

TRANSPORTATION LINKS

Views from 1979 and 1988 show the Broadway Bridge over the Harlem River Ship Canal (left) and a portion of the George Washington Bridge Bus Station.

Marble Hill Houses, 1987.

included refugees from the Holocaust, and the Mount Sinai Jewish Center of 1959, at 187th Street. The largest post-war development was Marble Hill Houses, a public project with eleven buildings, between 225th and 230th streets. (A tablet on the northernmost tower notes its proximity to the site of the old King's Bridge.) The project opened in 1951 and at the end of the 1980s, some 3,900 people lived there.

In the early 1960s, two major transportation projects were built on Broadway. The double-deck Broadway Bridge, the third to cross the Harlem Ship Canal, was finished in 1963. To accommodate river traffic, its center span could be hoisted up the 160-foot-high towers that dominate the surrounding low-rise landscape. Another striking structure, completed the same year, is the winged George Washington Bridge Bus Station, from 178th to 179th Street, on the site of the Great Maize Land.

For many years, the neighborhood kept one vital link to its pre-colonial farming heritage: the Benedetto farm, on Broadway between 213th and 214th streets, which was populated by chickens, rabbits, a goat and—at plowing time—a rented horse. The family sold eggs, corn, tomatoes, string beans, lettuce, peaches, and pears until 1954, when the property was sold to make room for a telephone company building.[21]

Broadway lost one of its finest functioning movie palaces in 1967, when the Loew's 175th Street Theater closed. It was purchased two years later for use as the United Church of Reverend Ike (the Reverend Frederick J.

204th STREET

W DYCKMAN PARK
[0.54 acres]

DYCKMAN HOUSE, No. 4881
1783-85, by William Dyckman; restored 1915-16, by Alexander McMillan Welch. Bake House (south wing), built between 1725 and 1750. Landmark. [3 stories]

COLONIAL GARDENS, No. 4915
1936, by H.I. Feldman. [6 stories]

4925-35 BROADWAY
1930. [5 stories]

207th STREET

W CHURCH OF THE GOOD SHEPHERD, No. 4967
1935, by Paul Monaghan.

E HARLEM SAVINGS BANK BRANCH, No. 4950
(Also known as the Apple Bank for Savings). 1930 [1 story]

4960-64 BROADWAY
1937, by I.L. Crausman. [6 stories]

ISHAM STREET

W WILLIAM B. ISHAM PARK
[20.09 acres]

ISHAM PARK PLAZA, No. 5009-21
1928, by Charles Kreymborg & Son. [7 stories]

ROSEWALL COURT, No. 5025-35
1926, by Charles Kreymborg & Son. [7 stories]

212th STREET

E GRENVILLE HALL, No. 5000-06
1912, by George F. Pelham. [6 stories]

215th STREET

W 215th STREET STAIRWAY

5057-61 BROADWAY
1939, by Charles Kreymborg. [6 stories]

MARBLE GATE, No. 5063-65
(Also known as the Jack Gallo Auto Body Shop, Seaman-Drake Arch). 1855. [2 stories]

216th STREET

E   **KINGSBRIDGE DIVISION DEPOT AND POWER HOUSE, THIRD AVENUE RAILWAY COMPANY**
(Also known as a Transit Authority Bus Garage). 1897, by Romeo Tomassek and Isaac A. Hopper.

218th STREET

W   **BAKER FIELD OF COLUMBIA UNIVERSITY**
1921-22. [22.5 acres] Soccer Stadium. 1985, by Richard Dattner. *Site of* Wonderland Park.

ALLEN PAVILION OF THE PRESBYTERIAN HOSPITAL, No. 5141
1986-88, by Skidmore, Owings & Merrill. [3 stories]

NINTH AVENUE

BROADWAY BRIDGE

1958-63, by George Ellenoff, Bureau of Bridge Design, Public Works Department. [312 feet long] *Site of* Broadway Bridge, 1907-08; Ship Canal Bridge, 1893-95.

HARLEM RIVER SHIP CANAL

(Also known as the United States Ship Canal). 1895, by Colonel George L. Gillespie.

225th STREET

W   *Site of* Kingsbridge Inn (also known as Hyatt's Tavern at the Free Bridge), 1773.

225th STREET I.R.T. STATION

E   **MARBLE HILL HOUSES**
1951-52, by John Ambrose Thompson.

5210-20 BROADWAY
[15 stories]

5240-50 BROADWAY
[15 stories] *Site of* Kingsbridge Hotel.

5360 BROADWAY
[14 stories] *Site of* Broadway Bridge (also known as the Borough-line Bridge), 1899-1900.

5470-96 BROADWAY
[14 stories]

228th STREET

W   **5365 BROADWAY**
[14 stories]

210 WEST 230th STREET
[14 stories]

Allen Pavilion of the Presbyterian Hospital, 1988.

Eikerenkoetter II), and has been carefully and respectfully maintained. The auditorium is whole, as is the Grand Foyer, the "Promenade of Jewels," and the Wonder Morton organ. A butterscotch-yellow haze of nostalgia floats under its iridescent chandeliers. The bronze gleam that suffuses the red-upholstered house is aged, mellow, and so warm that it seems to emerge from the filigreed walls themselves.

Another local landmark from the 1930s, the Jewish Memorial Hospital, did not fare as well. It was forced to close in 1983 and was razed not long afterward. The community waited five years to get another major medical facility: the Allen Pavilion, a 300-bed branch of the Presbyterian Hospital, situated in what had been the northeast corner of Baker Field.

With the completion of the Allen building in 1988, it could be said that Broadway had at last been developed from one end of Manhattan Island to the other. The task had taken 375 years.

Broadway does not stop where Manhattan ends. It goes through the Bronx and merges with the Albany Post Road at the city line. As South Broadway and North Broadway, it crosses Yonkers. Still called Broadway, it runs uninterrupted through Hastings-on-Hudson, Dobbs Ferry, Ardsley-on-Hudson, Irvington, Tarrytown, and North Tarrytown. After that, as Route Nine or the Albany Post Road, it travels through the rest of Westchester and then Putnam, Dutchess, Columbia, and Rensselaer Counties, all the way to Albany. It can be thought of as a 175-mile street, meaning that after Marble Hill, the journey has just begun.

George Washington Bridge and Bus Station, 1979.

NOTES

Listed below in boldface are the abbreviated names, which will be used throughout the notes, for recurring citations.

RECURRING CITATIONS

BLOOMINGDALE
Hopper Striker Mott, *The New York of Yesterday, A Descriptive Narrative of Old Bloomingdale* (New York: G.P. Putnam's Sons, 1908).

GREATEST STREET
Stephen Jenkins, *The Greatest Street in the World* (New York: G.P. Putnam's Sons, 1911).

HONE
Allan Nevins, ed., *The Diary of Philip Hone* (New York: Dodd, Mead & Company, 1927). Two volumes.

ICONOGRAPHY
I.N. Phelps Stokes, *The Iconography of Manhattan Island* (New York: Robert H. Dodd, 1915-28). Six volumes.

INSTITUTIONS
J.F. Richmond, *New York and Its Institutions, 1609-1872* (New York: E.B. Treat, 1872).

KING
Moses King, *King's Handbook of New York City*, 2nd ed. (Boston: Moses King, 1893).

NEW METROPOLIS
E. Idell Zeisloft, ed., *The New Metropolis* (New York: D. Appleton & Company, 1899).

NEW YORK 1900
Robert A.M. Stern, Gregory Gilmartin, and John Massengale, *New York 1900* (New York: Rizzoli International Publications, 1983).

OUR THEATRES
Ruth Crosby Dimmick, *Our Theatres To-Day and Yesterday* (New York: H.K. Fly, 1913).

PICTURE
A Picture of New-York in 1851 [Cover title: *Francis' Picture of New-York and Strangers Guide*] (New York: C.S. Francis & Company).

RIDER
Fremont Rider, ed., *Rider's New York City*, 2nd ed. (New York: Henry Holt & Company, 1923).

SHADOWS
James D. McCabe Jr., *Lights and Shadows of New York Life* (Philadelphia: National Publishing Company, 1872; reprint, New York: Farrar, Straus & Giroux, 1970).

STRONG
Allan Nevins and Milton Halsey Thomas, *The Diary of George Templeton Strong* (New York: Macmillan Company, 1952). Four volumes.

SUNSHINE
Matthew Hale Smith, *Sunshine and Shadow in New York* (Hartford, Conn.: J.B. Burr & Company, 1869).

TIMES
The *New York Times*, various dates.

VALENTINE
David Thomas Valentine, *Manual of the Corporation of the City of New York*, published between 1841-42 and 1870 (later edited by Joseph Shannon and John Hardy); and Henry Collins Brown, *Valentine's Manual of Old New York*, published between 1916-17 and 1928 (first titled *Valentine's Manual of the City of New York*). Cited are the manuals for 1849, 1850, 1851, 1855, 1856, 1857, 1863, 1864, 1865, 1916-17, 1917-18, 1919, 1921, 1923, 1924, 1926, 1927.

WONDER CITY
W. Parker Chase, *New York, The Wonder City* (New York: Wonder City Publishing, 1932; reprint, New York: New York Bound, 1983).

W.P.A. GUIDE
Federal Writers' Project of the Works Progress Administration, *New York City Guide* [also known as the *W.P.A. Guide*] (New York: Random House, 1939; reprint, New York: Random House, 1982).

SOURCES FOR THE INVENTORY

Besides data furnished by Christopher Gray and Michael R. Miller, basic information came from street atlases in the collection of the New-York Historical Society. Most frequently consulted were those by G.W. Bromley Company, Perris & Browne, REDI Real Estate Information Service, and Sanborn Map Company. The most generally helpful books and reports, including *Greatest Street, Iconography, King, Our Theatres, Rider, Valentine 1865, Wonder City,* and *W.P.A. Guide* were:

Apartment Houses of the Metropolis (New York: G.C. Hesselgren Publishing Company, 1908).

Apartment Houses of the Metropolis, supplement (New York: G.C. Hesselgren Publishing Company, 1909).

Robert F.R. Ballard, *Directory of Manhattan Office Buildings* (New York: McGraw-Hill Book Company, 1978).

Alan Burnham, *New York Landmarks* (Middletown, Conn.: Wesleyan University Press, 1963).

Cushman & Wakefield Directory of Manhattan Office Buildings (New York: Real Estate Data Inc., 1986).

R.M. De Leeuw, *Both Sides of Broadway* (New York: De Leeuw Riehl Publishing Company, 1910).

Margot Gayle and Michele Cohen, *The Art Commission and the Municipal Art Society Guide to Manhattan's Outdoor Sculpture* (New York: Prentice Hall Press, 1988).

Margot Gayle and Edmund V. Gillon Jr., *Cast-Iron Architecture in New York City* (New York: Dover Publications, 1974).

Paul Goldberger, *The City Observed: New York* (New York: Random House, 1979).

Hardy Holzman Pfeiffer Associates, *30 Theaters* (New York: Hardy Holzman Pfeiffer Associates, 1983).

Mary C. Henderson, *The City and the Theatre* (Clifton, N.J.: James T. White & Company, 1973).

A History of Real Estate, Building and Architecture in New York City (New York: Real Estate Record Association, 1898).

King's Photographic Views of New York (Boston: Moses King, 1895).

Landmarks Preservation Commission, *Ladies' Mile Historic District Designation Report*, vol. 1 (New York: Landmarks Preservation Commission, 1989).

Landmarks Preservation Commission, "Manhattan Survey" (June 20, 1986).

Landmarks Preservation Commission, *SoHo-Cast Iron Historic District Designation Report* (New York: Landmarks Preservation Commission, 1973).

John William Robson, ed., *A Guide to Columbia University* (New York: Columbia University Press, 1937).

Yale Robbins and Henry Robbins, *Manhattan Office Buildings, Downtown 1986* (New York: Yale Robbins, 1986).

Yale Robbins and Henry Robbins, *Manhattan Office Buildings, Midtown 1985* (New York: Yale Robbins, 1985).

John Tauranac, *Essential New York* (New York: Holt, Rinehart & Winston, 1979).

Norval White and Elliot Willensky, *AIA Guide to New York City*, rev. ed. (New York: Collier Books, 1978).

Elliot Willensky and Norval White, *AIA Guide to New York City*, 3rd ed. (New York: Harcourt Brace Jovanovich, 1988).

INTRODUCTION   Pages 1–9

1. Junius Henri Browne, *The Great Metropolis* (Hartford, Conn.: American Publishing Co., 1868), 339.
2. Reginald Pelham Bolton, *New York City in Indian Possession*, 2nd ed. (New York: Museum of the American Indian-Heye Foundation, 1975), 35-36; Rodman Gilder, *The Battery* (Boston: Houghton Mifflin Company, 1936), 4; *Iconography*, vol. VI, 67-b; De Vries, "Voyages from Holland to America," *Collections of the New-York Historical Society*, 2nd series, David Pietersz (New York: D. Appleton & Company, 1857), 102.
3. *Valentine 1851*, 361.
4. *Iconography*, vol. VI, 67-b, 589; Henry Collins Brown, *Glimpses of Old New-York* (New York: privately printed, 1917), 121; *Iconography*, vol. II, 349, pl. 87; Theodore S. Fay, *Views in New-York and Its Environs* (New York: Peabody & Company, 1831), 17; James Grant Wilson, ed., *The Memorial History of the City of New-York*, vol. I (New York: New-York History Company, 1892), 294.
5. *Iconography*, vol. IV, 254, 259.
6. *Iconography*, vol. V, 1297.
7. *Iconography*, vol. VI, plates 84B-b, 84B-c, 84B-d.
8. *Iconography*, vol. V, 1326, 1387.
9. *Iconography*, vol. V, 1475.
10. John Randel Jr. in *Valentine 1864*, 848.
11. Randel Jr., op. cit., 850.
12. *Hone*, vol. I, 434.
13. *Strong*, vol. I, 150.
14. *Iconography*, vol. V, 1739.
15. *Iconography*, vol. V, 1777-78.
16. James Fenimore Cooper, *New York* (New York: William Farquhar Payson, 1930), 13.
17. *Hone*, vol. II, 896.
18. Joel H. Ross, *What I Saw in New-York* (Auburn, N.Y.: Derby & Miller, 1851), 178-79.
19. *Strong*, vol. II, 203.
20. *Valentine 1856*, 520.
21. *Iconography*, vol. V, 1902.
22. *Institutions*, 113.
23. Edward Winslow Martin, *The Secrets of the Great City* (Philadelphia: National Publishing Company, 1868), 35.
24. Carin Drechsler-Marx and Richard F. Shepard, *Broadway* (New York: Harry N. Abrams, 1988), 8.
25. Charles Edwin Prescott, ed., *The Hotel Guests' Guide*, 2nd ed. (New York: Geo. W. Averell, 1872), 45.
26. Martin, *Secrets of the Great City*, 42, 45-7.
27. Browne, *Great Metropolis*, 340-41.
28. *Wood's Illustrated Hand-Book to New York* (New York: G.W. Carleton & Company, 1873), 147.
29. *Institutions*, 125.
30. Walt Whitman, "Broadway," in *Walt Whitman: The Complete Poems*, ed. Francis Murphy (London: Penguin Books, 1975), 530-31.
31. *New Metropolis*, 620.
32. *Greatest Street*, v, 276; "Want It Called Broadway," *Times* (February 26, 1898): 12.
33. *Interborough Rapid Transit* (New York: Interborough Rapid Transit Company, 1904), 18, 23.
34. "In the Real Estate Field," *Times* (October 23, 1904): 16.
35. *Broadway* (New York: Broadway Association, 1926), 9-10, 35, 102, 110, 118, 122, 137.
36. V.S. Pritchett, *New York Proclaimed* (New York: Harcourt, Brace & World, 1965), 14.
37. J.B. Kerfoot, *Broadway* (Boston: Houghton Mifflin Company, 1911), 117-18.

FINANCIAL DISTRICT   Pages 13–40

1. Martha J. Lamb, *History of the City of New York*, vol. I (New York: A.S. Barnes & Company, 1877), 34.
2. *Iconography*, vol. II, 216-18, 223, 226, 235; Henry Collins Brown, *The Story of Old New York* (New York: E.P. Dutton & Company, 1934), 127.
3. *Iconography*, vol. I, plate 23-a; Felix Oldboy, *Walks in Our Churchyards* (New York: Geo. Gottsberger Peck, 1903), 48.
4. E. Clowes Chorley, ed., *Quarter of a Millennium* (Philadelphia: Church Historical Society, 1947), 9.
5. *Valentine 1849*, 350.
6. *Iconography*, vol. IV, 530.
7. *Valentine 1850*, 416.
8. *A History of Columbia University* (New York: Columbia University Press, 1904), 21.
9. *Iconography*, vol. IV, 712.
10. "Bush, the Homeless and the Past to Meet at Service at St. Paul's," *Times* (April 24, 1989): B3; Chorley, *Quarter of a Millennium*, 28; *Valentine 1916-17*, 199.
11. *Iconography*, vol. IV, 819.
12. *Iconography*, vol. V, 992; *Greatest Street*, 22.
13. Thomas Jefferson Wertenbaker, *Father Knickerbocker Rebels* (New York: Charles Scribner's Sons, 1948), 101.
14. David Franks, *The New-York Directory* (New York: Shepard Kollock, 1786), 54-55.
15. *Strong*, vol. IV, 486.
16. *Iconography*, vol. V, 1262.
17. Benson J. Lossing, ed., *The Diary of George Washington* (New York: Charles B. Richardson & Company, 1860), 87; *Valentine 1855*, 583.
18. Robert Shackleton, *The Book of New York* (Philadelphia: Penn Publishing Company, 1917), 219.
19. Edmund M. Blunt, *Blunt's Stranger's Guide to the City of New-York* (New York: Edmund M. Blunt, 1817), 42.
20. *Iconography*, vol. V, 1309.
21. Philip N. Schuyler, ed., *The Hundred Year Book* (New York: A.S. Barnes & Company, 1942), 91.
22. *Iconography*, vol. V, 1672.
23. *Hone*, vol. I, 126.
24. *Iconography*, vol. VI, 55.
25. *Valentine 1927*, 350.
26. Advertisement in *Miller's New York As It Is* (New York: James Miller, 1866).
27. *Hone*, vol. II, 765.
28. *Picture*, xv.
29. *Iconography*, vol. V, 1871.
30. *New York 1900*, 145.
31. Henry Collins Brown, *Glimpses of Old New-York* (New York: privately printed, 1917), 138.
32. H. Wilson, *Trow's New York City Directory*, vol. LXXX (New York: John F. Trow, 1866), 375.
33. *Sunshine*, 515; *Strong*, vol. IV, 86.
34. Thomas Lloyd, *Lloyd's Pocket Companion and Guide* (New York: Thomas Lloyd, 1866), 148.
35. *King*, 732.
36. *Iconography*, vol. V, 1940; Robert Macoy, *How To See New York and Its Environs* (New York: Robert Macoy, 1876), 45.
37. *Sunshine*, 259, 261.
38. *Greatest Street*, 70.
39. Allan Nevins, *John D. Rockefeller* (New York: Charles Scribner's Sons, 1959), 155-6.
40. John A. Kouwenhoven, *The Columbia Historical Portrait of New York* (Garden City, N.Y.: Doubleday & Company, 1953), 394.
41. Nathan Silver, *Lost New York* (Boston: Houghton Mifflin Company, 1967), 102.
42. Robert Sobel, *N.Y.S.E.* (New York: Weybright & Talley, 1975), 250.
43. "The Birth of the New York Skyscraper—A Romance of Architecture," *Times* (May 21, 1905): sec. 4, p. 6.
44. Kouwenhoven, *Columbia Historical Portrait*, 394; "The Tallest in the World," *Times* (October 8, 1893): 17; "Francis H. Kimball Buried," *Times* (December 29, 1919): 9.
45. William H. Jordy and Ralph Coe, eds., *American Architecture and Other Writings by Montgomery Schuyler* (New York: Atheneum, 1964), 221; Montgomery Schuyler, *The Woolworth Building* (New York: privately printed, 1913), 8-9.
46. *New York, the Metropolis of the Western World* (New York: Foster & Reynolds Company, 1917), 30.
47. Deborah Nevins, *Palace of Commerce* (New York: New York Landmarks Conservancy, 1983), broadside.
48. Landmarks Preservation Commission, "U.S. Realty Building" (June 7, 1988), 3.
49. "Twin Skyscrapers on Broadway For Which Streets Will Be Moved," *Times* (May 27, 1906): 16; "Tall Buildings," *Times* (August 13, 1906): 6.
50. *King's Views, New York, 1908-1909* (Boston: Moses King, 1908), 39.
51. Landmarks Preservation Commission, "Woolworth Building" (April 12, 1983), 4-5.
52. S. Parkes Cadman, *The Cathedral of Commerce* (New York: Broadway Park Place Company, 1917), 6.
53. Schuyler, *Woolworth Building*, 3-4.
54. *New Metropolis*, 470.
55. "Skyscrapers Bad For City," *Times* (July 3, 1908): 1.
56. "World's Biggest Building," *Times* (September 19, 1912): 1; S.J. Makielski Jr., *The Politics of*

Zoning (New York: Columbia University Press, 1966), 14.

57. *Wonder City*, 177; City Planning Commission, *Zoning Handbook* (New York: Department of City Planning, 1981), 7.

58. "That Wonderful Year 1913," *195 Magazine* (February 1963): 13.

59. "New Cunard Building," *Times* (May 1, 1921): sec. 10, p. 1.

60. Arthur Bartlett Maurice, *Magical City* (New York: Charles Scribner's Sons, 1935), 17.

61. Sonny Kleinfeld, *The Biggest Company on Earth* (New York: Holt, Rinehart & Winston, 1981), 3-4.

62. "200 in Armed Guard Move Bank Billions," *Times* (March 23, 1931): 5.

63. Frank Moss, *The American Metropolis*, vol. II (New York: Peter Fenelon Collier, 1897), 182.

64. Alan Burnham, ed., *New York Landmarks* (Middletown, Conn.: Wesleyan University Press, 1963), 370; Axel Menges, *Architecture of Skidmore, Owings & Merrill, 1963-1973* (New York: Architectural Book Publishing Company, 1974), 144.

65. Burnham, *New York Landmarks*, 363; Silver, *Lost New York*, 212; Joseph P. Fried, "End of Skyscraper: Daring in '08, Obscure in '68," *Times* (March 27, 1968): 49.

66. Menges, *Skidmore, Owings & Merrill*, 150.

67. Rodman Gilder, *The Battery* (Boston: Houghton Mifflin Company, 1936), 250-51; Grover Whalen, *Mr. New York* (New York: G.P. Putnam's Sons, 1955), 89-90; "Ticker-Tape Parades: Which Were Biggest?" *Times* (October 29, 1986): B14.

68. John C. Goodbody, *One Peppercorne* (New York: Parish of Trinity Church, 1982), 99.

CIVIC CENTER/TRIBECA   Pages 45–64

1. *Iconography*, 537, 545.

2. James Hardie, *The Description of the City of New York* (New York: S. Marks, 1827), 191.

3. Frank Moss, *The American Metropolis*, vol. II (New York: Peter Fenelon Collier, 1897), 277; *Valentine 1865*, 567.

4. *Iconography*, vol. IV, 822.

5. A.J. Wall in *Valentine 1919*, 226.

6. *Iconography*, vol. IV, 940.

7. William J. Davis in *Valentine 1855*, 487.

8. Edmund M. Blunt, *Blunt's Stranger's Guide to the City of New-York* (New York: Edmund M. Blunt, 1817), 67.

9. *Iconography*, vol. V, 1394.

10. Evan W. Cornog, "To Give Character to Our City: New York's City Hall," *New York History* (October 1988): 389.

11. *Iconography*, vol. V, 1397.

12. Blunt, *Stranger's Guide*, 45.

13. Blunt, op. cit., 58.

14. Theodore S. Fay, *Views in New-York and Its Environs* (New York: Peabody & Company, 1831), 55.

15. Fay, op. cit., 45.

16. *King*, 544; James Grant Wilson, ed., *The Memorial History of the City of New-York*, vol. III (New York: New-York History Company, 1893), 234.

17. *Picture*, 51-2.

18. John Erskine, *The Philharmonic-Symphony Society of New York* (New York: Macmillan Company, 1943), 5.

19. *Our Theatres*, 34.

20. "Broadway Tabernacle History Is Reviewed by Dr. Chalmers," *New York Herald Tribune* (April 15, 1940).

21. Joseph Devorkin, *Great Merchants of Early New York* (New York: The Society for the Architecture of the City, 1987), 34.

22. *Hone*, vol. II, 729, 772; *Valentine 1921*, 192.

23. Andrew Scott Dolkart, *The Texture of Tribeca* (New York: Tribeca Community Association, 1989), 23-5; Margot Gayle and Lawrence Wodehouse, "The Sun Building N.Y.C." (New York: Victorian Society in America, 1974), 2.

24. Solyman Brown, ed., *The Citizen and Strangers' Pictorial and Business Directory* (New York: Charles Spalding & Company, 1853), 113.

25. *Francis's New Guide to the Cities of New York and Brooklyn* (New York: C.S. Francis & Company, 1857), 90.

26. *Iconography*, vol. V, 1855.

27. *Iconography*, vol. V, 1902.

28. *Institutions*, 373-74.

29. *The Metropolitan Life Insurance Company* (New York: Metropolitan Life Insurance Company, 1914), 61-62.

30. *Institutions*, 125.

31. *Rider*, 201.

32. Stan Fischler, *Uptown, Downtown* (New York: Hawthorn Books, 1976), 22.

33. "The Secret Accounts," *Times* (July 22, 1871): 1; "Concerning That Monument," *Times* (May 11, 1871): 4.

34. *Valentine 1924*, 113.

35. *Rider*, 202.

36. "Fate of the Old City Hall," *Times* (January 29, 1893): 17.

37. Ibid.

38. Art Commission, *City Hall* (New York: Art Commission, 1977), n.p.

39. "The Home's New Habitation," *Times* (October 22, 1893): 20.

40. Landmarks Preservation Commission, "Former New York Life Insurance Building Interior" (February 10, 1987), 2.

41. Montgomery Schuyler, *The Woolworth Building* (New York: privately printed, 1913), 10-11.

42. "Another Big Office Building," *Times* (October 29, 1893): 21.

43. Federal Writers' Project, *New York Panorama* (New York: Random House, 1938), 307.

44. *King*, 958.

45. *Valentine 1917-18*, 104.

46. "Old Sun's Site Sold for Erection of a $40,000,000 Skyscraper," *Times* (January 27, 1951): 9.

47. Landmarks Preservation Commission, "Tweed Courthouse" (October 16, 1984), 29.

48. *The Renascence of City Hall* (New York: Department of Public Works, 1956), 17-27; "A 'New' City Hall Gleams As of Old," *Times* (May 29, 1956): 29.

49. United States General Services Administration-Region 2, News Release (April 29, 1981).

SOHO   Pages 69–86

1. *Valentine 1865*, 604, 612.

2. William E. Dodge, *Old New York* (New York: Dodd, Mead & Company, 1880), 8.

3. Edwin Williams, ed., *New-York As It Is In 1834* (New York: J. Disturnell, 1834), 191.

4. *Sunshine*, 126; "Here Astor Once Lived," *Times* (February 16, 1896): 22.

5. *Doggett's New-York City Directory for 1845 & 1846* (New York: John Doggett Jr., 1845), 22, 311; *Institutions*, 361.

6. *Picture*, 133.

7. *Iconography*, vol. V, 1800.

8. *Picture*, 67.

9. *Iconography*, vol. V, 1845.

10. *Iconography*, vol. V, 1842-43.

11. "The St. Nicholas Hotel," *Times* (January 7, 1853): 6.

12. G. Danielson Carroll, *Carroll's New York City Directory* (New York: Carroll & Company, 1859), 76; *A Chronicle Recording One Hundred Twenty-Five Years* (New York: Brooks Brothers, 1943), 26.

13. "Marble Palaces on Broadway," *Times* (August 29, 1859): 4; Robert Hendrickson, *The Grand Emporiums* (New York: Stein & Day, 1979), 156.

14. *Carroll's Directory*, 148.

15. Bayrd Still, *Mirror For Gotham* (New York: New York University Press, 1956), 190; Philip N. Schuyler, ed., *The Hundred Year Book* (New York: A.S. Barnes & Company, 1942), 39.

16. *Carroll's Directory*, 100.

17. *The Sun's Guide to New York* (New York: R. Wayne Wilson & Company, 1892), 365.

18. Margot Gayle and Edmund V. Gillon Jr., *Cast-Iron Architecture in New York* (New York: Dover Publications, 1974), viii.

19. *Carroll's Directory*, 82.

20. Gayle, *Cast-Iron Architecture*, 141.

21. *King*, 874.

22. "Charles B. Rouss Dead," *Times* (March 4, 1902): 9.

23. *Appletons' Dictionary of New York and Its Vicinity*, 10th ed. (New York: D. Appleton & Company, 1888), 8.

24. Grace Glueck, "Neighborhoods: SoHo Is Artists' Last Resort," *Times* (May 11, 1970): 37.

25. Author's interview with Alfred Boyan Maw Sturtevant, March 3, 1989.

NOHO/EAST VILLAGE   Pages 91–108

1. Barnett Shepherd, *Sailors' Snug Harbor* (New York: Snug Harbor Cultural Center, 1979), 15.

2. William Rhinelander Stewart, *Grace Church and Old New York* (New York: E.P. Dutton & Company, 1924), 353-54; *Valentine 1865*, 644; Charles Hemstreet, *Nooks and Corners of Old New York* (New York: Charles Scribner's Sons, 1899), 175-76.

3. *Iconography*, vol. V, 1436; Edmund M. Blunt, *Blunt's Stranger's Guide to the City of New-York* (New York: Edmund M. Blunt, 1817), 136.

4. George E. DeMille, *Saint Thomas Church* (Austin, Texas: Church Historical Society, 1958), 20, 28.

5. *Picture*, 134.

6. Gene Schermerhorn, *Letters to Phil* (New York: New York Bound, 1982), 23.

7. Walter Barrett, *The Old Merchants of New York City*, vol. II, part 2 (New York: M. Doolady, 1872), 227.

8. Walter Barrett, *The Old Merchants of New York City*, 1st series (New York: Carleton, 1864), 12-13; Sturges S. Dunham in *Valentine 1917-18*, 212.

9. *Hone*, vol. I, 207.

10. Wayne Andrews, ed., *The Autobiography of Theodore Roosevelt* (New York: Charles Scribner's Sons, 1958), 6.

11. Charles Lockwood, *Bricks and Brownstones* (New York: Abbeville Press, 1972), 46.

12. E. Porter Belden, *New-York: Past, Present and Future* (New York: Prall, Lewis & Co., 1851), 124; *Picture*, 55.

13. Belden, *New-York*, 132.

14. *Strong*, vol. IV, 330.

15. *Hone*, vol. II, 754.

16. *Sunshine*, 38.

17. James D. McCabe, *New York By Sunlight and Gaslight* (New York: Union Publishing House, 1882), 147.

18. James L. Ford in *Valentine 1924*, 157-58.

19. "Prof. Bell's Telephone," *Times* (May 12, 1877): 2; *King*, 233.

20. Charles Hemstreet, *Literary New York* (New York: G.P. Putnam's Sons, 1903), 212; Lloyd Morris, *Incredible New York* (New York: Random House, 1951), 75.

21. *Our Theatres*, 36.

22. *Our Theatres*, 43; Mary C. Henderson, *The City and the Theatre* (Clifton, N.J.: James T. White & Company, 1973), 114.

23. *Our Theatres*, 44-48; Henderson, *City and the Theatre*, 117.

24. *New York Illustrated* (New York: D. Appleton & Company, 1869), 16.

25. Margot Gayle and Edmund V. Gillon Jr., *Cast-Iron Architecture in New York* (New York: Dover Publications, 1974), 161; Robert Hendrickson, *The Grand Emporiums* (New York: Stein & Day, 1979), 36; *New York Illustrated*, 18.

26. *New York Illustrated*, 18; *Shadows*, 378, 381.

27. *Shadows*, 378, 381.

28. *King*, 853.

29. Joseph Devorkin, *Great Merchants of Early New York* (New York: Society for the Architecture of the City, 1987), 22-23.

30. *Rider*, 204; *Shadows*, 126.

31. "Base-Ball," *Times* (February 7, 1876): 2.

32. Samuel White Patterson, *Hunter College* (New York: Lantern Press, 1955), 21, 23-24.

33. DeMille, *Saint Thomas Church*, 76.

34. *New Metropolis*, 202.

35. *King*, 581.

36. Christopher Gray, "The Ghost Behind a Huge Sign," *Times* (January 29, 1989): sec. 10, p. 12.

37. Robert Macoy, *How to See New York and Its Environs* (New York: Robert Macoy, 1876), 62.

38. Gayle, *Cast-Iron Architecture*, 159.

39. Richard Alleman, *The Movie Lover's Guide to New York* (New York: Perennial Library, 1988), 147-148.

40. "Broadway Cables Running," *Times* (May 11, 1893): 9.

41. Stephen Crane, "In the Broadway Cars," *The Empire City*, ed. Alexander Klein (New York: Rinehart & Company, 1955), 226.

42. Advertisement in *King's Photographic Views of New York* (Boston: Moses King, 1895), 476.

43. *New Metropolis*, 479.

44. *Golden Book of the Wanamaker Stores* (Philadelphia: John Wanamaker, 1911), 292-96; Robert A.M. Stern, Gregory Gilmartin, and Thomas Mellins, *New York 1930* (New York: Rizzoli International Publications, 1987), 336; "Wanamaker's Opens Airplane Department; First $25,000 Craft Due at Store Today," *Times* (October 8, 1925): 1.

45. Meyer Berger, "About New York," *Times* (July 16, 1956): 14.

46. Bayard Webster, "24 Killed in Broadway Loft Fire," *Times* (March 20, 1958): 1.

47. Murray Schumach, "Broadway Central Hotel Collapses," *Times* (August 4, 1973): 56.

48. Mary Peacock, ed., *The Village Voice Guide to Manhattan's Hottest Shopping Neighborhoods* (New York: Fawcett Columbine, 1987), 78.

49. Peter Kihss, "Hebrew College to Build Center at N.Y.U. and Share Facilities," *Times* (September 12, 1977): 26.

50. John Duka, "New Life Along Lower Broadway," *Times* (January 22, 1984): 45; Michael Gross, "New Life at LoBro," *Times* (September 20, 1985): A18.

51. Macoy, *How to See New York*, 60-61.

UNION SQUARE/LADIES' MILE   Pages 113–26

1. J. Sanford Saltus and Walter E. Tisné, *Statues of New York* (New York: G.P. Putnam's Sons, 1923), 28.

2. *Valentine 1857*, 480.

3. *Valentine 1865*, 648.

4. *Hone*, vol. II, 626

5. E. Porter Belden, *New-York: Past, Present and Future* (New York: Prall, Lewis & Co., 1851), 33.

6. *Strong*, vol. III, 359.

7. Brooks Peters, "An Unreal Estate," *Quest* (March 1989), 28.

8. *Miller's New York As It Is* (New York: James Miller, 1866), 68; M. Christine Boyer, *Manhattan Manners—Architecture and Style, 1850-1900* (New York: Rizzoli International Publications, 1985), 56.

9. Advertisement in *Miller's New York As It Is*; *King*, 294.

10. "Aaron Arnold," *Times* (March 19, 1876): 7; *Strong*, vol. IV, 211; Landmarks Preservation Commission, *Ladies' Mile Historic District Designation Report*, vol. I (New York: Landmarks Preservation Commission, 1989), 79, 83; Kenneth Holcomb Dunshee, *As You Pass By* (New York: Hastings House, 1952), 233.

11. *New Metropolis*, 484.

12. Gerard R. Wolfe, *New York, A Guide to the Metropolis*, rev. ed. (New York: McGraw-Hill Book Company, 1983), 220; John Crawford Brown in *Valentine 1921*, 99-100.

13. *Appletons' Dictionary of New York and Its Vicinity*, 24th ed. (New York: D. Appleton & Company, 1902), 85.

14. Advertisement in *Both Sides of Broadway* (New York: De Leeuw Riehl Publishing Company, 1910), 319.

15. *Institutions*, 129; "A Modern Trade-Palace," *Times* (November 27, 1870): 5.

16. Landmarks Preservation Commission, "Former Lord & Taylor Building" (November 15, 1977), 3; *Shadows*, 383-385.

17. "A New Dry-Goods Emporium," *Times* (September 29, 1872): 8.

18. John Disturnell, *New York As It Was and As It Is* (New York: D. Van Nostrand, 1876), 32.

19. James D. Ellsworth in *Valentine 1921*, 183-184; Bayrd Still, *Mirror for Gotham* (New York: New York University Press, 1956), 231.

20. Moses King, *King's Views New York 1908-1909* (Boston: Moses King, 1908), 91.

21. *King*, 851; Margaret Moore and Truman Moore, *End of the Road for Ladies' Mile?* (New York: The Drive to Protect the Ladies' Mile District, 1987), 40; Wolfe, *New York, A Guide to the Metropolis*, 220.

22. Landmarks Preservation Commission, *Ladies' Mile Designation Report*, 31, 70.

23. *King*, 846; *New Metropolis*, 484.

24. Landmarks Preservation Commission, "Gorham Building" (June 19, 1984), 6.

25. *New Metropolis*, 479.

26. Boyer, *Manhattan Manners*, 87.

27. *W.P.A. Guide*, 199.

28. Jeremy Gerard, "Michael Bennett, Theater Innovator, Dies at 44," *Times* (July 3, 1987): A1.

29. "A Historic Dedication to the Carpet Business," *Times* (August 4, 1986): B5.

MADISON SQUARE/
THE TENDERLOIN   Pages 131–42

1. *Valentine 1856*, 519.

2. *Valentine 1916-17*, opp. 61.

3. *Iconography*, vol. V, 1653.

4. Abram C. Dayton, *Last Days of Knickerbocker Life in New York* (New York: G.P. Putnam's Sons, 1897), 364.

5. *Strong*, vol. II, 125.
6. Gene Schermerhorn, *Letters To Phil* (New York: New York Bound, 1982), 23.
7. Henry Irving Dodge in *Valentine 1924*, 84.
8. William F. Mulhall in *Valentine 1923*, 132-133.
9. *Miller's New York As It Is* (New York: James Miller, 1866), 70.
10. *Valentine 1926*, 100.
11. Ibid.; James L. Ford in *Valentine 1924*, 163.
12. Mulhall, *Valentine 1923*, 129.
13. *Wood's Illustrated Hand-Book to New York* (New York: G.W. Carleton & Company, 1873), 38; Landmarks Preservation Commission, "Grand Hotel" (September 11, 1979), 5.
14. "Opening of the Gilsey House," *Times* (April 16, 1871): 6.
15. Ford, *Valentine 1924*, 164.
16. *Shadows*, 128; James D. McCabe, *New York By Sunlight and Gaslight* (New York: Union Publishing House, 1882), 152.
17. Herbert Asbury, *The Gangs of New York* (Garden City, N.Y.: Garden City Publishing Company, 1928), 177.
18. R.W. Stallman and E.R. Hagemann, *The New York City Sketches of Stephen Crane* (New York: New York University Press, 1966), 163.
19. McCabe, *New York By Sunlight and Gaslight*, 154-55.
20. McCabe, op. cit., 542, 544-45.
21. *King*, 238; Ford, *Valentine 1924*, 163.
22. *Greatest Street*, 251; Charles Edwin Prescott, ed., *The Hotel Guests' Guide to the City of New York*, 2nd ed. (New York: Geo. W. Averell, 1872), 101.
23. *The Sun's Guide to New York* (New York: R. Wayne Wilson & Company, 1892), 35.
24. *Our Theatres*, 57; *Greatest Street*, 251.
25. Richard Alleman, *The Movie Lover's Guide to New York* (New York: Perennial Library, 1988), 163-4; Matthew Josephson, *Edison* (New York: McGraw-Hill Book Company, 1959), 394.
26. Henry Moscow, *The Book of New York Firsts* (New York: Collier Books, 1982), 122.
27. Meyer Berger, *The Story of The New York Times* (New York: Simon and Schuster, 1951), 118.
28. *Valentine 1926*, 105.
29. Richard Harding Davis, "Broadway," *The Greatest Streets of the World* (New York: Charles Scribner's Sons, 1892), 24-25.
30. *New Metropolis*, 485
31. John C. Van Dyke, *The New New York* (New York: Macmillan Company, 1909), 120.
32. Department of Housing Preservation and Development, "SROs City Wide, Borough 1," December 1987.
33. Anna Quindlen, "About New York," *Times* (February 9, 1983): B4.

HERALD SQUARE/THE RIALTO/
GARMENT CENTER   Pages 147–60

1. *Iconography*, vol. VI, 98-99, 154.
2. James Grant Wilson, ed., *The Memorial History of the City of New-York*, vol. IV (New York: New-York History Company, 1893), 383.
3. *Valentine 1919*, 41.
4. *Valentine 1926*, 156-57; *King*, 592; S. Rosenbaum in *Valentine 1923*, 114, 121; *Greatest Street*, 260.
5. Francis Robinson, *Celebration: The Metropolitan Opera* (New York: Doubleday & Company, 1979), 12-15; *Opera Cavalcade* (New York: Metropolitan Opera Guild, 1938), 14; Wilson, *Memorial History*, vol. IV, 185.
6. *Opera Cavalcade*, 14.
7. Harvey O'Connor, *The Astors* (New York: Alfred A. Knopf, 1941), 200.
8. Mary C. Henderson, *The City and the Theatre* (Clifton, N.J.: James T. White & Company, 1973), 167; Ben M. Hall, *The Best Remaining Seats* (New York: Bramhall House, 1961), 16; *Our Theatres*, 55.
9. *King*, 594.
10. "Two Venerable Houses Bow to Broadway's Advance," *Times* (January 12, 1930): sec. 8, p. 4.
11. Brooks Atkinson, *Broadway* (New York: Macmillan Company, 1970), 11.
12. Leland Roth in *McKim, Mead & White, 1879-1915* (New York: Benjamin Blom, 1973), 41; Richard Kluger, *The Paper* (New York: Alfred A. Knopf, 1986), 162-63; "The Future Home of the New-York Herald" *Times* (May 11, 1893): 9.
13. *King*, 614.
14. Will Irwin, *Highlights of Manhattan*, rev. ed. (New York: D. Appleton-Century Company, 1937), 138.
15. Edward Hungerford, *The Romance of a Great Store* (New York: Robert M. McBride & Company, 1922), 67.
16. Tom Mahoney and Leonard Sloane, *The Great Merchants*, rev. ed. (New York: Harper & Row, 1974), 169.
17. Hungerford, *Romance of a Great Store*, 78.
18. *Greatest Street*, 259.
19. Isadore Barmash, "Saks-34th Street to Close Store at Herald Sq.," *Times* (June 2, 1965): 1.
20. *Rider*, 226.
21. "New York's Largest Hotel Will Cost Over $7,000,000," *Times* (January 1, 1911): sec. 6, p. 10; *Rider*, 26, 227.
22. "A.E. Lefcourt Dies Suddenly at 55," *Times* (November 14, 1932): 17; A.E. Lefcourt in *Broadway* (New York: Broadway Association, 1926), 136-137.
23. *Wonder City*, 223.
24. *Wonder City*, 220; *The Fashion Market Directory, 1400 Broadway*.
25. Richard Maney, "End of the Run for the Empire," *Times Magazine* (March 15, 1953): 22.
26. Carol Herselle Krinsky, *Rockefeller Center* (New York: Oxford University Press, 1978), 35-36; Paul Morand, *New York* (New York: Henry Holt & Company, 1930), 201.
27. Edgar B. Young, *Lincoln Center: The Building of an Institution* (New York: New York University Press, 1980), 13.
28. Nathan Silver, *Lost New York* (Boston: Houghton Mifflin Company, 1967), 226.
29. Robert A. Bennett, "Greenwich Acquisition Concluded," *Times* (November 5, 1981): D1.
30. Christopher Gray, "Grimy Grande Dame Housing the Homeless Off Herald Sq.," *Times* (September 27, 1987): sec. 8, p. 14.
31. Jonathan Kozol, *Rachel and Her Children* (New York: Crown Publishers, 1988), 28.
32. *W.P.A. Guide*, 164; Cecil Beaton, *Portrait of New York* (London: B.T. Batsford, 1948), 35; Harold H. Hart, *Hart's Guide to New York City* (New York: Hart Publishing Company, 1964), 421-22; Mahoney and Sloane, *Great Merchants*, 156 and 158; Isadore Barmash, *Macy's For Sale* (New York: Weidenfeld & Nicolson, 1989), 21-22.
33. *Macy's Thanksgiving Day Parade* (New York: Quarto Marketing, 1986), 14.

TIMES SQUARE/THEATER DISTRICT/
AUTOMOBILE ROW   Pages 165–200

1. *Iconography*, vol. VI, 171, pl. 84B-c; *Bloomingdale*, 3, 147-8; Martha J. Lamb, *History of the City of New York*, vol. II (New York: A.S. Barnes & Company, 1880), 125; Harvey O'Connor, *The Astors* (New York: Alfred A. Knopf, 1941), 18; Arthur D. Howden Smith, *John Jacob Astor* (Philadelphia: J.B. Lippincott Company, 1929), 258.
2. *Bloomingdale*, 8-9, 105-6.
3. "Broadway's New Line of Theatres Rising on Sites of Old Dutch Farms," *Times* (January 2, 1910): 14.
4. S. Rosenbaum in *Valentine 1923*, 117.
5. *New Metropolis*, 490; Rosenbaum, *Valentine 1923*, 118.
6. "Olympia Ready To Open," *Times* (November 24, 1895): 13; "Police Call in Olympia," *Times* (November 26, 1895): 1.
7. "Changes in Long Acre Square," *Real Estate Record and Guide* (November 16, 1907): 799.
8. John E. Meglio, *Vaudeville U.S.A.* (Bowling Green, Ohio: Bowling Green, 1973), 124.
9. Lloyd Morris, *Incredible New York* (New York: Random House, 1951), 262.
10. *Christopher Morley's New York* (New York: Fordham University Press, 1988), 35-36.
11. Christopher Gray, "Just Off Times Square, A Car Factory With Offices," *Times* (January 1, 1989): sec. 10, p. 4.
12. "Noteworthy Improvement at Broadway and 57th Street," *Times* (January 31, 1909): 14.
13. David Scott-Moncrieff, *The Veteran Motor-Car* (New York: Charles Scribner's Sons, 1956), 219.
14. Martin Clary, *Mid-Manhattan* (New York: Forty-second Street Property Owners and Merchants Association, 1929), 159.
15. "Tallest Broadway Building Above Times Square Section," *Times* (August 6, 1911): sec. 8, p. 1.
16. Paul Morand, *New York* (New York: Henry Holt & Company, 1930), 192.
17. Jill Stone, *Times Square, A Pictorial History* (New York: Collier Books, 1982), 107.
18. Mike Marqusee and Bill Harris, eds., *New York* (Boston: Little, Brown & Company, 1985), 140-41.
19. Stephen Graham, *New York Nights* (New York: George H. Doran Company, 1927), 13.

20. Bayrd Still, ed., *Mirror for Gotham* (New York: New York University Press, 1956), 323.
21. *Wonder City*, 126; Cecil Beaton, *Portrait of New York* (London: B.T. Batsford, 1948), 35.
22. *Rider*, 233.
23. "New Times Square Hotel Nearly Ready," *Times* (October 21, 1906): 12; Clary, *Mid-Manhattan*, 75.
24. *Greatest Street*, 269.
25. Meyer Berger, *The Story of The New York Times* (New York: Simon and Schuster, 1951), 154.
26. "City's Tallest Structure From Base to Top," *Times Building Supplement* (January 1, 1905): 3.
27. Mary C. Henderson, *The City and the Theatre* (Clifton, N.J.: James T. White & Company, 1973), 237; "Amazing Growth of the Great White Way," *Times* (September 11, 1910): sec. 6, p. 2.
28. *Our Theatres*, 74; "Newest Theatre in the Times Square Colony," *Times* (January 9, 1910): sec. 6, p. 9.
29. Landmarks Preservation Commission, "Winter Garden Theater" (January 5, 1988), 18; Louis Botto, *At This Theatre* (New York: Dodd, Mead & Company, 1984), 27.
30. Botto, *At This Theatre*, 46; Meglio, *Vaudeville U.S.A.*, 119.
31. Landmarks Preservation Commission, "Palace Theater" (July 14, 1987), 14, 17.
32. " 'Quo Vadis?' at Astor," *Times* (April 22, 1913): 11.
33. Adolph Zukor in *Broadway* (New York: Broadway Association, 1926), 109.
34. "New Strand Opens; Biggest of Movies," *Times* (April 12, 1914): sec. 3, p. 15.
35. Ben M. Hall, *The Best Remaining Seats* (New York: Bramhall House, 1961), 39; Federal Writers' Project, *New York Panorama* (New York: Random House, 1938), 289.
36. "New Strand Opens," *loc. cit.*; Benjamin B. Hampton, *A History of the Movies* (New York: Covici-Friede, 1931), 172.
37. Hall, *Best Remaining Seats*, 45, 51.
38. "The Rivoli, Newest Film Palace, Opens," *Times* (December 29, 1917); 9.
39. Zukor in *Broadway*, 111.
40. Hall, *Best Remaining Seats*, 57.
41. Zukor in *Broadway*, 113.
42. Landmarks Preservation Commission, "Embassy I Theater" (November 17, 1987), 1.
43. *Wonder City*, 69; Morand, *New York*, 209; Hall, *Best Remaining Seats*, 183.
44. "New Film Theatre," *Times* (April 27, 1930): sec. 9, p. 6; Landmarks Preservation Commission, "Mark Hellinger Theater" (November 17, 1987), 15.
45. Landmarks Preservation Commission, "Ed Sullivan Theater" (January 5, 1988), 2.
46. Hazel Meyer, *The Gold in Tin Pan Alley* (Philadelphia: J.B. Lippincott Company, 1958), 42.
47. Earl Wilson, *Earl Wilson's New York* (New York: Simon and Schuster, 1964), 43; *W.P.A. Guide*, 173.
48. "New Criterion Theatre Souvenir Program" (September 14, 1936).

49. *W.P.A. Guide*, 173.
50. Ibid.; "Night Club to Seat 1,000 Guests Is Planned for Brill Building," *Times* (November 16, 1932): 33; "Girls, Girls, Girls, Girls, Girls," *Fortune* (July 1939): 119.
51. *W.P.A. Guide*, 174.
52. Landmarks Preservation Commission, "Ed Sullivan Theater," 16.
53. Jim Haskins, *The Cotton Club* (New York: Random House, 1977), 116.
54. *W.P.A. Guide*, 167.
55. "Girls," *Fortune*, 119.
56. Gilbert Millstein, *New York: True North* (Garden City, N.Y.: Doubleday & Company, 1964), 257; "Site of the Latin Quarter Giving Way to a Tower," *Times* (February 13, 1989): B2.
57. *Earl Wilson's New York*, 39.
58. Nat Hentoff, "Birdland," *New York* (December 21-28, 1987): 92.
59. Edward Durell Stone, *The Evolution of an Architect* (New York: Horizon Press, 1962), 118.
60. Stone, *Times Square*, 109.
61. Meyer Berger, *New York, City on Many Waters* (New York: Golden Griffin Books, n.d.), n.p.
62. Marian Spitzer, *The Palace* (New York: Atheneum, 1969), 234-35.
63. Marya Mannes, *The New York I Know* (Philadelphia: J.B. Lippincott Company, 1961), 94-98.
64. William Laas, *Crossroads of the World* (New York: Popular Library, 1965), 144.
65. Thomas W. Ennis, "Hollow Shell Hides Remnants of Glory of Old Paramount," *Times* (June 25, 1967): sec. 8, p. 1.
66. Thomas Buckley, "Beatles Prepare for Their Debut," *Times* (February 9, 1964): 70.
67. Spitzer, *Palace*, 246.
68. Andrew L. Yarrow, "Movie Theaters: Facts and Figures," *Times* (June 26, 1987): C21.
69. Advertisement, *Times* (October 11, 1968): 78.
70. Rita Reif, "Tin Pan Alley in Distress," *Times* (April 11, 1976): sec. 8, p. 11.
71. Ada Louise Huxtable, "54-Story Hotel Expected to Revitalize Times Square," *Times* (July 11, 1973): 43.
72. New York Marriott Marquis promotional pamphlet.
73. Frank Rich, "Theater: Lloyd Webber's 'Cats,' " *Times* (October 8, 1982): C3.
74. "Automobile Row Bids Farewell to Broadway," *Times* (August 20, 1985): B5.
75. *Metropolis Times Square* (San Diego: The Hahn Company, 1989), 4.
76. City Planning Department, "Times Square: Summary of Urban Design Study and Proposed Zoning Controls" (January 1987), attachment F.
77. Martin Gottlieb, "Study on Project in Times Square Sees Rise in Jobs," *Times* (January 26, 1984): A1; Urban Development Corporation, "Forty-second Street Development Project, Draft Environmental Impact Statement" (February 1984), I-12.
78. Josh Alan Friedman, *Tales of Times Square* (New York: Delacorte Press, 1986), 178.

79. Henderson, *City and the Theatre*, 221.
80. Friedman, *Tales of Times Square*, 15.
81. Albert Scardino, "Builder Wants Green in Great White Way," *Times* (June 13, 1987): 32.

COLUMBUS CIRCLE/ LINCOLN SQUARE Pages 205–28

1. *Iconography*, vol. VI, 139.
2. The Rev. Carlos Martyn in *An Account of the Proceedings Incidental to the Opening for Public Worship of the Bloomingdale Reformed Church* (New York: Consistory of the Church, 1886), 17, 20.
3. Martyn, op. cit., 20, 33.
4. John Foord, *The Life and Public Services of Andrew Haswell Green* (Garden City, N.Y.: Doubleday, Page & Company, 1913), 72-73; *Iconography*, vol. V, 1929.
5. *Institutions*, 113.
6. *Greatest Street*, 276.
7. Barbara Cohen, Seymour Chwast, and Steven Heller, eds., *New York Observed* (New York: Harry N. Abrams, 1987), 86.
8. "The Grand Boulevard," *Real Estate Record and Guide* (July 13, 1889), 981; *King*, 297.
9. *King*, 536.
10. *King's Photographic Views of New York* (Boston: Moses King, 1895), 666.
11. *New Metropolis*, 267.
12. "Want It Called Broadway," *Times* (February 26, 1898): 12.
13. J. Sanford Saltus and Walter E. Tisné, *Statues of New York* (New York: G.P. Putnam's Sons, 1923), 94.
14. David Robinson, *Chaplin, His Life and Art* (New York: McGraw-Hill Publishing Company, 1985), 88-89.
15. Peter Salwen, *Upper West Side Story* (New York: Abbeville Press, 1989), 202, 204; Bennard B. Perlman, *Painters of the Ashcan School* (New York: Dover Publications, 1979), 190; *Rider*, 325.
16. Martin Clary, *Mid-Manhattan* (New York: Forty-second Street Property Owners and Merchants Association, 1929), 160.
17. Salwen, *Upper West Side*, 219.
18. Oliver Carlson and Ernest Sutherland Bates, *Hearst, Lord of San Simeon* (New York: Viking Press, 1936), 296-97; *New York 1900*, 168; Glenn Fowler, "Wreckers Find a Hearst 'Chapel,' " *Times* (March 12, 1966): 29; W.A. Swanberg, *Citizen Hearst* (New York: Collier Books, 1986), 426.
19. Michele H. Bogart, *Public Sculpture and the Civic Ideal in New York City, 1890-1930* (Chicago: University of Chicago Press, 1989), 199-200.
20. "Thousands in Riot at Valentino Bier; More Than 100 Hurt," *Times* (August 25, 1926): 1.
21. "French Plan Centre on the Century Site," *Times* (August 13, 1929): 1.
22. "Coliseum Opened; Crowds Flock in to See 3 Exhibits," *Times* (April 29, 1956): 1.

23. Robert A. Caro, *The Power Broker* (New York: Alfred A. Knopf, 1974), 1013-14; Ralph G. Martin, *Lincoln Center for the Performing Arts* (Englewood Cliffs, N.J.: Prentice-Hall, 1971), 11.

24. Edgar B. Young, *Lincoln Center, The Building of an Institution* (New York: New York University Press, 1980), 12, 13, 14; Francis Robinson, *Celebration: The Metropolitan Opera* (Garden City, N.Y.: Doubleday & Company, 1979), 19; Martin, *Lincoln Center*, 20.

25. Alan Rich, *The Lincoln Center Story* (New York: American Heritage, 1984), 84; Harold C. Schonberg, "Music: The Occasion," *Times* (September 24, 1962): 34.

26. Charlotte Curtis, "New Metropolitan Opera House Opens in a Crescendo of Splendor," *Times* (September 17, 1966): 1.

27. Martin, *Lincoln Center*, 129.

28. Young, *Lincoln Center*, 275.

29. Harold C. Schonberg, "Taj Mahal of Music," *Times* (October 3, 1969): 47.

30. John Canaday, "Art: Hartford Collection," *Times* (March 17, 1964): 32.

31. Anna Kisselgoff, "$3-Million Harkness Theater to Stage Dances Year-Round," *Times* (April 18, 1973): 40.

32. "Milstein Opens Throttle As Builder," *Times* (October 18, 1981): sec. 8, p. 1; "Plans Unit Backs Apartment Tower at Lincoln Center," *Times* (July 30, 1975): 36.

33. Susan Chira, "3d and Smallest Coliseum Plan Greeted by Signs of Approval," *Times* (April 20, 1989): 1.

UPPER WEST SIDE   Pages 233–56

1. *Iconography*, vol. VI, 95-96.

2. *Bloomingdale*, 95.

3. Hopper Striker Mott in *Valentine 1917-18*, 166.

4. *Valentine 1863*, opp. 272.

5. *Bloomingdale*, 87.

6. *Iconography*, vol. V, 1703; Abram C. Dayton, *Last Days of Knickerbocker Life in New York* (New York: G.P. Putnam's Sons, 1897), 362.

7. John A. Kouwenhoven, *The Columbia Historical Portrait of New York* (Garden City, N.Y.: Doubleday & Company, 1953), 250.

8. Charles Hemstreet, *Literary New York* (New York: G.P. Putnam's Sons, 1903), 158.

9. *Picture*, 23.

10. *Bloomingdale*, 97.

11. *Bloomingdale*, 361-62.

12. Harvey O'Connor, *The Astors* (New York: Alfred A. Knopf, 1941), 336; *Bloomingdale*, 96, 362.

13. I.M. Haldeman, *A History of the First Baptist Church* (New York: First Baptist Church, 1953), 4.

14. Christopher Gray, "A 'West End' Exception to the 'Men Only' Barrier," *Times* (December 6, 1987): sec. 8, p. 14; James Grant Wilson, ed., *The Memorial History of the City of New-York*, vol. IV (New York: New-York History Company, 1892), 241-42.

15. *King*, 242-43.

16. *Interborough Rapid Transit* (New York: Interborough Rapid Transit Company, 1904), 24-25.

17. Saul Bellow, *Seize the Day* (London: Penguin Books, 1974), 5.

18. Landmarks Preservation Commission, "The Ansonia Hotel" (March 14, 1972), 3.

19. Andrew Alpern, *Apartments for the Affluent* (New York: McGraw-Hill Book Company, 1975), 28.

20. *Apartment Houses of the Metropolis* (New York: G.C. Hesselgren Publishing Company, 1908), 33.

21. Steven Ruttenbaum, *Mansions in the Clouds*, (New York: Balsam Press, 1986), 45-46.

22. Landmarks Preservation Commission, "Hotel Belleclaire" (February 10, 1987), 11.

23. Advertisement, *Times* (September 6, 1914): sec. 6, p. 5.

24. Walter Barrett, *Old Merchants of New York City*, vol. III, part 2 (New York: M. Doolady, 1872), 41.

25. *Greatest Street*, 295.

26. "New Flathouse to Be Biggest in the World," *Times* (September 4, 1908): 1.

27. David Sinclair, *Dynasty, The Astors and Their Times* (New York: Beaufort Books, 1984), 218-220.

28. Christopher Gray, "A Closed Revival House That May Itself Be Revived," *Times* (July 5, 1987): sec. 8, p. 7.

29. *Broadway* (New York: Broadway Association, 1926), 158; Salwen, *Upper West Side Story*, 78.

30. *W.P.A. Guide*, 283; Advertisement in *Art in New York* (New York: Municipal Art Society, 1935), 133.

31. *Our Theatres*, 80.

32. *Our Theatres*, 75.

33. Records of the Theatre Historical Society.

34. Records of the Theatre Historical Society.

35. "Broadway Corner Sold to Builders," *Times* (February 14, 1922): 31.

36. Norval White and Elliot Willensky, *A.I.A. Guide to New York City*, rev. ed. (New York: Collier Books, 1978), 189.

37. *A Brief History of Rutgers Presbyterian Church* (New York: Rutgers Presbyterian Church, 1973), 12.

38. *Wonder City*, 146.

39. "Crowds at the Beacon, New Movie Palace," *Times* (December 26, 1929): 21.

40. Petronius, *New York Unexpurgated* (New York: Matrix House, 1966), 88.

41. Paul Goldberger, "Design Notebook: Rescuing the Ansonia From Its Rescuers," *Times* (June 26, 1980): C10.

42. Richard D. Lyons, "Belnord Tenants Turning to Preservation," *Times* (June 7, 1987): sec. 8, p. 9.

43. Department of Housing Preservation and Development, "SROs City Wide, Borough 1," December 1987.

44. Salwen, *Upper West Side Story*, 267.

45. Andreas Feininger and Kate Simon, *New York* (New York: Viking Press, 1964), 136.

46. "Divine Miss M. Is Set for a Tacky Gala," *Times* (December 29, 1972): 14.

47. Landmarks Preservation Commission, "Beacon Theater" (December 11, 1979), 8.

48. Susan Katz, *Zabar's Deli Book* (New York: Hawthorn Books, 1979), 15.

49. Richard D. Lyons, "The Zeckendorf Flag Flying High Again," *Times* (July 13, 1986): sec. 8, p. 1.

STRYKER'S BAY/ MORNINGSIDE HEIGHTS   Pages 261–76

1. *Iconography*, vol. IV, 527.

2. *Iconography*, vol. V, 1017.

3. *Iconography*, vol. V, 1280.

4. *Bloomingdale*, 21.

5. *Iconography*, vol. V, 1616.

6. *Picture*, 43.

7. *Institutions*, 296.

8. John William Robson, ed., *A Guide to Columbia University* (New York: Columbia University Press, 1937), 46.

9. Peter H. Wollenberg and Mark P. Shiff, "Henry Grimm Building (1871) and Rear Addition (1900)" (New York: Columbia University, Graduate School of Architecture and Planning, 1984), 4, 18.

10. "Isidor Straus's Home Sold," *Times* (May 19, 1912): 1; "Straus Home Sold to Builder," *Times* (May 26, 1912): sec. 8, p. 2.

11. *A History of Columbia University, 1754-1904* (New York: Columbia University Press, 1904), 161.

12. Frederick Paul Keppel, *Columbia* (New York: Oxford University Press, 1914), 79.

13. Frank Moss, *The American Metropolis*, vol. II (New York: Peter Fenelon Collier, 1897), 310; Leland Roth in *McKim, Mead & White, 1879-1915* (New York: Benjamin Blom, 1973), 31.

14. Robson, *Guide to Columbia*, 15-16.

15. *Rider*, 372.

16. *New York 1900*, 385.

17. Advertisement, *Times* (September 6, 1914): sec. 6, p. 10.

18. *Apartment Houses of the Metropolis* (New York: G.C. Hesselgren Publishing Company, 1908), 38.

19. *Greatest Street*, 309.

20. Records of Theatre Historical Society.

21. Andrew Alpern and Seymour Durst, *Holdouts!* (New York: McGraw-Hill Book Company, 1984), 96.

22. Daniel J. Fleming, *Education Through Stone and Glass* (New York: Union Theological Seminary, n.d.), 7.

23. Ralph G. Martin, *Lincoln Center for the Performing Arts* (Englewood Cliffs, N.J.: Prentice-Hall, 1971), 156.

24. James Trager, *West of Fifth* (New York: Atheneum, 1987), 70.

25. City Planning Commission, *Plan For New York City 1969, A Proposal*, vol. IV, Manhattan (New York: City Planning Commission, 1969), 124.

26. Charles Grutzner, "City 'Acropolis' Combating Slums," *Times* (May 21, 1957): 37.

27. "5 Families Move to Grant Houses," *Times* (August 21, 1956): 31.

28. Deirdre Carmody, "Birthday for Barnard: New Dorm's the Gift," *Times* (July 21, 1988): B1.

29. Charles Kaiser, *1968 In America* (New York: Weidenfeld & Nicolson, 1988), 165.

30. Andreas Feininger and Kate Simon, *New York* (New York: Viking Press, 1964), 136.

31. Advertisement, *Times Magazine* (February 14, 1988): 102.

32. Joseph Berger, "Hispanic Life Dims in Manhattan Valley," *Times* (September 11, 1987): B1.

HARLEM/MANHATTANVILLE/ HAMILTON HEIGHTS   Pages 281–96

1. Reginald Pelham Bolton, *Washington Heights Manhattan, Its Eventful Past* (New York: Dyckman Institute, 1924), 2-3, 19-20.

2. *Iconography*, vol. V, 1461.

3. *Churchyards of Trinity Parish* (New York: Corporation of Trinity Church, 1955), 73.

4. *Institutions*, 215.

5. Ibid.

6. John A. Kouwenhoven, *The Columbia Historical Portrait of New York* (Garden City, N.Y.: Doubleday & Company, 1953), 327; *Greatest Street*, 308.

7. *Institutions*, 302.

8. *Institutions*, 304.

9. Dorothy Levenson, *Montefiore* (New York: Farrar, Straus & Giroux, 1984), 45-46; *King*, 452.

10. "American League: New York Beat Washington In the Opening Game of the League in This City," *Times* (May 1, 1903): 7; "Yankees Start for Atlanta," *Times* (February 27, 1912): 10.

11. Landmarks Preservation Commission, "IRT Broadway Line Viaduct" (November 24, 1981): 1.

12. "Thirty Blocks of Broadway Transformed in Three Years," *Times* (April 26, 1908): sec. 6, p. 14.

13. J.B. Kerfoot, *Broadway* (Boston: Houghton Mifflin Company, 1911), 157-58.

14. *New York 1900*, 303.

15. *Greatest Street*, 312.

16. Advertisement, *Times* (September 2, 1906): 15.

17. Levenson, *Montefiore*, 91.

18. Records of the Theatre Historical Society; David Naylor, *Great American Movie Theaters* (Washington, D.C.: Preservation Press, 1987), 74.

19. Landmarks Preservation Commission, "Audubon Terrace Historic District" (January 9, 1979), 11.

20. *Museum of the American Indian*, brochure, n.d.

21. Landmarks Preservation Commission, "Chapel of the Intercession" (August 16, 1966), 2; E. Clowes Chorley, ed., *Quarter of a Millennium* (Philadelphia: Church Historical Society, 1947), 82-84.

22. *Rider*, 502; "Great Medical Centre Is Ready to Function," *Times* (March 11, 1928): sec. 9, p. 3.

23. Ethel Fleming, *New York* (New York: Macmillan Company, 1929), 78.

24. *Columbia-Presbyterian Medical Center Annual Report 1987* (New York: Columbia-Presbyterian Medical Center), 7-8; "Babies Hospital in New Quarters," *Times* (December 29, 1929): sec. 8, p. 16.

25. Rian James, *All About New York* (New York: John Day Company, 1931), 46-47.

26. "'Hello' to Gleam at Grant Houses," *Times* (August 20, 1956): 23; "5 Families Move to Grant Houses," *Times* (August 21, 1956): 31; *New York City Housing Authority Project Data* (New York: Housing Authority, 1989), 17, 24.

27. Lena Williams, "A Giant Looks Out Over Harlem," *Times* (June 13, 1976): sec. 8, p. 1.

28. Israel Shenker, "World Flattens For Old Society of Geographers," *Times* (November 26, 1978): 54.

29. Irvin Molotsky, "Compromise Is Reached to Keep Indian Museum in New York City," *Times* (April 13, 1988): A1.

30. "38 Held As Drug Dealers in Manhattan Raid," *Times* (March 30, 1989): B3; Ralph Blumenthal, "Life and Death in the Fateful Three-Four Precinct," *Times* (April 16, 1990): A1.

WASHINGTON HEIGHTS/ INWOOD/MARBLE HILL   Pages 301–14

1. Reginald Pelham Bolton, *Washington Heights Manhattan, Its Eventful Past* (New York: Dyckman Institute, 1924), plate I, 55-6, 59-60, 134-35; *Iconography*, vol. VI, 67-b.

2. Bolton, *Washington Heights*, 186, 191.

3. Short history by the Metropolitan Historic Structures Association.

4. *Iconography*, vol. IV, 643.

5. *Valentine 1864*, 855.

6. Bolton, *Washington Heights*, 198.

7. Christopher Gray, "Encrusted Relic of a Mid-19th Century Inwood Estate," *Times* (June 5, 1988): sec. 10, p. 14.

8. Bolton, *Washington Heights*, 160.

9. William A. Tieck, *Riverdale, Kingsbridge, Spuyten Duyvil* (New York: William A. Tieck, 1968), 134-35.

10. Tablet on 210 West 230th Street.

11. Tieck, *Riverdale*, 44-45.

12. *Greatest Street*, 331.

13. Records of the Theatre Historical Society.

14. *Rider*, 505.

15. Landmarks Preservation Commission, "Fort Tryon Park" (September 20, 1983), 3-4.

16. John William Robson, ed., *A Guide to Columbia University* (New York: Columbia University Press, 1937), 195; Bolton, *Washington Heights*, 163.

17. Advertisement, *Times* (February 22, 1930): 13.

18. "Dr. Reisner Dies; Noted Clergyman," *Times* (July 18, 1940): 19.

19. *Wonder City*, 54.

20. Rebecca Read Shanor, *The City That Never Was* (New York: Viking Press, 1988), 64.

21. Jeff Kisseloff, *You Must Remember This* (New York: Harcourt Brace Jovanovich, 1989), 222.

NOTES ON HISTORICAL ILLUSTRATIONS

(Furnished where information is available; numbers in the margin are page numbers.)

1. "A Description of the Towne of Mannados or New Amsterdam" as it existed in 1661, otherwise known as the Duke's Plan.

2. "Plan of New York, Surveyed in 1766 and 1767, By Bernard Ratzer."

3. Map of the city published in 1825 by David Longworth.

4–5. Illustrations taken from *Valentine 1865*, which contained 33 separate plates showing every building on Broadway between the Battery and Union Square. The blockfront elevations have been joined together for this book to show the street as a continuum.

6–7. "Sketch Map Showing Broadway From The Battery To Albany," published in *Greatest Street*.

13. "Pulling Down the Statue of George III," oil painting by Johannes A. Oertel.

14. Photograph by George P. Hall.

19. Photograph by Frank M. Ingalls.

21. Photographs by George P. Hall & Son.

47. "Broadway—gatan och Radhuset i New York," watercolor by Baron Axel Leonhard Klinckowstrom.

93. Photograph by Robert L. Bracklow.

140. Photograph by George P. Hall & Son.

147. Photograph by C.G. Hine.

148. Photograph of the Casino by Byron.

149. Photograph of the auditorium by Louis Mélancon.

165. Etching by Eliza Greatorex.

166. Photograph by George P. Hall.

167. Photograph by C.G. Hine.

170. Photograph by Browning.

171. Photograph by Frank M. Ingalls.

173. Photograph by Frank M. Ingalls.

174. Photograph by Frank M. Ingalls.

189. Photograph by Frank M. Ingalls.

207. Photograph by C.G. Hine.

208. Photograph by Boyette.

221. Photograph by Louis Melancon.

233. Photograph by C.G. Hine.

234. Wax paper negative by Victor Prevost.

235. Photograph by Robert L. Bracklow.

246. Photograph of the 95th Street Market by the Wurts Brothers.

247. Photograph by the Wurts Brothers.

INDEX

INDEX TO ARCHITECTS, ARTISTS, DESIGNERS, and SCULPTORS

Refers to buildings in the inventory. An asterisk means that the individual or firm was involved in more than one of the buildings listed on that page.

Abramovitz, Max, 212*
Abramovitz, Harris & Kingsland, 98
Abramson, Louis Allen, 139
Adams & Woodbridge, 24
Agam, Yaacov, 214
Ahlschlager, Walter W., 237
Ajello, Gaetan, 247, 248, 269, 272, 273*, 284
Allen & Collens, 273
Almirall, Raymond F., 194
Alswang, Ralph, 175, 186
Andersen, Henry, 270
Andrews, Frank M., 150, 214
Architects Unlimited, 126
Architectural Iron Works
   (see Daniel Badger)
Artkraft Strauss, 194
Attia, Eli, 31, 208
Audsley, George Ashdown, 14
Audsley, William James, 14

Babb, Cook & Willard, 20
Badger, Daniel D., 20, 27, 53, 54*, 58, 63, 64, 71, 73*, 76*, 79, 91, 139
Baer, Herbert M., 179
Baker, James B., 47
Barber, Donn, 38, 276, 301*
Bark, Victor, Jr., 158, 184
Bark & Djorup, 156
Barnard, George Grey, 272
Barney & Chapman, 195
Barnett, Hayner & Barnett, 21
Bartholdi, Frédéric-Auguste, 113, 132
Bartlett, Paul Wayland, 132
Batchelder, Evelyn Beatrice Longman, 31
Bates & Heindsman, 310
Batterson, James Goodwin, 133
Bauer, Otto, 175
Belluschi, Pietro, 212, 214*
Berger, A.G., 242
Bethlehem Engineering Corporation, 186
Beyer Blinder Belle, 118, 247
Bien, Sylvan, 103
Birge, Charles E., 99, 235
Birkmire, William H., 107, 126
Birkshire, William H., 63
Birnbaum, Philip, 131, 192, 210*, 214, 227, 248, 250
Bissell, George Edwin, 13, 24, 132
Bitter, Karl, 13, 24, 40
Bloch, Hesse & Shalat, 170
Bloodgood, William, 76, 235
Blum, George & Edward, 154, 158, 200, 250, 261, 271*
Boak & Paris, 250, 262, 269
Boak & Raad, 102, 103
Bond, Ryder & Associates, 296
Bosworth, William Welles, 31, 103, 200
Bowditch, Arthur H., 77
Boyd, John D., 234
Boylan, William H., 261
Brady, Joseph R., 91
Brounet, Arthur, 247
Brown, Henry Kirke, 113*
Browne, Frederick C., 58, 59, 96, 98
Brun, C.B., 287
Brunner, Arnold W., 272
Brunner & Tryon, 78, 93, 273
Buchman & Brunner & Tryon, 285
Buchman & Deisler, 73, 86*, 92, 99
Buchman & Fox, 77, 148, 289*

Bunshaft, Gordon, 212
Burgee (John) with Philip Johnson, 165, 166, 167
Burgee, John, 212
Burne, John C., 287
Burnham, Daniel H., 102, 131, 147, 168

Cady, Josiah Cleveland, 47, 157
Caffieri, J.J., 38
Calder, Alexander Stirling, 174
Candela, Rosario, 166, 233, 254, 270
Carles, Antonin Jean Paul, 151, 154
Carrère & Hastings, 18, 31, 157, 158, 171, 195, 200, 269
Carson, Lundin & Shaw, 208
Casey, Edward S., 263
Catalano, Eduardo, 214*
Chambers, Walter B., 14
Chagall, Marc, 212
Chanin, Irwin S., 157
Chapman, Henry Otis, 234
Chevalier, 21
Civiletti, Pasquale, 234
Clayton & Bell, 103
Cleverdon & Putzel, 79, 96, 99*
Clinton & Russell, 18, 19, 27, 30, 31, 53, 98, 108, 139*, 154*, 167, 170, 237, 242
Cobb, Henry Ives, 18, 165
Cohen & Siegel, 306
Cole, James W., 270
Collens, Willis & Beckonert, 273
Colles, Christopher, 59
Colt, Stockton B., 53
Cooper, Alexander, 250
Copeland, Peter, 234
Copeland, Novak & Israel, 148
Cornell, J.B. & W.W., 79, 106
Correja, John, 72, 79
Craig, Andrew, 234
Crausman, I.L., 313
Crisp, Arthur, 174
Cross & Cross, 19

Dattner, Richard, 284, 306, 314
Davis, Brody & Associates, 223, 272
De Francisci, Anthony, 113
Delano & Aldrich, 296
DeLemos & Cordes, 78, 92, 99, 115, 150
Del Gaudio, Matthew W., 310
De Rosa, Eugene, 170, 179, 188, 301
De Rosa & Pereira, 305
Deskey, Donald, 170
Dewey, F.H., 114
Diaper, Frederic, 55
Di Modica, Arturo, 13
Dinslow, L.E., 184
Dixey, John, 46
D'Oench & Yost, 256
Donnally & Ricci, 40
Donndorf, Karl Adolph, 113
Doyle, Alexander, 147
Duboy, Paul E.M., 235
Duncan, John H., 118, 207, 237, 247, 256, 290
Dunn, Joseph M., 106, 113
Dyckman, William, 313

Eberson, Drew, 212
Eggers & Higgins, 53, 70, 281
Eggers Partnership, 53, 272
Ehrenkrantz, Eckstut & Whitelaw, 26
Ehrenkrantz Group, 40
Eidlitz, Cyrus L.W., 26*, 133, 167
Eidlitz, Leopold, 45, 46
Ellenoff, George, 314
Embury, Aymar, II, 151
Engelbert, Henry, 93, 142

Faile, E.H., 47
Farrar & Watmough, 103
Faulkner, Barry, 15
Feingold, Joseph, 102
Feldman, H.I., 102, 216, 223, 306*, 313

Fellheimer & Wagner, 47
Felson, J.M., 254, 270
Fernbach, Henry, 92, 116
Flagg, Ernest, 18, 27, 78
Foster, Richard, 98
Fox & Fowle, 19, 20, 174, 187
Franklin, Bates & Heindsman, 310
Frazee, W. & J., 38
Fredericksz, Crijn, 13
Freedlander, Joseph H., 46
French, Daniel Chester, 13
Friedland, Louis H., 174

Gautier, Andrew, 38
Gaynor, John P., 76
Gehron, William, 276
Gilbert, A.F., 64
Gilbert, Bradford Lee, 19
Gilbert, C.P.H., 31, 216
Gilbert, Cass, 13, 40, 52
Giles, James H., 118*
Gillespie, George L., 314
Gillman & Kendall, 26
Ginsbern, Horace, 208, 310
Goldfine, Beatrice, 158
Goldstone, L.A., 301*
Gompert, William H., 102, 255
Goodhue, Bertram Grosvenor, 292
Graham, Ernest R., 26
Greene, Henry George, 97
Gregory, John, 15
Grimm, Henry, 262
Gronenberg & Leuchtag, 248, 263
Gross & Kleinberger, 290, 293*
Gruwé, Emile, 70
Gruzen Partnership, 186, 250
Gwathmey, Siegel & Associates, 175

Haas, Richard, 165
Haefell, Walter, 237
Haight, Charles Coolidge, 126, 233
Hall, R., 69
Hardenbergh, Henry J., 34, 147, 187
Hardenbrook, Theophilus, 46
Harding & Gooch, 46, 53
Harding, John, 223
Harney, George E., 96
Harris, Edward D., 52
Harrison, Wallace K., 212*
Harrison & Abramovitz, 276
Hastings, Thomas, 15, 132
Hatch, Stephen Decatur, 26, 55, 92, 96, 108, 139, 142
Hatfield, O.P., 77
Hatfield, Robert G., 46, 79
Hauser, John, 290
Hebald, Milton, 216
Hecla Iron Works, 132
Held & Rubin, 248
Heinigke & Bowen, 40
Heins & LaFarge, 24, 38, 46, 206, 233, 242, 270, 273
Henry, Leonard S., 223
Herter, Albert, 38
Herts & Tallant, 170
Herts, Henry B., 262
Hill & Turner, 248
Hill, George, 255
Hinchman, John R., 250
Hohauser, William S., 135
Hopper, Isaac, 314
Hoppin & Koen, 226
Horgan & Slattery, 261
Howe, William W., 244
Howells & Stokes, 31, 276
Hume, William H., 53, 150, 156, 284
Hunt, Richard Morris, 24, 27, 72, 138
Huntington, Anna Vaughn Hyatt, 292
Huntington, Charles Pratt, 292
Hutton, Addison, 156
Hurry, William, 31

Irrera, Raymond, 262

Jackson, Thomas R., 69, 108
Jacobs, Harry Allan, 263
Jacobs, Robert Allan, 170
Jacobs, Stephen B., 106
Jacobson, Frederick, 115
Jallade, Louis E., 272
Janes & Leo, 233, 242, 270
Jardine, David & John, 40, 53, 54, 59, 64, 78, 97, 101, 122, 138, 150, 186
Jardine, Hill & Murdock, 54, 63
Jennewein, C. Paul, 15, 40
Jerde Partnership, 171
Johnson, George, 73
Johnson, Joseph, 122
Johnson, Philip, 98, 165, 166, 167, 212*
Johnson, Tom, 40
Jordan & Giller, 64
Josselyn, Edgar H., 276
Josza, Igor, 91

Kahn, Albert, 192, 208, 310
Kahn, Ely Jacques, 134, 156, 157*, 159*
Kahn & Jacobs, 53, 157, 168, 184, 187, 188
Kajima International, 26
Karoly, Andrew B., 102
Katz & Feiner, 142
Keck, Charles, 172, 206, 272
Keister, George, 156, 171, 175, 210, 242
Kellum, John, 27, 40, 46, 78, 86, 103, 106
Kellum & Son, 54, 76, 102
Kelly, James Edward, 272
Kendall, Edward Hale, 14, 118
Kessler, S.J., 223, 228
Kight, A.B., 304, 305
Kilburn, Henry F., 233, 269
Kimball, Francis Hatch, 18, 20*, 21, 25, 26, 27, 34, 101*, 138, 157, 195*
King, David W., 91
King & Kellum, 63
Kirchoff & Rose, 175
Kjoldgaard, Valdemar, 237
Kleinberger, Joseph, 188
Kliment & Halsband, 271
Kling, Vincent G., 273
Koehler, Victor Hugo, 93, 269
Kofman, Peter, 223
Kohn Pedersen Fox Conway, 194
Kondylis, Costas, 178
Koppe & Moore, 188
Korn, Louis, 91, 101
Kornblath, Leo, 168
Krapp, Herbert J., 172, 186, 188, 192, 285, 293
Kreymborg, Charles, 305*, 306, 310, 313*

Lamb, Thomas W., 166*, 170, 171, 174, 175, 184*, 186, 187, 242, 247, 248, 250, 256*, 270, 271, 289, 296, 301
Lamb & Rich, 73*, 273
Lamb & Wheeler, 76
Lang, David S., 306*
Lapidus, Alan, 178
Lawrence, James Crommelin, 38
LeBrun, Napoleon, 47
LeGendre, Henri A., 284
Leigh, Douglas, 206
Leo, John P., 223, 289*
L'Enfant, Pierre Charles, 38
Lescaze, William, 192, 281
Levatan, B., 290
Levy, David, 276
Levy, Leon & Lionel, 206
Levy & Berger, 142
Liebman & Liebman, 223
Liebman Williams Ellis, 256
Lienau, Detlef, 114
Lillien, H. Herbert, 305*
Lindsey, E.D., 24
Lippold, Richard, 214
Little, Thomas, 46
Lober, Georg John, 172

Lord, James Brown, 179
Ludlow & Peabody, 14
Lukeman, Augustus, 269
Lyons, Robert T., 96, 122, 237

MacFadyen & Knowles, 276
MacKenzie, Andrew C., 167
MacMonnies, Frederick, 45
Magonigle, Harold Van Buren, 206
Malhotra, Avinash K., 93, 248
Mangin, Joseph François, 45
Manship, Paul, 31, 207
Marsh, Frederick Dana, 150
Marsh, Reginald, 13
Martine, Joseph, 122
Martiny, Philip, 34, 55
Marvin & Davis, 165
Maurer, Louis C., 216
Mayer & Whittlesey, 205
Mayers & Schiff, 172, 178
Maynicke, Robert, 55, 58, 63, 72, 86, 92, 101, 108, 227
Maynicke & Franke, 119, 122, 131, 135, 228
McBean, Thomas, 38
McComb, John, Jr., 45, 53
McElfatrick, John B. (& Son), 142, 147, 157*, 158, 159, 166, 170, 210, 214
McKim, Charles Follen, 272
McKim, Mead & White, 21, 55, 91, 119*, 142, 154, 216, 272*, 273
McNamara, John J., 175, 210
McVickar, John, 91
Meader, Herman Lee, 26
Meiére, Hildreth, 21
Mengelson, C.F., 34
Merrick, Frederic I., 210
Merrit, M.C., 242
Merry, F.C., 27
Mesbur, David K., 223
Mettam, Charles, 64, 77
Metzler, Henry Frederick, 79
Meyers, Charles B., 256, 262, 305–06
Milkowski, Antoni H., 132
Miller, George G., 262
Miller & Goldhammer, 301
Minuth, Francis A., 101
Monaghan, Paul, 313
Mook, Robert, 71
Moore & Landsiedel, 287, 289
Morris, Benjamin Wistar, 15, 20
Mullen, Buell, 38
Mullett, A.B., 45
Mulliken, Harry B., 248
Mulliken & Moeller, 192, 208, 226, 263, 290*
Munckowitz, Julius, 216
Myers, Forrest, 86

Nash, Thomas, 24*
Nervi, Pier Luigi, 304
Neville & Bagge, 254*, 255, 262, 270, 271*, 276*, 281*, 284*, 285*, 287*, 289*, 290*, 292*, 293*, 296*, 301*, 304*
New York City Public Works Department, 46, 314
Nichols, Charles H., 107
Niehaus, Charles Henry, 24
Nitchie, John E., 142
Noguchi, Isamu, 27

O'Connor & Kilham, 273*
Ogden, S.B., 263
Oltarsh, D.M., 69
Oppenheimer, Brady & Lehrecke, 216
Orlando, Joseph, 187

Pang, Daniel, 59
Parsons, William Barclay, 281
Partridge, William Ordway, 272
Patel, Kantilal B., 113
Peabody & Stearns, 25
Peabody, Wilson & Brown, 237

Petersen, F.A., 58
Pelham, George F., 192, 242, 244*, 250*, 263, 271, 284, 285, 287*, 289*, 292*, 293, 304*, 305, 313
Pelton, Henry Colden, 296
Perkins & Will, 296
Piccirilli, Attilio, 206
Platt, Charles A., 40, 250
Platt, F.P., 263
Polshek, James Stewart, 273
Poor, Alfred Easton, 53
Poor & Swanke, 53
Pope, George W., 114
Porter, A.V., 186
Portman, John C., Jr., 170, 171
Post, George B., 15, 21, 26, 34, 40, 86, 92, 98, 107
Potter, Edward T., 103
Potter, William A., 255
Prentice & Chan, Ohlhausen, 165
Price, Bruce, 21, 25, 134, 165

Rambusch Studios, 174, 187, 188, 237, 296, 301
Rapp, C.W., 168
Rapp, George L., 168
Reed, S.B., 226
Reid, Charles A., 228
Reinagle, Hugh, 54
Renwick, James, Jr., 93, 103*, 106
Renwick, William W., 103
Renwick, Aspinwall & Russell, 106
Renwick, Aspinwall & Tucker, 20
Rhind, John Massey, 19, 24, 26, 150
Ritch, J.W., 27
Roberts, Ebenezer L., 18, 64
Robertson, R.H., 116, 234
Robinson, James, 13, 24
Roche & Roche, 171
Roche Dinkeloo, 184
Rogers, Butler, Burgun, 296
Rogers, Isaiah, 40
Rogers, James Gamble, 296
Rogers, Randolph, 132
Roiné, Jules Edouard, 103
Ross & McNeil, 256
Rossiter & Wright, 96
Roth, Emery, 237, 247, 248*, 262, 284, 285, 290, 292
Roth, Emery (& Sons), 15, 19, 46, 108, 158, 165, 175, 192, 195, 210
Rouse, William L., 270
Rouse & Goldstone, 139, 148, 165, 250*, 254, 261, 262
Rouse & Sloan, 106, 256
RTKL, 147
Rubin Architects, 119
Russo, Gaetano, 206

Saarinen, Eero, 212
Safdie, Moshe, 228
Saint-Gaudens, Augustus, 132
Salkowitz, A.H., 106
Sass, S., 107
Sayles, Allen, 186
Schickel & Ditmars, 138
Schimenti, Don, 91
Schlanger & Irrera, 255
Schloss, Newton, 187
Schultze & Weaver, 186
Schuman, Lichtenstein, Claman & Efron, 148, 228, 250*, 256
Schwartz & Gross, 122, 135*, 156, 234, 237, 242, 254*, 256, 261, 269, 284, 287*, 289, 292, 293*, 296*, 304*
Schwarzmann, Herman J., 92
Schweinfurth, J.A., 248
Schweitzer, August, 70
Seelig & Finkelstein, 126
Severance, H. Craig, 18

Severance & Van Alen, 18
Shampan, Louis, 138
Shaw, Howard, 200
Shaw & Anderson, 18, 142
Shire & Kaufman, 178
Shreve & Lamb, 147, 200
Shreve, Lamb & Blake, 18, 195, 269
Shreve, Lamb & Harmon, 38, 46, 142, 194, 272*, 276, 301
Skidmore, Owings & Merrill, 26, 27, 167, 171, 207, 208, 234, 296, 314
Slade, Jarvis Morgan, 63, 96
Sloan & Robertson, 19
Smith, Perry Coke, 113
Smith, William Wheeler, 55, 97, 116
Smith, H.W., 71
Smith, Smith, Haines, Lundberg & Waehler, 21, 167
Snook, John B. (or Snook & Sons), 27, 47*, 52*, 59*, 71, 73, 76, 79, 86, 91*, 114, 119, 133*, 165
Snyder, C.B.J., 114
Sommerfeld & Steckler, 156, 207, 287
Specter, David Kenneth, 131
Springsteen & Goldhammer, 310
Stanley, Thomas E., 208
Starkweather & Gibbs, 102
Starrett & Van Vleck, 27, 142, 159
Steele, William, 101
Stent, Thomas, 79*
Stephenson, Abner, 24
Stevens, John W., 77, 97
Stone, Edward Durell, 171, 205
Stoughton, C.W. & A.A., 237
Stuckert & Sloan, 172
Styles, Thomas H., 115
Sugarman & Berger, 248, 255, 270, 310
Sugarman & Hess, 235, 242
Sutcliffe, Arthur, 115
Swanke Hayden Connell, 25, 26
Swasey, William Albert, 186
Sweet & Shaw, 166
Swift, Joseph, 276

Tachau & Vought, 310
Taylor, Alfred H., 216
Thain & Thain, 285
Thomas, Griffith, 26, 40, 55, 69, 70, 71, 76, 108, 115, 116, 126
Thomas & Son, 58, 73
Thompson, Benjamin, 93
Thompson, John Ambrose, 314
Tillion & Tillion, 237
Tomassek, Romeo, 314
Townsend, Ralph S., 70, 71, 78, 107
Townsend & Oppenheimer, 237
Townsend, Steinle & Haskell, 142, 151, 194, 271, 284
Tracy, Evarts, 269
Tracy & Swartout, 255
Trench & Snook, 52
Trench, Joseph, 52
Trimble, John M., 92, 96
Trowbridge & Livingston, 47, 165
True, Clarence, 289

Upjohn, Richard, 24, 25, 113
Urban, Joseph, 207

Vaux & Company, 103, 292
Vaux & Radford, 292
Vaux, Withers & Company, 292
Very, Brown & Behr, 233
Volz, Charles, 244

Waid & Willauer, 200
Walker, Ralph, 21
Walker & Gillette, 25, 64, 167
Walker & Hazzard, 250
Wank, Adams & Slavin, 98
Ware & Styne-Harde, 227

Ware, F. & A., 158, 234
Ward, John Quincy Adams, 113, 132, 151
Warner, Samuel A., 59, 77, 86
Warren & Wetmore, 212
Washburn, William, 131
Webster, John Averit, 247
Wechsler, Max, 284
Weekes, H. Hobart, 250
Weiser, Arthur, 233
Welch, Alexander McMillan, 313
Westermann & Miller, 214*
Westervelt, J.C., 34
Westervelt & Austin, 166
Whinston, B.H. & C.N., 207, 244
White, Stanford, 45, 132
Whitenack, J. Odell, 86
Whitney, Gertrude Vanderbilt, 296
Whyte, Nicholas, 63
Wickes, Walter H., 34
Williams, John T., 53, 59, 71
Williams, Frank, 234
Wills & Dudley, 91
Wilson, Thomas, 135
Wilton, Joseph, 13
Winnam, A., 71
Winter, Ezra, 15
Wiseman, Harrison G., 248
Withers, Frederick Clark, 24
Wood, J.A., 97
Wright, Charles, 59

Ximenes, Ettore, 212

Yellin, Samuel, 15, 235
York & Sawyer, 27, 40, 156, 235
Young, Harold L., 276
Young & Gronenberg, 290
Youngs & Cable, 19*

Zion & Breen, 70
Zucker, Alfred, 71, 73, 78, 99*, 133, 138

INDEX TO ILLUSTRATIONS

A. & S. Plaza (*see* Gimbel Brothers
  Department Store)
Adele Lehman Hall-Wollman Library
  (Barnard), 268
Albemarle Hotel, 133
Alexander Hamilton, 280
Alexandria, 256
Allenhurst, 262
Allen Pavilion of Presbyterian Hospital, 314
American Bible Society Building, 210, 223
American Circle Building, 208
American Express Building, 20
American Geographical Society, 291, 292
American Surety Building, 25, 26
American Telephone & Telegraph Building (*see*
  Telephone & Telegraph Building)
Ansonia Hotel, 234, 235, 238–39, 256
Apple Bank (*see* Central Savings Bank)
Appleton (D.) & Company Building, 4, 73
Apthorp, 232, 242, 245
Arch Bridge (*see* Stone Bridge)
Argonaut Building (*see* Demarest Building and
  Peerless Building)
Armory of the 22nd Regiment, 207
Arnold, Constable & Company Store, 112, 115
Arragon, 261
Astor Hotel, 171
Astor House, 4, 21
Astor Place Building, 90, 102, 108
Astor Place Plaza, 90
Astor Plaza, (One), 143, 145, 180
At Our Place Restaurant, 255
Audubon Park Apartments, 279
Audubon Terrace, 291, 292
Audubon Theater, 288
Avery Fisher Hall (*see* Philharmonic Hall)

Babies Hospital, 293
Ball, Black & Company Store, 4, 81, 85
Bancroft House (*see* Jacob Cram house)
Barnard College, 268
Barrett House, 168
Baudouine Building, 139
Bayard Building, 77
Beach Pneumatic Subway Terminal, 47
Beacon Theater, 251
Bel Canto, 206
Belding Brothers Building, 72
Belleclaire Hotel, 232, 237, 242
Belnord, 246
Bennett (James Gordon) Memorial, 154
Bimberg's Broadway Theater, 276
Bingham Building, i
Bloomingdale Asylum for the Insane, 262
Bloomingdale Reformed Dutch Church, 205
Bloomingdale Road, 2
Bond Store (*see* International Casino)
Bonta Hotel, 243, 255
Boricua College (*see* American
  Geographical Society)
Boulevard (apartments), 257
Bowling Green, 11, 13
Bowling Green Offices, 15, 27
Bretton Hall Hotel, 243
Bricken Casino Building, 146
Bricken Textile Building, 159
Bridewell, 45
Brill Building, 175, 184–85
Brinckerhoff Hall (Barnard), 268
Broadway, (Two), viii
Broadway, (325–31), 4, 54
Broadway, (380-82), 5, 54, 56
Broadway, (388), 5, 54
Broadway, (390), 5, 54, 57
Broadway, (392), 5, 57
Broadway, (394), 57
Broadway, (473–75), 67
Broadway, (491), 73, 81

Broadway, (550), 76
Broadway, (552–54), 76
Broadway, (530), 77
Broadway, (540), 78
Broadway, (560–66), 80
Broadway, (580–90), 82
Broadway, (678), 97
Broadway, (716), 99
Broadway, (810), 109
Broadway, (862–68), 114
Broadway, (1161–75), 138
Broadway, (1250), 143
Broadway, (1400), 146
Broadway, (1407), 143, 145, 157, 158
Broadway, (1500), 197
Broadway, (1585), 175, 194, 198, 200
Broadway, (1675), 187, 198
Broadway, (1745), 194
Broadway, (1845–47), 207
Broadway, (1981–87), 206
Broadway, (2270–76), 247
Broadway, (2840–48), 271
Broadway, (3470–78), 284
Broadway, (3680–90), 285
Broadway, (4080–84), 311
Broadway, (4720–28), 300, 311
Broadway Barber Shop, 277
Broadway Bridge, 312
Broadway Chambers, 52
Broadway Fashion Building, 250
Broadway-Franklin Building, 55
Broadway Mall Center, 256
Broadway Place, (One), 171, 197, 199, 200
Broadway Tabernacle Congregational Church
  (34th Street), 147, 151
Broadway Tabernacle Congregational Church
  (56th Street), 167
Broadway Temple, 306
Broadway Theater (*see* Colony Theater)
Bromley, 257
Brooks Brothers Store (Bond Street), 96, 100
Brooks Brothers Store (Grand Street), 5
Brooks Brothers Store (22nd Street), 122
Brown (John Crosby) Memorial Tower (Union
  Theological Seminary), 260, 275
Buck's Horn Tavern, 113
Bunny Theater, 290
Butler Brothers Store, 73, 81

Cable Building, 91, 103
Campbell Funeral Chapel (*see* Welden Hotel)
Casino, 148
Central Park South, (240), 205
Central Savings Bank, 235, 252–53
Centre Hotel, 244
Chemical Bank, 4
Chequers, 210
Christ Church, 233, 236
Churchill's Restaurant (46th Street), 190
Churchill's Restaurant (49th Street), 178
Church of the Intercession (*see* Intercession)
Circus Cinema, 179
City Hall, 3, 5, 45, 47, 48–51
City Hall I.R.T. Station, 58
City Hall Park, 45
City Hotel, 20
Claremont Hall, 270
Coliseum Theater, 307
Colonnade Building, 200
Colonnade Houses, 5, 93
Colonial Bank (66th Street), 207
Colonial Bank (68th Street), 212, 226
Colonial Club, 235, 256
Colony Theater, ii, 188
Colorado, 232
Colored Orphan Asylum, 284
Columbia (apartments), 257
Columbia-Presbyterian Medical Center, 293, 314
Columbia University, 261, 264–69
Columbus Center project, 207, 228
Columbus Circle, 203, 225

Columbus Circle, (10), 206
Columbus Memorial, 203, 209, 224–25
Conran's (*see* 81st Street Theater) Continental
  Building, 159
Copley, 223, 227
Corbin Building, 34
Cornwall, 243
Coronado, 228
Cotton Club (*see* Palais Royal)
Cram (Jacob) house, 114
CrossLand Savings Bank (*see* Greenwich
  Savings Bank)
Crossroads Building, 165
Crystal Court, 280
Cunard Building, 36–37
Custom House (*see* United States
  Custom House)

Dante Alighieri statue, 209
Dante Park, 209
Delmonico's Restaurant, 135
Demarest Building, 169
Devlin (D.) & Company Store, 4, 72
District Health Center, 293
Dittenhoffer (A.J.) Warehouse, 69, 78–79
Domestic Sewing Machine Building, 108
Dorilton, 233, 240–41
Duffy, Father Francis P. statue, 172
Duffy Square, 161, 163, 172, 191, 199
Dyckman House, 302–3

Earl Hall Center (Columbia), 266
Edison Theater (*see* Bimberg's Broadway)
Ed Sullivan Theater (*see* Hammerstein's)
Edwards (Nancy S.) house, 113
Eighty-first Street Theater, 247, 255
Embassy Hotel (*see* Ormonde)
Embassy I Theater, 174, 179
Embassy Suites Times Square Hotel, 175
Embassy Theater Building, 234, 254
Empire Building, 21
Empire Hotel, 209
Equitable Building (first), 24
Equitable Building (second), 12
Eternal Light Monument, 132
Euclid Hall Hotel, 231
Evangelical Lutheran Church of the Advent, 255
Exchange Court, 5

Federal Plaza, 43
Fifth Avenue Building sidewalk clock, 132
Fifth Avenue Hotel, 133
First Baptist Church, 233, 236, 244
Flatiron Building, 129, 131, 140–41, 146
Fort Amsterdam, 1
Fort Tryon Park, 299
Fourth Universalist Church, 5
Franconi's Hippodrome, 131
Furniture Workers Building, 98, 102

Gaiety Theater, 164
Gallery of Modern Art, 203, 205
George III statue, 13
Georgetown Plaza, 108
George Washington Bridge Bus Station, 312, 315
Georgia, 280
General Motors Building, 203
Germania Building, 4, 30
Gershwin Theater (*see* Uris)
Gilsey House, 136–37
Gimbel Brothers Department Store, 147, 154, 160
Goelet Building, 120–21
Goelet Garage, 211
Goelet (Robert) house, 113
Good Sheperd, Church of the, 310
Gordon Novelty Company, 126
Gorham Silver Manufacturers Building, 112, 119
Gotham National Bank Building, 214
Grace Church (Rector Street), 20

Grace Church (10th Street), 5, 44, 89, 92, 94–95
Grand Central Hotel, 101
Grand Hotel, 133
Greenwich Savings Bank, 156
Grimm (Henry) Building, 263
Grosvenor Buildings, 64
Gulf & Western Building, 207, 225
Gunther's (C.G.) Sons Store, 5, 77

Hamilton Theater, 289
Hammerstein's Olympia, 166
Hammerstein's Theater, 188
Harkness Plaza, (One), 223, 229
Harlem Heights battle marker, 261
Harlem River Ship Canal, 305
Harrigan & Hart's New Theatre Comique, 101
Haughwout (E.V.) & Company Store, 5, 73, 74–75
Havemeyer Building, 82–83
Havemeyer Hall (Columbia), 265
Hawaii Kai Restaurant, 187
Hendrik Hudson Addition, 271
Howard Johnson's Restaurant, 187, 190
Heere Straat, 1
Herald Center (see Saks & Company Store)
Herald Square, 147, 154
Hess Building, 116
Hoffman House, 133
Holiday Inn Crowne Plaza Hotel, 179, 198, 200
Hollywood Theater (see Warner Hollywood)
Home Life Building, 59
Hopper (Andrew) homestead, 165
Horace Mann School, 260, 269

Imperial Hotel, 134
Independence Flagstaff, 127
Interborough Rapid Transit subway, 24, 58, 233, 235, 254, 256, 259, 286
Intercession, Chapel of the, 279, 294–95
International Casino, 170, 186, 196, 199
International Hotel, 4, 58
International Mercantile Marine Building (see Washington Building)
Irving Trust Headquarters (see One Wall Street)

Jewish Memorial Hospital, 311
Jewish Theological Seminary, 272
Johnson Building, 152, 154
Johnston Building, 139
Johnston (J. & C.) Store (see Mortimer Building)
Juilliard School of Music, 214, 222

Kelly family villa, 235
Kennedy (Captain Archibald) Mansion, 4, 14
Knickerbocker Hotel, 173
Knowlton Court, 287

La Farge House, 4
Langham Hotel, 270
Latin Quarter (see Palais Royal)
Le Boutillier Brothers Store, 69
Lefcourt Normandie Building, 146, 157
Lester Building, 233
Liberty Plaza, (One), 12, 27
Lincoln, Abraham statue, 113
Lincoln Arcade, 210
Lincoln Center, 204, 212, 214, 217–22, 229
Lincoln Plaza, (One), 204, 226
Lincoln Plaza, (30), 210, 225, 226
Lincoln Square Building, 216
"Little Cary" Building, 5, 98
"Little" Singer Building, 84–85
Loew Building, 171, 196–97
Loew Footbridge, 38
Loew's 175th Street Theater, ii, 308–09
Loew's Lincoln Square Theater, 210
Long Acre Building, 167
Lord & Taylor Store (Grand Street), 4
Lord & Taylor (20th Street), 117, 118
Loubat Stores, 68

MacIntyre Building, 114, 124–25
Macy (R.H.) & Company Store, 151, 152–53
Macy's Thanksgiving Day Parade, 161
Madison Square, 130, 132, 135
Maine Monument, 206, 213, 224
Manhasset, 271
Manhattan Life Insurance Building, 31
Manhattan Mercantile Building, 82
Manhattan Savings Institution, 105
Manhattan Towers Hotel, 237
Manhattan Valley Viaduct, 286
Mansfield, 290
Marble Gate, 304
Marble Hill Houses, 313
Marie Antoinette Hotel, 208
Marine Midland Building, 26
Mark Hellinger Theater (see Warner Hollywood)
Marlborough Hotel, 154
Marquis Theater, 193
Marriott Marquis Hotel, 193, 199, 200–1
Marseilles Hotel (see Langham Hotel)
Martinique Hotel, 147, 154
Martyrs' Monument, 23
McAlpin Hotel, 150
McCreery (James H.) & Company Store, 97, 99, 100, 109
Medical Center Concourse, 293
Meir, Golda bust, 158
Merchants Bank Building, 82
Metropolitan Hotel, 5, 71
Metropolitan Life Home Office (Thomas Street), 54, 56
Metropolitan Opera House (39th Street), 149
Metropolitan Opera House (Lincoln Center), 204, 212, 217, 220–21
Metro Theater (see Midtown)
Midtown Theater, 273
Midway Hotel (see Allenhurst)
Montana, 257
Morningside Gardens Houses, 272
Mortimer Building, 116, 126
Miller (I.) Building, 174, 185
Mills & Gibb Building, 72
Mott (Dr. Valentine) summer house, 234
Museum of the American Indian, 291
Mutual Life Insurance Company (MONY) Home Office, 194

National Park Bank, 45
Navarre, 261
Nevada Towers, 227
New York Coliseum, 206, 215
New York County Court House (see Tweed Court House)
New York Herald Building (Ann Street), 24
New York Herald Building (35th Street), 147, 151
New York Hospital, 3, 4, 46
New York Hotel, 4
New York Institute of Technology, 210
New York Life Home Office (first), 55
New York Life Home Office (second), 62
New York Mercantile Exchange, 92
New York Society Library, 5
Niblo's Garden, 70
Ninety-fifth Street Market, 247, 255
Nova Theater (see Bunny)
Novotel Hotel, 198
Nuevo Edison Theater (see Bimberg's Broadway)

Olympia (see Hammerstein's Olympia)
Olympic Theater, 5, 70
107th Street, (245 West), 270
116th Street Gateway (Columbia), 264
125th Street I.R.T. Station, 259, 286
Opera (see Manhattan Towers Hotel)
Ormonde, 227

Palace Theater, 176

Palace Theater Building, 175
Palais Royal, 178
Panama, 290
Paramount Building, 168, 180–81, 197
Peerless Building, 169
Philharmonic Hall, 212, 217–19, 229
Prescott House, 4
Presidential Mansion, 19
Produce Exchange, 15
Pupin Physics Laboratories (Columbia), 267
Pussycat Cinema (see Churchill's Restaurant)

Red Cube sculpture, 26
Reeves Teletape Studio (see 81st Street Theater)
Renwick, 109
Rialto Building, 166, 184
Rialto Theater, 166
Riverside Park Community Apartments, 297
Riviera Theater, 248
Rivoli Theater, 164, 178, 195
RKO Coliseum Theater (see Coliseum)
RKO Hamilton Theater (see Hamilton)
RKO Warner Twin Theater (see Strand Theater)
Rogers, Peet Store, 81
Roosevelt Building (Broome Street), 72, 78, 87
Roosevelt Building (13th Street), 104
Roosevelt (Cornelius V.S.) house, 4
Rossmore Hotel, 174
Roxborough, 254
Rutgers Building, 234
Rutgers Church, 235

St. Denis Hotel, 4, 96–97
St. James Building, 134
St. Nicholas Hotel, 4, 68, 71
St. Paul's Chapel, 4, 16–17, 18, 38
St. Thomas Church, 4, 92
Saks & Company Store, 148, 159
Samler (Casper) farmhouse, 131
San Franscisco Minstrel Hall, 4
Saxonia, 284
Saxony, 243
Schiff (Jacob I.) Building (Jewish Theological Seminary), 272
School of Engineering (Columbia), 264
School of Journalism (Columbia), 266
School of Mines (Columbia), 264, 267
Seaman-Drake Arch (see Marble Gate)
Seminole, 227
Seventh Avenue, (750), 184, 199
Seventy-second Street I.R.T. Control House, 235, 254, 256
Seventy-seventh Street, (233 West), 232
Sherman Square, (One), 227
Sherman Square Hotel, 228
Silk Exchange Building, 68, 83
Sinclair Building, 90
Singer Building, 31
Singer Building, "Little," 84–85
Sloane (W. & J.) Store (Bleecker Street), 93
Sloane (W. & J.) Store (19th Street), 116, 118
Spencer Arms Hotel, 226
Standard Oil Building, viii, 11, 18
Statue of Liberty in Madison Square, 135
Stewart (A.T.) Store (10th Street), 5, 99
Stewart's "Marble Palace," 5, 52–53
Stone Bridge, 69
Strand Theater, 177, 194, 201
Straus Park, 269
Studebaker Building, 168, 199
Stuyvesant Institute, 4
Sun Building (see Stewart's "Marble Palace")
Symphony House, 195

Tattersall's Stables, 70
Teachers College (see Horace Mann School)
Telephone & Telegraph Building, 17, 31, 35, 40, 45
Temple Apartments, 306
Theater Arts Building, 191
Thompson's Saloon, 4

Ticker-tape parade, 41
Tiffany & Company, 5
Times Square, 170, 199
Times Square Plaza, (One), (see Times Tower)
Times Square Theater Center (TKTS), 163, 172, 191
Times Tower, 163, 165, 167, 174, 180, 189
Tower Building, 19
Trinity Building (first), 4
Trinity Building (second), 11, 12, 25, 32
Trinity Church (first), 18
Trinity Church (second), 19, 20
Trinity Church (third), 4, 22–23
Trinity Church Cemetery, 281, 282–83
Trinity Church Yard, 14–15, 23
Tryon Gardens, 311
Tweed Court House, 5, 46, 60–61

Union Dime Savings Bank, 134
Union Square, 111, 113, 127
Union Theological Seminary, 260, 274–75
Union Trust Building, 21
Unitarian Church of the Messiah, 5
United States Custom House, ii, viii, 13, 28–29
United States Post Office, 45
United States Rubber Company Building, 170, 203
Uris Building, 143, 184, 190
Uris Theater, 186

Varian (Isaac) homestead, 132
Verdi, Giuseppe statue, 234, 235

Wall, 1
Wallach Building, 142
Wallack's Theater, 5
Wall Street I.R.T. Station, 24
Wall Street, (One), 12, 39
Wanamaker (John) Store, 90, 106
Ward (Samuel) house and art gallery, 5
Warner Hollywood Theater, 182–83, 187
Warren Building, 119, 123
Warren-Nash Motor Corporation Garage, 281
Washington Building, viii, 14
Washington, George statue, 111
Washington Hall, 46
Welden Hotel, 207, 208, 216
Western Union Building, 34
White (James) Building, 55
Wien (Lawrence A.) Center for Dance and Theater, 119
William, 261
Wilson Building, 148
Windsor Court, 280
Winton Motor Carriage Garage, 212
Woodward Hotel, 192
Woolworth Building, 11, 32–33, 40, 43
World Apparel Center, 189
Worth Monument, 133

Zabar's (see Centre Hotel)

4/24/91